Economic Development and Reforms in India and China

A Comparative Perspective

BY THE SAME AUTHOR

The Ideology of India's Modern Right

Hindus Under Siege: The Way Out

Sri Lanka in Crisis: India's Options

Terrorism in India: A Strategy of Deterrence for India's National Security

Rama Setu: Symbol of National Unity

Corruption and Corporate Governance in India: Satyam, Spectrum and Sundaram

Hindutva and National Renaissance

India's China Strategic Perspective

Virat Hindu Identity: Concept and its Power

Building the Sri Rama Temple in Ayodhya

2G Spectrum Scam

Economic Development and Reforms in INDIA and CHINA

A Comparative Perspective

Subramanian Swamy

Former Professor of Economics, Indian Institute of Technology, Delhi and Faculty, Harvard University; Chairman, Board of Governors, School for Communication and Management Studies (SCMS) Cochin; Former Union Cabinet Minister of Commerce, Law and Justice (GOI)

HAR-ANAND
PUBLICATIONS PVT LTD

Reprint, 2023

Published by Ashok Gosain and Ashish Gosain for
HAR-ANAND PUBLICATIONS PVT LTD
E-49/3, Okhla Industrial Area, Phase-II, New Delhi-110020
Tel: 41603490
E-mail: info@haranandbooks.com/haranand@rediffmail.com
Shop online at: www.haranandbooks.com

Printed in India

PREFACE

India and China face new challenges in the 21st century as their economies stand at cross roads of policy making. The challenge is formidable. What stands between economic slow down and accelerated growth, is essential financial sector reforms. A wide ranging financial sector reform is essential for the sustainability of their growth performance.

This would require India to implement a major push for second generation reforms. China can raise or even sustain its growth rate only through new set of reforms that raise productivity and greater efficiency in use of resources. That also requires wide ranging new financial reforms.

This book, therefore, looks comprehensively at the various dimensions of economic development in terms of growth, structural changes, equity and productivity and the associated factors of globalization, information technology, governance, and demographic trends.

In writing this book, I have benefitted from the last ten years of teaching this topic as a course at Harvard University during the summer term. I have been tirelessly assisted by my secretaries Pran Nath Mago and Subbulakshmi in the word processing of various drafts. Madan Raj and Hari Singh also were very helpful in photocopying and collating the pages. But in trying to meet a deadline for this summer, some mistakes may still remain for which I am responsible. My publisher has been a dream for any author.

SUBRAMANIAN SWAMY

Definitions

Asian economies classified as geographic groupings are follows:

Association of Southeast Asian Nations (ASEAN) comprises Brunei Darussalam, Cambodia, Indonesia, Lao People's democratic Republic, Malaysia, Myanmar, Philippines Singapore, Thailand and Viet Nam.

Central Asia comprises Armenia, Azerbaija, Georgia, Kazakhastan, Kyrgyz Repubnlic, Tajikstan, Turkmenistan, and Uzbekistan.

East Asia comprises People's Republic of China; Hong Kong, China; Republic of Korea; Mongolia and Taipei, China.

South Asia comprises Islamic Republic of Afghanistan, Bangladesh, Bhutan, Indian, Maldives, Nepal, Pakistan and Sri Lanka.

Southeast Asia comprises Brunei Darussalam, Cambodia, Indonesia, Lao People's Democratic Republic, Malaysia, Myanmar, Philippines, Singapore, Thailand and Viet Nam.

Contents

Chapter I

INTRODUCTION

Economics is a science of optimization, that achieves a maximum or minimum value for an objective goal, by efficient allocation within the constraints of scarce resources and by a choice from amongst feasible alternatives.

Thus Economic Policy is structured by specifying objectives, setting priorities amongst the objectives, a strategy, and a balance sheet of resources available for financial mobilisation. Economic logic is special and distinguished from common sense by: (i) *Comparability*: we compare only those alternatives that serve the same objectives. It is thus difficult, for example, to optimize by minimizing costs when comparing defence and development since we need both. (ii) *Relativity:* items are cheap or costly in terms of costs of available *comparable* alternatives, which is termed as Opportunity Cost or the Rate of Social Discount. For example, no price for water is too high when dying of thirst, or cost of water if there is an acute water shortage since there are no alternative to water. More importantly and less obvious is the theory of comparative advantage which postulates that nations may find it to profitable to trade even if each of one country's output costs is exceeded, one to one, by the output costs in another country. Profitability of multi-product international trade depends on the relative cost structure and not on one to one absolute costs differentials. (iii) *Marginal analysis*: optimal decisions are made not on averages, but at the margin. Average costs depend on sunk costs, but for the firm only the rate of change of variable costs matter when optimizing profits.

The mathematical sophistication and technique for economic analysis was provided by Paul Samuelson in a systematic way, by Simon

Kuznets through his indefatigable attempts at quantifying the concepts and collecting real life data for testing propositions, and by Milton Friedman who led the field to a global consensus on the optimality of market principles which postulates a Government to umpire or a delegated Regulator to enforce Rules and correct for market failures or exploit external economies. Samuelson-Kuznets-Friedman may be called the Holy Trinity of modern economics

Since, controlled experiment in economics is quite impossible, we rely on cross-section and time series data from the comparative experience of nations to contrast alternative economic systems, to test propositions, and to make inferences inductively about macroeconomic causation. Thus the need for theories and models.

However, with the collapse and unraveling of the USSR in 1991, comparative economics *has changed focus* from *alternative systems* to *alternative market models in a democracy* i.e., inferences on how much freedom and how much choice we do and should have; how much public sector and how much private enterprise is appropriate etc., since now democracy is considered as the best or in any case the least worst political system, and market [as distinct and different from *Laissez Faire*] as best for the efficient allocation of resources-provided market failures are rectified by well defined and designated Regulators, especially since decision making is not transitive in democracy when choice is made on majority principle from amongst alternatives.

There are also contradictions between democracy and market system which need to be resolved. But first we define economic development and then consider the resolution of conflict between democracy and market economy.

DEFINITION OF ECONOMIC DEVELOPMENT

We begin with a definition of *economic development* of a nation: as consisting of modern economic growth [Simon Kuznets], increasing equity [measured by Gini coeff, HDI, social security and safety nets], rising productivity [measured by TFP], a sophisticated financial architecture, efficient governance, and associated ideological structures of freedom, democracy, transparency, and cultural values [rationality, punctuality, incentive and merit based not birth or cronyism based rewards]. This is presented in Chart I below:

CHART 1

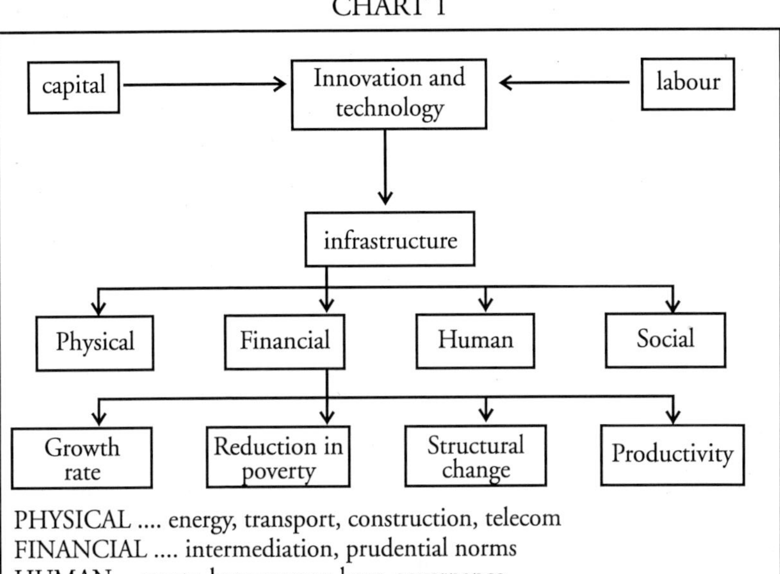

Kuznets definition of modern economic growth [1] is: "a long-term rise in capacity [measured by GDP growth rate and its per capita] to supply increasingly diverse goods to its population [structural changes], this growing capacity based on advancing technology [*epochal innovation*], and the institutional and ideological adjustments that it demands [e.g., arising now from globalization]."

Kuznets had observed 'an inverted U' in population growth and inequality, and explained why. Thus, according to him, failure to exploit the opportunities provided by modern technology makes a country less developed. The US stays ahead because of its capacity to transform knowledge into cutting edge technology, and incentives into rewards through open competitive market system.

Economic development is thus multifaceted. If per capita income was the only standard to measure development as it is sometimes in UN publications, then we find that (a) not all less developed nations are poor e.g., oil-rich Shiekhdoms (b) not all developed countries are rich e.g., Southern Europe. Other criteria are also being popularized, for example: HDI, 'Green' GDP, GNW etc.

Kuznets in recognising the crucial role of *epochal innovation,* laid the foundation for the subsequent development of Solow's theory of technical change, thus demolishing diminishing returns concept of earlier thinkers such Smith, Marshall, Malthus and Marx, that had dominated development literature, and which had rendered economics as a "dismal science."

While the descriptive model of Kuznets, and of Solow have survived, the prescriptive Soviet model [closed autarkic state-controlled], Singer's Vicious Circle Theory; Rostow's model [stages and take-off], East Asia [export-driven] model, and now the Washington Consensus [WB/IMF] have now fallen on the way side of time.

The search is now on within the broader framework of macroeconomic environment, quality of public institutions, and technology. 'One size' no more fits all, nor do *laissez faire* or command economy. Hence, the international organizations such as the United Nations, IMF and World Bank have began to rely more on goals or targets. One such set of targets is the Millennium Development Goals (MDG) adopted by the UN in 2000 for every country to achieve by 2015 [see Box 1 and Goals 1 to 8 below, and India's and China's achievements of the same].

There is also the question of how to make the transition from an authoritarian command structure to a competitive market system in a democratic framework, as also which: democracy or development comes first? Lee Kuan Yew of Singapore had advocated that the latter must come first. Sharansky, a long time prisoner of the brutal KGB, and now a Minister in Israel, sees the world divided between fear and free societies, wherein in the first, it is essential to find people with inner strength to confront evil, and in the second to develop moral clarity to see evil and oppose it. Hence, he advocates that democracy must be a pre-condition. That is what Karl Popper also wrote in 'Enemies Within'. The answer of course is that it is neither. We need both together but democracy must receive priority attention.

Box 1: Millennium Development Goals

Goals and Targets (from the Millennium Declaration	Indicators for Monitoring Progress
Goal 1: Eradicate extreme poverty and hunger Target 1A: Halve, between 1990 and 2015, the proportion of people whose income is less one dollar a day	1.1 Proportion of population below $1 (PPP) per day1 1.2 Poverty gap ratio 1.3 Share of poorest quintile in national consumption
Target 1B: Achieve full and productive employment and decent work for all, including women and young people	1.4 Growth rate of GDP per person employed 1.5 Employment-to-population ratio 1.6 Proportion of employed people living below $1 (PPP) per day 1.7 Proportion of own-account and contributing family workers in total employment
Target 1C: Halve, between 1990 and 2015, the proportion of people who suffer from hunger	1.8 Prevalence of underweight children under-five years of age 1.9 Proportion of population below minimum level of dietary energy consumption
Goal 2: Achieve universal primary education Target 2A: Ensure that, by 2015, children everywhere, boys and girls alike, will be able to complete a full course of primary schooling	2.1 Net enrollment ratio in primary education 2.2 Proportion of pupils starting grade 1 who reach last grade of primary 2.3 Literacy rate of 15-24 year-olds, women and men
Goal 3: Promote gender equality and empower women Target 3A: Eliminate gender in primary and secondary education, preferably by 2005, and in all levels of education no later than 2015	3.1 Ratios of girls to boys in primary, secondary and tertiary education 3.2 Share of women in wage employment in the non-agricultural sector 3.3 Proportion of seats held by women in national parliament
Goal 4: Reduce child mortality Target 4A: Reduce by two-thirds, between 1990 and 2015, the under-five	4.1 Under-five mortality rate 4.2 Infant mortality rate 4.3 Proportion of 1-year-old children immunized against measles
Goal 5: Improve maternal health Target 5A: Reduce by three quarters, between 1990 and 2015, the maternal mortality ratio	5.1 Maternal mortality ratio 5.2 Proportion of births attended by skilled health personnel
Target 5B: Achieve, by 2015, universal access to reproductive health	5.3 Contraceptive prevalence rate 5.4 Adolescent birth rate 5.5 Antenatal care coverage (at least one visit and at least four visits) 5.6 Unmet need for family planning
Goal 6: Combat HIV/AIDS, malaria and other diseases Target 6A: Have halted by 2015 and begun to reverse the spread of HIV/AIDS	6.1 HIV prevalence among population aged 15-24 years 6.2 Condom use at last high-risk sex 6.3 Proportion of population aged 15-24 years with comprehensive correct knowledge of HIV/AIDS 6.4 Ratio of school attendance of orphans to school attendance of non-orphans aged 1-14 years

Target 6B: Achieve, by 2010, universal access to treatment for HIV/AIDS for all those who need it	6.5 Proportion of population with advanced HIV infection with access to antiretroviral drugs
Target 6C: Have halted by 2015 and begun to reverse the incidence of malaria and other major diseases	6.6 Incidence and death rates associated with malaria 6.7 Proportion of children under 5 sleeping under insecticide-treated bednets 6.8 Proportion of children under 5 with fever who are treated with appropriate anti-malarial drugs 6.9 Incidence, prevalence, and death rates associated with tuberculosis 6.10 Proportion of tuberculosis cases detected and cured under directly observed treatment short course
Goal 7: Ensure environmental sustainability Target 7A: Integrate the principles of sustainable development into country policies and programmes and reverse the loss of environmental resources	7.1 Proportion of land area covered by forest 7.2 CO_2 emissions, total, per capita, and per $1 GDP (PPP) 7.3 Consumption of ozone-depleting substances 7.4 proportion of fish stocks within safe biological limits 7.5 Proportion of total water resources used
Target 7B: Reduce biodiversity loss, achieving, by 2010, a significant reduction in the rate of loss	7.6 proportion of terrestrial and marine areas protected 7.7 proportion of species threatened with extinction
Target 7C: Halve, by 2015, the proportion of people without sustainable access to safe drinking water and basic sanitation	7.8 Proportion of population using an improved drinking water sources 7.9 Proportion of population using an improved sanitation facility
Target 7D: By 2020, to have achieved a significant improvement in the lives of at least 100 million slum dwellers	7.10 Proportion of urban population living in slums[2]

INTRODUCTION TO THE MILLENNIUM DEVELOPMENT GOALS

At the Millennium Summit in September 2000, the largest gathering of world leaders in history adopted the United Nations Millennium Declaration, committing their nations to a new global partnership to reduce extreme poverty and setting out a series of targets, with a deadline of 2015. These have become known as the Millennium Development Goals (MDGs). In 2007, the MDG monitoring framework was revised to include four new targets agreed on by member states at the 2005 World Summit, namely, full and productive employment and decent work for all, access to reproductive health, access to treatment for HIV/AIDS, and protection of biodiversity. The indicators for these new targets became effective in January 2008 and this is the framework used here to monitor progress toward achieving the MDGs.

The first MDG targets the poor directly—those living on less than one dollar a day—while the next six focus on the underlying causes of poverty, such as lack of access to education, health care, and employment; gender inequality; poor housing conditions; and environmental degradation. The eighth goal is to develop a global partnership for development, and focuses on how the industrialized countries can work with the poorer countries to enhance the latter's standard of living. The MDGs thus complement the Asian Development Bank's vision of a region free of poverty, and its mission to help its developing member countries reduce poverty and improve the quality of life of their citizens. Box 1 lists the eight MDGs and the corresponding targets and indicators for monitoring progress.

Chart 2
International Comparisons of MDG and Achievements

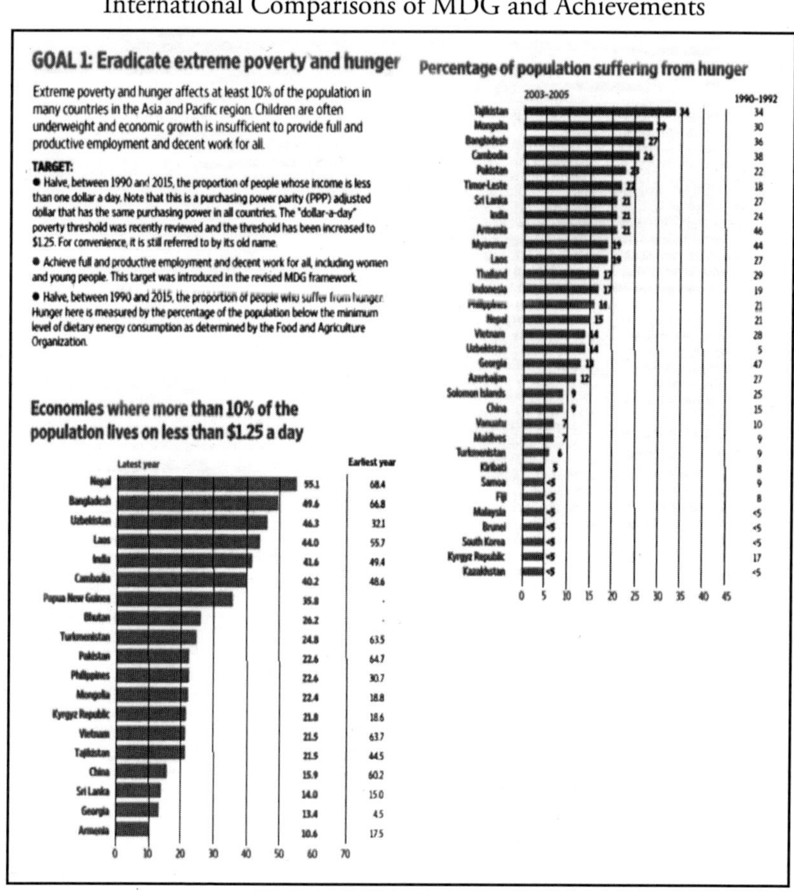

Chart 3

GOAL 2: Achieve universal primary education

Substantial progress has been made towards achieving universal primary education and basic reading and writing skills. But in economies with lower literacy rates, there are clear gender disparities—women are still more likely to be illiterate than men.

TARGET:

- Children everywhere, boys and girls alike, will be able to complete a full course of primary schooling.

Total net enrolment ratio in primary education

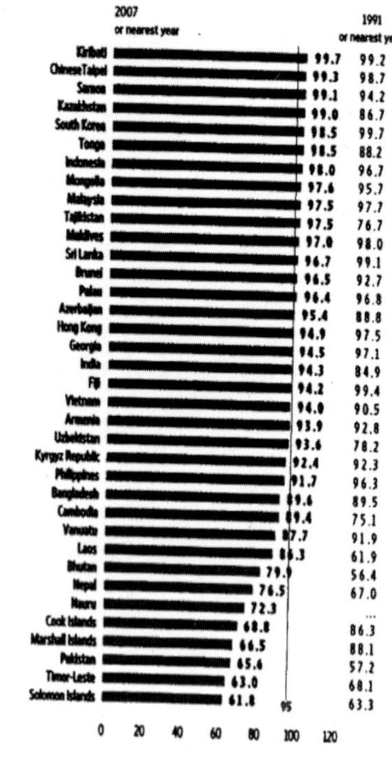

Percentage of children starting grade 1 and reaching last grade of primary education

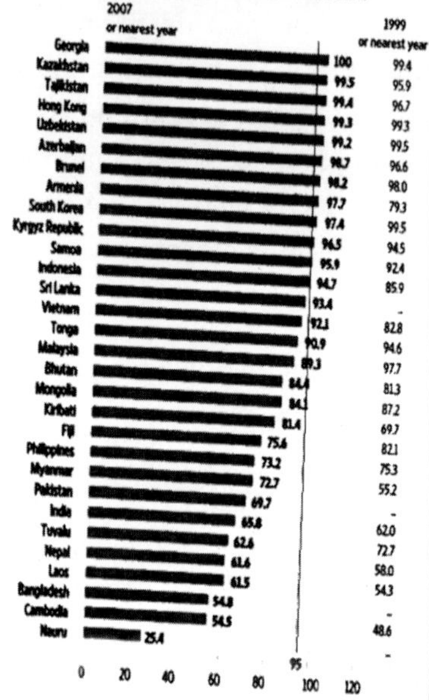

Chart 4

GOAL 3: Promote gender equality and empower women

Male-female equality in primary school enrolment has now been achieved in most economies in the region and good progress has been made at the secondary level, but fewer countries have achieved gender equality in tertiary education. When women do enrol in school, they tend to study longer than men.

TARGET:

- To obtain equality of males and females in primary, secondary, and tertiary education enrolment.

Primary school female-male enrolment ratios

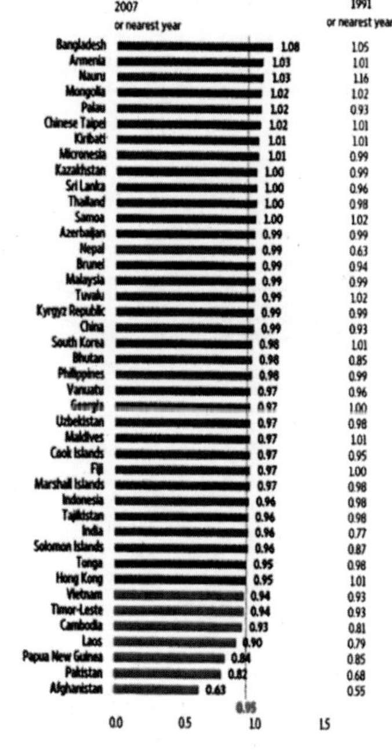

Secondary school female-male enrolment ratios

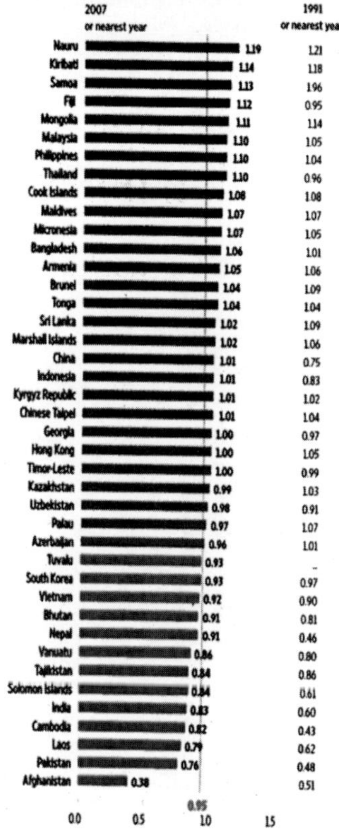

Chart 5

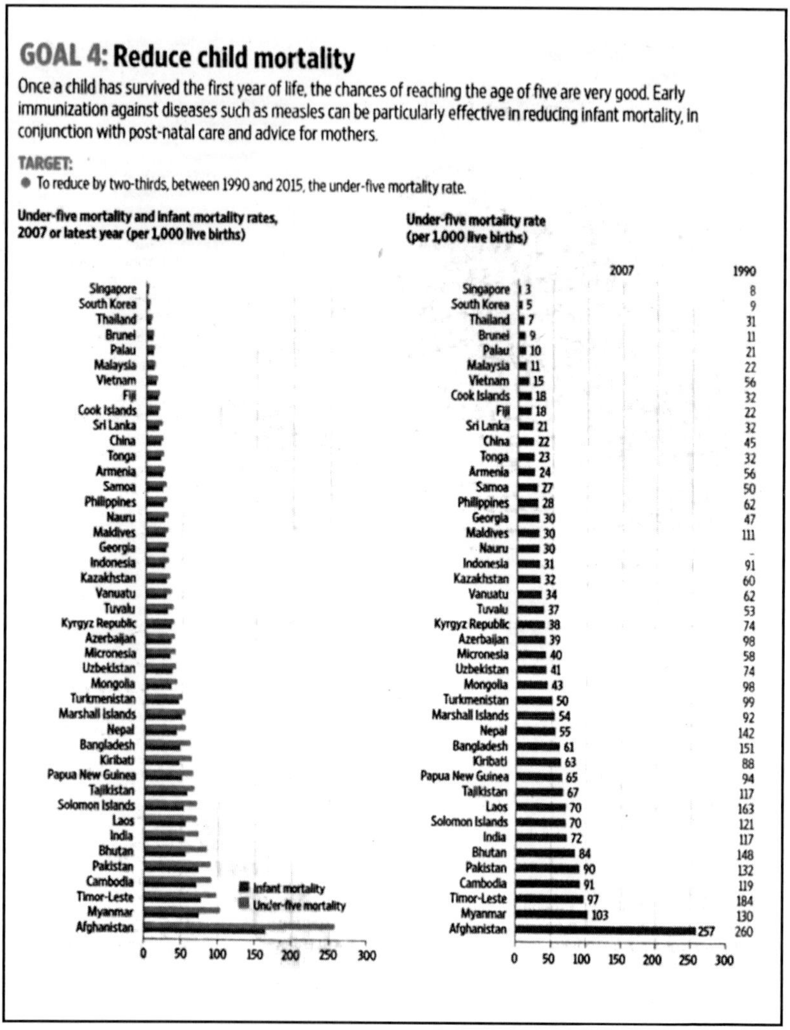

Once a child has survived the first year of life, the chances of reaching the age of five are very good. Early immunization against diseases such as measles can be particularly effective in reducing infant mortality, in conjunction with post-natal care and advice for mothers.

TARGET:

- To reduce by two-thirds, between 1990 and 2015, the under-five mortality rate.

Under-five mortality and infant mortality rates, 2007 or latest year (per 1,000 live births)

Singapore
South Korea
Thailand
Brunei
Palau
Malaysia
Vietnam
Fiji
Cook Islands
Sri Lanka
China
Tonga
Armenia
Samoa
Philippines
Nauru
Maldives
Georgia
Indonesia
Kazakhstan
Vanuatu
Tuvalu
Kyrgyz Republic
Azerbaijan
Micronesia
Uzbekistan
Mongolia
Turkmenistan
Marshall Islands
Nepal
Bangladesh
Kiribati
Papua New Guinea
Tajikistan
Solomon Islands
Laos
India
Bhutan
Pakistan
Cambodia
Timor-Leste
Myanmar
Afghanistan

0 50 100 150 200 250 300

Infant mortality
Under-five mortality

Under-five mortality rate (per 1,000 live births)

	2007	1990
Singapore	3	8
South Korea	5	9
Thailand	7	31
Brunei	9	11
Palau	10	21
Malaysia	11	22
Vietnam	15	56
Cook Islands	18	32
Fiji	18	22
Sri Lanka	21	32
China	22	45
Tonga	23	32
Armenia	24	56
Samoa	27	50
Philippines	28	62
Georgia	30	47
Maldives	30	111
Nauru	30	-
Indonesia	31	91
Kazakhstan	32	60
Vanuatu	34	62
Tuvalu	37	53
Kyrgyz Republic	38	74
Azerbaijan	39	98
Micronesia	40	58
Uzbekistan	41	74
Mongolia	43	98
Turkmenistan	50	99
Marshall Islands	54	92
Nepal	55	142
Bangladesh	61	151
Kiribati	63	88
Papua New Guinea	65	94
Tajikistan	67	117
Laos	70	163
Solomon Islands	70	121
India	72	117
Bhutan	84	148
Pakistan	90	132
Cambodia	91	119
Timor-Leste	97	184
Myanmar	103	130
Afghanistan	257	260

0 50 100 150 200 250 300

Chart 6

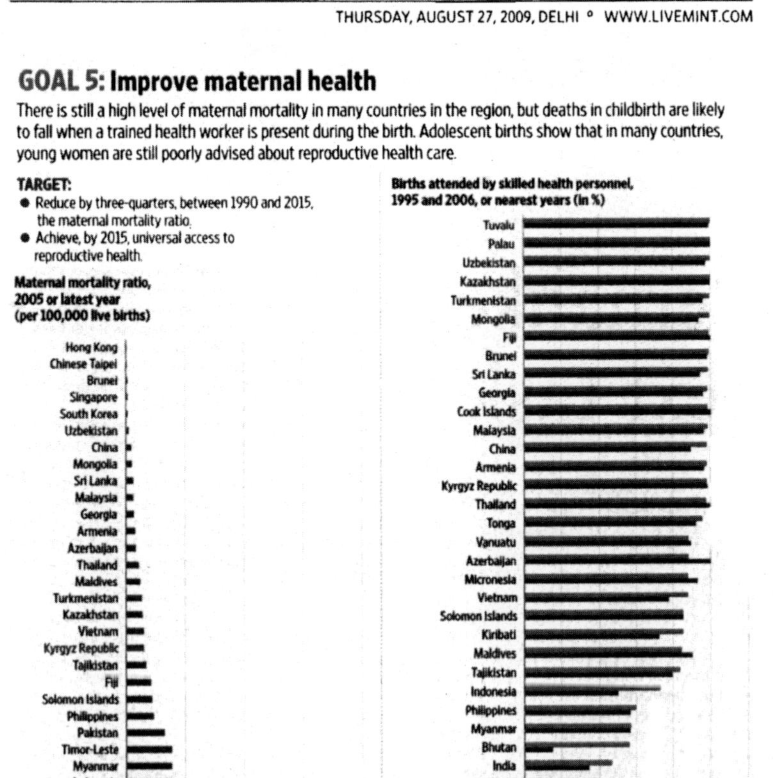

THURSDAY, AUGUST 27, 2009, DELHI ° WWW.LIVEMINT.COM

GOAL 5: Improve maternal health

There is still a high level of maternal mortality in many countries in the region, but deaths in childbirth are likely to fall when a trained health worker is present during the birth. Adolescent births show that in many countries, young women are still poorly advised about reproductive health care.

TARGET:

- Reduce by three-quarters, between 1990 and 2015, the maternal mortality ratio.
- Achieve, by 2015, universal access to reproductive health.

Chart 7

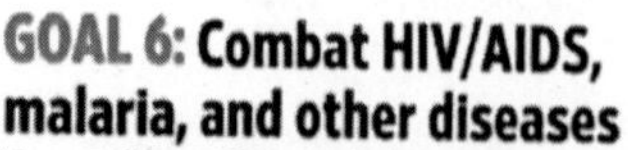

The prevalence of tuberculosis has been reduced in most economies. Many adults still live with HIV. The incidence of HIV is heavily concentrated in six economies and in most cases, those in need of them do not currently have the necessary access to antiretroviral drugs.

TARGET:

- Have halted, by 2015, and begun to reverse the spread of HIV/AIDS.
- Achieve, by 2010, universal access to treatment for HIV/AIDS for all those who need it.
- Have halted, by 2015, and begun to reverse the incidence of malaria and other major diseases.

Percentage of the population with advanced HIV infection with access to antiretroviral drugs, 2006 and 2007

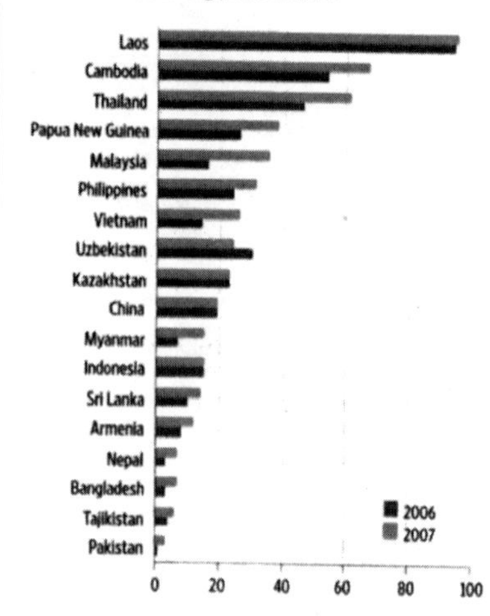

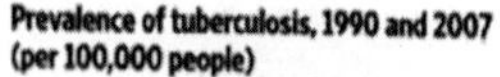

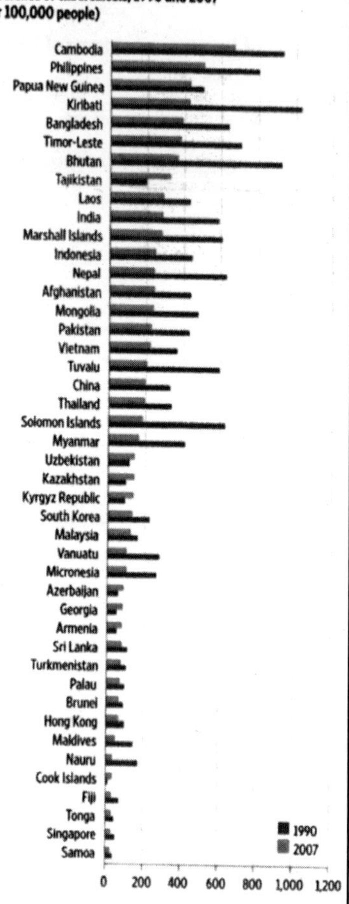

Chart 8

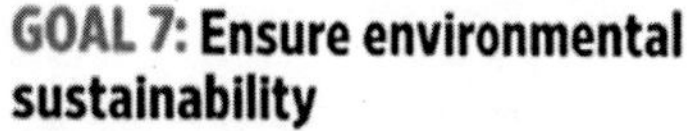

GOAL 7: Ensure environmental sustainability

Deforestation and rising per capita emissions of carbon dioxide continue to pose a threat to environmental sustainability. Although emissions by the five most populous economies in the Asia and Pacific region are still low compared to those in the industrialized countries, rising living standards will inevitably increase global emissions with serious consequences for climate change unless this is offset by reductions in developed countries.

TARGET:

- Integrate the principles of sustainable development into country policies and programmes and reverse the loss of environmental resources.
- Reduce biodiversity loss, achieving, by 2010, a significant reduction in the rate of loss.
- Halve, by 2015, the proportion of people without sustainable access to safe drinking water and basic sanitation.
- By 2020, to have achieved a significant improvement in the lives of at least 100 million slum dwellers.

Change in forest area between 1990 and 2005 ('000 sq. km)

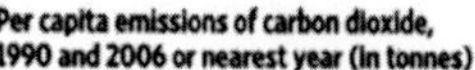

Per capita emissions of carbon dioxide, 1990 and 2006 or nearest year (in tonnes)

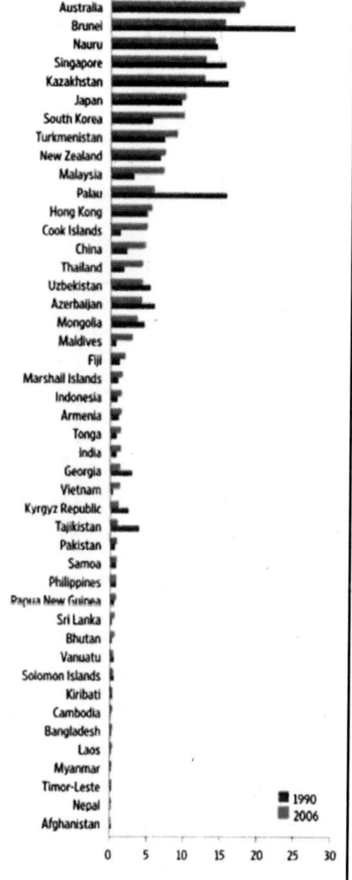

Chart 9

GOAL 8: Develop a global partnership for development
While the burden of debt has been falling for most countries in the region since 2000, less progress has been made in spreading the benefits of new technologies more widely. The digital divide still means that 50% or more of the population in eight economies have Internet access, while the rate is less than 20% in the majority of countries.
TARGET:
● Deal comprehensively with the debt problems of developing countries through national and international measures in order to make debt sustainable in the long term.
● In cooperation with pharmaceutical companies, provide access to affordable essential drugs in developing countries.
● In cooperation with the private sector, make available the benefits of new technologies, especially information and communications.
Debt service as a percentage of exports of goods And services, 2000 and 2007, or nearest years
2000
2007
Pakistan
Nepal
Philippines
Tonga
Samoa
Sri Lanka
Indonesia
Papua New Guinea
Bangladesh
Maldives
Laos
Georgia
India
Tajikistan
Kyrgyz Republic
Mongolia
Malaysia
Armenia
Solomon Islands
Vietnam
Afghanistan
Myanmar
Kazakhstan
Thailand
Vanuatu
Fiji
China
Azerbaijan
Cambodia
Telephone lines and cellular subscriptions, 2008 or latest year (per 100 population)
Cellular subscriptions
Telephone lines
Hong Kong
Singapore
Maldives
Thailand
Chinese Taipei
New Zealand
Australia
Malaysia
Kazakhstan
South Korea
Brunei
Japan
Vietnam
Azerbaijan
Philippines
Fiji
Armenia
Indonesia
Georgia
Sri Lanka
Palau
Pakistan
Cook Islands
Tonga
China
Samoa
Uzbekistan
Kyrgyz Republic
Tajikistan
Mongolia
India
Cambodia
Afghanistan
Bangladesh
Laos
Micronesia
Bhutan
Tuvalu
Nauru
Nepal
Vanuatu
Turkmenistan
Timor-Leste
Papua New Guinea
Solomon Islands
Marshall Islands
Myanmar
Kiribati

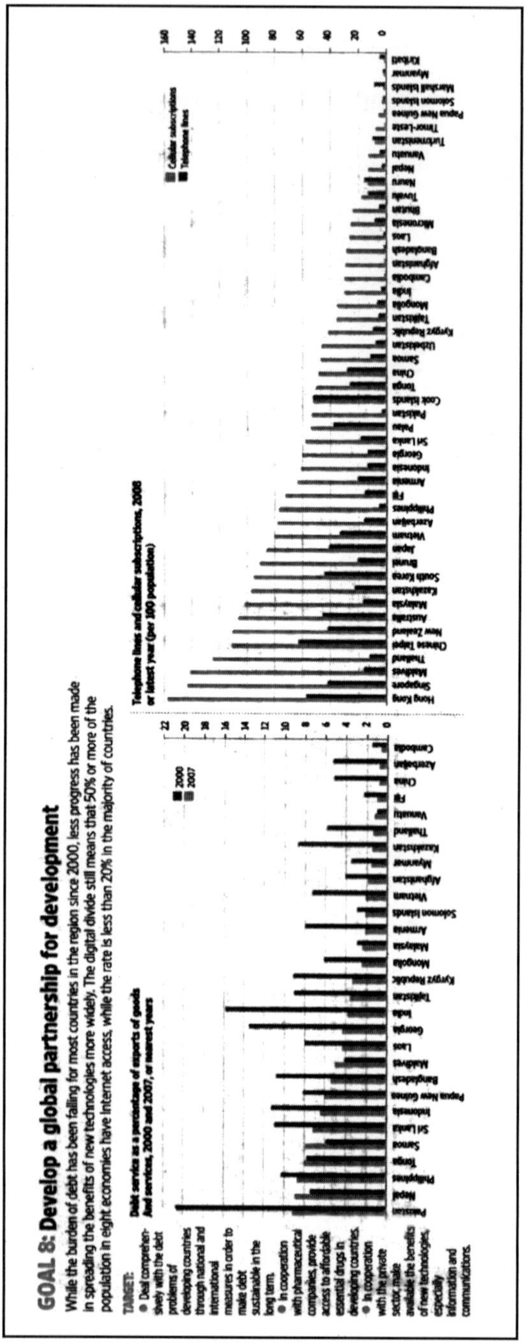

Below is a summary of the UN System in China's collective assessment of China's situation *vis a vis* the MDGs.

Table 1

Overview of China MDG Status

Goals and Targets	State of Goal Achievement	State of Supportive Environment
Eradicate Extreme Poverty & Hunger by 2015		
Halve the proportion of people living in extreme poverty	On track	Well developed
Halve the proportion of population below minimum level of dietary energy consumption	On track	
Halve the proportion of underweight children under five years old by 2015		
Universal primary education by 2015		
Achieve universal primary education by 2015	On track	In place
Gender equality		
Achieve equal access for boys and girls to primary and lower secondary schooling by 2005	May be not on track	In place
Achieve equal access for boys and girls to upper secondary education by 2005	May be not on track	In place
Under-five mortality		
Reduce under-five mortality by two-thirds by 2015	On track	In place
Reproductive health		
Reduce maternal mortality ratio by three-quarters by 2015	On track	In place
Universal access to safe/reliable reproductive health services (contraceptive methods) by 2015	On trace	Well developed
Combat disease (HIV/AIDS, TB & Malaria)		
Halt and reverse the spread of HIVS/AIDS by 2015	May be not on track	May be not on track
Halve the prevalence of TB by 2015	May be not on track	In place
Reduce the incidence of malaria	On track	In place
Environment		
Implement national strategies for sustainable development by 2005 so as to reverse the loss of environment resources by 2015	May be not on track	Well developed
Basic amenities		
Halve the proportion of people unable to reach or afford safe drinking water by 2015	On track	Well developed
Improve the proportion of rural people with access to improved sanitation	On track	In place

On current official information, China will probably achieve most of MDG goals by 2015. While China is on course nationally for achieving most of the goals, inequality has increased and thus there is a need to work towards balanced regional economic growth. National figures however mask large and growing development gaps between the relatively rich coastal areas and poorer centre and Western regions of China.

Table 2: India: Millennium Development Goals, 1990-2006

	1990	1995	1998	2001	2004	2006
Eradicate extreme poverty and hunger 2/						
Income share held by lowest 20%	–	–	–	–	8.1	–
Malnutrition prevalence, weight for age (% of children under 5)	–	–	44.4	–	43.5	–
Poverty headcount ratio at national poverty line (% of population)	–	36.0	–	28.6	27.5	–
Prevalence of undernourishment (% of population)	–	25.0	21.0	–	20.0	–
Achieve universal primary education 3/						
Literacy rate, youth total (% of people ages 15-24)	61.9	–	–	76.4	–	–
Persistence to grade 5, total (% of cohort)	–	–	59.7	61.4	73.0	–
Primary completion rate, total (% of relevant age group)	63.8	77.1	69.7	72.4	83.8	85.7
School enrolment, primary (% net)	–	–	–	78.5	89.4	88.7
Promote gender equally 4/						
Proportion of seats held by women in national parliament (%)	5.0	–	7.0	9.0	9.0	8.3
Ratio of girls to boys in primary and secondary education (%)	70.3	–	82.1	79.8	90.3	91.4
Ratio of young literate females to males (% ages 15-24)	67.1	–	–	80.5	–	–
Share of women employed in the non-agricultural sector (% of total non-agricultural employment)	12.7	14.4	16.0	16.8	17.9	–
Reduce child mortality 5/						
Immunization, measles (% of children ages 12-23 months)	56.0	72.0	51.0	53.0	58.0	59.0
Mortality rate, infant (per 1,000 live births)	80.0	74.0	72.0	68.0	61.6	58.7
Mortality rate, under 5 (per 1,000)	114.9	101.5	–	89.3	–	78.4
Improved maternal health 5/						
Births attended by skilled health staff (% of total)	–	34.2	42.3	42.5	–	46.6
Maternal mortality ratio (modeled estimate, per 100,000 live births)	–	–	–	–	–	–

Combat HIV/AIDS, malaria, and other diseases 7/						
Children orphaned by HIV/AIDS	–	–	–	–	–	–
Contraceptive prevalence (% of women ages 15-49)	43.0	–	–	46.9	–	56.3
Incidence of tuberculosis (per 100,000 people)	167.8	–	–	–	–	–
Prevalence of HIV, female (% ages 15-24)	–	–	–	–	–	–
Prevalence of HIV, total (% population ages 15-49)	–	–	–	–	–	0.3
Tuberculosis cases deleted under DOTS (%)	–	0.3	1.6	23.1	55.3	53.8
Ensure environmental sustainability 8/						
CO2 emissions (matric ions per capita)	0.8	1.0	1.1	1.1	1.2	–
Forest area (% of land area)	21.5	–	–	22.7	–	22.6
GDP per unit of energy use (Constant 2000 PPP and per kg of oil equivalent)	3.2	3.4	3.7	3.9	4.3	4.5
Improved sanitation facilities (% of population with access)	14.0	–	–	23.0	–	28.0
Improved water source (% of population with access)	71.0	77.0	–	82.0	–	89.0
Nationally protected areas (% of total land area)	–	–	–	–	–	–
Develop a global partnership for development 9/						
Aid per capita (current US$)	1.5	1.9	1.6	1.6	0.6	1.2
Debt service (PPG and IMF only, % of exports of G&S excl. workers' remittances)	–	–	–	–	–	–
Fixed line and mobile phono subscribes (per 1,000 people)	0.6	1.3	–	3.6	–	24.3
Internet users (per 1,000 people)	–	–	–	0.5	–	17.8
Total debt service (% of exports of goods, services and income)	31.9	29.7	21.2	14.7	13.8	7.7
Unemployment, youth female (% of female labour force ages 15-24)	–	8.0	–	10.2	10.8	–
Unemployment, youth male (% of male labour force ages 15-24)	–	8.4	–	10.1	10.4	–
Unemployment, youth total (% of total labour force ages 15-24)	–	8.3	–	10.1	10.5	–
General indicators						
Fertility rate, total (births per woman)	3.8	3.4	3.3	3.1	2.7	2.5
GNI per capita, Atlas method (current US$)	390.0	380.0	420.0	480.0	630.0	820.0
GNI, Atlas method (current US$) (billions)	330.9	350.2	415.1	478.6	680.6	914.7
Gross capita formation (% of GDP)	24.2	26.6	22.6	24.2	31.6	38.0
Life expectancy at birth, total (years)	59.1	51.4	52.2	62.9	63.4	64.5
Literacy rate, adult total (% of people ages 15 and above)	48.2	–	–	61.0	–	–
Population, total (millions)	849.5	932.2	982.2	1,032.5	1,079.7	1,109.8
Trade (% of GDP)	15.7	23.1	24.0	26.4	37.9	47.2

Source: *World Development Indicators* database, September 2008.

1/ In soem cases the data are for earlier or later years than those stated.

2/ Halve, between 1990 and 2015, the proportion of people whose income is less than one dollar a day.

3/ Ensure that by 2015, children everywhere, boys and girls alike, will be able to complete a full course of primary schooling.

4/ Eliminate gender disparity in primary and secondary education preferably by 2005 and to all levels of education no later than 2015.

5/ Reduce by two-thirds, between 1990 and 2015, the under-five mortality rate.

6/ Reduce by three-quarters, between 1990 and 2015, the maternal mortality ratio.

7/ Have halted by 2015, end begun to reverse, the spread of HIV/AIDS. have halted by 2015, and begun to reverse, the incidence of malana and other major diseases.

8/ Integrate the principles of sustainable development into country policies and programs and reverse the loss of environmental resources. Halve, by 2015, the proportion of people without sustainable access to safe drinking water. By 2020, to have achieved a significant improvement in the lives of atleast 100 million slum dwellers.

9/ Develop further an open, rule based, predictable, non-discrimination trading and financial system. Address the Special Needs of the Least Developed Countries. Address the Special Needs of landlocked countries and small island developing states. Deal comprehensively with the debt problems of developing countries through national and international measures in order to make debt sustainable in the long term. In cooperation with developing countries, develop and implement strategies for decent and productive work for youth. In cooperation with pharmaceutical companies, provide access to affordable, essential drugs in developing countries. In cooperation with the private sector, make available the benefits of new technologies, especially information and communications.

It is clear that transparency and accountability are essential for sustainability of the market vitiated with asymmetric information. Hence Democracy must come first in priority. Otherwise oligarchy will flourish in the name of development. In every nation, democracy must be structured on four pillars: electoral legitimacy, constitutional safeguards, functionally independent institutions, and embedded accountability. Mere elections is not sufficient of be termed as democracy. But as Table below reveals, the comparative performance of two nations artificially partitioned on political reasons, but of the same people and same civilization perform so differently because of the contrast between authoritarian command economy and democracy with competitive market system.

Why should we be interested in discussing democracy in an economic development book? A comparison of East & West Germany show how democracy and market system together perform better for economic development than dictatorships and command economy [see Table 1] same result emerge from North and South Korea, China and India before reforms and after. Because democracy is spreading, now 115 countries, and no two modern democracies go to war. The best human political structure is provided in a democracy.

But there is a conflict between the market and democracy that requires to be resolved: (i) a flourishing and vibrant democracy that empowers a relatively poor majority to vote and hence can influence legislation against the relatively rich capitalist and entrepreneurial minority, *and* (ii) a thriving market economy driven by a rich empowered minority with disproportionate access to capital, skills, and media and other networks with capacity to undermine the electoral system through strategic funding of the same.

Table 3: Economic Indicators—South/North Korea (1995-96) and West/East Germany (1989) Compared

	South Korea	North Korea	South/ North ratio	West Germany	East Germany	West/ East ratio
1	2	3	4	5	6	7
Population Million	44.9	23.9	1.9	62.1	16.6	3.8
GNP Billion $	451.7	22.3	20.3	1,207	96	12.6
Per capita income $	10,067	957	10.5	19,283	5,840	3.3
Economic growth in% p.a. 1990-1995	+7.6	-4.5	—	3.0	-0.8	—
Government expenditure billion $ (as % of GNP)	97.1 (21.5)	19 85	5.1	547.7. (45.5)	61.8 (64.4)	8.9
Defence expenditure billion $ (as % of GDP) Per capita ($)	14.4 (3.2) 318	5.2 (23) 218	2.8 1.5	28.5 (2.4) 459	11.2 (11.6) 675	2.6 0.7
Foreign trade billion $ (as % of GNP)	260.2 (57.6)	2.05 (9.2)	126.9	611.1 (50.6)	47.0 (49)	13.0
-Export of goods billion $	125.1	0.74	169	341.3	23.7	14.4

-Import of goods Billion	135.1	1.31	103	269.8	23.3	11.5
Foreign debt billion $ (as % of GNP)	79 (17.5)	11.8 (53)	6.6	106.7 (8.8)	22 (23)	4.9
Life expectancy In years (1995)	72.0	70.5	1.02	75.0	74.0	1.01
Infant mortality Per 1,000 births (1995)	10	26	0.28	7.4	7.5	0.99
Rural population % of total (1995)	19	39	0.49	3.7	10.8	0.34
Radios[1] Per 1,000 inhabitants (1989)	1,003	207	4.9	83%	99%	0.84
Television[2] Per 1,000 Inhabitants (1989)	207	14	14.8	94%	57%	1.65

[1]For West and East Germany: percentage of households with ratio.

[2]For East and East Germany: percentage of households with colour television.

Source: National Unification Board, Bank of Korea; Statistisches Bundesamt, Statistisches Jahrnuchder DDR; Weltbank.

Table 4: Ethnic Chinese Population of Southeast Asia and Taiwan

Country	Total Population	Chinese Population	% Chinese
Brunei	299,939	42,800	15.0
Cambodia	11,163,861	250,000[2]	2.0
Indonesia	209,774,138	5,244,353	2.5
Laos	5,116,959	66,520	1.3
Malaysia	20.491,303	6,147,391	30.0
Myanmar	46,821,943	8,193,840[2]	17.5
Philippines	76,103,564	1,522,071	2.0
Singapore	3,440,693	2,669,978	77.6
Taiwan	21,699,776	21,048,783	97.0
Thailand	59,450,818	8,323,115	14.0
Vietnam	75,123,880	1,051,734	1.4
Total	529,086,894	54,560,585	10.3

Notes. [1]Figures are compiled from the US Census Bureau, World Population Estimates, a n d *the* East Asia Analytical Unit of the Australian Department of Foreign Affairs and Trade.

[2]*Approximate* figure only.

Source: George T. Haley, Tan Chin Tiong, and Usha Haley, New Asian Emperors (Oxford: Butterworth-Heinemann, 1998); table compiled from Far Eastern Economic Review, February 26, 1998 and East Asia Analytical Unit estimates- Reproduced by permission of Butterworth-Heinemann Publishers, a division of Reed Educational & Professional Publishing Ltd.

Table 5: Ethnic Chinese Population of Southeast Asia and Taiwan

Country	Chinese as % of population	% of market capital controlled by Chinese
Brunei	15.0	0.0[1]
Cambodia	2.0[3]	70.0[4]
Indonesia	2.5	73.0
Laos	1.3	0.0[2]
Malaysia	30.0	69.0
Myanmar	17.5	0.0[2]
Philippines	2.0	50-60.0
Singapore	77.6	81.0
Taiwan	97.0	95.0[5]
Thailand	14.0	81.0
Vietnam	1.4	45.0[6]

Notes:

[1]In Brunei, ethnic Chinese often do not hold citizenship, and business are held in partnership with local citizens.

[2]Economies are currently moving away from strict socialist systems: figures still unavailable.

[3]Very rough estimates.

[4]Pre-Pol Pot figure.

[5]Percent of economy controlled by ethnic Chinese, not market capitalization.

[6]Estimate for Ho Chi Minh City only.

Source: George T. Haley, Tan Chin Tiong, and Usha Haley, New Asian Emperors (Oxford: Butterworth-Heinemann, 1998); table compiled from Far Eastern Economic Review, February 26, 1998 and East Asia Analytical Unit estimates. Reproduced by permission of Butterworth-Heinemann Publishers, a division of Reed Educational and Professional Publishing Ltd.

Box 2

INDIA

DIASPORA FACTS
There are 20 million Indians living overseas

NORTH AMERICA

U.S.	1,700,000
Canada	850,000

EUROPE

Britain	2,200,000
Netherlands	217,000
Italy	72,000
Portugal	70,000
France	65,000
Germany	35,000
Spain	29,000

MIDDLE EAST

Saudi Arabia	1,500,000
United Arab Emirates (mostly Dubai)	950,000
Oman	312,000
Bahrain	130,000
Yemen	100,900

[illegible]

Trinidad & Tobago	500.000
Guyana	396,000
Suriname	150,000
Jamaica	62,000

Source: Indian External Affairs Ministry

[illegible]

South Africa	1,000,000
Mauritius	716,00
Reunion islands	220,000
Kenya	103,000
Nigeria	25,000

SOUTHEAST ASIA

Malaysala	1,700,000
Fiji	337,000
Australia	190,000
Indonesia	55,000
New Zealand	55,000

Source: Far Eastern Economic Review, Jan 23, 2003, p. 32.

If this minority is an identifiable ethnic group as the Chinese were in Indonesia[or in many other countries—see Table 6] or Indians in Uganda, then this contradiction becomes explosive. Then the dynamics of the conflict can lead to the overthrow of the minority or the subversion of the majority by bribery and corruption. This is Yale Professor Amy Chua's thesis.

To avoid such an eventuality, either democracy will be subverted by the rich by broking the voter or market economy will be sabotaged by controls and regulation by those who get elected on the mandate of the numerous poor.

Hence, this potential conflict must be defused and institutions must come into play to resolve this conflict satisfactorily. China has proposed a *Harmonious Society*, while India has suggested *Inclusive Society*. We therefore need to understand the dynamics of democracy especially since, in India, economic reformers have consistently lost elections. Thus, designing of reforms becomes important because leaders initiating reforms must win elections. Or understand how a democratic Japan came to have such an opaque financial system with no prudential norms or accountability because of cronyism, or how the US had no proper regulation in place for the new sophisticated financial products and thus gave free play to so much greed?

That is, economic reforms can be electorally successful if it is so designed that the losers from it, mostly touts who organise quotas and licences for the rich for a price, and who immediately lose the "rent" because de-regulations implicit in reforms makes them redundant while the unorganized poor see early returns from reforms, which benefits they do not see in the usual top- down reforms.

De-regulation should also not mean that we reject government intervention for safety nets, affirmative action, market failure and creating level playing field. Democratic institutions have to empowered to guard against public disorder arising from rapid de-regulation as it happened in Russia post-1991.

Institutions should not however be so empowered, as in the Singapore case, in order to contain disorder and to deal with market failures, to end up threatening democracy itself. Or in other extreme, as was Yeltsin's Russia democracy end up threatening market institutions. Institutions must thus work out the trade-offs such as between public order and de-regulation, through affirmative action, social security and safety net to create a stake for the poor in the system, leveling the playing field to create hope, ensure transparency, accountability, and trusteeship [philanthrophy] as also corporate governance to legitimise profit making that drives the market system. Such a compromise for a market system has led some conservatives to call it the death knell of capitalism. Market system is not free for all. It is capitalism with rules of transactions. With that proviso, market system is capitalism since the principle driver is capital and its deployment.

On April 21, 1980, Time Magazine ran a cover story that asked the question: "Is Capitalism Working?" The yes answer was affirmed through Reagonomics and Thatcherism in the 1980s. Almost three decades later, the same Times Correspondent, George M. Taber and author of the 1980 Time Story(of March 4, 2009), revisited this same question. He wrote: "There was no doubt about my (1980) conclusion, and I still agree with the story's final sentence: For all its obvious blemishes and needed reforms, capitalism alone holds out the promise: the power of the free, ambitions individual."

Ironically, the period between the 1970s and present second decade of the 21st century, capitalists enjoyed a two-decade long golden age of capitalism. The U.S. economy flourished in an unprecedented period of strong growth, minimal inflation, low unemployment and great innovation. During that time, many other countries also turned to freer economies. China in 1978 opened its state-controlled economy to a greater role for the private sector and de-regulation [socialism with Chinese characteristics"], while India took the same path starting in the mid-1980s. As *Chart II and Graph 1* below reveal, the correlation between economic freedom and prosperity is undoubtedly positive and very high.

The collapse of the Soviet Union in the late 1980s led to freer economies throughout Eastern Europe. While India continues to deepen its democratic roots, there is concern since the 1989 Tiananmen episode, as to where China will head after reforming its economic system. 1989 events showed a steely resolve of the Chinese Communist Party not to

Graph 1
Economic Freedom and Income

1999 per Capita GDP in Purchasing Power Parties

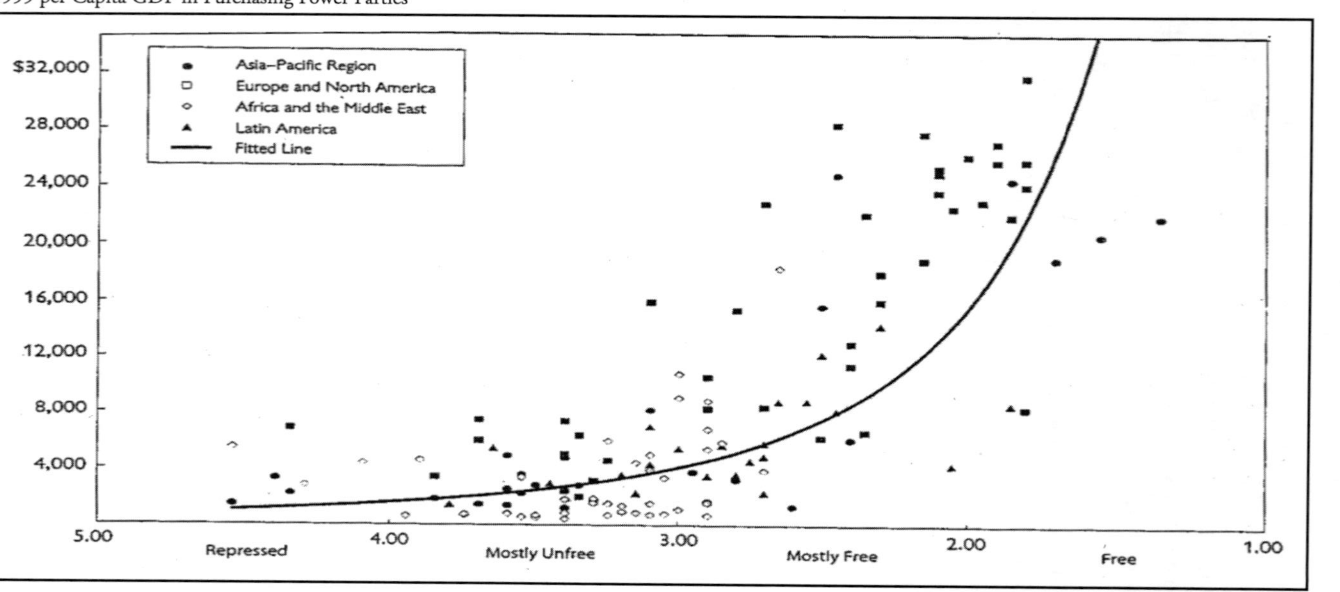

Note: Per capita GDP figures were not available for the following countries; Armenia, The Bahamas, Bahrain, Bosnia, Democratic Republic of Congo, Cube, Djibouti, Iraq, North Korea, Kuwait, Lebanon, Libya, Malta, Oman, Qatar, Suriname, Taiwan, Tajikistan, United Arab Emirates, Yugoslavia. Per capita GDP figures are in current international dollars and are from 1999.

Source: The World Bank, 2001 *World Development Indicators on CD-ROM.*

Chart 10

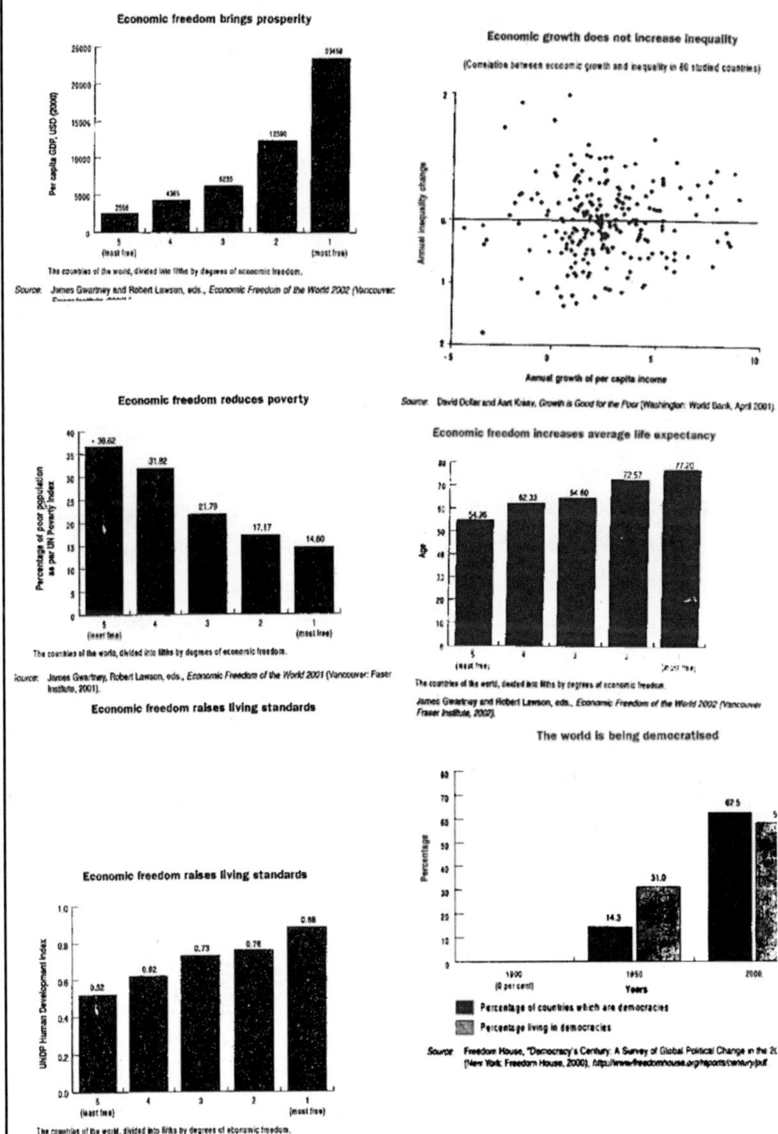
Economic freedom brings prosperity
Per capita GDP, USD (2000)
25000
20000
15000
10000
5000
0
2556
4365
6235
12390
23450
5 (least free)
4
3
2
1 (most free)
The countries of the world, divided into fifths by degrees of economic freedom.
Source. James Gwartney and Robert Lawson, eds., Economic Freedom of the World 2002 (Vancouver:
Economic growth does not increase inequality
(Correlation between economic growth and inequality in 80 studied countries)
Annual inequality change
Annual growth of per capita income
-5
0
5
10
Source. David Dollar and Aart Kraay, Growth is Good for the Poor (Washington: World Bank, April 2001).
Economic freedom reduces poverty
Percentage of poor population as per UN Poverty Index
40
35
30
25
20
15
10
5
0
38.62
31.82
21.79
17.17
14.60
5 (least free)
4
3
2
1 (most free)
The countries of the world, divided into fifths by degrees of economic freedom.
Source. James Gwartney, Robert Lawson, eds., Economic Freedom of the World 2001 (Vancouver: Fraser Institute, 2001).
Economic freedom raises living standards
Economic freedom increases average life expectancy
Age
80
70
60
50
40
30
20
10
0
54.26
62.33
64.60
72.57
77.20
5 (least free)
4
3
2
1 (most free)
The countries of the world, divided into fifths by degrees of economic freedom.
James Gwartney and Robert Lawson, eds., Economic Freedom of the World 2002 (Vancouver: Fraser Institute, 2002).
The world is being democratised
Percentage
80
70
60
50
40
30
20
10
0
14.3
31.0
62.5
1900 (0 per cent)
1950
2000
Years
Percentage of countries which are democracies
Percentage living in democracies
Source. Freedom House, "Democracy's Century: A Survey of Global Political Change in the 20th Century" (New York: Freedom House, 2000), http://www.freedomhouse.org/reports/century.pdf
Economic freedom raises living standards
UNDP Human Development Index
1.0
0.8
0.6
0.4
0.2
0.0
0.52
0.62
0.73
0.76
0.88
5 (least free)
4
3
2
1 (most free)
The countries of the world, divided into fifths by degrees of economic freedom.
Source. James Gwartney and Robert Lawson, eds., Economic Freedom of the World 2001 (Vancouver: Fraser Institute, 2001).

dilute its hold over the state apparatus, even as it permitted unprecedented de-regulation of the economic system. Economic reform thus could legitimize the Chinese authoritarian political structure, but not undermine it or even relax it.

Democracy with Chinese Characteristics

China's first *White Paper* on political democracy was issued by the State Council Information Office on October 19, 2008. Fang Ning, Deputy Director of the Institute of Political Science under the Chinese Academy of Social Sciences, gave an interview to the People's Daily in which he stated:

> "Since the 16th National Congress of the Communist Party of China (CPC) in November 2002, the CPC Central Committee, the National People's Congress (top legislature) and its sanding committee, and the State council have promulgated more than 30 documents and statutes on promoting political democracy in total. We can say that the building of China's political democracy is in full swing and there have been noted achievements in this period."

The *White Paper* is China's first government document on its political democracy, with focus on consensus building, because amid social evolution in China, political democracy encounters many new challenges. In this *White Paper*, an elaboration of China's practice political democracy and China's concept of democracy are disclosed.

The White Paper states, "The history and reality of human political civilization have proved that *there is no single and absolute democratic mode in the world that is universally applicable*. To say whether a political system is democratic or not, the key is to see whether the will of the overwhelming majority of the people is fully reflected, whether their rights as masters of the country are realized, and whether their legitimate rights and interests are fully guaranteed." This is the centerpiece of China's concept of democracy, which comes from "longtime practice of the CPC, the Chinese Government and the Chinese people."

It adds that the "CPC's leading status was a choice made by history and by the people. It conforms to the needs of China's social development and the fundamental interests of the masses of Chinese people. Western media have always held biased views on China's political democracy, because they apply their own criteria on China but turn a blind eye to the country's progress in this regard. Over the past 20-plus years, the Chinese economy has maintained an average annual growth rate of more than 9 percent. Without the strong guarantee of political democracy and social stability, such a rapid development speed is impossible".

Three expositions are worthy of close attention of scholars: The most important one is about the relationship between the CPC leadership and the people's status as 'masters' of the State. The White Paper points out that the CPC leads and supports the people to be masters of the state. It also translates the objective requirement for the Party's leadership into the "Four Needed" theory (see Note 1 below) clarifying its historic certainty and rationality.

Second is the proposal of five guiding principles for the development of China's political democracy (Note 2) in the White Paper's "conclusion" part. They are all new, which are based on summarization of both positive and negative experiences of previous practices, with references to lessons in foreign countries.

Last, the white paper expounds the internal concept of democracy. Democracy in China and other countries have a lot of fields to share but also differ from each other evidently, due to China's typical conditions. Real democracy is not dependent on formalities. It should resonate with a country's national conditions and cater to national development. China needs democracy that can make it strong and prosperous.

According to the White Paper, in building socialist political democracy, *China has always adhered to the basic principle of combining the Marxist theory of democracy with China's realities*. In addition, the useful including Western democracy, would be assimilated into the democratic elements of China's traditional culture and institutional civilization, with the following mandatory Notes:

Note (1) "Four needed" theory: The CPC's leadership and rule is needed for promoting socialist modernization and realizing great national rejuvenation; the CPC's leadership and rule is needed for safeguarding China's unification and keeping Chinese society harmonious and stable; the CPC's leadership and rule is needed for making the state power stable; and the CPC's leadership and rule is needed for uniting hundreds of millions of people to work in concerted efforts in building a beautiful future.

Note (2) Five guiding principles for the development of China's political democracy; Upholding the unity of the leadership of the CPC, the people being masters of the country and ruling the country by law; giving, play to the characteristics and advantages of the socialist system; being conducive to social stability, economic development and the continuous improvement in the people's living standards; safeguarding national sovereignty, territorial integrity and state dignity; and being in accord with the objective law of the progress step by step and in an orderly way.

Thus real democracy requires enlightened political leadership with moral vision. Otherwise democracy can legitimize a Hitler, or a Mugabe can manipulate the electoral verdict. Politics and economics are hence the two main determinants of policy choices in development. Handle it well or we shall have a failed or an oppressive state.

Political Structure and Economic Reforms

Do political compulsions in a country determine economic policy, or is that the economic imperatives shape politics in a country? If both are true, then which is the dominant vector?

It is my contention that as far as India and China are concerned, it is the political compulsion that has been the main driving force and causation of economic reforms. However, it is my further contention that in the decade ahead, political compulsion will become the main constraint that will limit further economic reforms in the two countries – especially reforms that are essential to avoid a possible financial crisis. The consequences of the political constraint in India and China, in implementing further necessary economic reforms, are serious. Unattended, it may be even become catastrophic.

The first fundamental premise that underlies the causation from politics to reforms is that any package of reforms must promote the political legitimacy and stability of the reigning authority. Otherwise there will be no incentive to adopt reforms in the first place. That is, of course, the basic political compulsion in any society but more so in India and China. Since governments in the two countries impinge on almost every aspect of the lives of their citizens and enjoy a near-paternalist status amongst the people. Reforms become more easily possible especially when the legitimacy of political authority has been eroded by policy failures as had happened in China in the 1970s and India in 1990-91.

Hence any reform that erodes the reach or hold of the government will ipso facto be resisted by those in authority, unless such erosion in the hold of government (e.g. because of deregulation or decentralization) is hedged against the future by being compensated by an increase in legitimacy of political authority. Reforms may be popular with people, but these could undermine the legitimacy of authority. There is therefore often a trade-off to be explored in design of reforms.

The second fundamental premise that underlies the causation between politics and reforms in India and China is that invariably those who will stand to lose from economic reforms are those who are relatively rich, a minority of the people, but organized and already entrenched in the political system. These people belong to the party officials in China and the rentier class and crony capitalists in India. They are able to perceive their losses from reforms immediately. In particular, the loss of patronage and perquisites of the party cadre and the denial of a 'soft-budget constraint' arising from a 'moral hazard', directly hits this minority in China. The windfall and leakage gains from distributing licences and quotas, and through protectionist trade that are to be forgone by the cronies in India causes severe opposition to reforms of deregulation.

Moreover, those who may be expected to benefit from reforms are those who are poor, although in a majority are disorganized and passive in the political system. These poor also may not perceive immediately the future stream of benefits that is to accurate to them especially if the reforms are based on the 'top-down and trickle' principle as most reforms are.

Hence, the losers will discredit the reforms without fear that the beneficiaries from these reforms will rise in its defence.

Economic reforms thus must take into account these two premises, and thus be designed on consistent objectives, a clear ordering of priorities, a well-defined political strategy, and which reforms must be embedded in a sustainable financial architecture. In structuring such reforms, there will be a number of variables whose values will have to be determined by a clear calculus that takes into account the constraints to be met – the equivalent of the mathematical truism that a solution could exist only if the number of variables equals the number of equations, a concept glorified by Jan Tinbergen into a 'mantra' decades ago. Such a calculus, dependent on the nature of political strategy, will be different in its authoritarian political order from a strategy in a democracy, a distinction made ably in Amy Chua's seminal study.

In a multi-party pluralistic democracy, these poor are empowered to vote but it is the rich who have the resources to organize the campaign and information dissemination in an election. Unless there is a mass consciousness developing out of a defining event, as it happened in India in 1977 and 1984, the poor can be manipulated to serve the rich, or alternatively the losers from reforms, although a minority of voters, can 'persuade' the majority of voters to reject reforms, Thus if subsidies or doles made in programmes such as food-for-work that leak funds to the entrenched political interests are discontinued in the interest of a competitive market economy on the promise of benefits on the trickle down principle, the majority will reject the reforms. This happened in India in 1996 and in 2004.

Therefore, reforms have to be whetted politically and designed to frustrate this manipulation by dividing the potential losers, or by enabling a section of the rick to see further gains in endorsing the reforms or by incorporating in the name of reforms such ad hoc projects that generate immediate if temporary employment for the poor. In a single party system, the calculus will be dependent on understanding the nature of political control. In such a system, the financial system and cronyism ('gunashi') are crucial to retaining the authority of the party. This would mean that independent sources of economic power such as a private sector with non-state access to markets and finance cannot be permitted. No reform that promotes that will be politically feasible. This has been noted in China to be so by one representative of a multinational corporation, George Gilboy and recorded in interesting article.

Politics and Reform in India and China

Hence, the politics of economic reforms in India and China will be healthy if the design of reforms is cognizant of, and based on an understanding of these two fundamental premises. The design of reforms should thus resolve the basic contradiction between the requirements of economic efficiency in the allocation of resources and challenge of political compulsions. The failure to do so has already led to set backs in the reforms process in India and China during the last eight years.

This has nothing to do with the conventional wisdom that strong stable and authoritarian governments with cohesive parties in power can deliver reforms better than weak unstable governments. It instead entirely depends on how the ruling authority wants to politically hedge against the future and how economic interests are represented in the party in power. Rajiv Gandhi had received the largest ever mandate to govern India as prime minister in 1984. Despite being a truly modern person who understood what needed to be done, the Congress Party's economic interests backed by the pro-Soviet establishment made him climb down from radical reforms within a year in office. His inability to effect structural reforms left India with a huge balance of payments crisis in 1990.

In early 1991, the Soviet Union was already unraveling which enabled a minority government of Prime Minister Chandrashekhar (in which this author was the senior-most Cabinet Minister) to draft and adopt a blue print for economic reforms that was however implemented by the successor Narasimha Rao government, also perceived as a politically weak minority government.

But Rao in mid-1991 brought reforms as a hedge against the uncertain political future arising out of the BoP crisis, but his failure to get re-elected five years later was not because of results of the reforms that he got implemented – which were in fact spectacular – but in the failure to design the reforms in such a way that beneficiaries could see some gains as quickly as the losers could feel the losses.

Despite rescuing India from a financial and balance of payments abyss, and placing the Indian economy firmly on the path of fast economic growth for five continuous years (1991-96), peaking at 8 per cent per year, Narasimha Rao's government was soundly defeated at the polls in 1996. He was formally disowned and disgraced since then by his party – now led by Italian born Sonia, who is a widow of former Prime Minister Rajiv Gandhi.

The Congress subsequently disowned these reforms as delivered in the verdict of the party's Antony Committee, mainly because these reforms had violated the second fundamental premise. The Congress is dominated by those who had become entrenched in the power structure during the highly regulated Soviet type system. The Rao - guided reforms therefore obviously had threatened these elements in the party.

Since then, five successive governments have not found it necessary to launch the required 'second generation reforms', but have adopted reforms piecemeal to meet *ad hoc* objectives. This has helped to postpone the day of financial reckoning, but it will not be for long. As we shall see, India is already in a comprehensive fiscal failure, even if it is an international secret today. Indian coalition politics of today will not permit the essential fiscal reforms to correct for this failure. A crisis seems thus inevitable as was in 1990-91. Only in the midst of a crisis will the politics of India, to hedge against the future, permit essential reforms. An analysis of past achievements such as the 'green revolution' onwards shows that it has taken a crisis to overcome or re-define political compulsions in India to permit essential reforms. Hence, as an Indian I look forward to the next crisis.

In China, the 1989 Tianamen incident may be analysed in the context of the first premise. According to a study edited by Harvard's Roderick Macfarquhar the student revolt for 'democracy' staged in Tiananmen Square was crushed because the Communist Party feared 'spiritual pollution', a euphemism for the dilution in legitimacy of authority. This had its roots in the decades of economic planning.

In 1950, India and China had adopted the Soviet style planned economy framework for change in their respective civil strife-wasted and imperialist-bled economy. The leadership that came to power had the aura that liberators and founding fathers are gifted with, and hence, not only had the legal authority, but the moral mandate as well to expect sacrifices from the people for the change.

In China, an authoritarian political structure immediately launched on a complete restructuring of the production relations and achieved the same by 1956. By this, the leadership wiped out whatever resistance there may have been from the previous feudal order, and consolidated thereby the Communist Party's legitimacy. But in securing its control on society by authoritarian measures, the party also alienated those sections who could be motivated only by incentives and security – especially farmers with small holdings, and also professionals such as doctors etc. broadly called the intelligentsia. Only when the 'Hundred Flowers' campaign was launched in 1956, did the permitted free criticism of the restructuring become vehement and shocked the leadership. It was clamped down by a successor campaign of 'Rectification' in which the unorthodox sections of the intelligentsia were severely punished. The legitimacy of the Communist Party of China had been threatened and hence the leadership acted swiftly.

Further re-structuring of the production relations followed in the Great Leap Forward (1958-60) campaign. But a number of exogenous factors such as the Soviet Union's breach of faith with China by withdrawing all its technicians and blue-prints from the construction of 146 industrial projects along with a severe drought caused havoc in China with 16 to 32 million perishing in a famine of epic proportions. The GLP campaign had thus to be abandoned by a new leadership of the party, that came to office by 'elevating' chairman Mao to an ornamental position. One of the prime movers, Deng Xiaoping, initiated in 1961 a number of reforms to restore the health of the economy, such as backyard plots for commune households and opening of trade with west European and Japanese markets. By 1965, just as the legitimacy of the party had been restored by a rapid economic recovery, a power struggle erupted in the form of Great Proletarian Cultural Revolution (1966-76), unseating

Deng and his colleagues, and which struggle nearly destroyed the credibility of the party.

Once again Deng Xiaoping re-emerged in 1977 and launched one of the most impressive reforms and graduated deregulation of the economy, while refurbishing and preserving the legitimacy of the party. Deng told me, when he received me in April 1981 in Beijing, that he had decided on such far-reaching reforms when he was in the political wilderness and saw that people unhappy with their economic situation had begun doubting the party. The impressive economic reforms were thus clearly for restoring the legitimacy of the party but needed Deng's political skill and hold over the party to sell it to the world as 'secularism with Chinese characteristics'.

Hence, what this narration suggests is that understandably reforms will continue or new reforms will be initiated in China only if these will enhance the legitimacy of the Chinese Communist Party. Which reforms will be barred on this consideration and which will not, have to be inferred from the context of the proposed reforms.

In India and China the reforms to date have been driven by political compulsions. New political compulsions may now block future essential reforms. Hence, we need a clear set of consistent objectives, an ordering of priorities, an effective strategy of growth based on a realistic model and accurate data availability for course corrections, a modern financial architecture, and an enabling environment or soft infrastructure.

Thus, given that the best economic system is market-driven, and best political order and human infrastructure is constitutional democracy, it is the harmonization of market and democracy that is sustainable and stable.. For market *with* democracy we need [i] growth *with* income equity [ii] technological progress, new innovations *with* job creation [iii] merit –based choices *with* affirmative action [iv] Philanthropy *with* profit [v] regulation *with* transparency. The US has nearly perfected this system but 'greed' derailed the system in August 2007. The economic man must not only be driven by profit but also tempered by moral values.

Stripped down to its core and at its best, American capitalism is ideologically close to the theories espoused by Joseph Schumpeter, a Harvard economist, born in 1883 in what is now the Czech Republic and educated in Austria. He taught at Harvard from the 1920s to the 1940s.

Schumpeter's most important work was *Capitalism, Socialism* and *Democracy,* which was first published in 1942. The centerpiece of his thinking is the concept of "creative destruction," a theory based on earlier work by the Russian Mikhail Bakunin as well as the Germans Friedrich Nietzsche and Werner Sombart. Schumpeter, though, popularized it.

Creative destruction means that old established companies under capitalism tend to lose their dynamism with time and atrophy under a layer of corporate bureaucracy and complacency. Then entrepreneurs, who usually have few links to the past, introduce bold and fresh ideas for new products, manufacturing techniques, or distribution and displace the old order. The process is often destructive, but also creative. This corporate life cycle has repeated itself again and again in numerous fields: Ford Motor Company was innovative in the early 20th century, but Japanese auto companies passed Ford and other American auto makers in the 1970s; Sears Roebuck dominated U.S. retailing in the 1950s, but Wal-Mart has now eclipsed it; IBM in the 1960s reigned supreme over mainframe computers, yet Apple and Dell ushered in personal computers in the 1980s.

According to Schumpeter, innovation and entrepreneurs are the driving force of economic vitality and growth. The implication for American public policy is that government should foster policies – such as low capital gains taxes and few barriers to starting new companies – that encourage entrepreneurs to practice their craft.

Since 1947, the only alternative ideology of economic development and progress to Capitalism and Marxism came from India propounded by Deendayal Upadhyaya. But his Integral Humanism Theory (IHT) was ignored because no political party including the successors of his Jan Sangh party, the BJP, gave the theory any substantive importance.

What distinguishes IHT from Marxism and Capitalism is the latter's one dimensional concept of the human pursuit of material progress. Hence while Marx talks of economic interpretation of history and class struggle of annihilation, capitalism focuses on maximization of profit and consumption, as well the survival of the fittest [see Table 7 below].

Table 6

Dimension	Capitalism (Adam Smith)	Ideology Socialism (Harold Laski)	Communism (Karl Mars)	Integral Humanisam (Deendayal Upadhyaya)
1. Objectives	Maximum profit and Maximum consumption Energy-intensive	Maximum material welfare and hedge against risk: safety nets	Maximum production	Optimum synthesis of national development and global welfare. Swalambhana (self reliance)
2. Priorities	Energy-intensive exploitation of resources	Guaranteed minimum material standards of pay, pension and unemployment	primacy of the system based on coercion in the extraction of funds from the people for the state	Primary of man through balanced development of Chaturvidha Purushartha [Artha, Kama, Dharma, and Moksha]
3. Development strategy	Primacy to labour saving capital-intensive technology that energy consuming Free trade globally	Nationalization of commanding heights and public distribution of essential commodities	Total ownership of all the means of production. Foreign trade discouraged	Conflict resolution and harmonisation through complementaries
4. Resource Mobilization	Incentive and propensity to spend. Environment destructive	Taxation and controls and Licensing	Total control over incomes received and permitted consumption. Administered prices and terms and trade	Trusteeship and austerity; Four sources of wealth, vidya sashtra, dhan, bhoomi distributed without concentration in one hand.
5. Institutional	Survival of the fittest laissez faire in a free market. Invisible hand.	Administrative controls, licences and Government regulation in a quota system	Dialectical Materialism, Class struggle and Dictatorship of the Proletariat	Decentralization, Panchayati Raj and self-employment of the people

Sources: Smith, Adam: *Wealth of Nations;* Laski, Harold: *Grammar of Politics;* Marx, Karl: *Das Kapital;* Upadhaya, Deendayal: *Integral Humanism.*

But now it is acknowledged that Marxism has failed world wide, in contrast with and relative to market economy and democracy, as we saw in cases evidenced by Germanys, Koreas, or China and India before and after reform. Moreover the crucible of Marxism, the USSR, has disassembled and dissolved. Capitalism is racked with instability continuously. Capitalism has produced wealth and prosperity but not internal contentment of the individual. Hence there is a search for a new theory of development.

IHT is a two dimension theory of harmonization of material progress with spiritual advancement. This harmonization is achieved by new objectives, priorities, strategy and resource mobilization techniques [see Table 7] by permitting competitiveness and seeking adjusting complementarities.

Democracy thus is not enough, because of two reasons viz., intransitivity in majority decision and contradictions that Amy Chua has elaborated. *Varna* system in India was one effective way to resolve these contradictions but the system degenerated and became purely birth-based. It is discredited today as retrograde and against human freedom..

Gross National Product and National Income (GNP and NI)

Gross national product is the sum total of goods and services produced in a country during a year. There are several stages in arriving at national income (Net National Product (NNP)) from gross national product. That is done by first estimating obsolescence.

A bicycle bought today in US is worth $500. Are you likely to get the same amount for the bicycle, if you sell it after two years? No! Because it has become old and depreciated due to use. Thus, the current price of the cycle is calculated by deducting depreciation charges from the original price. Similarly, in the production process a country may use machines and equipments. When there is depreciation, we have to repair or replace machines and equipments. The expenses incurred for this is called the depreciation expenditure. Net National Product is calculated by deducting depreciation expense from gross national product. But since it is difficult to get accurately the decline in value due to wear and tear and "going out of fashion" therefore, in national accounts an educated guess is made which is called obsolescence. That is, NNP = GNP – Obsolescence.

National income is arrived from NNP, by deducting indirect taxes and adding subsidies. Sales tax is an example for indirect tax. This is collected by adding tax to the price of commodities. Then if you want to know the original price, you have to deduct sales tax from the selling price of the commodity.

You might have noticed that products are given rebate during festival seasons. Say 20% rebate is given for a product. If you want to know the original price of a product sold during the festival season, naturally you have to add the subsidy given to the sale price of the product. This process is followed in the calculation of National Income also. National Income is calculated by deducting indirect taxes from Net National Product and adding subsidies. Thus, NI = NNP - Indirect Taxes + Subsidies. Per Capita Income (PCI) is the average annual income of the people of a country. It is obtained by dividing national income by the population of a country.

PURCHASING POWER PARITY

Why are things expressed in terms of US dollars when the value of the dollar has fallen so much since 2005? Because the United States economy is the largest in the world, it is convenient to use the US dollar as the *numeraire* currency. But we can either use the foreign exchange market rate to convert values in other currencies to the dollar or we can construct a Purchasing Power Parity [PPP] conversion rates based actual market prices prevailing various countries and thereby calculating the price ratio for each commodity by dividing it by price prevailing in the US market.

Purchasing power parity thus is "...the number of currency units required to purchase an amount of goods and services equivalent to what can be bought with one unit of currency of the base country, for example the United States dollar. PPP conversion rates allow users to compare real economic outputs across countries at a common set of average international prices ..."

A detailed description of the methodology underlying PPPs is set out in the World Bank's *ICP 2003-2006 Handbook* [World Bank 2007a chapter 1]. In practice, any currency can be used as the numeraire currency. In Asia and the Pacific region and in this publication, Hong

Kong, China was used as the base economy, which means that results are presented either in terms of values expressed in Hong Kong dollars or as an index with Hong Kong, China = 100. In addition, results are also presented in terms of regional average for Asia 1 to enable comparisons to be made readily between individual economies and the average for all 23 economies. It is important to note that the relative volume and price comparisons across economies remain unchanged when a different currency is used as the numeraire or when the results are expressed in index number form.

Table 7: Ethnic Chinese Population of Southeast Asia and Taiwan

Consumer Goods	Unit	Indian Market Price (S/unit)	(1) Chinese Market Price (S/unit)	(2) Ratiu (2) + (1) (yuan/rupee)
1. Rice	1 kg	0.47	0.36	0.76
2. Milk	1 litre	0.28	0.60	2.14
3. Cooking Oil	1 litre	1.02	1.45	1.42
4. Pork	1 kg	0.62	1.81	2.92
5. Cabbage	1 kg	0.32	0.24	0.75
6. Pears (Asian)	1 kg	1.42	0.72	0.51
7. Oranges	1 kg	0.19	0.72	3.81
8. Apples	1 kg	1.08	0.97	0.89
9. Coca Cola	1 can	0.32	0.28	0.87
10. Ice Cream	Indigenous	0.17	0.70	4.12
11. Haagen-Dazs Ice Cream	One Scoop	0.26	3.02	11.61
12. Pizza Hut (Cheese)	Large	3.02	7.85	2.60
13. Toothpaste (Colgate)	Large	1.19	0.72	0.61
14. Toothpaste (Indigenous)	120 g	0.90	0.31	0.34
15. Taxi	5 kms	0.65	1.69	2.60
16. Gasoline	1 litre	0.63	0.32	0.51
17. Movie	1 Ticket	0.65	2.20	3.39
18. Bicycles	1 unit	28.508	36.303	1.27
19. Electric Fans	1 unit	20.958	4.937	0.23
20. Color Television Sets	1 unit	254.465	65.741	0.26
21. Tyres	1 unit	29.912	8.883	0.30
22. Primary Cells and Batteries	1 unit	0.225	0.048	0.21
Major Exports for China and India		**Indian FOB Value**	**Chinese FOB Value**	
23. Trousers of Cotton Handloom	1 unit	4.180	3.310	0.79
24. Jacket and Blazers	1 unit	6.800	6.710	0.99
25. Men Suits of Wool	1 unit	21.400	55.900	2.61
26. Women Suits of Cotton	1 unit	6.300	5.590	0.89
27. Women Suits of Wool	1 uinit	8.000	30.200	3.78
28. Skirts and Divided Skirts	1 unit	5.800	2.940	0.51
29. Dresses of Wool	1 unit	9.600	11.210	1.15
30. Footwear	1 unit	11.800	7.440	0.63

31. Travel Goods of Leather	1 unit	16.000	3.790	0.24
32. Leather Handbags for Ladies	1 unit	8.800	4.210	0.48
33. Electric Clock Movements	1 unit	3.452	0.140	0.04
34. Wrist Watches (Automatic)	1 unit	17.949	1.060	0.06
35. Electric Alarm Clocks	1 unit	4.918	0.370	0.08
36. Sewing Machine Needles	1 kg	38.801	10.740	0.28
37. Melamine	1 kg	2.901	0.830	0.29
38. Anthraquinone	1 kg	7.758	2.730	0.35
39. Saccharin and its salts	1 kg	6.860	2.420	0.36
40. Ampicillin salts	1 kg	39.312	14.770	0.38
41. Barium Carbonate	1 kg	0.316	0.190	0.60
42. Chloramphenicol and its derivatives	1 kg	26.442	17.250	0.65
43. Citric Acid	1 kg	1.160	0.800	0.69
44. Xylene	1 kg	0.370	0.470	1.27
45. Full Automatic Washing Machine Unit	1 unit	118.537	156.030	1.32
46. Cathode Ray TV Picture Tube	1 unit	52.132	73.130	1.40
47. Sodium	1 kg	0.580	1.360	2.34
48. Vitamin B1 and its derivatives	1 kg	6.048	14.790	2.45
49. Calcium	1 kg	1.037	4.050	3.91
50. Pyridine and its salts	1 kg	5.704	28.100	4.93

Source: Gopalan R: "China's Competitiveness" Ministry of Commerce, New Delhi, May 9, 2001, and US-China Business Council quoted in China Business Review, May-June 2001 and author's collection of data. Official exchange rate are: 1 Yuan = 5.56 rupees; 1$ = 8.28 yuans; 1 rupee = 0.18 yuan.

This gigantic project of the UN is called the International Comparisons of Prices [ICP] project. There are 146 countries and territories participating in the ICP. This is a record number. China was included for the first time, but India has not participated since 1985. Africa included 48 countries. Estimates of purchasing power parities have been made for an additional 39 non-participating countries. The ICP is a voluntary programme. A record number of countries participated in this round but resource constraints and other reasons prevented some countries from participating. Many have indicated their willingness to participate in the next round.

The data in *World Development Indicators* are based on previous benchmark surveys. For developing countries, where benchmark data existed, they are based on the previous ICP round in 1993 and are quite of date. For countries with no previous benchmark, data were imputed. So it is not surprising that there will be some changes with the introduction of new and better data. One of the biggest changes is for China which has participated in the ICP for the first time.

The data for GDP, population, and exchange rates were provided by national sources. For a few countries they differ from the data published by international agencies such as the World Bank because of differences in vintage or statistical methods. When the ICP results are published in the *World Development Indicators,* they will be made consistent with other indicators in the WDI database.

The most celebrated example of a PPP is the "Big Mac Index" compiled and regularly published by *The Economist* magazine [see Table 9] The Big Mac Index is a PPP that is based solely on the price of a Big Mac in various countries—a commodity that is comparable in quality and available in most locations.

TABLE 8

THE TOP TEN

Country	GNI (PPP) (2007) in $ billion
US	10914
China	8435
Japan	3641
India	3068
Germany	2267
France	1640
UK	1639
Italy	1543
Brazil	1322
Russia	1279

GNI: Gross National Income
PPP: Purchasing Power Party

Big Mac Index

The Economist's Big Mac Index is based on the theory of purchasing-power party (PPP), the idea that exchange rates should move to equalise the prices of a basket of goods and services across different countries. our basket is the Big Mac. For example, the cheapest burger in the chart is in China, at $1.26, compared with an average American price of $3. This implies that the yuan is 58% undervalued relative to its Big Mac dollar - PPP. On the same basis, the euro is 25% overvalued, the yen 17% undervalued.

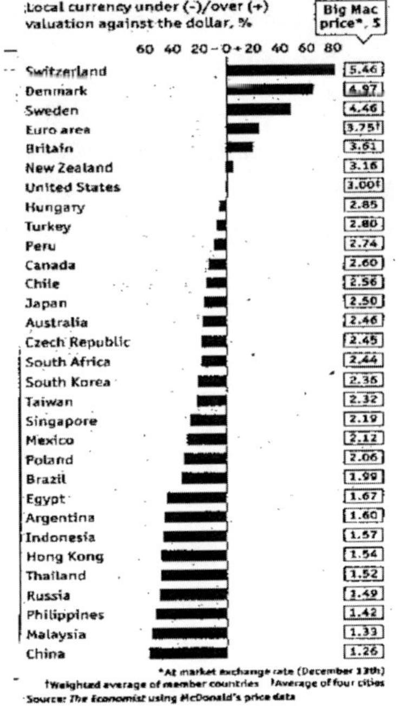

TABLE 9

ECON S-1316 Economic Development in India and East Asia
Dr. Subramanian Swamy

Q: How is the Big Mac Index Calculated?

The hamburger standard

	Big Mac price in dollars*	Implied PPP[†] of the dollar	Under (-)/ over (+) valuation against the dollar, %
United States[‡]	3.06	—	—
Argentina	1.64	1.55	-46
Australia	2.50	1.08	-18
Brazil	2.39	1.93	-22
Britain	3.44	1.63[§]	+12
Canada	2.63	1.07	-14
Chile	2.53	490	-17
China	1.27	3.43	-59
Czech Republic	2.30	18.4	-25
Denmark	4.58	9.07	+50
Egypt	1.55	2.94	-49
Euro area	3.58**	1.05[††]	+17
Hong Kong	1.54	3.92	-50
Hungary	2.60	173	-15
Indonesia	1.53	4,771	-50
Japan	2.34	81.7	-23
Malaysia	1.38	1.72	-55
Mexico	2.58	9.15	-16
New Zealand	3.17	1.45	+4
Peru	2.76	2.94	-10
Philippines	1.47	26.1	-52
Poland	1.96	2.12	-36
Russia	1.48	13.7	-52
Singapore	2.17	1.18	-29
South Africa	2.10	4.56	-31
South Korea	2.49	817	-19
Sweden	4.17	10.1	+36
Switzerland	5.05	2.06	+65
Taiwan	2.41	24.5	-21
Thailand	1.48	19.6	-52
Turkey	2.92	1.31	-5
Venezuela	2.13	1,830	-30
Aruba	2.77	1.62	-10
Bulgaria	1.88	0.98	-39
Colombia	2.79	2124	-9
Costa Rica	2.38	369	-22
Croatia	2.50	4.87	-18
Dominican Rep	2.12	19.6	-31
Estonia	2.31	9.64	-24
Fiji	2.50	1.39	-18
Georgia	2.00	1.19	-34
Guatemala	2.20	5.47	-28
Honduras	1.91	11.7	-38
Iceland	6.67	143	+118
Jamaica	2.70	53.9	-12
Jordan	3.66	0.85	+19
Latvia	1.92	0.36	-37
Lebanon	2.85	1405	-7
Lithuania	2.31	2.12	-24
Macau	1.40	3.66	-54
Macedonia	1.90	31.0	-38
Moldova	1.84	7.52	-40
Morocco	2.73	8.02	-11
Nicaragua	2.11	11.3	-31
Norway	6.06	12.7	+98
Pakistan	2.18	42.5	-29
Paraguay	1.44	2941	-53
Qatar	0.68	0.81	-78
Saudi Arabia	2.40	2.94	-22
Serbia & Montenegro	2.08	45.8	-32
Slovakia	2.09	21.6	-32
Slovenia	2.56	163	-16
Sri Lanka	1.75	57.2	-43
Ukraine	1.43	2.37	-53
UAE	2.45	2.94	-20
Uruguay	1.82	14.4	-40

*At current exchange rates [†]Purchasing-power parity [‡]Average of New York, Chicago, San Francisco and Atlanta [§]Dollars per pound **Weighted average of member countries [††]Dollars per euro
Sources: McDonald's; *The Economist*

Country	(1) Big Mac price in local currency	(2) Exchange rate (05/04) foreign/domestic	(3) Big Mac price in dollars	(4) Implied PPP of the dollar	(5) Local currency under(-)/over(+) valuation
United States	$3.06	--	$3.06	1.00	--
China	10.51	8.2765	$1.27	3.44	-58.50%

Column (1): Prices in local currency
Column (2): Actual exchange rates on June 9, 2005
Column (3): column (1) / column (2)
Column (4): column (1) / $~~[illegible]~~ (the price of a Big Mac in the U.S.) $3.06
Column (5): ([column (4) / column (2)] - 1)

Teaching Assistant

Although it is a simple example of a PPP, in practice it is of little use for making international comparisons because it is not representative of all the goods and services included in GDP. More reliable measures of PPPs, such as those compiled as part of the 2005 ICP, are constructed using a large amount of data on the prices of a broad range of goods and services that make up GDP. In ICP Asia Pacific, the participating economies priced items from a list of around 800 household and nonhousehold products in 2005 and early 2006.

To calculate PPPs, it is necessary to identify goods and services of similar quality that are *comparable* across all the countries involved in the comparison and that are broadly *representative* of the goods and services purchased in each participating country. Differences in income, lifestyle, and sources of products make it difficult to identify products that meet these two competing criteria, so compromises have to be made. Once the full range of price data is collected, relative prices of the items are weighted using GDP data to compute PPPs for different commodity groupings, ranging from detailed component expenditures to broad aggregates, such as individual consumption expenditures by households, and to total GDP, measured from the final expenditures that make up GDP (for example, household expenditures, investment, and government expenditures). PPPs are compiled for different GDP aggregates, including GDP itself, to convert them to a numeraire currency.

Using exchange rates to convert aggregates in local currency units can be misleading because exchange rates do not reflect relative domestic price levels and are influenced by extraneous factors (interest rates and financial flows, for example).

The most common use of PPPs is their application to national accounts data to provide estimates of levels of GDP and GDP per capita that are comparable directly across countries. In other words, PPPs are an intermediate step in determining the levels of outputs expressed in a common currency for all countries included in the comparison. Apart from the obvious use of comparing the levels of GDP and its major components, the main uses of these data are for comparing productivity levels and aggregating real expenditures into regional and subregional totals (as, for example, total GDP in 2005 for ICP Asia Pacific).

Apart from its importance as an intermediate step in calculating the real levels of GDP and its major components, PPPs are an essential input in calculating the price level indexes (PLIs) that enable one to compare the relative price levels in countries (that is, determining whether goods and services in a country are either relatively expensive or relatively cheap). While the PLI for GDP measures the overall price level in a country, PLIs can also be calculated for the main aggregates, such as household consumption, capital formation, and government expenditures; and for more detailed levels of expenditures such as food, clothing, transport, and construction. Policymakers can use this information to identify goods or services whose price levels are high compared with other countries in the region, and then determine if these high levels are due to market imperfections that may be remedied by policy measures. PPPs can also be used to make a wide range of intercountry comparisons that are relevant for economic and social policy. For example:

While PPPs are a powerful tool for several kinds of economic analysis, a word of caution is needed. First, PPPs do not tell us what the exchange rate "should be." When the theory of PPPs was first developed, it was argued that these would be close to "equilibrium exchange rates." But the PPPs from the 2005 round cover not only tradable but also nontradable products, such as construction goods and government services. In any event, exchange rates are determined by the total demand for a particular currency; financing foreign trade is only one component of this demand. PPPs, therefore, cannot be used to indicate a country's "correct" exchange rate, which is determined by international currency markets.

Second, PPPs are statistics and so are subject to sampling errors. GDP statistics that are used as weights in the calculation of PPPs at basic heading level also contain similar errors (Basic headings are the lowest level of aggregation at which expenditure-share weights are available). Obviously, some components of GDP are more challenging to compare than others. For example, nonmarket services such as the provision of health, education, and other government services remain difficult, despite research efforts that aim to address long-standing problems. Construction projects are another area of weakness in the ICP because of differences in building codes, quality of materials, type and amount of equipment used, and labor skills. Striking a balance between comparability and representativity of products and services makes the challenge even more compelling. This is particularly true when countries in comparison are different in terms of expenditure patterns, as well as in economic and social development. Hence, results in difficult-to-compare sectors must be approached with greater caution than other GDP components.

Finally, time series of GDP (in PPP terms) are misleading. Real GDP provides a snapshot of the relative real GDP levels among participating countries for a given benchmark year. When benchmark PPP estimates are placed side by side, these snapshots may appear to provide a moving picture of relative real GDP levels over the years, but this apparent time series of real GDP is actually similar to a current price time series showing the combined effect of changes in relative price levels and changes in relative real GDP levels. Within each year, the indexes are at a uniform price level, which changes from one reference year to the next.

HOW FAST IS CHINA REALLY GROWING?

It must be stated at the outset that much of the assessment of China's economic performance in the literature, leave alone in the media, is based on an uncritical acceptance of Chinese official statistics. Although in this study we do not share the alarmist view that the Chinese authorities "cook their statistical books", nevertheless officially released data from China do require re-working to bring them in conformity with international practice. Some but relatively little re-working of Indian data is also essential.

Otherwise, data on GDP, FDI and foreign trade of the two countries are not comparable, and would lead to wrong inferences. A re-working of Chinese data lowers of the growth rate estimate, increases inequality, reduces FDI inflow, and makes a less impressive export performance. Nevertheless, despite all this, Chinese performance based on corrected data are still very impressive and in many ways better than India's performance.

India, with a relatively more open and free press, however suffers from adverse comparisons across the board with China because of media-induced perceptions on economic performance, and more so because

Chinese data are less UN Statistical Office compliant in concepts and accuracy than India, a hazard we have to live with, but as scholars need to correct for.

In fact, the US based Institute of the Management Accountants which has carried out extensive research on the Chinese firms' costing has recently warned us about the vagaries of the Chinese cost accounting systems. And yet there is little awareness about it amongst the general readers of China affairs.

The International inter-governmental organizations that publish data on the Chinese economy do not, for political correctness, re-construct the Chinese data for scope, valuation and netness errors before publication. Most of the scholars with nouveau interests on China, such as Amartya Sen and T.N. Srinivasan, have been recently writing on India-China comparisons, but have not bothered with or are unable to read the original Chinese sources for data concepts but rely on uncorrected official data published by the World Bank or IMF and therefore generally get their conclusions wrong.

Does China "cook the books' on its growth rate figures as international media is quoting some scholars as saying? According to this author it is clearly: *No* !. But what has been true for long is that Chinese data lack internal consistency, and the inherent biases in official data collection methodology have resulted inconsistently over-stating the growth rate of the economy. For the period-78, Chinese official data had revealed a growth rate in net material product [NMP] of about 8 percent per year, which scholars spliced with their estimates of the non-material sectors to get a growth rate in GDP of 6 to 8 percent per year for that period, and this estimate of how fast China was growing held the field for sometime. Percapita income in 1978 was placed at $1000 by some scholars.

There were however a few [Swamy [53](1973), Michael Field (1975), and Kang Chao[8] (1978)] who had opined then that the NMP estimates in scope, netness and valuation errors were inflated, and needed to be re-worked but this had little scholarly support, till 1980, when to conform to UN statistical standards the Chinese officially admitted that the earlier published data had been inflated, and the 1980 percapita income was not more than $253, i.e., about the same as India's.

In a later publication, *Dwight Perkins* [35] (1997) demonstrated the type of inherent biases in Chinese data by re-calculating the 1957-78 NMP figures at 1990 prices [which were closer to the market besides being in conformity with Paasche's Index] and showing that an annual 6 percent growth rate in 1957 prices had to be replaced with 3.6 percent in 1990 prices as more accurate. This growth rate also put China in the same growth league as India—for the period till China began its reforms. If such re-evaluation and downward revision had not been done, the $1000 percapita figure projected forward at the post-reform Chinese officially claimed growth rate of 10.1 percent year would put China's percapita income today in 1980 prices at $8000, making it a G-7 developed country.

Today some of the same scholars are erring on the other extreme. Rawski[1980] who in the 1970s was all for accepting Chinese officially published data without correction, today is quoted by Newsweek Magazine as supporting the view that China cooks her data books and the growth rate in recent years could be negative! This implies a fraud on part of the Chinese authorities as also a decline in data quality since the 1970s.

On the contrary, Chinese official data have vastly improved in quality over the years since 1980 thanks largely to the discipline of the UN statistical system of reporting to which China is increasingly conforming. It has to be said to the credit of the Chinese authorities that on the contrary when glaring data malfeasance was brought their notice by subsequent events, they made on an open admission and corrected the data as the following illustrates:

(i) In 1958, in the aftermath of Mao's Great Leap Forward adventure, grain output was to claimed to have doubled. Later the Prime Minister Chou En lai himself announced the correction.

(ii) In 1998, following Premier Zhu Rongji's announcement that he will strive for a 8% growth rate in GDP, all provinces, except Yunnan, reported growth of provincial domestic product in excess of 8%. But Yazhou Kan of March 27, 2000 reported in an article "Numbers Lie: Premier Uncovers Lies" that NBS scaled down the figures after Zhu's intervention. In 1999 too the problem persisted. While officially growth rate was put at 7.1% only two provinces reported below 7.1% and 10 provinces reported above 10% growth rate.

(iii) Following the 1995 Industrial Census, the NBS made a 20% downward correction in the gross value of output of the Collective Sector [mostly TVEs] retrospectively for four previous years.

(iv) *Guangming Ribao* [July 24, 1998], in an article titled "Statistical Fraud in China" carried a stern warning from the NBS of prosecutions for falsifying data. It reported that in 1997 about 60,000 cases had been registered!

Recently *Allyn Young* [61] has for the NBER done an excellent review of the current status of official statistics and reworked the data. Young is of the considered opinion that there is no willful fudging or falsification of data by senior Chinese authorities nor is there is any direction to do that from above. China has in fact enacted a new law for statistical purity. The Chinese National Bureau of Statistics has also suo moto revised downwards data earlier published on gross value of industrial output.

Hence, with Allyn Young, Dwight Perkins and others, I too join in debunking the view that China at the National Bureau of Statistics level cooks the books to make it's economic performance look good. That does not mean that we accept the Chinese official statistics as it is or that we deny at the lower levels officials here and there may for career interests fudge or fabricate the data. Or that under pressure to report fast to meet some deadline, a county office may report for example, current price data as in constant prices. Thus Chinese data certainly need re-working, cross-checked, and be made internally consistent.

There are principally the following reasons why it is responsible to assume that Chinese authorities will not and do not wilfully fudge or fabricate data as a national policy:

(i) To do so would require maintaining two sets of files, one strictly "neybu" for internal policy makers use, and another for publication. It will require two parallel hierarchies since it will be necessary to keep the neybu files from those who handle others. This is a horrendous task administratively, and it is therefore easier to decide just not to publish data as had happened between 1966 and 1976 than fabricate data.

(ii) Inflating a percentage increase for one year makes it a little harder each year without sooner or later inviting ridicule since growth is a cumulative process that snowballs in a compound rate calculus.

(iii) Some of the statistics such as wages, prices, incomes are verifiable from personal experience, but have to be falsified as well to maintain internal consistency. This is dangerous because not only the task is enormous, but it could end up discrediting the whole effort. Foreign trade data can be independently verified from other countries data.

Based on my study, I would say that Chinese data on national income aggregates require three types of correction: (a) In scope to remove double counting (b) netness in ensuring that value added is measured and not gross value (c) valuation in choosing the right deflator for calculating in constant prices, PPP, and making corrections for substitution effects while converting to common dollar numbers while making international comparisons [see *Samuelson and Swamy* [44] (1974) and (1984)].

That the Chinese official estimate of GDP growth of 10.1 percent per year for the period 1980-00 is an overestimate emerges from the from following:

(a) It implies an unprecedented efficiency in the use of energy. On basis of official data, the energy use in standard coal equivalent as a ratio of official GDP [1990 prices] declined from 900,000 [1978] to 600,000 [1985] to 400,000 [1994] to 310,000 [1999]. This makes the Chinese energy elasticity of income 0.31 which is half India's and equal to the US. It also implies that energy use efficiency quintupled in two decades. If we assume as the World Bank 1996 study shows that energy use efficiency improved at the annual rate of 2.2 percent since 1992, then the GDP growth rate cannot exceed 6.6 percent per year. And if we plug in the same data on energy use in the World Competitiveness Report (2000) cross-section regression, then also we get the same growth rate for China.

(b) Since there is a high correlation between the rate of inflation over time and the constant price GDP growth rate over the same period, a presumption is raised that a substantial part of the stated constant price GDP is in fact in current prices. In fact, after reforms the valuation problem has become harder because the private sector which may be about one-third of the economy and the Town and Village Enterprises [TVEs] which is about half of the industrial sectors, have not only growth fast but are largely out of reach of the

> Chinese statistical system and discipline. We have just a vague idea of how constant price are estimated in these sectors. The World Bank and Harry Wu [2000] have thus recalculated the industrial production index using alternative deflators. The results of these research couped with estimates of agriculture and service valued added show again that the 1980-99 growth rate of GDP could not be 10.1 percent but about 1.7 to 2 percent points less.

Using these guideposts, the data for China were reworked, making adjustments for scope netness, and valuation using Index Number theory, and arrive the following estimates of annual growth rates period-wise: 1980-92 : 8.4. percent; 1992-00 : 6.5 and overall 1980-00: 7.4.

Whether using official data or in the corrected data, a common interference is that since 1992, Chinese growth rate has been slowing continuously over the decade due to slackening demand largely because rural incomes have been stagnant. Since 1997 there has been an attempt by the reform-minded Prime Minister Zhu Rongji to keep up demand for production by pump priming. But the soft budget constraint having the State Owned Enterprises (SOEs), the consequent huge level of NPAs at nearly 50 percent, the run on banks that could result from WTO mandated opening for foreign banks, the inconsistency in defending a fixed exchange rate, while pursuing a reckless monetary policy [15% growth in M2] and while still hoping to globalise, makes for a heady mixture. China thus is sitting on top of a financial volcano that could erupt if financial reforms are not carried out. That is a Catch-22 situation because financial reforms would erode the hold of the Communist Party. So far the incremental reforms have legitimized the Party and maintain its hold, but financial reforms that are necessary will cut the coots of that hold.

However, China in its official publications rebutted the usually made allegations about Chinese official data. In "Fallacies of 'China Collapse' and Overblown Official Statistics" [NEWS *FROM CHINA;* MARCH 16 - 31, 2003] a Chinese author wrote: "Some Western scholars have written books questioning the truthfulness of China's economic prosperity. They are echoed by some mainstream Western media, which claim that China's prosperity is false due to overblown official statistics and untrustworthy

GDP growth rate, and that the country's investment environment is not as good as believed. Some even predict that the country's WTO entry, like opening a Pandora's box, will cause the collapse of its economic system.

In 2000, Professor *Thomas G. Rawski* [39] then from the University of Pittsburgh published an article, "What's Happening to China's GDP Statistics?" questioning the authenticity of Chinese statistics. He studied economic data released by various provinces, autonomous regions and municipalities, and found they did not add up to those announced by the National Statistics Bureau, the country's highest statistics authority.

Rawski's viewpoint, saying China's economic growth is false and the Chinese economy will collapse, soon became a prime subject for the Western mainstream media, as it met the needs of those who foiled in achieving what they had expected through preaching the "China threat" theory.

In his 2002 book *The China Dream,* Joe Studwell [47], founder and editor of The China Economic Quarterly, said China's economic foundation have been "laid on sand". He went on to predict the eruption of large-scale political and economic crisis in China arid warned investors not to throw billions of dollars in this bottomless pit.

A research report by Credit Lyonnais Securities Asia estimated that China's ratio of public debt to GDP stood at 139 per cent in 2000, compared with the officially announced 23 per cent. If this situation cannot be reversed, the Hong Kong brokerage company concluded, China would suffer a financial crisis. It even declared, "The date that shows China as the fastest growing economy in the world is not worth the paper if is written on."

In response to overseas rumors, Qiu Xiaohua, Deputy Director of the National Statistics Bureau, commented that Rawski's incorrect conclusion is a result of his hasty scholarly work, and if some people with ulterior motives intend to make a fuss of his viewpoint, it is no longer an academic matter.

Deeming that, throughout the world, no GDP statistics are a hundred percent correct, Xu Xianchun, Director of the National Economic Accounting Department under the National Statistics Bureau, holds that the current GDP (statistics of China basically reflect me objective situation / of its economic development.

In fact, the authenticity of China's official statistics has never been. a problem to unbiased analysts. For example, the World Bank directly quoted China's official statistics in its analysis reports in the 1980s. In the early 1990s, however, it cast doubts on the truthfulness of China's statistics and adjusted them consciously. This was because China's accounting system was not in line with international practices at that time. In the wake of the country's continuous improvement in this regard, the World Bank stopped adjusting China's statistics at the end of the 1990s and resumed the practice of directly quoting them in its publications.

Fan Gang, a celebrated Chinese economist, at the World Bank had made a thorough study of China's accounting system in 1998, which showed that the 'average error rate of the country's GDP growth rate was only 1 percent. However, Fan said, this result has never been publicized by the Western media.

Fan said false statistics are common in developing countries, and their impacts on the real conditions of the economy should be examined from a comprehensive perspective. He added that although the ongoing debate on the truthfulness of China's economic statistics mainly focuses on overblown local data, it is very true that some localities, especially developed areas and private enterprises, preferred understating their achievements.

"A lot of statistics such as import and export volume, paid-in foreign investment, balance of international payments and residents' savings deposits, are actually immune to falsification," noted Fan. "The savings deposits of Chinese residents are increasing more than 10 percent year on year. Where is the money coming from? It probably indicates that the growth in the Chinese residents' income has been underestimated. If anybody is reluctant to accept official GDP statistics, they can reach their own conclusion based on these indisputable indicators."

Before China joined the World Bank in 1979 and sought to receive the IDA concessional loans which required its exchange rate-converted per capita income to be below $400 to qualify for the loan, the Chinese national income estimates in the field [except that of this author's] placed the 1970s per capita in the range between $600 and $1000, and the growth rate at around 6 to 8 percent per year (The Chinese official uncorrected series had placed it at 8 percent).

In 1979, China decided to revise the data and the revised data revealed an estimated per capita income in 1980 at $253 below India's $260. The $253 figure published by Deng's China, projected *backward* at an assumed 6 to 8 percent GDP growth rate, or the $600-$1000 per capita income figure projected *forward* to year 2000 at the currently accepted growth rates, *would clearly lead to ridiculous results.* Hence, estimates of per capita and growth rates that had acceptability till then in the 1970s have now to be decisively rejected.

Even state-controlled media reports and editorials have in recent days raised questions over their accuracy.

The Global Times, controlled by the People's Daily, the Communist party mouthpiece, said the public reacted with "banter and sarcasm" to NBS figures showing average urban wages in China rose 13 per cent in the first half to $2,142.

It quoted an online poll showing 88 per cent of respondents doubted the official numbers.

An editorial in the China Daily (06/08/2009) the government's English-language mouthpiece, quoted another survey that *found_91 per cent of respondents sceptical of official data, up from 79 per cent in 2007.*

Economists abroad have also questioned the data. Derek Scissors of the Washington-based Heritage Foundation, referring to the time it took for the bureau to produce the figures after the end of the first half this year stated: "Despite starkly limited resources and a dynamic, complex economy, the state statistical bureau again needed only 15 days to survey the economic progress of 1.3bn people."

The NBS itself is often wary of data provided by local governments and tends to revise down preliminary estimates using its own statistical model. According to official economists "...provincial officials have enormous incentives to improve their career prospects by exaggerating local economic growth".

CONCLUSION

Thus, in this study, based on corrected and refined data, we shall focus on China and India for four reasons:

[a] because India and China are more easily comparable—in size, population, economic history, in initial conditions of modern economic growth, and that both were considered just two centuries ago, by the then prevailing standards as the two most developed countries, but which regressed to underdeveloped status by mid twentieth century. Besides, both are neighbours with profound historical contacts.

[b] Furthermore, the development models adopted by both countries since 1950 have been similar-socialist till 1980, followed by market oriented reforms. In the 21st century, the combined effect of the growth of the two economies will be staggering. Together, today they are 38% of the global population, 2 and 4th in PPP GDP, contributing 45% of the global growth rate today. IT superpowers, and preferred outsourcing destinations. There is also the half glass full or empty syndrome.

[c] India is a pluralistic democracy while China is not. Hence the political dynamics of economic choices and strategy, i.e., what is feasible and what is not, is interesting.

[d] The ideology of each may indicate some convergence at a future date since India has begun to advocate "Inclusive Growth" while China now preaches "Harmonious Society", both mean therefore to attain the same aims.

Chapter 2

HISTORICAL SETTING (1870-1951)

China and India are two geographically large countries with the longest span of civilized history, as also the only two nations of the globe with more than a billion each in population. The two ancient nations together constitute 38 per cent of the world's population today.

Three centuries ago, the two nations were considered by then contemporary standards as the two most economically developed nations of the world accounting for more than 50 per cent of the world GDP. India and China thus up to eighteenth century were areas of immense wealth and wisdom for Europeans travelers and traders to flock to, as well for the university centres of Europe to seek knowledge in mathematics, science and technology.

In 1820, China generated a third of world output, and India, which had already declined during the three earlier centuries of Islamic invasions and plunder, about another 16%[**Tables 10-15 and Graphs 2-5**]. In mid-20th century, China's and India's share of global GDP had fallen to less than 5% each. During the 18th and 19th century, the two Asian countries thus fell far behind the rapidly growing economies propelled by the epochal innovations of the steam engine and Bessemer converter, of Western Europe and North America.

The two nations had then a combined population in excess of half a billion in 1820 and by 1900 it rose to 700 million. By the end of the twentieth century, their combined population had more than trebled.

And surprisingly, and unprecedented in the global historical context, except during a brief decade in the latter half of the twentieth century, these two neighbouring nations over two millenniums, never went to war or even had tense relations, but interacted productively and in a spirit of cooperation. How these two nations perform and progress is, therefore, of widespread and defining global interest.

Graph 2

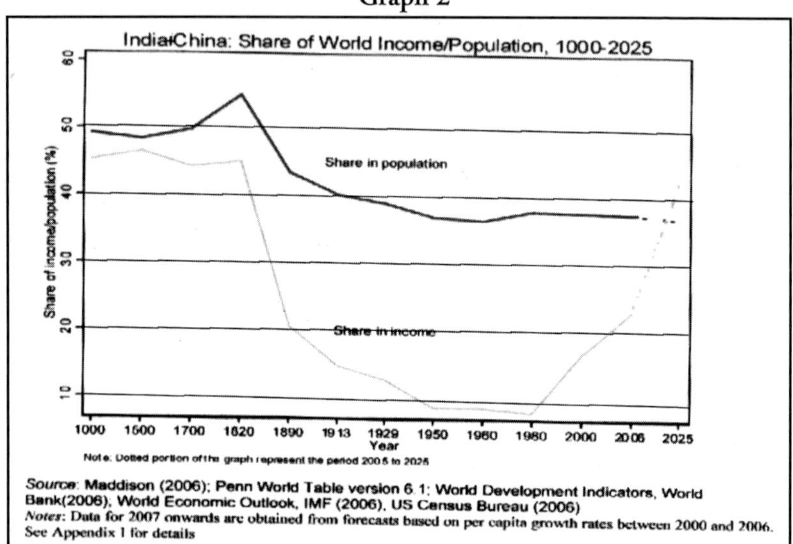

Source: Maddison (2006); Penn World Table version 6.1; World Development Indicators, World Bank(2006); World Economic Outlook, IMF (2006), US Census Bureau (2006)
Notes: Data for 2007 onwards are obtained from forecasts based on per capita growth rates between 2000 and 2006. See Appendix I for details

Table 10: World Regions, Annualized growth (in %)

	1500-1700	1700-1820	1820-1950	1950-1980	1980-2006	2006-2025
West	0.12	0.13	1.23	2.9	1.9	2.1
Asia	0.01	0.01	0.16	3.3	4.0	5.3
Latin America	0.07	0.12	0.95	2.8	0.7	1.8
Africa	0	0.01	0.73	1.5	−0.1	1.7
Developing Economies	0.01	0.01	0.34	2.7	3.2	4.9
Developed Economies	0.1	0.14	1.17	3.1	1.9	2.2
China	0	0	−0.24	2.7	7.1	6.2
India	0	−0.03	0.11	1.7	4.2	8.3
World	0.04	0.06	0.89	2.5	1.9	3.4

Source: Penn world Table 6.1: Maddison (2006), World Bank WDI (2006); International Monetary Fund WEO (2006 sep). Appendix I for details on construction of real incomes.

Note: West includes all of Europe, Eastern Europe, Northern America, Australia, New Zealand, former Soviet Union. Asia includes Japan, as does the region "developed economies". Developing economies is the entire world excluding the West and Japan.

Table 11: Yearly per capita income with respect to USA, (1996 PPP $)

	1500	1700	1820	1950	1980	2006	2025
West	189.4	181.5	89.1	58.2	69.9	66.6	69.1
Asia	139	107.4	45.6	7.4	10.1	16.5	31.4
Latin America	131.7	114.8	55.7	25.2	29.5	20.8	20.2
Africa	100	76.5	32.4	11	8.7	4.9	4.6
Developing Countries	135.8	104.3	44.6	9.1	10.4	13.9	24.5
Developed Countries	187	172.2	86	51.8	66.1	62.8	65.9
China	145.5	110.5	46.4	4.5	5	18.6	41.9
India	139.8	106.2	43	6.6	5.4	9.5	31.6
Russia	252.0	210.0	95.8	39.6	41.4	32.2	43.4
United Kingdom	172.4	229	131.3	70.3	67.1	67.9	69.4
World	148	121.6	54.9	23.1	24.7	23.5	31.4
United States	100	100	100	100	100	100	100
United States (actual)	449	591	1409	10702	21334	36715	52746

Source: Maddison (2006); Penn World Table version 6.1; World Development Indicators, World Bank (2006); World Economic Outlook, IMF (2006).

Notes:

1. West includes all of Europe, Eastern Europe, former Soviet Union. Asia includes Japan, as does the region "developed economies". Developing economies is the entire world excluding the West and Japan.
2. All figures are relative to incomes except for USA (actual) which reports the actual figures for USA. See Appendix I for details.

Graph 3

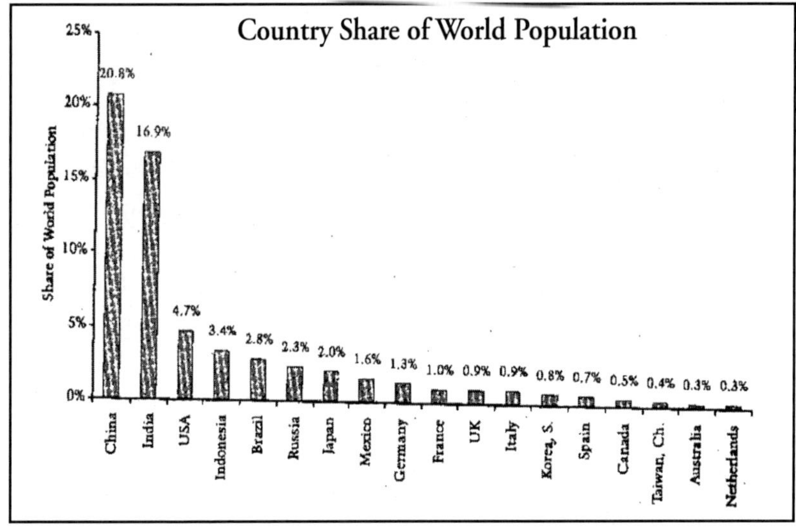

Graph 4

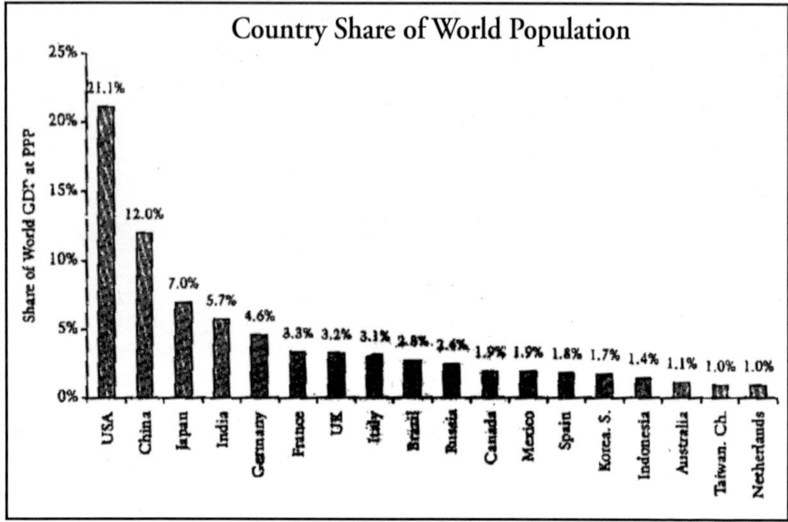

In his address titled *The Indianisation of China: A Case of Cultural Borrowing,* at the Tri-centennial Celebrations at Harvard University in 1936, noted poet and President of Peking University **Dr. Hu Shih** declared these interactions as having led to unprecedented "peaceful cultural borrowing from India by the Chinese people".

Both countries however have had in the eighteenth, nineteenth, and the twentieth centuries the common experience of foreign invasions, plunder, and imperialism, as also Soviet socialism, and the more positive recent phase of three decades of economic reforms leading to rapid and accelerating economic growth which has uplifted their world status.

Somewhere between the middle eighteenth century and early nineteenth centuries both these countries came under Imperialist European control. The Chinese also had a taste Japanese imperialism during the 1937-45 period which was even more traumatic—if not as devastating economically because of the relatively short period of Japanese occupation.

The two nations today possess similar demographic and economic strengths, share the same economic and social challenges, of transforming themselves into market-driven societies, and are expected to be among the top three in world economy along with the US, by this mid-century.

Being the territorial and demographic giants of the region, these countries have the potential for establishing a new political and economic world order on behalf of Asian nations arising from an East Asia Union to parallel and later to overtake the EU.

In terms of these attributes and historical facts, therefore, these two nations are unique in the world. If they cooperate or confront in the decades to come it will have cataclysmic restructuring convulsions for the world. Hence these two nations are invariably compared and contrasted in any debate on the future of global economic development and growth.

In this study we seek answers to five interesting questions in these Chapters: First, whether the initial historical economic and institutional conditions obtaining in China and India in the late 1940s, and at the advent of economic reforms (1978 onwards) were different? And if so, the consequence on economic developments in these two nation since the commencement of Reforms due to those differences (this Chapter). Second, in terms of the Kuznetsian structural changes, in equity and productivity in a comparative appraisal of Chinese and Indian economic performance over the last six decades, whether after due correction in the data of the two countries, there is a significant difference in outcomes and a trend towards narrowing or widening of the gap in the economic distance between the two countries i.e., a convergence or divergence in the growth paths of the two economies (Chapter III). Third, whether in the globalization process, information technology use, governance structures such as in the financial architecture in the two nations, and the potential Demographic Dividend, there exist significant differences (Chapter IV&V). Fourth, on the basis of answers to the above questions whether it is plausible to infer that India, which is behind China today in material terms, will catch up with China in the foreseeable future, e.g., by 2025, and even overtake China (Chapter VI).

The distinctive and accelerated economic performance of the Indian and Chinese economies began with the advent of economic reforms in 1980. These reforms differed in sequencing and in intensities of implementation in the two countries. In 1978, in both countries new political dispensations in respective governments had emerged that enabled the subsequent ushering of economic reforms. In India, in the

1977 General Elections held in the aftermath of the authoritarian rule under a State of Emergency (1975-77), Ms. Indira Gandhi's pro-Soviet government was defeated by the Janata Party led by a "conservative liberal" Morarji Desai.

For the first time since the advent of Soviet type economic planning in 1951 a few deregulation measures were adopted thereafter in India reversing the trend of increasing state control over the previous three decades. Trade liberalization measures were also tentatively put in place (**see Swamy** [**50**]). In China, after the Gang of Four was dethroned in 1978, and Deng Xiaoping was firmly in the saddle, deregulation and decentralizing measures in agricultural and foreign trade sectors were incrementally and sequentially implemented following the Resolutions passed in the Communist Party Congress held in December 1978. These resolutions had authorized the sequencing of reform measures termed "Four Modernisations", which were (at least till 1992) the 'Pareto Optimal' type, namely adoption of only those measures where "no one was worse off, but some were better off."

In 1950, when both countries, had achieved liberation from Imperialist domination of over a century, and chose to embark on national centralized planning to develop their respective economies, the initial conditions prevailing [Table below] were different in the two nations and reflected the differential impact of imperialism on their respective economies over the previous hundred years.

The decline of China and India as economic powers had begun coincidentally with Industrial Revolution in Europe. By 1870, the Indian and Chinese economies entered into a long phase of decline, which decline by 1950 (i.e., seven decades later), transformed the two nations from prosperous countries by pre-modern standards to poor under developed nations by modern industrial criteria of the twentieth century.

When the British first arrived in force in India in the eighteenth century, the central authority in Delhi was in a state of decline following the autocratic reign of the Moghul Emperor Aurangzeb. His successors in the dynasty had lost both the will and power to enforce the directives from capital city of Delhi. An alternative force to fill the vacuum was emerging, but the British imperialists, by then already in India as traders, nipped that emergence in the bud. Thus, the Peshwa aristocracy attempt to fill the void was effectively scuttled by Lord Cornwallis who thereby as British Crown's resident representative, fresh from defeat in the United States, vindicated himself in India in the eyes of the British Crown. In contrast in China, when the British and other foreign powers arrived, the Ching dynasty was well established and a force.

The Opium Wars of 1838-42 in China were almost eight decades later than the decisive battle of Plassey (1757) in India waged by Robert Clive who had set up a British fortress in Bengal earlier exploiting India's internal divisiveness. Thereafter, except for the 1857 Great Uprising or the First War of Independence, India did not put up much of a resistance to the West in the latter part of the nineteenth century. At the time the British had subdued India in 1857, the Chinese people were still fighting against foreign onslaught. In the last five decades of nineteenth century, China had in fact put up a stiff fight against the foreigner. The back of Chinese resistance was broken only after a decisive defeat in the last decade of the nineteenth century, at the hands of the Japanese which culminated in the signing of the Treaty of Shimonseiki (1895).

During the course of the century, China was under siege from five imperialist countries each of which were extracting one concession after another, while India was in complete control of a single Imperialist country, viz., Britain. As a colony of the British, India was free from upheaval even if under challenge from a non-violent movement led by Mahatma Gandhi in the latter half of the period of hundred years. Accounts of visiting dignitaries and travelers over several centuries earlier had opined that by the prevailing standards of the times, China and India were prosperous developed countries and perhaps remained so till mid-nineteenth century.

The level of inequality, and the extent of poverty in a section of the people, were perhaps excessive and oppressive, but nevertheless it remained a fact that trade of the world with China and India flourished with a favourable balance over several centuries because the two countries were producing and trading what a large part of the world did not or could not produce. For example, in trade with US, Indian Kings agreed to import ice blocks from Belmont, Mass., because the America importers of

Indian goods did not want the ships to India from US to go empty. India enjoyed a "massive" balance of trade surplus with Europe as well, and with most other parts of the world. Merchants came from all over the world to purchase goods from Indian markets.

In the nineteenth century and before World War I, Indian exports generated large surpluses with the USA even as India had a nominal and increasing deficit with the UK (**Saul** [36]). India sent a large tribute to Britain in the shape of 'Home Charges' (that is, costs of British civil and military establishment in Britain maintained by Indian revenues along with interest on British loans to India all of which was charged to Indian revenues), and British traders, shippers, and insurers realized a profit, going up to 40 per cent of India's external trade: most of that trade was monopolized by European—mainly British—traders (**Bagchi** [1]). Much of British investment in India owed its origin to the reinvestment of profits made by the Europeans in India. While some of those profits originated in new enterprises, the Europeans had privileged access to those resources such as land for plantations, charters for railways, or mining properties which made the enterprises profitable.

Eight generations had to endure exploitative British Colonial Rule. By the time it was over, all memories of those who valued freedom and fought the 'firingee'— as the foreigner was called—had been obliterated. History had been distorted to make out that India entered a modern industrial stage due to British imperialism and colonialism. But hidden from general public attention was the fact that India had been plagued by frequent famines from the impoverishment that recurred through two centuries of British loot.

Before British Rule and during Islamic Rule (pre 1745 AD)

11th century	:	Two famines, both local
13th century	:	One famine around Delhi
14th century	:	Three famines, all local
15th century	:	Two famines, both local
16th century	:	Three famines, all local
17th century	:	Three 'General' area, not defined
18th century	:	Four in North-Western Provinces

Under British Rule since 1857

1868-69 : Punjab, Hyderabad, Southern

1873: Bengal and Bihar, Bombay, Deccan

NWFP and Oudh, Gujarat, Marvar

1874-77 : Bombay, Hyderabad

1876-78 : Madras, Mysore

1977-78 : NWFP and Oudh

1884 : Punjab

1884-85 : Lower Bangal, Madras

1886-87 : Central Provinces

1888-89 : Bihar

1889 : Orissa (Tributary States) Madras (Ganjam)

1889 : Kumaon and Garhwal

1890-92 : Ajmer Marwara

1892 : Madras, Bombay (Deccan) Bangal, Bihar Upper Burma

1897-98 : Madras, Bombay, Central Provinces, NWFP

1899-1900 : Bombay, Punjab, Central Provinces,

Rajputana, Central India, Hyderabad, Deccan, Berar.

This drain of resources from India to Britain made a once prosperous India a victim of endemic shortage and famine The list below of famines given below may not be exhaustive. It is put forward on investigations made independently and at different times:

In 1866, Sir George Campbell M.P., who had served in India at all levels from writer to Lt. Governor, was asked to enquire into famines. He confined himself to the British period and he records—769 droughts, 1770 famines, and with great loss of life. He also records that the revenue collections of 1771 were higher by Rs. 5.30 lakh than they had been in 1768, before any failure of rain was reported. Sir George states, "The British authorities were early alive to this evil and much sympathized with it, but always with an overriding consideration for the revenue."

The testimony of a witness, that of William Digby, CIE, rebuts this colonial propaganda of the British concern. "The history of famines prior to, and during, early British period is not exact or abundant. One thing however stands out most clearly. All famines were local; not one approached in extent or intensity the three great distresses of the last quarter of the nineteenth century"—when British colonial rule dominated the land of India.

Digby, writing in 1901, continues, "A reporter of the last famine—that of 1900—might have used precisely the same words of the events of one hundred and thirty years later. "Whatever the condition of the country, the revenue is squeezed out of the people. Stated roughly famines have been four times as numerous during the last 30 years of the nineteenth century, as they were one hundred years earlier and four times more widespread."

Thus, we may summarize the record of famines under British Imperialist Colonial Rule of undivided India over a century of administration since 1850 to 1950 as below:

1st 25 years five famines, deaths occurring perhaps of one million

2nd 25 years, two famines, deaths of about half million

3rd 25 years, six famines, deaths, recorded nearly five million

4th 25 years, eighteen famines, deaths estimated at twenty six million.

Digby poignantly observed: "In the last 25 years of the past (19th) century, more than a half million people died of famine, and its effects in a British ruled country, two each minute, 120 each hour, 2,880 each day. During the last 10 years, the average has been four every minute, 240 each hour and 5,760 each day."

Digby next quoted the census figures' population in 1801, all India: 287,223,431. Population as it ought to have been in 1900 with normal increase, put forward by the government of India as "normal": 330,306 945. Population actual in 1901: 294,000.000. Missing 36 million, three hundred and six thousand nine hundred and forty five (36,306,945). Digby concludes thus that famines were more destructive of human life under the British than they had been at any time earlier in Indian history.

It is significant that the governments of Independent India since 1947, however inefficient or bumbling, have prevented a famine from occurring. A history of famine is thus required to put the British Raj in perspective, and especially its propagandist view that British rule benefitted the "natives of India".

John Maynard Keynes [21] discounted even the private British investment in India as "exaggerated figures" and estimated that over the period 1902-09, the remittances from India by foreign investors in private enterprises exceeded the investments made by them in those enterprises. Pandit, taking the 16 years from 1898 to 1914, calculated Britain's private investments in Indian private firms was positive in only two years (viz., 1900-01 and 1905-06) and negative in all the other years. The net outflow on account of private enterprises in which British investors were involved, according to Pandit, came to £ 15.5 million over these years.

The cost of conquest of India and pacification operations was routinely borne by the Indian peoples themselves. For example, the whole cost of suppressing the Indian uprising of 1857-58 was passed on as the budgetary burden of British India. In the period between the two world wars, when the export-earnings of primary producers suffered severely, colonial government's normal revenues which were tied closely to exports, suffered a decline. But the governments defrayed their expenses by borrowing in metropolitan money markets and the debt-service burdens of the colonial peoples went up tremendously.

In the Indian case, the interest on the debt accumulated by the British Indian government had almost from the beginning of British rule (originally in the form of dividend on the East India Company stock) provided a method of extracting and transferring a part of the surplus.

Very few would be aware of the horrendous calamities inflicted on Indians by the British. The annual death rate in 1877 in British labour camps during the Deccan famine was about 94%. Extraordinarily low population growth between 1870 and 1930 (due to famine, malnourishment-exacerbated disease and cholera, plague and influenza epidemics) was due to this exploitative policy. In 1943, Bengal Famine in British-ruled India about 5 million people were perished, but it was never mentioned in the British history books, because it was caused by a deliberate British "scorched earth policy" to deprive the Azad Hind Army and the Japanese to receive any material support from the local people.

The annual death rate in India before 1920 was about 4.8% but this declined to 3.5% by 1947 and is presently about 0.9% . Using a baseline "expected" annual death rate value of 1.0% and assuming an "actual" pre-

1920 value of 4.8% one can estimated that the avoidable (excess) mortality was about 0.6 billion during 1757-1837, 0.5 billion during 1837-1901 and 0.4 billion during 1901-1947. Thus the British rule of India was associated with an excess (i.e. avoidable) mortality totaling 1.5 billion - surely one of the greatest crimes in all of human history.

An extraordinary feature of the appalling record of British imperialism with respect to genocide and mass, worldwide killing of huge numbers of people (by war disease and famine) is its absence from public perception. There is no mention of famine in India or Bengal in the British textbooks of history. Now historians in India are now putting the blame on the victims! Meghnad Desai in his article in Cambridge History of India puts the blame on the Indian speculators; **Amartya Sen** has suggested that people in that area had eaten too much to create the famine!

('Ingredients of Famine Analysis', *Quarterly Journal of Economics,* Vol XCVI, 1981).

The progress thus made in India under British Rule like the coming of Railways, Postal System, Telegraphic Communications, etc., were all undertaken by the British Administration to facilitate their rule. The costs were however borne by Indians. The aim of British policy was to integrate the Indian economy with that of the British in way such that India supplied Great Britain with cheap raw material for being manufactured into final products and then exported back to India and other colonies.

But after the first World War, as the 'tribute' became less important as a component of the total Budgetary surplus, interest on the India debt became more important for extracting and transferring the surplus, and became a powerful argument for pursuing a basically deflationary fiscal and monetary policy throughout the period between the two world wars.

In China, starting in 1870 from a similar level to India's in agricultural yields, and despite the neglect of agriculture in terms of investment, had achieved a growth rate in foodgrains [at 0.6 per cent per year] of about six times India's, while in non-foodgrains crops, the Chinese growth rate was higher but by a small margin. In terms of per capita consumption in calories, thus, China by 1952 as Table above reveals, had 24 percent higher consumption per capita than India.

Expectation of life at birth in China, at 40 years, was higher by 25 percent. China was however behind India in output of textiles, cement, crude oil, rail and road transport a by-product of the circumstances of imperialist presence in the two countries. India was also ahead in literacy and enrolment in higher education. Per capita income (in 1970 base purchasing parity prices) in 1952 was 54 percent higher in India [at $154] compared to China. How these initial conditions in 1950s reflected the nature of imperialism is discussed in **Swamy** [52].

National liberation struggle against foreigners had however unified the Chinese and Indian societies in terms of political consciousness of the elite, and created a reservoir of goodwill in the masses for governance by these elites who took position of power after liberation from foreign rule or hegemony in these two countries. This is best an unintended but a positive outcome of the two nations 'association' and confrontation with the West.

To understand the process by which the post-liberation initial conditions came to be, we propose to look at some of the data that have become available in the two countries to estimate the national income and its structure for the period 1870-1952. The data, especially for China, are scattered and fragmentary. Some are even of doubtful value. However, some scholars have attempted to collate these data and have derived consistent series on yield per acre, manufacturing output, and national income. One such effort of collating is that of this **author** [53].

We begin first with agriculture. **Perkins**[34] has done impressive work in deriving the per capita output in Chinese agriculture for the period stretching from the Ming Dynasty to the early 1950's. For India, equally painstaking research is the work of **Blyn**[6]. In this section, our analysis will be based on the collated data of Perkins and Blyn.

According to Perkins, the foodgrains yield per cultivated acre in China more or less doubled between the fourteenth and nineteenth or twentieth centuries. Furthermore, there were few institutional changes in agriculture between the fourteenth century and the campaigns of the 1950's of land reform and cooperative formation. Perkins calculates that the per capita grain output between 1850 and 1933, and between 1933 and 1957, remained about constant.

Since the growth rate of population during this period, implicit in Perkins' population data, was 0.6 per cent per year, therefore a per capita constant output implies that output of grain in this period also grew at 0.6 per cent. Perkins also gives grain yield data, according which yield per acre rose by 0.11 percent per year. Therefore the acreage under grain must have expanded at 0.49 per cent per year during this period.

In India, according to Blyn, the yield per acre in foodgrains declined substantially, at the annual rate of 0.20 per cent during the 56 years (1891-1947). During this same period, acreage under foodgrains cultivation rose at the annual rate of 0.31 per cent. Since population growth during these nearly eight decades was at the rate of 0.67 per cent per year, this implies that the per capita foodgrains output in India declined at the annual rate of 0.56 per cent per year. In other words, assuming that the 1870-91 trends are the same, the per capita grain output of India in 1870 would have been 1.55 the level in 1950.

Thus, by 1950, when India and China founded their republics, and commenced development through economic planning, China had a relatively comfortable food surplus which enabled it to engage and finance rapid industrial growth, while for India which had suffered a two century long decline in foodgrain yields, no such cushion or surplus existed. This forced India to slow down its industrialization program following a food crisis in 1966-67. The adopted Soviet model of planning had to be modified to enable expending resources for the simultaneous improvement in agriculture with industrialization plans.

Although the yield per acre in China increased relative to India for all three crops, the relative increase in China is the maximum for rice crop. The question that is of interest is why China which had been ruled by a feudal oligarchy during the entire period of 1870-1950, and had gone through political and military turbulence of the kind that India had not experienced, yet in agricultural performance especially in terms of grain output, was superior to India's in this period.

This contrast in performance raises questions of technological as well institutional issues. Data on irrigation, multiple cropping, and chemical fertilizer application all show China in 1952 to be more advanced than India. There was 42 percent more land in China under irrigation, 22 per cent more land under multiple cropping, and 140 per cent more chemical fertilizer application per acre than in India. In India, irrigation facilities and fertilizers were diverted, as a part of British policy, to "cash" crops marked for exports. The relatively higher level agricultural technology in China achieved under much more difficult political circumstance therefore points to the negative role of colonial Indian government in the nineteenth and early twentieth centuries. Indeed this is further supported by the fact that in 1939-40, the small share of the total area irrigated by government canals.

Since Chinese per capita grain output had remained constant and in 1950 the per capita grain output in China was 1.54 times that of India's, therefore in 1870 the per capita grain output was about the same in China and India.

Table 12: Long Term Growth Rate of Crops in China and India

	CHINA[1] (percent per year)	INDIA[2]
Output		
Foodgrains	+0.60	+0.11
Non-Foodgrains	1.37	+1.31
Area		
Foodgrains	+0.49	+0.31
Non-Foodgrains	+0.25	+0.42
Yield per Acre		
Foodgrains	0.11	–0.20
Non-Foodgrains	+1.12	+0.89
Population	0.60	0.67
Per Capita Output		
Foodgrains	+0.00	–0.56
Non-Foodgrains	+0.77	+0.64

1.1871-1957; 2.1891-1947

Source: China: Perkins, D.H.: *Agricultural development in China 1368-1968,* Chicago (1969). India: Blyn, George: *Agricultural Trends in India (1871-1947)* University of Pennsylvania Press (1966).

Table 13: Ratio of Rice, Wheat and Cotton Yields: (China to India)

Crop	1921-25	1947
Wheat	1.20	1.50
Rice	1.52	3.29
Cotton	2.00	2.07

Source: 1921-25: Buck, J.L: China's Farm Economy, University of Chicago Press, 1930, page 208. 1947: Economic Development in India and Communist China, Staff Study No. 6, Committee on Foreign Relations, U.S. Congress Washington D.C., 1956, page 9.

Thus, the 1950 gap, which was not there in 1870, in grain production per capita between China and India was due to the decline in per capita grain output in India.

For non-grain crops, the Perkins and Blyn data can be similarly used to show that yield per acre rose both in China and India during 1870-1950, but the growth was faster in China. In India, non-foodgrains crop output per acre rose at the rate of 0.89 per year, while in China the annual increase was at the rate of 1.2 per cent. All these figures are summarized in the **Table-12.**

What clearly emerges from **Table-12** is that during the eight decades preceding the founding of the popular Republics of India and China in the late forties, agricultural crops performed distinctly better in China than India, in aggregate, in per capita, and in terms of productivity (as measured by changes in the yield per acre). However in terms of output of cash crops, India's performance was not much inferior to that of China, reflecting British imperialist trade needs for cheap agro-raw materials from India for industry in Britain.

More significantly, in 1870 per capita grain production in China and India was about the same. By 1950, Chinese level rose 54 per cent above India's, not due a faster per capita increase in China (in fact per capita output was constant), but because of a *decline* in per capita grain production in India. This higher per capita grain output in China translated itself in terms of higher Chinese consumption in caloric terms.

In China, during the period of the Ch'ing dynasty from 1753 to 1908, land tax grew at an average rate of 0.4 per cent per year which was lower than the growth rate of output from agriculture. **Phillip Kuhn** [25] has pointed out that the Ch'ing dynasty, although weak in the later periods, nevertheless saw to it that the local elites did not come between the central government and the collection of the land tax. Indeed as **Feuerwerker notes,** it is the overall stability of the Chinese agriculture system that is most remarkable [13].

In India, the situation was the opposite. A government of foreigners needed a comprador local elite to govern securely. The colonial government encouraged the growth of an intermediary class which was obliged to deliver a fixed and unchanging amount of revenue to the colonial Government. As an incentive to perform, this class was fully empowered and permitted by Imperialist power to extract what it could from the tenant cultivator and keep the difference. Thus, if a peasant in debt ran away or had died, the revenue collector could ask his neighbour to pay his debts! The character of the Indian colonial agricultural system was thus really feudal. In contrast, the Chinese system was not feudal but bureaucratic (if even not dynamic). Thus, there had under colonialism been a regression in the institutional frame work of Indian agriculture.

The British colonial government's decision to build such a feudal system in India for collecting land revenue was motivated by the political need to secure collaborators for Imperial rule. After the 1857 Great Uprising, it became clear to the British that the peasantry especially in Rohilkhand and Oudh areas had aided and financed the revolt against British Rule. Therefore, to strengthen their political control on India, keeping the pressure on the peasants through the land revenue system seemed necessary to the colonial administration.

Thus, in India the Government had an oppressive land revenue system, while spending the mobilised resources on defence (40%) and administration. Even during the terrible famines, land revenue collected were over 95% of the assessment. In China however, the land tenure and tax system had stabilized for centuries.

As a consequence, China had much fewer famines than India. Between 1870 and 1947, India had 12 major famines causing deaths to

13-18 million people. China during this period had two major famines, 1876-79 and 1920-21 causing deaths to 13.5 million people (**Perkins** p.166). However, although India had larger number of famines, yet the average deaths per famine was less than in China, because of India's transportation network (railways plus highways plus traction animals). This transportation strength helped India post-1947 to escape famine while the lack of the same made China lose 16-32 million people in a famine in 1959-61.

During 1870-1950, Indian railway network expanded relatively faster than China's. In India, track length increased from 7,678 kilometers in 1870 to 65,217 kms in 1946-7. In China, it increased from 15 kms (1876) to 25,700 kms in 1950. China's geographical area is in fact three times India's.

In China, the railways took its time coming because of the fierce debate of whether or not it should be allowed. There was no such debate within India although there was some opinion in Britain on whether railways should be taken to India. But the 1846-50 Sikh wars and the so-called '1857 Mutiny' [the correct terms is: "The First War of Indian Independence] and later the nineteenth century Russian invasion of Afghanistan, convinced the 'doubting Thomases' otherwise.

As Davis concludes: "If the history of British rule in India were to be condensed to a single fact, it is this: there was no increase in India's per-capita income from 1757 to 1947." [in M. Davis: *Late Victorian Holocausts: E1 Nino famines and the Making of the Third World,* London, Verso Books, 2001].

The contrast between the response of an indigenous government faced with a peasant-inspired rebellion which is the case of China after the Taiping Rebellion, and that of a colonial government in India after the 1857 revolt, is thus striking. The Chinese government responded by becoming more accommodative to the peasants, while the colonial Indian government hardened in its approach to peasants. This is reflected in the growth rates of out put, yield and area an agriculture.

This difference in response also may also be a reason why during the whole period 1870-1950, China had only two major famines, while India had twelve.

The contrast between an indigenous government and a colonial one can also be seen in the experience of the British-ruled and the Indian princely states. During 1920-21 to 1940-41, the states ruled by Indian princes compared to British India experienced a faster growth in output of grains and in the yield per acre as **Table** below shows.

Table 14: Comparative Performance and British Ruled and Princely States: India

	Units	Level 1940-41	Growth Rate (per cent/year) (1920-21 to 1940-41)
Foodgrains Output	million tons		
British India		38.15	−0.35
Princely States		6.41	+1.52
Area under Foodgrains	million acres		
British India		136.20	+0.25
Princely States		29.11	+0.18
Yield Per Acre	tons/acre		
British India		0.28	−0.60
Princely States		0.22	+1.34
Population	millions		
British India		295.81	+1.34
Princely States		93.20	+1.36

Source: Subramanian, S.: *Statistical Summary of the Social and Economic Trends in India* (Inter-War Period), Office of the Economic Advisor, Government of India, New Delhi, 1945, pp. 6-9.

From Table above we can infer that for the period for which data are available, namely 1920-21 to 1940-41, the states ruled by Indian princes compared to British India experienced a *faster* growth in output of grains and in the yield per acre. Because of this high growth rate in yield, the difference in the level of output per acre in foodgrains narrowed considerably to just 0.06 tons per acre. That is, while the. per acre grain yield in 1940-41 in British-ruled India was 1.27 times the level in the Princely states, in 1920-21 the yield per acre of grain in the former area was about double the yield in the latter. The reason for the initially much lower yield per acre in Princely states was that the British-India comprised of the most fertile parts of India, while the Princes ruled in states most of which were of poor quality lands or plain desert areas.

Why an indigenous Govt. of China, but in local chaos and a foreign government in India but with at least 90 years stability failed to industrialize? Why Japan was different? The answer is: in China it was the resistance to the foreigner that lasted till 1895. In India it was the obstruction of the British Government in London, and the bleeding of agriculture as a policy of the Colonial Government.

Obstructions for example in 1854, Maneckla1 Petit set up a Textile plant, but was isolated by the British authorities on the pressure of Lanchashire lobbies who remained in revolt till 1913 when Belgium threatened British exports to India.

In 1870's Jamshed Tata sought permission for a steel plant but was denied it by London. Then WWI then changed the scenario because of the rising demand for steel in the war efforts. Tata was then given permission. Jamshedji then raised the capital on the nationalistic "Swadeshi" call, and thus 100% of the funds came from India. Tata Iron and Steel became the cheapest producers steel [see Table below] and remained so for six decades.

Table 15: Comparison of Works Costs, United States of America and Canada with TISCO: 1923.

	Canada	USA	Jamshedpur	
	(Tons/$)	(Ton/$)	(Rs)	(Ton/$)
Pig Iron				
Total Materials cost	24.70	24.00	36.12.0	12.27
Labour cost	0.85	1.00	2.11.0	0.87
Steel Ingots				
Total materials cost	24.75	30.00	70.4.	23.42
Labour cost	1.10	1.50	5.12.0	1.92
Blooms				
Materials	29.50	35.00	88.3.0	29.40
Labour	0.65	1.50	1.11.0	0.56
Rails				
Materials		41.00	123.0.0	41.00
Bars				
Materials	39.00	45.00	134.15.0	44.98
Labour	4.50		11.15.0	3.98

Note: TISCO mentions that "cost of pig iron at the blast furnace does not agree with the price charged to ingots in United States of America and Canada as they use an average price when charging to the open hearth furnaces".

Source: ITB, Evidence by the Tata Iron and Steel Company, Calcutta 1924, op. cit., pp 256-57. Quoted in Datta, S: "Role of the Indian Worker in Early Phase of Industrialization", Economic and Political Weekly, XX, No.48, Nov. 30, 1985.

In 1844, Dwarkanath Tagore owning a mining company wanted to build a railways from Kolkata port to Burdwan shines. The British authorities denied him permission.

In 1850s and 60s two impetuses changed the situation: In 1857, the Indian rebellion against British colonial rule, and in 1865 the US Civil War that blocked cotton exports to Britain, coupled fear of a possible Russian invasion of India via Afghanistan. So East India Rail under East India Company was set up. The company entered into a counter guarantee agreement with the colonial Indian government, of 5% dividend for British investors for 99 years. Railways remained in deficit, so 0.2 to 0.3% of GNP paid to cover deficit till 1900. Because of this 4 largest rail system in 1947. But no structural changes in the economy resulted because freight rates designed to price internal trade so high as not worth it. Locomotives could be produced in Byculla as early or 1865, but British exported them (20000 1865-1941) – 22% of UK production. Even engine drivers down to plate layers from were Englishmen.

The slow industrialization of India (1870-1950) cannot be attributed to lack of Indian 'native' entrepreneurship or the size of market or even unacceptable rates of return. It was the British India Government obstruction to epochal innovations of Industrial Revolution being brought to India.

Agriculture too as we saw it was the same. Cash crops encouraged. From 1914 till 1947, India continued to bleed. Entire defence expenditure including for wars was paid for by India. India thus bled –7% of GDP on defence.

As a consequence, the GDP growth rates and per capita income increases were stunted. In comparison with the industrializing nations India and China fell behind.

Table 16 : Net Domestic Product and Growth Rates in China and India: 1870-1952 (billion parity yuan)

Year	*(1) China 1952 prices*	*(2) India 1948-49 prices*	*(3) Ratio of Product 1/(2) (3)/(4)*	*(4) Ratio of Populations China/India*	*(5) Ratio of per capita product*
1870	27.96	16.83	1.66	1.68	0.99
1914-18	44.75	28.98	1.54	1.71	0.90
1933	59.49	32.36	1.84	1.79	1.03
1952	69.99	49.83	1.40	1.58	0.89

Table 17: Annual average growth rates (%/year)

	Non domestic Product		*Per Capita Population*		*Per Capita Product*	
	China	*India*	*China*	*India*	*China*	*India*
1870/1914/18	1.0	1.2	0.5	0.4	0.5	0.8
1914-18/1933	1.7	0.6	0.8	0.9	0.9	-0.3
1933/1952	0.9	2.3	0.7	1.2	0.2	1.1
1870/1952	1.1	1.3	0.6	0.7	0.5	0.6

Sources: China: For 1870-1933, Table 5: For 1952 see Subramanian Swamy, *Economic Growth in China and India* (Chicago: University of Chicago Press, 1973).: The yuan estimates for India have been obtained at the parity rate of Rs. 1.8 = !¥.: India; For 1870-1933, figures given in Heston, A: "National Income" *Cambridge Economic History of India:*

1750-1970 (Cambridge, 1982). For 1952, see Swamy, *op. cit.,* using the 1946-47 base prices. The ratio of population calculated from data in two sources. For China population calculated from data in two sources. For China population figures are from Perkin.s, D.H.: *Agricultural Development in China:* 1368-1957, Aldine, 1970. For India, the data are from *The Cambridge Economic History of India.* Angus Maddison, by a different method, has estimated the Indian per capita growth rate for 1870-1913 at 0.7 per cent per year. For source see Heston *op. cit.*

Table 18: Growth of National Product, Population and Per Capita Product: [Selected Countries]

Country	*Duration of period Years*	*Total (years)*	*Rate of growth per decade(%)* Product	*Population*	*Per Capita Product*
England & Wales	1855/59-1857/59	112	21.1	6.1	14.1
France	1841/50-1960/62	106	20.8	2.5	17.9
Germany	1871/75-1960/62	88	31.1	11.2	17.9
United States	1839-1960/62	122	42.5	21.6	17.2
Japan	1879/81-1959/61	80	42.0	12.3	26.4
European Russia	1860-1913	53	30.2	13.8	14.4
China	1870-1952	82	11.4	6.1	5.3
India	1870-1952	82	13.2	7.2	6.0

Source: For China and India, see Table 17. For the remaining countries see Simon Kuznets, *Modern Economic Growth* (New Haven: Yale University Press, 1966), p. 64.

Table 19: Structure of National Product in China and India (1885-1936)

Sector	*(Percentage)*			
	China	*India*	*China*	*India*
	1885		*1936*	
Agriculture (A)	66.8	51.9	62.9	43.8
Manufacturing (M+)	5.2	10.1	18.9	15.2
Service (S)	28.0	38.0	18.2	41.0

Source: China: 1885: Feuerwerker, A: "Economic Trends in Late Ching Empire 1870-1911", *The Cambridge History of China,* Vol. II, Part 2, (Cambridge University Press, U.K. 1982) p. 5. The reference year, of Feuerwerker is '1880s', which we take as 1885. 1936. 1936: K.C. Yeh's estimate quoted in Ramon Myers: *Chinese Economy—Past and Present* (Wadsworth, Calig, 1980). India: Heston, Alan "National Income", *The Cambridge Economic History of India,* Vol. II, 1750-1970. The years 1885 and 1936 are financial years starting April 1.

Table 20: Level of Key Indicators: China and India (at around the time of founding of the republic)

	Indicator	*Unit*	*Year*	*China*	*India*	*Ratio*
1.	Per Capita	1970 parity$	1952	101	154	0.66
2.	Population	millions	1952	574.8	367.0	1.57
3.	Birth Rates	per 000	1950	37.0	40.0	0.93
4.	Death Rates	per 000	1950	18.0	28.0	0.64
5.	Life Expectancy	years	1950	40.0	32.0	1.25
6.	Infant Mortality	per 000	1950	175.5	190.0	0.92
7.	Adult Illiteracy	per cent	1950	25.0	20.0	1.25
8.	Calories	per capita	1952	1917.0	1540.0	1.24
9.	Foodgrains	mill. tons	1952	163.9	69.9	2.35
10.	Yield	tons/ha	1931-37			
		Rice		2.5	1.3	1.90
		Wheat		1.0	0.6	1.56
11.	Sugar	tons	1952	0.5	1.8	0.25
12.	Irrigation	per cent	1949	20.7	14.6	1.42
13.	Cropping	Index	1949	135.4	111.1	1.22
14.	Ammonium Sulphate	000 tons	1951	129.0	53.7	2.40
15.	Steel	mill. tons	1952	1.4	1.1	1.25
16.	Cotton Textiles	million				
		spindles	1956	7.2	12.4	0.58
		000 looms	1956	115.0	207.0	0.56
17.	Coal	mill. tons	1952	66.0	39.3	1.68
18.	Electric Power	billion KWH	1952	7.3	6.1	1.20
19.	Crude Oil	mill. tons	1952	0.4	0.4	1.01

20.	Cement	mill. tons	1952	2.9	4.1	0.71
21.	Railways	000 kms	1950	25.7	54.8	0.47
22.	Highways	000 kms	1949	130.2	391.8	0.33
23.	Literacy	percent	1951	14.3	16.7	0.86
24.	Students Enrolled in Higher Education	(OOOs)	1954	253.0	594.1	0.43
25.	College Graduates	(OOOs)	1952	32.6	72.1	0.45
	Percentage in techno-logics subjects			31.4	17.8	

Source: Data called from official statistical abstracts of the two countries. For China the primary sources are publications of the State Bureau, Beijing, the World Bank, and Tsao, James: *China's Economic Development Strategies and their Effects on U.S. Trade,* USITC Publication No. 1645, February 1985, Washington D.C. For India, we have relied on *Basic Statistics Relating to the Indian Economy,* Centre for Monitoring Indian Economy, Bombay, August 1984. The per capita dollars figures have been obtained from Table 34. The grain yield figures for India are different for the year 1936-39.

In 1950, thus India had a per capita income which was higher than China's, a light industry which was more developed, and a well developed administrative system relative to China. But India was behind China in the largest sector of economic activity – viz., agriculture. India and China nevertheless despite a prolonged decline to underdeveloped status by modern standards had, because of a prolonged liberation struggle, united their peoples and raised their mass consciousness. However, both countries thereafter gradually squandered the legacy of the their respective liberation struggles and public goodwill by adopting the unsuited Soviet planning framework for development. Three distinguishing negative features of this framework were: (1) an anti-export inclination coupled with blind import substitution that disregarded the law of comparative advantage; (2) the concept of maximum postponement of consumption through levies, quotas, and taxes, and according high priority for investment in "heavy" capital goods industry; (3) financing of the plan by squeezing agriculture through unfavourable terms of trade, by compulsory procurement, administered prices, and forced savings. In the 1950s, China collectivized agriculture, nationalized industry, banking, trade, restricted freedom of choice of jobs, as well as freedom to migrate, internally or externally. India also adopted a similar approach although from a different route. But there was less "cushion" for India to compress agriculture since that sector had bled during British Rule and hence had little surplus to spare. The insensitivity to the plight of farmers during this socialist phase in India is brought out in Table below wherein it is apparent that while the terms of trade moved in favour of agriculture in China, it was adverse in India.

There was a private sector in India, unlike in China, but it was a captive shackled one because of partial nationalization [i.e., some key sectors nationalized e.g., airlines, insurance and banks, while others not], a land reform [which was prone to fraud and corruption, and insensitive to considerations of economies of scale], labour laws that made it almost impossible to fire without expensive litigation and compensation, and an Industrial Development Act and other legislation that meant effectively state - controlled financial and investment decisions, administered prices of key inputs, rigid Exit policy, and public sector occupying the "commanding heights" of the economy. India thus adopted with modifications a framework that could be called a closed hybrid Soviet planning model while China adopted the closed Soviet model in it's pristine form.

Table 21: Agricultural terms of trade over time: China and India (1952-80)

Year	China Purchasing Price of farm and sideline products (1)	India Price of industrial goods in rural areas (2) (Base 1952=100)	Index of agricultural terms of trade (1)÷(2)×100	Year	Purchasing price of farm products (3)	Prices paid for industrial goods in rural areas (4) (Triennium ending 1971-72=100)	Index of agricultural terms of trade (3)÷(4)
1952	100.0	100.0	100.0	1952-53	48.3	53.0	91.1
1956	116.6	100.4	116.1	1957-58	50.2	55.9	89.8
1957	122.4	101.6	120.5	1965-66	77.7	75.5	102.9
1958	125.1	99.4	125.9	1970-71	100.5	100.5	100.0
1962	161.9	114.7	141.2	1971-72	102.5	105.1	97.5
1965	155.0	107.3	144.5	1972-73	116.9	112.9	103.5
1966	162.0	102.6	157.9	1973-74	145.0	132.3	109.6
1977	168.8	99.5	169.6	1974-75	166.8	166.9	99.9
1978	173.5	99.5	174.4	1975-76	142.4	168.3	84.6
1979	211.8	100.2	211.4	1976-77	157.0	173.2	90.7
1980	226.9	101.1	224.4	1977-78	164.8	181.6	90.8
1981	240.3	102.8	233.8	1978-79	157.1	183.9	85.4
				1979-80	185.4	209.3	88.6

Source: Economic and Political Weekly, July 14, 1999, Mumbai, India.

While China had a justification of sorts in choosing the Soviet model —since the liberation of the nation in 1949 was led by the Chinese Communist Party, in India the adoption of the Soviet model was a reversal by Prime Minister Jawaharlal Nehru of the principles laid down by Mahatma Gandhi and Deputy Prime Minister Vallabhai Patel. Gandhi was assassinated in 1948, and Patel died of natural causes in 1950.

Nehru as Prime Minister, unfettered thereafter, and in cooperation with the newly grafted portion of the bureaucracy of expatriate Indians from England, who had been influenced as tutors by the "Oxbridge" intellectuals led by Kim Philby and Harold Laski of the London School of Economics, saw a profitable transition from feudalism to socialism in the Soviet model. Indians who could afford to study in England then, had by and large been from the families of the British - appointed land revenue collectors (called zamindars) and thus progeny of the comprador class that, by exorbitant revenue extraction mandated by the colonial government, had starved Indian agriculture. This class had been enabled with enormous discretionary power for appropriation and confiscation to dispossess the peasants of their lands for failure to meet the near impossible demands for revenue.

Nehru, and then his daughter Indira Gandhi as Prime Ministers for a total of 33 years of the five decades of Independence then set about making the State achieve "commanding heights of the economy that made the Indian system a hybrid Soviet set-up via pervasive licenses and controls. The first barrier to entry came with the Industries (Development and Regulation) Act 1951 (IDRA), which made it incumbent upon all existing and proposed private sector industrial units to obtain licenses from the central government. The IDRA continued for 40 years before being dismantled in the first wave of reforms after June 1991. By creating an encompassing licensing regime, the IDRA fostered not only entry barriers via preemption of licenses, but also an environment of rent seeking. Over the years, licensing became increasingly stringent and required clearances from a large number of uncoordinated ministries. By the time licensing was abolished in 1991, a typical private sector manufacturing company needed government permission to establish a new plant, manufacture a new article, expand capacity, change location, import capital goods and to do many other things that fell under the rubric of normal corporate activity.

A more serious barrier to entry occurred in 1956, when the Industrial Policy Resolution (IPR) adopted the maxim of 'a socialist pattern of society' and prescribed that the public sector would occupy 'the commanding heights' of the economy. Schedule A of the IPR listed 17 industries whose future development would be "the exclusive responsibility of the State" and 12 Schedule B industries where "the State will increasingly establish new undertakings". By a single stroke, India succeeded in creating yet another restraint on private investment.

The late 1960s and early 1970s witnessed an intensified trend to limit the scope of private investment. The Monopolies and Restrictive Trade Practices Act, 1969 (popularly known as MRTP) linked industrial licensing with an asset-based classification of monopoly. Interestingly, MRTP did not apply to state owned enterprises—on a tenuous assumption that public monopolies were not inimical to either the nation's or the consumer's interest. With the passing of MRTP, private businesses whose assets exceeded a fairly paltry amount varying from Rs.10 million to Rs.1 billion had to apply for additional approvals to increase capacities. Quite often, the applications were rejected. Thus, instead of building on core competencies, business houses used their free cash flows to set up capacities in unrelated activities.

MRTP was followed by widespread nationalization. It began with the insurance companies and banks, and spread to petroleum and collieries. With nationalization came employment preservation, which saw successive governments in the 1970s and early 1980s taking over financially distressed private sector textile mills and engineering companies—thus converting private bankruptcy to public debt. As if these distortions were not enough, the State adopted the fetish of 'small is beautiful' and encouraged the setting up of mini-plants. The 1980s saw the mushrooming of technologically nonviable mini-steel, mini-cement and mini-paper units that were set up with heavy tax concessions, high initial leveraging and subsidized long term finance. This proliferation of non-competitive manufacturing capacities was exacerbated by reserving over 800 product lines for the small scale sector.

These dysfunctional policies and procedures flourished in an administratively controlled, closed economy buttressed by high tariffs and import quotas. Import substitution of the 1970s and early 1980s made it incumbent upon a company to demonstrate the 'essentiality' of any import; and 'indigenous availability' forced producers to purchase domestic inputs even at higher price-lower quality configurations. Import quotas came in the firm of various types of licenses. Among the many were Actual Users (Industrial) Licenses, Actual Users (Non-industrial) Licenses, Capital Goods Licenses, Customs Clearance Permits, Supplementary Licenses, Import Replenishment Licenses, Special Import Licenses, Additional Licenses, canalisation of imports and Open General Licenses. Over the years, industrial tariffs continued to be raised according to demands pressed by industry until the peak rate exceeded 300%. By 1985, the mean tariff rate for intermediate goods was 146% (standard deviation 56%); and for capital goods it was 107% (standard deviation 48%). That China's mean tariff was 79% and 63% respectively.

To be sure, some of these policies helped set up industrial capacities, especially in engineering, drugs and pharmaceuticals, chemicals, fertilizers and petrochemicals. But they also created highly protected markets, fostered uncompetitiveness and promoted large scale rent-seeking. In 1969, the government introduced yet another distortion by nationalising banks. Now, as the sole shareholder, the state could order banks to do whatever it wanted, without going through the regulatory loop of the Reserve Bank of India. Thus, by the mid-1970s, all the ingredients were in place for steadily destroying the foundations of the financial system.

Thus, when the Janata Party was voted to power in 1977, India was only nominally not a "scientific" socialist state as was formally China then, but in practical terms India was state-driven not market driven.

Chapter 3

Economic Growth, Structural Change, Equity and Productivity (1952)

By 1950, when India and China founded their republics, the two nations commenced development through the Soviet model of economic planning, China although had a relatively more comfortable food surplus which enabled it to better finance industrial growth, it lacked the industrial infrastructure to put it to good use.

While India, which had suffered a two century long decline in foodgrain yields, had no such cushion or surplus in agriculture in 1950 and thus had to slow down its industrialization programme mid-way following a food crisis in 1966-67. The adopted Soviet model had thus to be modified by India beyond recognition to enable the simultaneous improvement in agriculture with industrialization planning following this food crisis. The model ought to have been jettisoned in the mid-sixties, but the influence of the Soviet lobby in academia and government was so strong that it could be done till 1991. By then there was no Soviet Union.

Why India and China had to adopt a thoroughly unworkable Soviet model of planning for their development? During the entire period of 1870-1950, China had been ruled by a feudal oligarchy and had gone through political and military turbulence of the kind that India had not experienced in the same period, and yet in agricultural performance especially in terms of grain output, China was ahead of India's at the end of this period.

The contrast is thus striking between the response of an indigenous government faced with a peasant-inspired rebellion which was the case of China after the Taiping Rebellion, and that of a colonial government in

India after the peasantry financed 1857 revolt which it had crushed. The Chinese government responded by becoming more accommodative to the peasants, while the colonial Indian government hardened its already harsh approach to peasants. This contrast in response also may also be a reason why during the whole period 1870-1950, China had only two major famines, while India had twelve!

The difference in economic consequences between an indigenous government and a colonial one was seen in Chapter II in the experience of the British-ruled and the Indian princely states [which reigned over about one-third of undivided India]. That is, during 1920-21 to 1940-41 for which we have data, the states ruled by Indian princes, compared to British—held India, experienced a faster growth in output of grains and in the yield per acre. Therefore, and for much the same reason, Chinese agriculture under an indigenous government performed much better than a revenue extracting foreign ruled Indian agriculture, especially in food crops.

In the 1950s, China collectivized agriculture, nationalized industry, banking, trade, restricted freedom of choice of jobs, as well as freedom to migrate, internally or externally. India also adopted a similar approach although it permitted a private sector.

After gaining independence in the late 1940's, both countries adopted different political frameworks, with India becoming the world's largest democratic Republic, and China becoming a Communist doctrinaire Peoples' Republic. Despite having different political ideologies, both embraced similar economic ideas on planning. Both had suffered exploitation, economic stagnation, impoverishment and innumerable injustices of so-called capitalist and free trade policies imposed by the imperialist forces.

This had instilled a deep rooted fear of *laissez faire* capitalism. Both then saw capitalism as an inefficient mechanism which perpetuated inequalities. The level of poverty and deprivation in both countries grew steadily during that Imperialist phase, more than half the population becoming poverty-stricken by mid-twentieth century. During those days, the Soviet model of socialism, due to press censorship in the USSR, apparently was working wonders in rapid industrial development. Hence, a closed or autarkic economy became emotionally acceptable in both countries.

This portrayal of socialism along with inherent distrust for capitalism led to both countries adopting the centralized economic planning. On one hand, China became a state controlled autarky since its private sector was almost non-existent. Indian policies, on the other hand, were influenced by a more moderate form of socialism sometimes known or caricatured as Fabian Socialism but really it was the lasting influence of Mahatma Gandhi and his espousal *of Ram Rajya* and *Swadeshi,* that made Nehru and others adopt a more democratic version of socialism, Nehru spared no effort to whittle down the economic freedom to bring the structure within the Soviet scheme of public sector dominance.

Thus, because of the Gandhian legacy, India chose the path of a mixed economy from 1951 itself whereby both the public and private sector were allowed to co-exist and participate in the economic development of the country. However, under Soviet influence, Prime Minister Nehru directed that the public sector be increasingly accorded the more dominant role, 'the commanding heights', for reviving the economy with the bureaucracy being put in charge of regulating the private sector. His daughter Mrs. Indira Gandhi went further and nationalized banks, wholesale trade, and imposed suffocating restrictions, quotas, and licence requirements on the private sector.

In mid-twentieth century thus, though the two nations became independent republics, the two nations launched on the path of planned development on a borrowed ill-suited Soviet growth model that called for squeezing an already depleted agriculture to finance capital-intensive nationalized producer goods industry that had few buyers for those goods because of poor purchasing power of the masses. Thus, both nations suffered devastating food shortages and foreign exchange short fall, rise in inventories, poor quality, and inevitably had to impose rationing by quotas and permits that made the situation even worse.

The pursuit of self- sufficiency or autarky, a strategy of the Soviet model, however failed in both countries. By the 1970's, neither country had even begun to regain its historic position of developed nations. Bad policies, inefficient allocation and improper implementation, with corruption emaciating the bureaucracy, all resulted due centralized Soviet planning. Thus, both economies performed dismally at a 3.5 per cent annual growth rate in GDP which was insufficient to curb poverty and reduce unemployment while population growth rates rose.

China had a major famine in 1959-61 which was initially hidden, perhaps more from China's own ruling elite than from its people or the world at large, that had followed swiftly upon the debacle of Great Leap Forward—a memorable piece of policy making by fantasy—and the Soviets walking away with all the blueprints of the turn-key industrial projects they had originally brought to China to express socialist solidarity. These setbacks was followed by 11 years of a chaotic Cultural Revolution, a failed coup by the Defence Minister, and utter autocracy of the Gang of Four. In 1978, China was in a mess of Great Wall proportions.

India's foreign exchange crisis of 1957, and the double harvest failure in 1965 and 1966 brought the nation to its proverbial knees in terms of foreign policy and dependence on monthly sanctioned US food aid. So poor was India's stature in the world then that the now forgotten book: *Famine: 1975,* published in 1966 by two US State Department officials, brothers by name Paddock, had predicted that by 1975 India would be 'unfeedable' and 'fit' to be abandoned by the West much as a grievously wounded soldier would be considered as not worth rescuing from the battlefield.

The Paddocks had predicted that there would be a massive famine in India in 1975 and millions will die. They even predicted food riots, chaos and cannibalism! None of it, of course, came to pass. The opposite in fact happened. India not only became self-sufficient in food but began exporting food!

Thus India fell behind China in the then largest sector of economic activity – viz., agriculture. India nevertheless attained a higher level in per capita GDP than China's by 1950, despite a lagging agriculture, but because of India's light industry which was more developed. Nevertheless, India and China despite an overall decline (by the then prevailing standards) from developed to underdeveloped status (by modern standards), had because of a prolonged liberation struggle, united their peoples, and raised their mass consciousness. This became indispensable human capital for national renewal and nation-building.

Both countries however gradually squandered this legacy of their respective liberation struggles and public goodwill, by adopting the unsuited Soviet planning framework for development and thus failing to raise the people's standard of living adequately. Three distinguishing negative features of this Soviet framework were: (1) an anti-export inclination coupled with blind import substitution that disregarded the law of comparative advantage; (2) the concept of maximum postponement of consumption through levies, quotas, and taxes, and according high priority for long-gestation period investment in "heavy" capital goods industry risking a food crisis; (3) financing of the economic five year plan by squeezing agriculture through an unfavourable terms of trade, by compulsory procurement, administered prices, and forced savings. This deprived the rural sector of purchasing power, and hence the products of capital-intensive industrialization ended up as inventory.

The short answer to the question why India and China adopted an unworkable Soviet model of economic planning after their hard and grim struggle, is that China was liberated by a Communist Party which then owned allegiance to the USSR, while in India several Freedom Struggle leaders including Nehru, who as students in Cambridge, Oxford and London School of Economics, had come under the influence of anti-Imperialist ideological propaganda of the then unmasked KGB agents such as Kim Philby and others.

In 1978, with new dispensations, Janata Party-led government in power in India, as well Deng Xiaoping led one in China, both nations embarked on reforms, moving away incrementally from the unsuccessful closed Soviet model. The initial conditions of 1980 were in substance unchanged from 1950, although China had achieved parity with India in per capita incomes at $250 through a much lower population growth. China also had a more egalitarian society in terms of social indicators and Gini index, while India distinguished itself through its vibrant democratic polity.

Table below brings out the initial conditions prevailing in 1978 in the material sectors in terms of physical output ratios, before the commencement of Reforms in the two countries. The Table reveals that it is in the industrial sector that China had sped ahead of India during the period 1952-78, while India kept apace in the agricultural sector. This ironic since Mao had led a peasant resolution and thought that India was a "feudal society full of exploitation of the peasantry." During this period, India had forged ahead in the service sector which not reflected in the Table.

Table 22: Ratio of Outputs: China to India 1952-78

Product	1952	1957	1965	1970	1978
1	2	3	4	5	6
1. Rice	1.99	2.01	1.06	2.8	2.04
2. Wheat	2.42	2.67	1.26	2.23	1.54
3. Foodgrains	2.35	2.46	2.07	2.01	2.07
4. Oilseeds	0.79	0.76	0.47	0.45	0.49
5. Tea	0.27	0.32	0.26	0.81	0.45
6. Milk	0.01	0.01	0.02	0.05	0.04
7. Meat	5.23	6.65	8.22	9.74	9.84
I. Farm Output	**2.03**	**2.27**	**2.13**	**2.28**	**2.30**
8. Cotton cloth	0.77	0.77	0.85	1.20	1.17
9. Sugar	0.25	0.34	0.42	0.36	0.39
10. Paper & Boards	2.72	1.22	3.09	3.09	4.35
11. Light Bulbs	1.20	1.60	2.56	3.24	3.72
12. Bicycles	0.67	1.03	1.13	1.81	2.53
13. Radios	1.31	1.84	1.15	1.83	5.84
14. TV Sets	0.00	2.00	4.00	1.20	0.86
15. Sewing Machines	1.43	1.66	2.87	10.01	35.16
II. Light Industrial	**0.80**	**0.92**	**1.72**	**2.17**	**3.54**
16. Coal	1.68	3.00	3.30	4.64	6.0
17. Crude Oil	1.01	3.47	2.43	4.51	8.97
18. Electricity	1.20	1.70	2.04	2.08	2.50
19. Natural Gas	0.15	0.29	1.50	1.99	4.88
III. Energy	**1.61**	**3.30**	**3.16**	**4.37**	**6.83**
20. Steel	1.25	2.55	1.87	2.69	3.19
21. Cement	0.71	1.12	1.51	1.80	3.32
22. Fertilisers	2.40	1.15	5.09	2.30	3.21
23. Machine Tolls	2.94	6.95	3.30	9.33	2.00
24. Motor Vehicles	0.01	0.28	0.57	1.01	1.98
25. Tractors	0.22	0.44	0.72	1.60	2.38
26. Rail Wagons	0.84	1.22	0.09	1.24	1.46
IV. Heavy Industrial	**1.75**	**2.02**	**2.04**	**3.02**	**3.63**
V. Total Output	**1.51**	**1.66**	**1.94**	**2.51**	**3.26**
VI. Population	**1.57**	**1.59**	**1.54**	**1.51**	**1.47**

Note: Rows I, II and IV have been calculated using Chinese shares in gross value of output, Row III has been derived from shares in coal equivalents.

Source: China: Data for China have been called from diverse sources, including documents of Party Congress, The Ten Great Years, Beijing 1959, the Statistical Year Book of China (1985), Beijing and U.S. Congress, Committee on Foreign Relations, Economic Development in India and China, 1956. India: The 1986-87 (and earlier) *Economic Survey,* Ministry of finance, New Delhi. February 1987.

Between 1952 and 1978, the growth rate in China and India, calculated by this author using Indian prices [**Swamy 1989**] to be almost the same, at about 3.8 percent per year for India, and 4.0 for China. Although earlier these estimates arrived by this author did not find much favour with scholars then being considered for China as too low, but now there is greater acceptability for this estimate of GDP growth rates for 1952-78 for China.

Eminent Harvard scholar **Dwight Perkins** [35] recently stated that "... having just redone the Chinese GNP in 1990 prices, [I have] recalculated the Chinese growth rate between 1957 and 1978 at 3.6% per year", which is down from 6 per cent estimated by him earlier.

Therefore, Chinese and Indian growth rates in GDP for this period was about the same around 4% per year, which resulted from a fast growing services sector in India offset by the fast growth rate of manufacturing sector in China, while in agriculture, however, the performance of the two economies was about the same. In per capita terms, because of a lower population growth in China, a gap did develop in growth rates of per capita GDP in favour of China. These growth rates were inadequate for wiping out unemployment, or even for containing it.

THE ADVENT OF ECONOMIC REFORMS

In 1978 under the astute leadership of Deng Xiaoping, a chastened China, essentially to redeem the credibility of the Communist Party, took up reforms and effected the gradual transition of the economy from state-controlled to market-driven and from an autarky to international economic integration.

China commenced, *albeit* incrementally, on economic reforms step by step towards openness and market orientation. India in 1977 under a new elected dispensation of which this author was a part, began with smaller measures in deregulation in 1978, and then shifted gears to an open hybrid Soviet model in 1980, in which emphasis was on export growth, liberal imports financed by short term loans in the international capital market, and by a hefty IMF loan. Because of the extensive continued Soviet influence with Indian political leaders, India however could not make a clean break with the Soviet model till 1991.

China had in contrast made an explicit political break with the Soviet Union even as early as 1960s, and had already begun to trade significantly with Japan and democratic European countries. But the Cultural Revolution and the activities of the Gang of Four had stunted these moves till 1978. In fact, as early as in 1961 after the Soviet's total pullout with blueprints from the 156 key large industrial projects and a massive famine that had led to the starvation deaths of over 30 million Chinese, Liu Shao chi and Deng Xiao ping had advocated some relaxation in controls on agriculture, by allowing household backyard plot cultivation outside the Maoist commune system with liberty to farmers to sell the produce in a free market in rural trade fairs, and to the State to import grain and essential industrial items from Japan and Europe.

This "liberalization" and the subsequent experience gathered in working such relaxation of controls, enabled the Chinese peasants to make an easy transition to the Household Responsibility System [HRS] adopted in 1980. Both in agriculture and exports thus, China had already some experience in market functioning and in handling openness, before the Four Modernisation slogan was adopted in December 1978. This may partially explain why China's transition toward market economy and international trade has been less painful and disrupting than for other erstwhile Soviet systems of Russia and East Europe.

India, reluctantly took up partial reforms in the late 1970s and 80's such as import liberalisation. Growth rate in India accelerated, but it was not sustainable since it was powered by the now permitted short-term loans from abroad that was not matched by rising foreign exchange reserves due to lagging exports. Huge Government short-term borrowings also led to high fiscal deficits, along with a worsening current account and evaporating foreign exchange reserves.

The imminent collapse of the USSR which was India's major trading partner, and the first Gulf war which caused a spike in oil prices, caused a major balance of payment crisis for India. Foreign exchange reserves sunk to levels that could not cover even two months imports bill. Added to that was the payments that became due on short-term loans from abroad, and a consequent panic run of the NRI deposits to the tune of $2 billion.

The crisis however enabled India to shake-off the vice-like grip of the ideas that had been promoted by pro-Soviet Indian economists for half a century. These ideas had condemned India to a less than 4 percent annual growth rate for four decades after 1950, which is a better growth rate of course, as a feeble consolation, than under British imperial rule. This failure in achieving a high growth rate that was witnessed in East Asia, was palmed off by these Left-wing economists as inevitably the "Hindu rate of growth" when in fact it was the Soviet rate. Fortunately, these economists soon thereafter migrated to the US thus enabling Indians who stayed home, to come out of harm's way.

Economic reforms were ushered in—quickly and sequentially—in China, while haltingly in India during the first decade since 1980. But reforms uncorked the bottled up entrepreneurship inherent in the peoples of the two countries. Growth accelerated and continues to do so even now. The two most populous nations are thus counted today amongst the world's fastest growing economies, with their GDPs on the basis of corrected data, increasing at the trend rate estimated over the five years 2003-08, of about 9 per cent annually.

In purchasing power parity (PPP) terms, China today is the second largest economy in the world, next to the United States, followed by India [having overtaken Japan last year]. At current trend growth rates, China is estimated, *ceteris paribus,* to become the world's largest economy in three decades hence, overtaking the US, while India will be the world's third largest economy.

These conclusions have to be qualified by the words *ceteris paribus,* because the US can, as it has often in the past, re-invent itself by new epochal innovations, to retain its global economic lead as it did in the 1990s by inventing the Internet and the PC and thus changed forever the way business is transacted domestically and transnationally. And China and India, as we shall see in Chapter IV, could also suffer a financial crisis as did Japan and other East Asian "tigers" in 1997-98, and thus not be able to catch up with the US.

The Growth Rate and Structural Changes

The gap today in GDP levels between India and China, and the difference in the growth rates averaged over the past three decades between two economies, had emerged during the 1980-93 period, when China had jettisoned the Soviet planned economic system and was rapidly reforming while India remained shackled by it and haltingly reformed till 1992. This enabled China to grow at twice the rate as India for nearly a decade and a half. That gap has remained unreduced even if it has not widened since [see **Graphs**].

Reforms in India since 1992 have helped in unleashing the massive potential of both the countries and led to a convergence in growth rates by 1998. Both have now witnessed spectacular and similar growth rates at 9 percent per year, or thereabouts, in recent years. But the gap of 1980-93 period has yet to be closed and will remain intact unless India growth rate exceeds the Chinese rate in the future and for some length of time. By the periods 1952-80, 1980-93, 1993-2003, and 2003-2008, on the basis of PPP calculations and after data correction, this author's estimates are as follows:

Table 23: Growth Rates in GDP and Population

[Annual Percentage]

Period	GDP		Population	
	China	India	China	India
1952-80	4.0	4.0	1.8	2.2
1980-93	10.0	5.5	1.4	2.0
1993-03	8.0	6.5	1.1	1.9
2003-08	8.7	8.5	0.8	1.7

Source: Author's estimate using corrected PPP data on moving averages.

India's savings/GDP ratio increased dramatically to nearly 38% during the period 2003-04 to 2007-08 while China's crossed 43%. In details there is a sharp contrast between the two countries.

Graph 5: GDP Growth: China vs. India 1950-2006

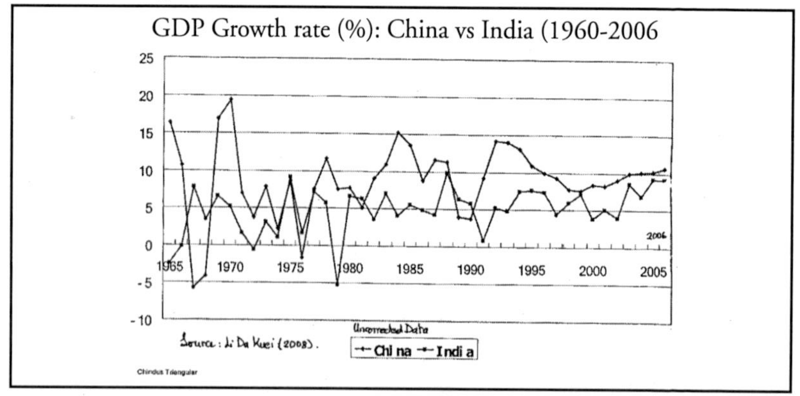

Graph 6: Growth in GDP, China (%)

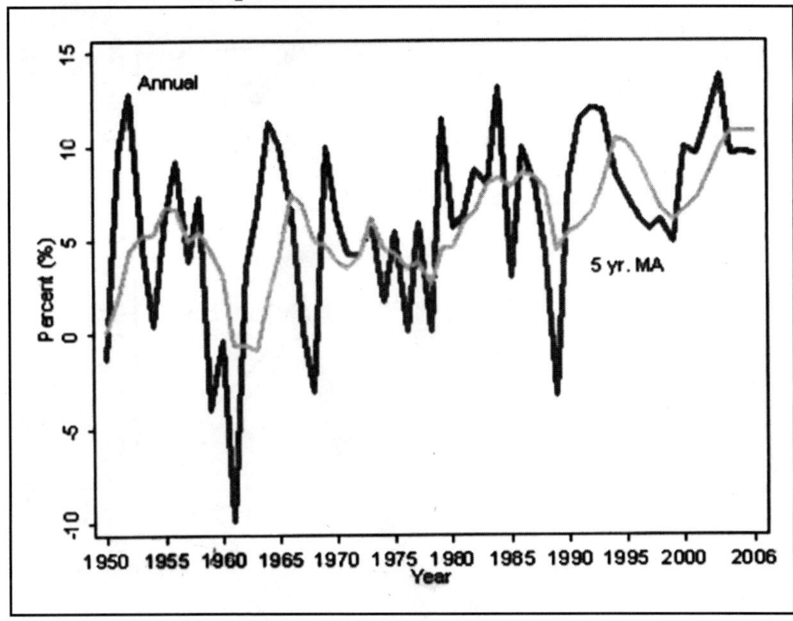

Graph 7: Growth in GDP, India (%)

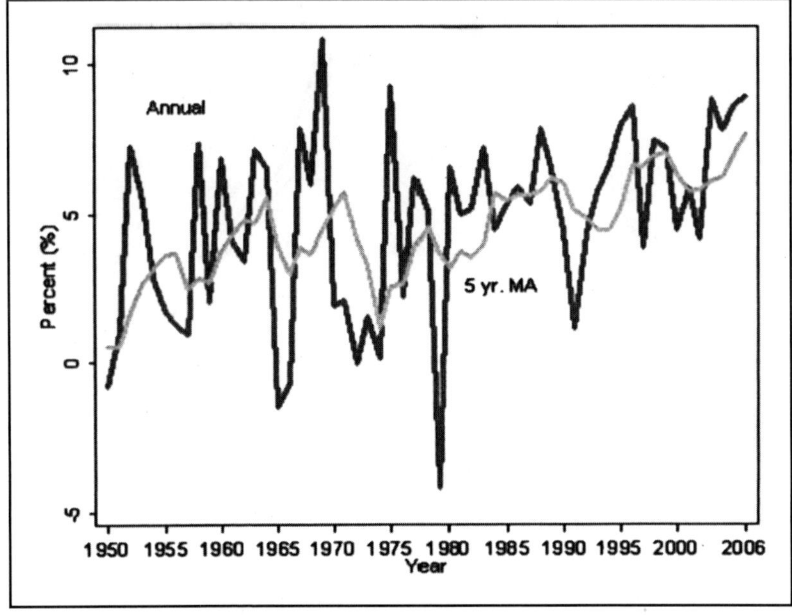

Graph 8: Growth rates in China and India

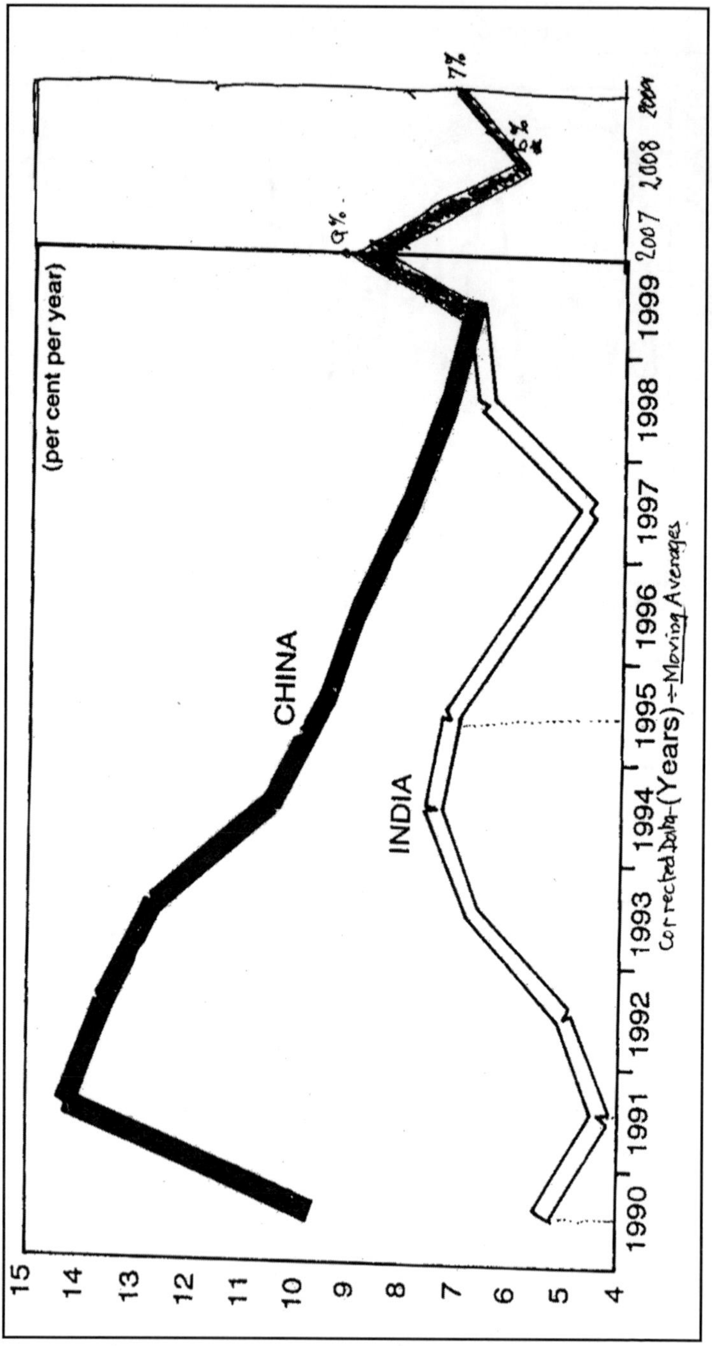

Source: India's Economic Performance and Reforms by Subramanian Sway (Konark Publishers (P) Ltd., 2000)

In China, savings ratio has been extraordinarily high. As a consequence, China's investment/GDP ratio has crossed 50%. Modigliani et al have opined that China's saving rate has reached a ceiling, ruling further increases [ ]. Since the mid-1980s, as a share of GDP, it first peaked at 43.3 percent of GDP in 1993. Investment has been high since throughout this period, with household and government investment stable at rates comparable to other countries. Enterprise investment, ranging between 27 and 35 percent of GDP makes China's investment high. Analysis based on Graphs and Table above reveal the following points:

- Although discussions on investment and saving traditionally focus on household saving, China's high saving rate is as much driven by high saving of enterprises and the government as by high household saving. This is in sharp contrast with India.
- Investment by households and direct investment by the government has been relatively steady at levels comparable to other countries (around 7 and 3-4 percent of GDP, respectively).
- Investment by the enterprise sector distinguishes China from other countries, and shows most of the variation over time. In recent years, the differential ranged between 11 (Korea), 13%(India), and 20 (US) percentage points of GDP.
- High enterprise investment is financed partly by a large excess of saving over investment of households—channeled by the banking system—and the government—transferred to enterprises.
- But with enterprise own saving having risen as profitability has improved, over one-half is financed by enterprise retained earnings.
- High government saving is a result of a policy favoring government-financed investment over government consumption, and not having to pay dividend to government.
- Reasons for relatively high saving by enterprises include a high share of capital intensive industry in GDP and dividend policies.

Graph 9: Gross Domestic savings (% of GDP): China vs. India (1960-2006)

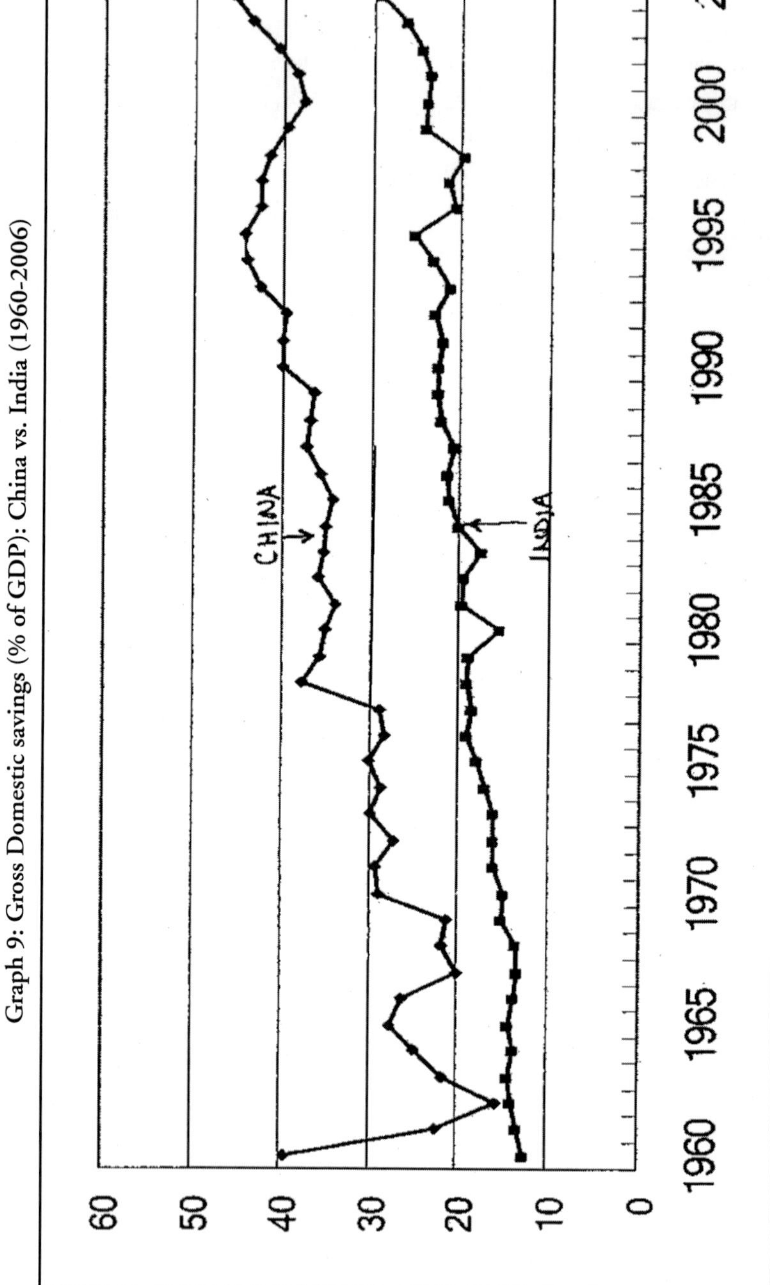

Table 24: China: Comparing Saving with other Countries[1]
(in percent of GDP)

	China	United States	France	Japan	Korea	Mexico	India
Total Domestic Savings	42.5	14.3	20.7	25.5	31.0	20.8	29.7
Difference China-others due to:	42.5	28.2	21.8	17.0	11.5	21.7	12.8
Household saving	42.5	11.8	5.8	8.4	12.1	8.6	−6.6
Enterprise saving	42.5	8.6	9.4	−0.5	4.1	8.3	9.6
Government saving	42.5	7.9	6.7	9.2	−4.7	4.8	9.8

Source: NBS (national accounts), via CEIC, and OECD National Accounts.
[1]Data for China is for 2003, for Mexico for 2001, and for other countries for 2002.

On the other hand, the main component of India's savings, household sector savings, accounts for over 60% of domestic savings, which share however rose a little (2%). Add to that the fact that more than 50% of household savings continues to be in relatively unproductive assets—land, gold and silver—and, clearly it is financial, not physical, savings that are the key to future higher investment and growth for India. Savings in physical assets accounted for about 66% of household financial assets in 1994-95. But by 2007-08, the share of such assets in total household savings had come down to 52%.

Graph 10: Savings rate, China

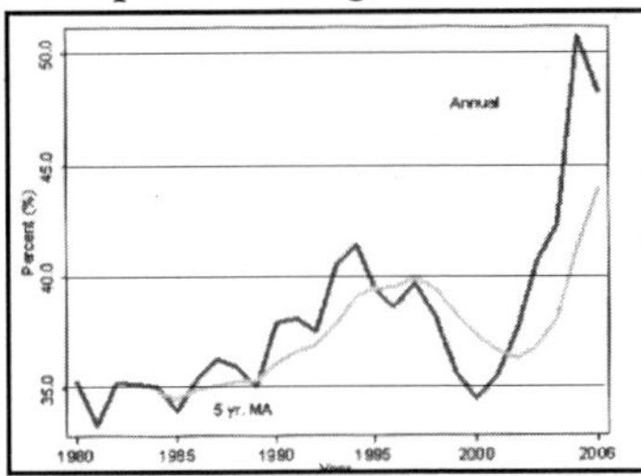

Graph 11: Investment rate, China

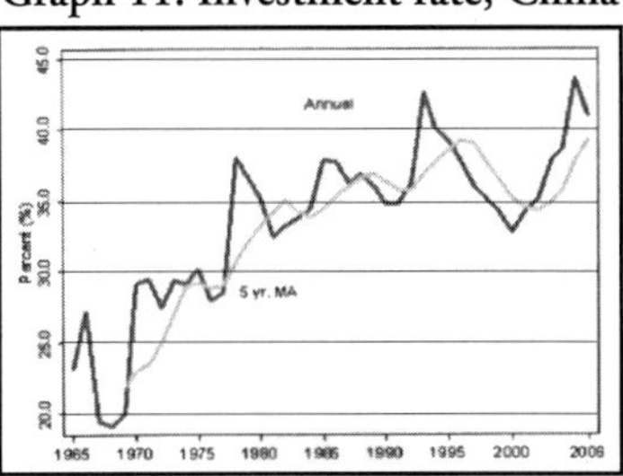

Graph 12: Savings rate, India

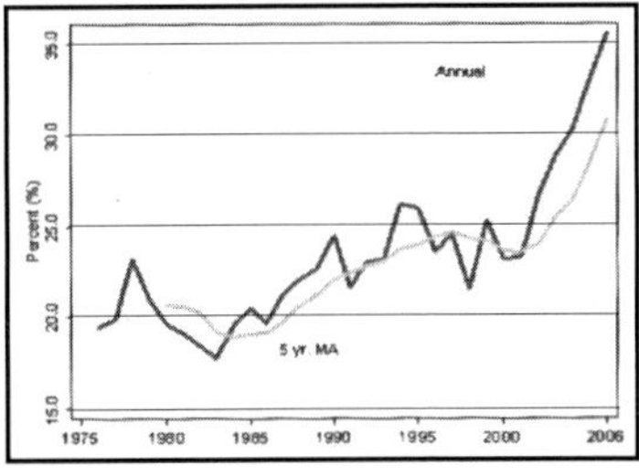

Graph 13: Investment rate, India

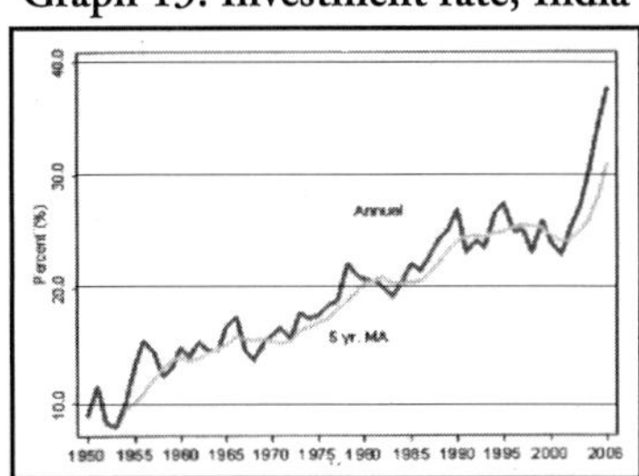

Graph 14: Investment Rate: China/India

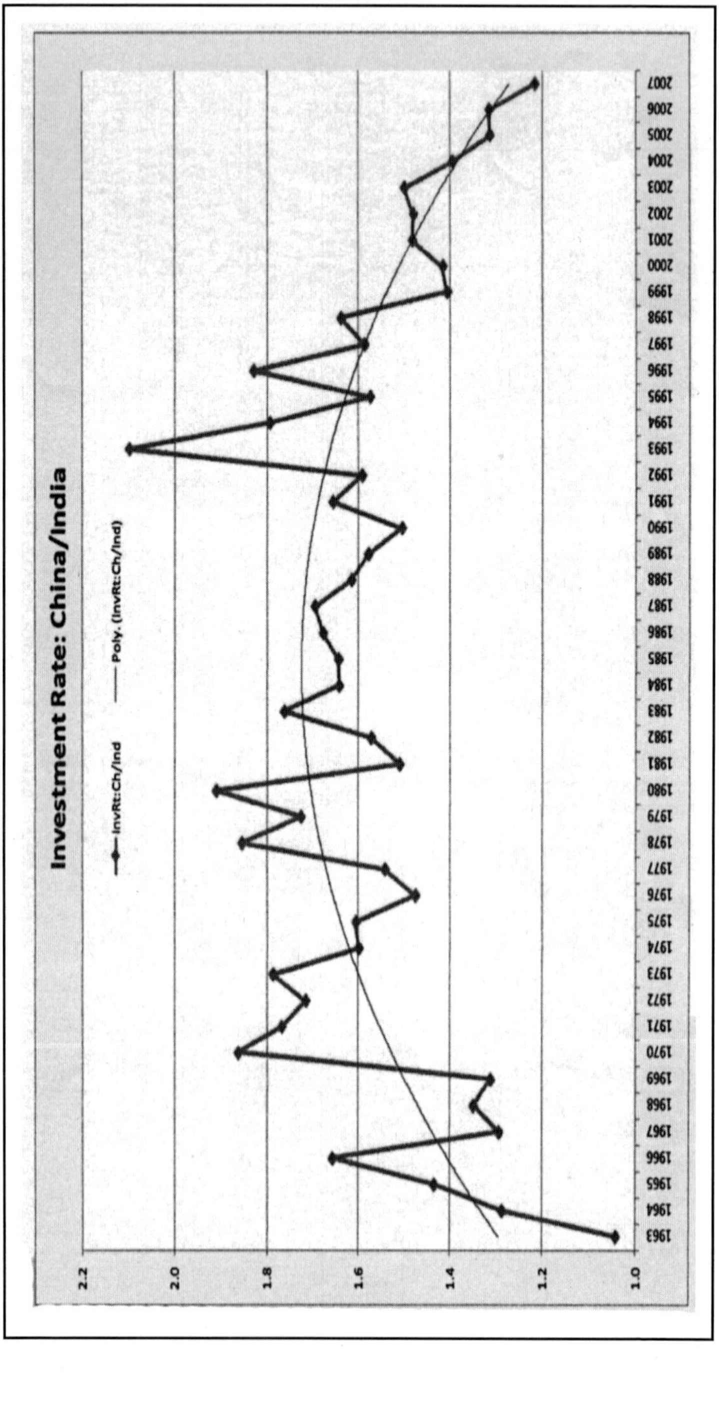

19 March, 2009 CPR: AV

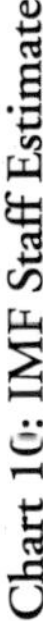

Chart 10: IMF Staff Estimate

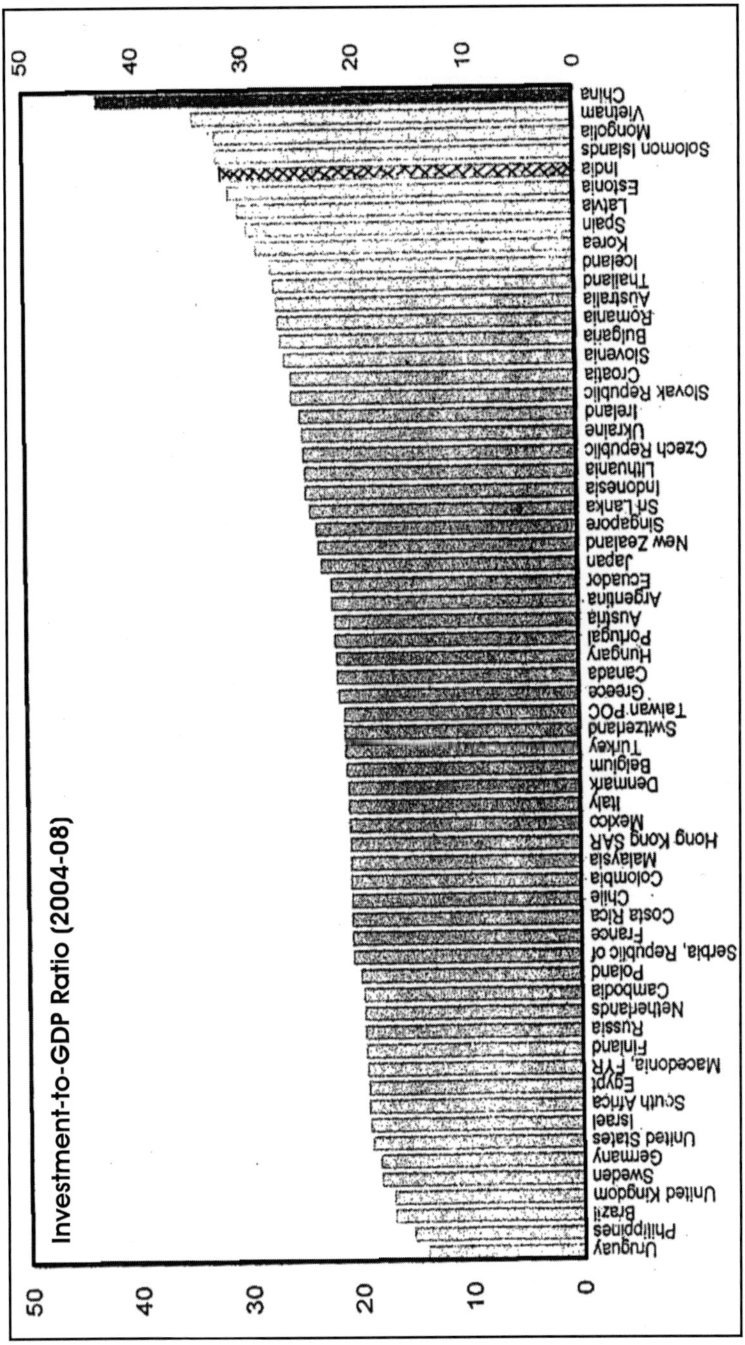

Investment-to-GDP Ratio (2004-08)

Table 25: Gross Domestic Savings/GDP
INDIA

	2003-04	2004-05	2005-06	2006-07	2007-08	Increase over 5 years
House hold savings:	23.8	23.0	24.1	24.1	24.3	2.0
Of which financial assets	11.3	10.1	11.7	11.7	11.7	3.5
Physical assets	12.4	12.9	12.4	12.4	12.6	1.6
Private corporate sector	4.7	6.6	7.7	8.3	8.8	87.0
Public sector	1.2	2.2	2.4	3.3	4.5	275.0
Gross domestic savings	29.7	31.8	34.2	35.7	37.7	27.0

As far as private corporate savings is concerned, though Indian corporates have turned in a performance compared to their counterparts elsewhere in the world, this has come by paring costs rather than from expanding top lines. Hence, corporate private sector savings are also likely to plateau out in the next few years, or at least till the global recovery is complete.

The net result is that the improvement in the India savings/GDP ratio witnessed during the past few years which while cannot be dismissed, is more illusory than real. The predominance of savings in physical assets, for long the bane, is changing, albeit not changing fast enough and enough to power India ahead of China.

Even within the broad spectrum of financial assets, Indian households seem to prefer safe bank deposits to shares and debentures. A detailed breakup of the components of financial savings shows [Table above] that bank deposits account for a high and increasing share of financial savings of households. Indeed, even as the share of bank deposits in financial savings of households increased from 48% in 2006-07 to 58% in 2008-09, savings in shares and debentures fell from 9% to 2.6%.

Why is it that when it comes to savings, Indian households demonstrate such a strong aversion to risk? Do Indians have a strong liquidity preference that made Keynes once remark: "The history of India at all times has provided an example of a country impoverished by a preference for liquidity"— have ironically turned even more risk averse, post-reform? Faced with a fast-changing economic environment, the end of job security, breakup of traditional family structures and absence of any social safety net, compounded by gigantic stock market corruption, even better-off households now put a premium on safety rather than the rate of return on financial assets.

STRUCTURAL CHANGES

In terms of structural changes, the Chinese and Indian economies differ sharply. While the share of agriculture declined in both countries, the Chinese industrial sector's share rose to exceed 50 per cent of GDP, in India it was the Service sector whose share rose over the years to exceed 50 per cent of GDP.

Table 26: On Value of Output and Employment

(A) VALUE OF OUTPUT	**2003-04**	**2014-15**
Total Value of output (Rs crore)	5,125,606	5,864,466
Value of output due to the		
Communications Section (Rs crore)	93,170	571,173
Communications output multiplier	1.9401	1.9401
Share of Communications sector to total value of output (%)		
Direct		
Direct and Indirect		
(B) EMPLOYMENT	**2003-04**	**2015-15**
Total Employment (Million)	368.9	391.7
Employment in the Communications Sector (Million)	1.68	10.31
Communications sector employment multiplier to employment	1.3383	1.3383
Share of the Communications sector employment to total employment (%)		
Direct	0.46	2.63
Direct of Indirect	0.61	3.52

(At 2003-04 Prices)

The question is why Services rose so relatively fast in India? The answer lies in the fact that unorganized services were always in the private sector, and that the IT revolution in India especially in Communication and Financial Services after the 1999 de-regulation led this growth as the Table above reveals.

According to two Fellows of NCAER, Rajesh Shukla and R.A. Siddiqui, the share of the communications sector, which include postal, telephone and telegraph services, to the total GDP has risen from a meager 0.7% in the 1980s to 5.7% in 2007-08. It emerged as the fastest growing sector in the period 2001-08 recording a growth rate of 25.7%. By 2014-15, its share in total GDP is expected to rise to 15.4%, making the communications sector the largest contributor to GDP.

This has been possible largely due to the telecom reforms which gave an enormous boost to private sector participation. The expansion of telecom infrastructure has given a huge boost to the services sector—particularly the BPO, information technology and information-technology-enabled services. The software industry and the financial industry sectors too have grown, largely due to the support provided by a strong communication sector. So much so that the US-based Gartner Inc has projected mobile services revenues to grow at a compounded annual growth rate of 12.5% between 2009 and 2013, taking the telecom subscriber base to nearly 770 million connections. Despite the recessionary trends, the IT and IT-enabled services are expected to post a growth rate of almost 11% (2009).

How has the communications sector performed vis-à-vis other growth sectors? Consider the three sectors—trade, registered manufacturing and communication—that have contributed more than 10% to GDP growth during the period 2001-08. While trade's contribution was highest at 16.7%, that of registered manufacturing and communications were 11.7% and 12.2% respectively, the importance of the communications sector looks more promising when we see the relative share of the sector's GDP to the total GDP and its contribution to overall growth.

Shukla Siddiqui analysis shows that the "output multiplier" of the communications sector is 1,94. Assuming the communications sector continues to grow at the same pace that it did during 2001-08 (25.7%), the value of output of the communications sector will be Rs.5,711 billion in 2014-15, growing from its level of Rs.931 billion in 2003-04. As a result of linkages that the communications sector shares with electronic equipment and business services sectors, these sectors too are being positively impacted by the growth.

What will be the impact of an increase in the overall GDP on GDP due to the communications sector? To assess this, it is calculated the elasticity to measure the impact of increase in overall GDP on communication GDP which comes out to 2.45. The sector's elasticity suggests that a 1% increase in the overall GDP results in an increase in communications GDP by 2.85%. And a 1% increase in the communications GDP will lead to 0.35% increase in the overall GDP.

Graph 15: Structural Changes in China and India GDP

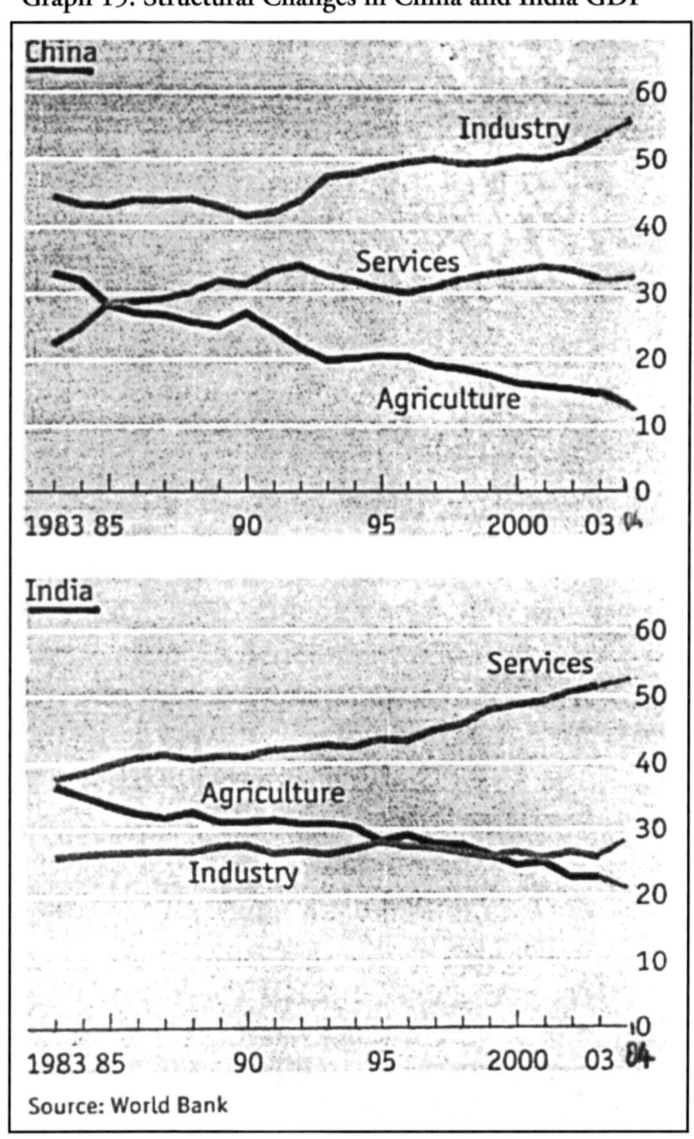

Table 27: Value – Added and Employment by industry as Share of Total

Percent

		Primary	Secondary	Tertiary	Total
			Value added		
1978	China	28	48	24	100
	India	44	24	32	100
1993	China	17	51	33	100
	India	33	28	39	100
2004	China	9	58	33	100
	India	22	28	50	100
			Employment		
1978	China	71	17	12	100
	India	71	13	16	100
1993	China	56	22	21	100
	India	64	15	21	100
2004	China	47	23	31	100
	India	57	18	25	100

Source: China Data Center and CSY: India National Accounts; India NSSO.

Table 28: Sectoral GDP: China, 1960-2006

	Growth (in %)			Share in GDP		
	Agriculture	Industry	Service	Agriculture	Industry	Service
China						
1960s	2	5.9	2.9	39.2	34.8	26.1
1970s	2.9	10.4	5.9	32.3	44.5	23.1
1980s	5.1	10	11.9	29.3	44.6	26.1
1990s	4.2	12.1	8.9	20.3	45.5	34.2
2000s	3.3	9.8	9.4	13.6	45.6	40.7
2003-06	4.29	11.31	8.58	12.85	46.03	41.01

Source: World Bank World Development Indicators (2006)

Table 29: Sectoral GDP: India, 1960-2006

	Growth (in %)			Share in GDP		
	Agriculture	Industry	Service	Agriculture	Industry	Service
1960s	4.5	4.7	4.1	43.7	18.5	31
1970s	1.0	3.6	4.5	38.8	20.5	32.3
1980s	4.2	6.6	6.3	31.2	23.5	35.3
1990s	2.9	5.6	7.3	26.7	24.4	39.6
2000s	1.8	6.0	7.3	21.1	24.3	45.9

Source: World Bank World Development Indicators (2006)

Table 30:
Services form the largest part of the Indian economy

Country	Service	Manufacturing	Agriculture
South Korea	65.1	35.9	3.0
India	53.6	27.4	19.0
Thailand	46.0	44.1	9.9
Malaysia	41.8	49.8	8.4
Indonesia	40.8	45.8	13.4
China	40.2	47.3	12.5
Vietnam	38.1	41.0	20.9

Figures are composition of GDP in per cent in 2005. *Source:* Asian Development Bank

Table 31: India has been unable to reduce the proportion of its population employed in agriculture

Country	Agriculture	Manufacturing	Services
India*	60.0	12.0	28.0
Vietnam*	56.8	37.0	6.2
Thailand#	49.0	14.0	37.0
China*	45.0	24.0	31.0
Indonesia**	43.3	18.0	38.7
Malaysia#	14.5	36.0	49.5
South Korea*	6.4	26.4	67.2

2000 *2003 **2004 *2005
Figures are labour force by occupation in per cent
Source: CIA Factbook

Table 32: International Comparisons of yield Selected Commodities—2004-5

Rice/paddy		Wheat		Maize	
Egypt	9.8	China	4.25	U.S.A.	9.15
India	2.9	France	7.58	France	7.56
Japan	6.42	India	2.71	India	1.18
Myanmar	2.43	Iran	2.06	Germany	6.69
Korea	6.73	Pakistan	2.37	Philippines	2.1
Thailand	2.63	U.K	7.77	China	4.9
U.S.A	7.83	Australia	1.64		
World	**3.96**	**World**	**2.87**	**World**	**3.38**
Cotton		**Major Oilseeds**			
China	11.10	Argentina	2.51		
U.S.A	9.58	Brazil	2.48		
Uzbekistan	7.98	China	2.05		
India	4.64	India	0.86		
Brazil	10.96	Germany	4.07		
Pakistan	7.60	U.S.A	2.61		
		Nigeria	1.04		
World	**7.33**	**World**	**1.86**		

Source: Ministry of Agriculture and Cooperation.

Table 33: Yields (a/ha) of crops & National Demonstrations for the Year 1987-88
Annual Report of the Department of Agricultural Research &Education, 1949-50

Crop	National Average	Average Yield in National Demonstrations	Highest Yield in National Demonstrations
Rice	19.53	42.87	78.25
Wheat	20.02	37.18	54.00
Sorghum	7.62	37.56	58.37
Perimittes	3.78	18.54	35.0
Chickpes	6.29	11.31	30.20
Pigeonpea	6.25	16.37	18.00
Groundnut	8.35	17.32	35.30
Mustard	7.47	19.00	23.57

Source: Economic-Survey 2006-2007(GOI ,Delhi).

Table 34: Yield of Some Selected Commodities, 2002

Commodity (Country	Highest	World	India
Rice/paddy (Egypt)	9135	3916	2915
Wheat (UK)	8043	2720	2770
Maize (Italy)	9550	4343	1705
Sugar cane (Egypt)	119893	65802	68049
Groundnut (China)	2986	1381	794

Source: Economic Survey 2005-06.

Table 35: Compound Growth Rates of area, production and yield

(as % per annum with Base T.E. 1981-82=100)

Growth rates	1949-50 to 1964-65	1967-68 to 2008-09*
	Rice	
Area	1.21	0.50
Production	3.50	2.46
Yield	2.25	1.99
	Wheat	
Area	2.69	1.20
Production	3.98	3.69
Yield	1.27	2.46
	Coarse Cereals	
Area	0.90	–1.41
Production	2.25	0.67
Yield	1.23	1.99

	Pulses	
Area	1.72	0.01
Production	1.41	0.75
Yield	–0.18	0.72
	Sugarcane	
Area	3.28	1.69
Production	4.26	2.64
Yield	0.95	0.94
	Cotton	
Area	2.47	0.42
Production	4.55	3.06
Yield	2.04	2.63
	Nine Oilseeds	
Area	2.53	1.44
Production	3.12	3.16
Yield	0.00	1.69

Source: Department of Agriculture and Co-operation.
Note: *Growth rates are based on fourth advance estimates for 2008-09.

Not surprisingly, these factors have also influenced the employment generation capacity of the communications sector. Keeping in mind the above assumptions, the sector is projected to employ 10.31 million people by 2014 15 and a total of 13.8 million jobs (including in allied sectors) are expected to be created (see the Table above).

What is even more interesting is that India enjoys a significant potential advantage over China in agriculture. Besides being the lowest cost producer of agricultural products in the world, India has the most under utilized fertile farm land and one of the lowest yield per hectare in the world. As Table below shows, even with the existing agricultural technology and know-how, Indian experimental plots produce on best current practices between 2.5 to over 4.0 times the national average.

INFRASTRUCTURE

We have in Chapter I presented Chart I in which infrastructure is defined to include both hard and soft infrastructure.

As China is to manufacturing, India is to services – an over simplification but a telling one. Manufacturing prowess is typically the yardstick that is used internationally to measure the prosperity of emerging nations. But that depends on infrastructure. China has plowed its huge reservoir of domestic saving – about 40% of GDP – into some of the best infrastructure you will see anywhere in the world.

The Empowered Sub-Committee {of the Cabinet Committee on Infrastructure headed by the Prime Minister} in its meeting held under the chairmanship of Deputy Chairman, Planning Commission, decided on including the following in the definition of infrastructure for India, which is similar to that internationally for hard infrastructure.

COMPONENTS OF INFRASTRUCTURE

Electricity (including generation, transmission and distribution) and R&M of power stations,
Non-Conventional Energy (including wind energy and solar energy),
Water supply and sanitation (including solid waste management, drainage and sewerage) and street lighting,
Telecommunications,
Roads and bridges,
Ports,
Inland waterways,
Airports,
Railways (including rolling stock and mass transit system),
Irrigation (including watershed development),
Storage,
Oil and gas pipeline networks.

Infrastructure development has been accorded key priority in India's 11th Five-Year Plan for the years 2007-2012 and the 12th plan period of 2012-2017, with projected investment requirement of $500 billion and $1.5 trillion, respectively, by the Prime Minister's Committee on Infrastructure.

But these initiatives pale when compared to China a nation that spends about 11% of its GDP on infrastructure development against India's 6% in 2007-08 (as compared to 4.5% in 2003-04) indicative of the scope and extent of scaling up needed in infrastructure development in India to match global standards.

But as an astute observer, Cait Murphy, a Managing Editor of Fortune observed in 2006: “But in important ways, India’s economic software is superior” citing bank health, capital markets, human resource quality and the system of independent judicial oversight. It is always easier to close the hardware deficit than that of software.

Table 36: Basic Infrastructure Sector Performance Indicators

		India			China		
		1980	1990	2005	1980	1990	2005
Communications[a]	**Units**						
Telephone Connections	per 1,000	2.3	5.07	185	4.3	11.1	626
Mobile Phones	person	n.a.	0	148	n.a.	.02	348
Energy[b]							
Power Capacity	1000 mwh	33.3	71.8	137.6	65.9	126.6	444.4
Power Generation	billion kwh	119.3	275.5	661.6	285.5	590.3	2371.8
Primary Energy Production	10^{15} BTU	3.1	6.8	11.7	18.1	29.4	63.2
Per Capita Energy Consumption	10^{6} BTU	5.9	9.4	14.8	17.8	23.5	51.4
Energy Intensity	$ GDP/kg	3.4	4.0	5.5	1.3	2.1	4.4
Transport[c]							
Roads	1,000 km	644	2,000	2,526	883	1,181	1,931
Paved Roads	%	n.a.	47	57	n.a.	n.a.	82.5
Road Freight	million tons	195.9	318.4	557.4	3,820	7,240	11,600
Rail Lines Route Length	km	61,240	62,367	63,465	49,940	53,378	62,200
Rail Freight	billion ton-km	158	236	407	571	1,060	1,934
Water and Sanitation Access[c]							
Safe Drinking Water	% population	42	70	86	n.a.	70	77
Sanitation		7	14	33	n.a.	23	44

n.a. = not available.

Source: [a]International Telecommunications Union (2008). [b]Energy Information Administration website http://www.eia.doe.gov/. [c]World Development Indicator (2007), supplemented by national source such as Economic Survey (various issues) for India and National Bureau of Statistics for China.

Table 37: Infrastructure Development in China and India
(in annual compounded growth rate, %)

	India			China		
	1950-80	1980-90	1990-2005	1950-80*	1980-90	1990-2005
Electricity Generation	10.8	9.4	6.5	14.2	8.4	9.5
Road network length	4.6	3.4	3.8	7.2	1.7	3.4
Railway network	0.5	0.2	0.1	2.8	0.8	1.1
Telephone subscribers	10.2	8.9	28.7	6.6	13.8	40.9
Annual GDP Growth	3.7	5.7	6.4	5.2	9.8	10.2

Source: China Data Online and National Accounts for India Various Issues.
*Data for China refers to 1952-1980.

Graph 16: Infrastructure Investments (in % of GDP)

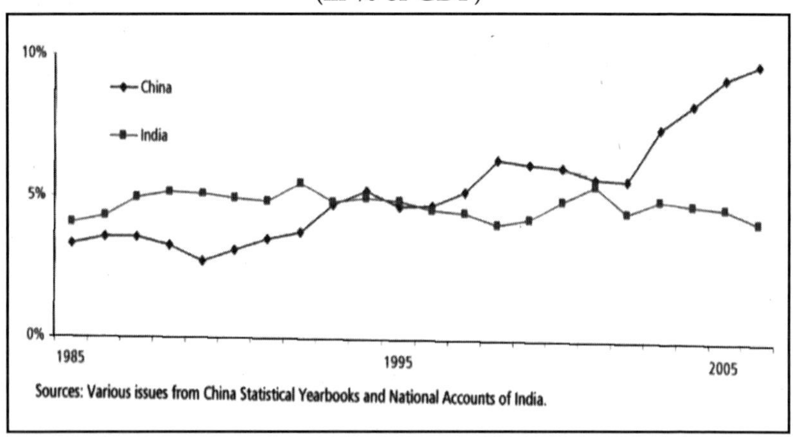

Chart 11: India: Infrastructure Indicators

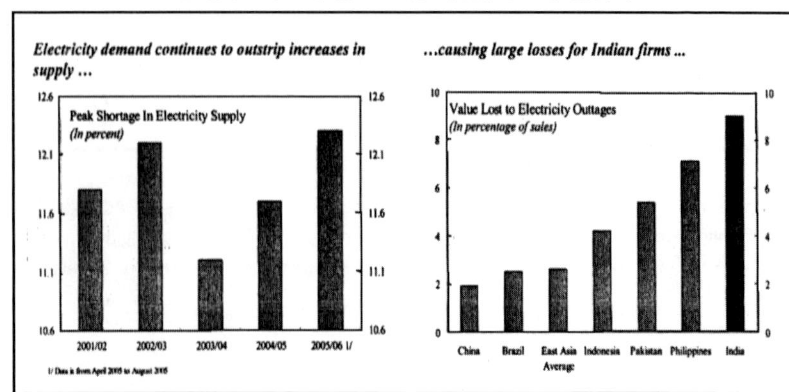

Chart 12: India: Infrastructure Indicators (Contd..)

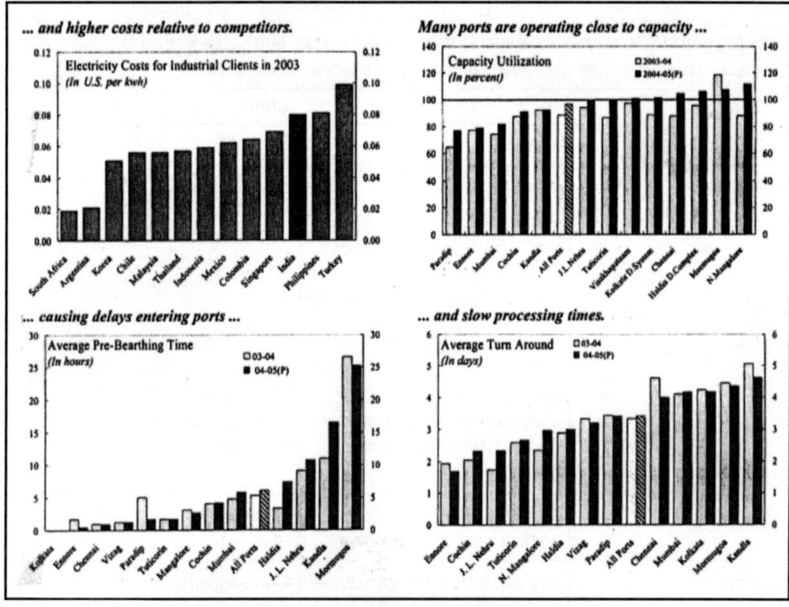

Box 3

India plans to spend $514 bn on infrastructure during the 11th 5-Year Plan*

Sector	Amount
Power and roads	245
Forts	22
Telecom	65
Airports	8
Railways	65
Irrigation and water supply	98
Others	11

2007-12

If figures in $ billion... Planning Commission.

Table 38

Production	Unit	2003-04	2004-05	2005-06
Electricity	Billion Kwh	559	587	512.27
Coal	Million tonnes	361	375	320.7
Finished steel	'000 tonnes	36,957	38,325	34,777
Cement, all kinds	'000 tonnes	117,035	125,338	120401
Petrol and products	'000 tonnes	146,686	152,197	126,335

Box 4

The big gap between India's physical infrastructure needs, current as well as projected, and the actual reality is illustrated by the following comparative examples:

Sector	India	Comparative Example
Roads	Out of India's 3.3 million km road network, only 2% of the total are national highways. Only 8,000 km (12%) of the national highways are dual carriageways, and not all of them are four-lane.	By the end of 2007, China had some 53,600 km of highways with four lanes or more.
Railways	By 2012, China's railroad will expand from 79,000 km today to 1,10,000 km. By the same date, India's railway network will inch 2,000 km ahead to reach 65,300 km.	This year alone, China will begin construction of 5,148 km of new lines—more than twice India's target for new lines over the next four years.
Ports	It takes an average of 20 days to clear import cargo in India.	In Singapore it takes 3 days.
Power	In 2007, India achieved capacity addition of only about 7,000 MW.	China added nearly 100,000 MW in the same year.
Telecom and IT Infrastructure	India has 2.8 crore PCs, 0.54 crore broadband subscribers and 5.2 crore internet users.	China has 16.2 crore PCs, 8.5 crore broadband subscribers and 29.8 crore internet users.
Urban Infrastructure	The average driving speed in Delhi has fallen from 27 kph in 1997 to 10 kph in 2009. Other lesser-endowed cities have for worse transportation systems. Walkways for pedestrians and space for cyclists have disappeared.	In spite of having four times more vehicles than India, China's death toll in road accidents is 60% of India's. (Nearly 130,000 people die in road accidents in India).
Water Supply	None of the 35 Indian cities with a population of more than 1 million distribute water for more than a few hours per day.	Paris which supplies about 100 litres of water per days per citizen is able to manage 24 × 7 water supply, where as cities like Delhi, which supply 300 liters of water per day per citizen is unable to do so.
Sewerage	Only 13% of the sewage produced in Indian cities is treated.	By the end of 20078, China's sewage treatment capacity has reached 80 million tons per day, and urban sewage treatment rate has hit 58%.

Box 4 (contd.)

Housing	India's urban population is expected to double over the next two decades, to 57.5 crores, yet its cities are already choking. Mumbai has 1.7 crore inhabitants, half of whom live in slums.	
Health Infrastructure	India has an abysmal 0.7 hospital beds per 1000 population, at	World average is 3.96 hospital beds per 1000 population.
Vocational Training	1/5th the world average. India has only 5,000 ITIs with just 5% of the existing workforce in India receiving skill training.	China has 5,00,000 institutes of vocational training, 100 times more than India. 96% of Korean, 75% of German, and 80% of Japanese workforce received skill training.

In 1980, both India and China were comparable on infrastructure data. However, as teh above examples show, India has badly lagged behind China in the past three decades. It is principally on account of this Infrastructure gap that China's economy has grown bigger, faster and on a more sustainable basis than India's.

Chart 13: Indicators of Infrastructure Bottlenecks

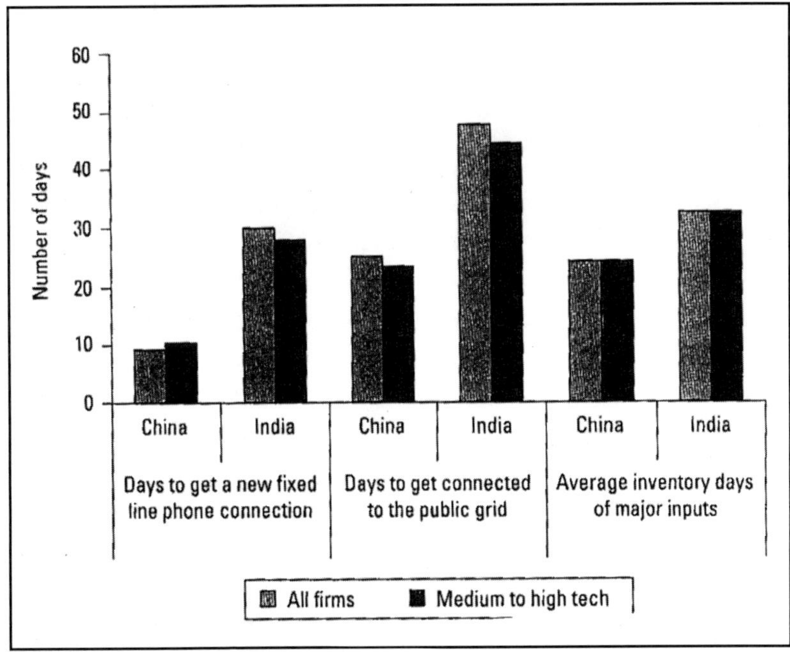

India's slow and steady race to the top has been praised by many an author comparing India to China's 'break neck' speed of growth, drawing an analogy between the hare and tortoise. But equally pertinent is for us to remember President Hu Jintao's remark: "Only if the hare takes a nap". So far China has shown no such intention. But some observers recall a blockbuster Hollywood film titled "Speed", where a terrorist plants a explosive device in a public transportation bus that will automatically explode if the bus speed drops below 50 mph on a crowded rush hour traffic ! The Chinese economy is compared to that bus.

Fast growth of the economy places increasing stress on hard infrastructure such as electricity, railways, road, ports, airports, irrigation, and urban and rural water supply and sanitation, all of which already suffer from a substantial deficit [**See Table below**]. But the soft infrastructural growth has to keep apace, otherwise the fate of Latin America (1980s) and East Asia (1990s) awaits India and China in the (2010s). *The growth in GDP achieved can be sustained only if this overall, hard and soft infrastructure deficit is overcome.*

According to the World Development Report on Infrastructure, developing countries, on average, invested 4% of GDP on infrastructure (World Bank, 1994). Infrastructure investments however in India slowed down after reaching a peak level of 5.5% of GDP in the early 1990s (**see chart below**).

The gap between infrastructure investments between China and India is widening not only as share of GDP, but also in absolute levels given that India's GDP is only one third that of China.

China has out-performed India in hard or physical infrastructure largely due to liberal policies on FDI especially in construction and real estate, but in soft-infrastructure of financial architecture, social and civic services, and human rights, the record compared to India is mixed.

In the early fifties and sixties both countries had fairly similar levels of infrastructure assets and services. For example, China's electricity output at 7.3 billion kWh in 1952 compares well with India's power output of 6.3 billion kWh in 1950-51. The Indian road network in 1950s was extensive at 400.000 kms compared to about one third obtaining in China. In both countries, about 40% of roads were paved then. India's railway network at 53,000 kms was more than double that of China at 23,000 kms. India and China had similar number of telephone subscribers. But due to the varying importance given to infrastructure development in China and India, overall outcomes today are very different.

Following the 1991 fiscal crisis in India, the Government of India adopted several reform measures to make the economy globally competitive. It recognized that the success of these policies would crucially depend on the expansion and improvement of physical infrastructure.

For India to maintain its target growth of 7.9% per annum it was found that its infrastructure investments would need to increase from the 4-5% of GDP level in the 1980s and 1990s, to 8% in 2005 requiring a threefold increase in absolute levels. However, compared to what was needed, actual levels of investments have remained well below the suggested levels. For example, the 2005 target of 8% of GDP investment in infrastructure, even as of 2009, the level reached is about 6% of GDP. Now, to match China, India would need to invest $2 trillion over the next seven years.

Chart 14: Infrastructure Indicators in 2005 (in percent of GDP)

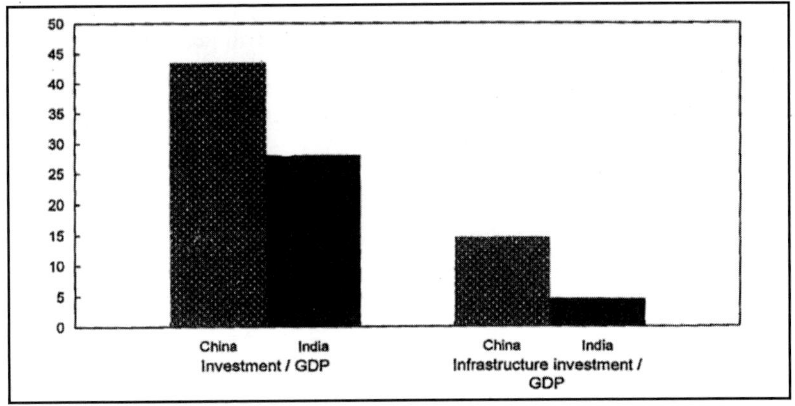

Table above presents annual compound growth rate for basic infrastructure access for three periods, 1950-1980, 1980-1990 and 1990-2005. It indicates the significant growth achieved by China in the last 25

years. India was not able to continue higher levels of growth achieved in earlier years after liberation in 1947.

One area of vast difference is electricity. In the case of China, the rate of growth of electricity generation seemed much too high compared to the Chinese growth rate in GDP. Again, a drop in electricity consumption is not matched by a similar drop in GDP growth rate (**Chart**). This again raises questions about the reliability of the growth rate of GDP. Based on a trend income elasticity of electric power output, once again we get the 2009 growth rate of GDP as 6 per cent, not 8% as Chinese official statistics show. There was a similar mismatch in the use of other key industrial inputs as Table below shows:

Today, China is facing its worst power shortages because government-set prices mean many plants lose money with every spark of electricity they generate. More than a dozen provinces are rationing power to industrial users, and Beijing is struggling to guarantee enough electricity for the Olympics. Top executives from State Grid Corp. which controls most of China's power lines, have been dispatched to other cities hosting events to guarantee supplies, reported Wall Street Journal (August 12, 2009).

"We are moving into a period where electricity outages are returning as a potential cap on economic growth," quoting Glenn Maguire, Chief Asian economist for Societe generale.

But, the squeeze is while the price increases will get power plants to produce more electricity, they will add to already high inflation. They also could end up squeezing corporate profits when are already hurt by higher wages and raw material prices.

The Chinese government is aiming for 15 percent of the country's primary energy to come from non-hydro renewable sources by 2020, an increase of nine percent over 2006 levels. In 2006 the Renewable Energy Law became effective, setting out a detailed plan for the development of hydroelectricity, wind power and solar energy.

Hydroelectricity accounts for most of China's current "renewable" electricity output, with 171 GW installed capacity at end 2008. Of this, the massive Three Gorges Dam project accounts for 22.4 GW.

Chart 15: Economy, Power Consumption Drop Off

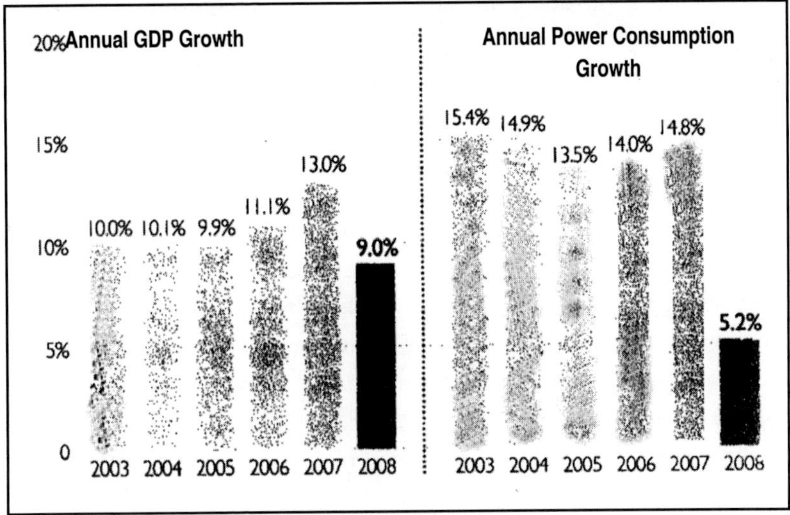

Source: China Monthly Statistics, Vol. I 2003 - Vol. 12, 2008; "China 2008 Power Consumption up 5.23 pct, Lowest Rise in 10 years-Association," XFN-ASIA, January 5, 2009, at http://www.forbes.com/afxnewslimited/feeds/afx/2009/0//05/afx.5882229.html (January 22, 2009).

The coal-based power generation market is dominated by the "Big Five Gencos" of Huaneng, Huadian, Dateng and China Power investment. Since the deregulation of coal prices, all Gencos have suffered from margin squeeze. However, the global downturn has offered some respite as coal prices dropped on lower demand.

The government is committed to improving efficiency in the sector and has implemented programmes such as "Program of Large Substituting Small" to close China's least efficient coal power stations. From 2006 to the first half 2009, it shut down 54 GW worth of those least efficient coal fired power plants and plans to close an additional 31 GW of other small plants in the next three years Those plants are being replaced by medium and large ones, with the larger ones lover 600 MW required to be ultra-supercritical."

Thus, China's primary energy consumption of commercial fuels has doubled since 2000 to about 1.9 bn tones of oil equivalent. The increase over the seven years is more than double India's total primary energy consumption of 410m tones of oil equivalent in 2007. Unsurprisingly, China's carbon dioxide emissions had soared to 5.6bn tones by 2006, compared with 1.3bn tones from India. In per capita terms China's emissions were almost four times higher than India's, with China's economy three times as large as India's today and given her disproportionately large footprint in international trade, capital flows, energy consumption and carbon emissions, China's potential role in helping solve the major global economic issues of the day is correspondingly greater. For example, in the global recession, China's massive fiscal stimulus over the past year has already helped revive China's growth and imparted a significant stimulus to other Asian economies. But the vital question remains: Is it sustainable, or will it explode into a triggered crisis?

In *Is China's Energy Sustainability: The Shrinking Window of Opportunity* [October 2006, (ISBN 0-8213-6753)], the authors use historical data from 1980 and alternative scenarios through 2020 to assess China's future energy requirements and the resources available to meet them. They find that current trend of energy use are putting China on an unsustainable insecure energy growth path.

Power outages

It is surprising that India claiming to be on a growth path to global status finds corporate India and households face day after day. 'a power shutdown', or an outage which is a disruption in power supply. Very simply, power is not available for use. This disruption or outage, if you please, costs India Inc Rs. 45800 crores [$ 18 billlion] every year. This ugly truth has been unraveled in a study by IT hardware industry body: Manufacturers' Association for Information Technology (MAIT), and Emerson Network Power. The study, covering 800 companies across 14 sectors in seven major cities, including Delhi, Pune, Bangalore and Mumbai reveals the rot in the power sector and its impact on the economy, presently 1% of GDP.

India has the capacity to generate 203,000 MW of electricity (this includes 148,000 MW generated by power plants and 55,000 MW generated by captive power plants set up by individual companies). Of this nearly a third – 27 per cent—is lost in transmission and distribution (T&D) and theft. According to the study, power outages, huge T&D losses and poor capacity additions have become a feature of the power industry GDP output and productivity. The loss from outages has doubled from Rs. 22,000 crore in 2003 to Rs. 45,800 in 2009. This is 1% of GDP and an opportunity cost of 6% of GDP. The loss due to power outage grew at an average of 11.9 per cent in the past five years. In fact despite nearly two decades of reform nothing really seems to have changed for the power sector.

After 60 years of Independence, a power project has still to go through 60-65 clearances and approvals and a good 18 months for it to take off, and thus trip at every point – funding, government clearances, generation, distribution and even tariffs. This contrasts sharply with China as the following Chart shows:

The electricity sector in the Indian federal system remains on the "concurrent list" in the Constitution, implying responsibility for the sector by both the central government and the state governments. One of the most important factors that remained uncoordinated was the funding issue. A large number of states had followed the practice of subsidizing power for agriculture and, as a result, there was ambiguity regarding who was going to pay for the power. The financial status of most of the State Electricity Boards (SEB) was grim, with most experiencing large and unsustainable deficits. In the early 1990s, the rate of return on all SEBs combined was highly negative (-13.5% of capital employed). A large number of private projects were also approved with guarantees by the state governments to private project sponsors representing a significant share of the cumulative state GDP.

India may have third largest PPP GDP but the fifth largest electricity generation capacity in the world. The installed generation capacity including thermal, nuclear, hydro and others is about 155859 MW {as on Nov. 09}.

According to MAIT (Manufacturing Association of Information Technology), India Inc. registered a loss of {around INR 44,000 crore in 2008-09} due to power outages, around 5% of GDP. Roughly 20% of villages remain off-grid. Around 300-400 million Indians have no access to power!

During the 11th Plan period, India hopes to add 78,000 MW of capacity and the 12th Plan (2012-17) targets additions of another 100,000-110,000 MW. So far, between 2007-08 and 2008-09, about 12,000 MW has been added and from April to November, 2009, only 6017 MW has been added. Many projects in various stages are in the pipeline. Much of this will be privately funded and managed. Bureaucratic bosses abound. India requires an additional 100,000 megawatts of power by 2012. The country currently has a peak deficit of 12.2% and an overall energy deficit of 7.9%.

In the power sector, the search for a "personal" solution has led to a buoyant market in power back up equipment. A whopping Rs.100,000 crore or about $20 billion has been invested by households and companies in back-up power equipment, according to a recent study commissioned by Wartsilla India. To top it, another Rs. 30,000 crore is the spend every year to keep this equipment humming as in many areas.

Back-up power is expensive and polluting (think diesel gensets) though it is better than no power at all when seen from the users' perspective. Clearly, it points towards a sub-optimal allocation of resources. If Rs.100,000 crore had been spent on setting up a thermal power plant, its capacity would have been over 25,000 MW. That would have covered the peak deficit of 13,500 MW recorded in July this year twice over.

The obvious thing to do is to funnel the spending capacity of individual consumers and companies towards the actual construction of large-scale power plants. This construction needs to be incentivised. This is the suggestion of Dr. Vandana Gombar. One way of doing it is to allow these plants to cater exclusively to those who have the ability and willingness to pay higher charges for the power they consume. If there is a willingness to pay anywhere upwards of Rs.10 per unit of power from a diesel genset—as long as the power is assured—why not create a new power-market?

There is an existing alternate market model which has been tried in Pune city to assure 24 × 7 power. A premium is charged from all households consuming above a certain minimum threshold which goes towards buying expensive power to plug the demand supply gaps. To go further corporate and farmers can be given an option to get reliable 24 × 7 power at premium tariffs or opt for the cheaper power with zero reliability.

Nuclear power, which accounts for 14 per cent of the world's electricity, is undergoing a revival as fossil-fuel generators are retired and governments seek to curb carbon output. Today, many countries—trying to scale up their nuclear power capacities—are finding it difficult to source critical components due to a demand-supply mismatch. Experts believe that as the demand for nuclear power increases, India will emerge as a major sourcing base for nuclear equipment and technology.

India has a large engineering talent pool and manufacturing base. It has already become a recognized source base for a number of industries. There is no reason why the same will not happen for nuclear components.

Still, more groundwork needs to be done. India's Atomic Energy Act 1962 prohibits private-sector players from setting up nuclear power stations. The Act also restricts the nuclear generation business to government-owned companies. Then, the US Department of Energy has not issued the mandatory licence to American companies for doing any kind of civilian nuclear trade with India unless there is an "assurance" from New Delhi on nuclear non-proliferation.

Per capita energy use varies globally from 100 kilowatt hour (kWh) in some countries to 18,000-19,000 kWh in some developed countries. In India, it is about 700 kWh per year. It is undeniable that there is a direct relationship between energy use and quality of life in a country. Hence, we need to explore what India's option is.

Nuclear energy offers an option: Firstly, from per kilogram of material excavated, you get more energy from a nuclear source as compared to a fossil source. Secondly, it is free from greenhouse gas emission, Third, nuclear power variable costs are extremely low; it is not prone to escalation.

India's energy resource profile originally was based on a perception that there is plenty of coal. But the coal reserves will last for 130 years. Hydrocarbons will however run out much earlier. Even for nuclear energy, there is hardly any uranium in India, unless India recycles on thorium reactors.

India's three-stage nuclear power programme comprises building uranium-fuelled pressurized heavy-water reactors (PHWRs), development of fast breeder reactors and an advanced nuclear power system based on thorium-uranium fuelled reactors. Our uranium reserves will support 10,000 mw, which is not much. But it is the starting point for setting up fast reactors. The same uranium, through recycling in fast reactors, would offer a capacity of 200,000-500,000 MW. That is another distinctive feature of nuclear energy: it produces fuel even while it is consumed.

India has been successful in fast-reactor technology. In the third stage, India's ambition is to unleash the huge potential in thorium that is available in large quantity in the southern coastal districts. As expected, the lobbies for and against thorium (which is on the verge of commercialization) are going strong.

The lobby working against thorium states that the established reactor builders, technology providers and nuclear-plant operators, would rather milk their investments in uranium fuel technology they are currently using rather than spend millions on learning and ratifying a new technology. But then, thorium reactors produce 70 per cent less nuclear waste compared to uranium reactors. Thorium fuel is 5-10 per cent cheaper and less price-volatile than uranium fuel.

Box 5: World's largest thorium reserves

Country	Reserves
Australia	300,000
India	290,000
Norway	170,000
US	160,000
Canada	100,000
South Africa	35,000
Brazil	16,000
Others	95,000

(Figures in tones)
Source: BW research

After all, India is the only country to be setting up a 300-MW plant at Kalpakkam near Chennai that will be a step-away from commercial thorium power generation. It had been conceived after a trial-run in a 30-KW reactor, also at Kalpakkam. As the next step, a thorium reactor is currently being vetted at Bhabha Atomic Research Centre (Bare) in Mumbai for technology and design. It should be operational in 2011-12.

Thorium backers, however, believe that the Kalpakkam project, scheduled for commissioning in 2011-12 will be the first major technology demonstrator, and that India can begin developing larger commercial thorium reactors within 8 years. A two-year wait from now for a nuclear project that has an average lifecycle of 60 years is acceptable. Besides, the Kalpakkam plant is being designed for 100-year lifetime. But the opportunity to lead the world will be gone if resources and infrastructure get diverted (towards uranium and light-water reactors). Though the government has not explicitly indicated it, but the implications of Indo-US Nuclear deal is just that.

The magnificent 5.6 KM long Bandra-Worli sea link epitomizes what is right and what is wrong with India's infrastructure sector. The architectural marvel has cut what used to be a one-hour commute between Bandra and Worli in Mumbai to a 10-minute zip. But the bridge, which was first proposed by me in 1982 as an MP of Mumbai was conceived in 1999 but had to wait until 2009 – five years later than originally envisaged – to become operational. And it cost Rs. 1,600 crore – more than five times the original estimate of Rs. 300 crore.

Delayed approvals, cost over-runs, and poor planning and execution have dogged infrastructure projects in the country over the years. According to the World Bank, 70% of projects in India seek an extension. In the UK, this figure stands at 25%. About 40% of road contracts in India have cost over-runs of 25-50% and an estimated Rs. 9,000 crore is locked up in disputes. Over 75% of the respondents in a recent PMI-KPMG survey of 100 C-suite executives from the infrastructure, construction and financial businesses cited regulatory and land acquisition issues s the primary causes for project delays. India thus lags in infrastructure.

While the Prime Minister has set a target of $1 trillion for infrastructure for the 12th five year plan (2012-17), which is the size of the present Indian economy, it is difficult to visualize its mobilisation.

India is already behind in her spending on infrastructure and spends about $60-70 billion as opposed to the targeted $100 billion per annum under the current five year plan[2007-12]. If the extra $30 billion was spent, it would generate incremental GDP of approximately $45 billion and push GDP to double digits.

A survey conducted by Execution Noble an investment banking group and the City of London with a range of investors and data from various well known research bodies and consultants suggest that infrastructure investments for FY 07-12 may not be more than $350 billion as against the planned $500 billion, a shortfall of 30 per cent. The irony is that presently too much capital is chasing too few bankable projects with the result that the return on equity is reduced and this is keeping equity investors at bay.

However, the report says that capital for infrastructure projects is not really the issue and that it will flow in if certain contentious issues are resolved. Some of the issues that the government need to sort out are put on a priority basis issues relating to tax holidays, transparency in the private public participation (PPP) tender bidding and awarding process and lastly issues concerning resolving the delays in regulatory and land clearances.

Generally in China highway and expressway construction and maintenance are the responsibility of local city governments. Since the establishment of the first Build, Operate and Transfer (BOT) concession, the private sector especially PDI-based foreign companies has been actively courted to participate in the toll roads sector. In fact, there are now more toll roads in China than any other country, and the Chinese network of toll roads represents more than 70 per cent of the world's total.

In addition to green field construction, there is an increasingly active secondary market, as entitled such as local authorities and domestic construction companies look to release capital from their asset portfolios in order to invest in new highway and other infrastructure projects.

However, with the large level of capital available in the domestic market, and with the expected growth in direct and indirect investment by domestic insurance and pension funds into infrastructure, pricing for good operating assets is likely to become increasingly competitive, putting pressure on returns.

New opportunities may also present themselves from the recent permitting of private participation in government funded toll-road concession projects, subject to a competitive bidding process.

Other opportunities for investors are mainly in related construction materials and heavy equipment businesses, which are seeing rapid demand growth from the stimulus investment programme – though even then care must be taken as there is a possible risk of oversupply in certain sectors, such as cement, in some provinces.

Over the last 10 years, while China's crude oil production has grown from 3.3 million to 3.7 million barrels per day, its demand for oil has continued to grow rapidly, such that by 2025 China is expected to import more than three quarters of its oil.

Downstream, refining capacity has increased from 4.6 million barrels per day in 1997 to 7.6 million barrels per day in 2007, while consumption reached 7.9 million barrels in 2007.

According to BP, China's natural gas reserves are 1.88 trillion cubic metres. Consumption hit 67.3 billion cubic metres in 2007 and continues to grow. To cope with this growing demand for natural gas as well as to take advantage of stimulus monies, there is currently heavy investment in pipeline systems, the bulk of it by Petrochina.

And it has attracted massive inflows of foreign direct investment as the means to acquire technology, managerial expertise, and factories on a scale and with scope that is a wonder. China has, in fact, leapt to the fore as the largest recipient of FDI in the world – some US$70 billion per year in 2007-08. India suffers in comparison basically from having none of the above. India has a 34% national saving rate, much less that of China. As a result, it has far less in the way of internally-generated funds available to plow back into infrastructure. And it does not take much sight-seeing in into to learn about its infrastructure constraint in India . But India seems to cope with it and produce world class software and automobile ancillaries.

As Professor Penelope Prime has noted, the most common reason cited for China's lead in FDI is better infrastructure. But yet, she states, comparing infrastructure in the two countries, surprisingly shows that *there are not major differences* in China and India in telecommunications and transportation infrastructure, and in terms of the airports, ports and rail terminals, India appears to outdo China in numbers and generally in quality of services.

In India, fixed and mobile telephone density be low now at about 35 for each 100 persons nationwide and much lower for persons in rural areas; extremely rapid growth in cellular service with modest declines in fixed lines. A comparison of the internet infrastructure in the two countries shows that China has had higher percent of users and penetration of internet within the population, but the percent of user growth is higher in India in the 2000-08 period.

But, despite India's recent economic growth and slow and steady improvement in infrastructure, a number of barriers still exist. The challenges in implementing projects in infrastructure sector are still immense. Each sector in the infrastructure sector has its own specificities, be it of land acquisition, environment, regulation, financing or of designing of contracts. In case of land acquisition, the problems are well known as in several cases, the entire process of land acquisition has to pass the judicial test.

The need to develop appropriate mechanisms for financing infrastructure is necessary. It is also important to develop different types of infrastructure through effective coordination between different agencies. Which growth path India embarks on in the future will depend on how well the government and private sector can work together to create common understanding of where the economy should be headed, and most of all what it needs get there. This is now being attempted at the highest level in Government. For China, as Prem Shankar Jha has noted in his recent study, it is a questions of the efficiency in the use of resources for China.

Thus summarizing Jha's findings, the consumption coefficient for steel per percentage increase of the GDP rose from 0.54 in 1980-85 to 2.02 in 2000-04 and that of soda ash, a base material in the chemicals industry, rose from 0.37 to 1.36. The consumption coefficient of plastics rose equally sharply from 0.58 to 1.27. The consumption of cement and plate glass, both prime building materials especially for office buildings, showed a more mixed trend, because of its close correlation with booms and recessions in the building industry.

China is still suffering from the overhang of unsold apartments and office space left over by the previous boom. The ratio of cement consumption to GDP growth had risen sharply from 1.26 in 1980-85 to 1.74 in 1990-95, before falling back to 1.07 in 2000-04. The consumption of plate glass, a prime office building material, showed a similar trend. The high figure for 1990-95 reflects the frenzy of overbuilding that followed the opening of thousand of SEZs and development zones in the late 1980s and early 1990s. In 1997, Chinese investors found themselves saddled with a huge property bubble of unsold flats and office space.

China's experience is in striking contrast to that of India, where, as Table below shows, there has been a decrease in the incremental use of energy and raw materials for growth after the economy was liberalized in 1991.

This was not the concern in China during the period of 1952-78 because of the Soviet model. In fact in 1979-80, Chinese were wasting their resources for every dollar of output as the following table show.

Table 39: Intermediate Input Levels Per Dollar of GNP (1979-80)

	Steel (grams)	Sulphuric acid (grams)	Cement (grams)	Energy (kilograms of coal equivalent)
China	146	31	319	3.21
USSR	136	21	116	1.49
USA	42	17	27	1.16
Japan	109	7	87	0.48
FDR	61	7	47	0.56

Source: World Bank, *China: Socialist Development*, Washington D.C.,1982.

Table 40: Materials Intensity of Growth in China (in percentage)

Year	GDP	Rolled Steel	Cement	Plate Glass	Soda Ash	Plastics
1980-85	66	36	83	100	25	38
2000-04	41	83	44	51	56	52

Source: Calculated from *China Statistical Yearbook* 2005, Tables 14-19 by Prem Shankar Jha.

Table 41: Materials Intensity of Growth in India (in percentage)

Year**	GDP	Energy	Finished Steel	Cement
1980-85	32	29	44	78 (50)*
2000-05	33	21	41	52

Source: Ministry of Finance, Government of India Economic Surveys 1995-96 and 2006-07. Op. cit.

Notes: *The high figure here probably reflects the emergence of clandestine production and sales after cement price and distribution controls were lifted in 1981.

** The fiscal year begins on 1 April, so these data relate to 1 April of the given year till 31 March of the next year.

The conclusion is thus obvious: Since the 1990s, China's growth has become progressively more raw materials-intensive. Corrected for its data-inflated growth figures, even after 1995 this has happened but now data have hidden this from view. Can China sustain its present rate of growth, or even a somewhat lower average rate, if it needs ever larger and larger amounts of capital, energy and raw materials to sustain dollar of increase in its GDP? These trends are visible even if one accepts the official rate of growth of GDP. But they become starkly apparent if one concludes from the data on the consumption of inputs, prices, investment and raw materials consumption, that there was a sharp recession after 1996 that lasted till at least 2000, and brought down the growth rate between 1995 and 2000 substantially below the official estimate. But if we lower the growth rate between 1995 and 2000 to the 4.2 per cent recorded in 1989 and 1990, then in the period 1995 till 2004 a 73 per cent growth of GDP required a 167 per cent increase in the consumption of steel, an 81 per cent increase in the consumption of cement, a 77 per cent increase in the consumption of plate glass, a 116 per cent increase in the consumption of soda ash and a 219 per cent increase in the consumption of plastics.

The rising materials intensity of China's growth has become a matter of concern not only in international organizations and research institutes across the world but even more in China. In August 2005, shortly after China formalized its 11th Five Year Plan, Pan Yue, deputy environment minister, put the issue in stark terms in an interview in Der Spiegel: 'We are using too many raw materials to sustain this growth', he said. 'To produce goods worth US$ 10,000, for example, we need seven times more resources than Japan, nearly six times more than the US and, perhaps most embarrassingly, nearly three times more than India'(Ching 2005). He might have also added that China was using more than twice as much energy per dollar of GDP, measured in real consumption, than India.

The 11th Plan set a target of bringing down the energy consumed per unit of incremental GDP by 20 per cent that is by 4 per cent a year. The State National Development and Reform Commission (SDRC) turned this into a set of concrete goals in a report published in August 2006. Central to it was a reduction of the consumption of coal by 300 million metric tones a year. This accounted for 13.5 per cent of the energy consumed in 2005. But to do so, it warned, China would have to close down, install anti-pollution equipment, or otherwise modernize the vast majority of its $500,000 small and medium-sized coal-fired boilers. These consumed 400 million tones of coal each year and were responsible for most of the country's serious atmospheric pollution. Up to 70 million tones could be saved by upgrading the technology and management of these boilers. But Chinese leadership's determination is not in dispute. How much Provincial Party bosses co-operate only time will tell.

Again as Jha has noted China's hunger for energy pales before its consumption of other key non-renewable resources. Table below which compares its consumption with that of the United States and India, brings this out:

With one-tenth of the world's GDP in purchasing power terms, China is consuming between one-third and one-sixth of the world's traded raw materials including one-third of its coal, and one-eights of its total energy. It consumes substantially more than the US of everything except crude oil, despite the fact that it has barely 15 per cent of its GDP.

Table 42: Share in Global Energy Consumption

Energy Source	CHINA	INDIA Percentages in 2003	USA
Coal	32.9	7.1	20.6
Oil	7.4	3.4	25.3
Electricity Generation	11.4	3.8	24.3
Energy in coal equivalent	12.6	3.6	23.4

INNOVATION

Presently we are in the era of 'Knowledge Economy" due to the advent of information technology. Hence, the young population need to be skill-empowered to reap the demographic dividend in terms of productivity gains which requires designing an educational system to endow skills on the young population. That ability would depend on a host of factors including hard [physical] and soft [financial, human and social] infrastructure.

Thus both, the reaping of the demographic dividend and the induction of new innovations in the economic system, would depend on the quality and empowerment of the population through a modem educational system. In this regard, China is better equipped because of a wise decision to allow FDI in education. Thus Harvard, Stanford, and Princeton not to mention a host of European and Australian universities entered the field in China and set up world class educational institutions and supplied the faculty for it too.

India is still debating this question of how to structure the permitting of FDI in education. Thanks to IT, it is no more essential to invest heavily in overheads to impart education. Online facilities can now take education to the villages obviating the need for villagers to enable their children to go to schools far away.

India needs to modify the capital market for education. It should be possible to access funds from the capital market and financial institutions for education on an assessment of the present value of future income streams from education instead being weighed down for mortgages.

*Thus the **factor** in determining the future trends in economic growth of China and India would be the education system in the two countries and its capacity for skill empowerment and development of the innovation motivation in the 5-25 years age group. We shall discuss this question in detail in Chapter VI.*

The effect of innovation will be seen in the measurement of Total Factor Productivity [TFP] and its rate of change [TFPG]. The key factor thus is not only the level of capital and labour deployed in production and creation of services, but innovation and technology used in maximizing the returns from that deployment, in short, from productivity increases from epochal innovation as Nobel laureate Simon Kuznets had observed.

This author had earlier estimated that total factor productivity (for 1952-78) to be declining in China, at minus 0.5 percent per year, while TFP for India grew at 1.1 percent per year.

Thus the Total Factor Productivity [TFP] growth has remained at a trend rate of 40 percent throughout for both countries. Efficiency in use of the Chinese intermediate output especially of heavy industry, was in question just as reforms were being introduced after 1978.

At present, both China and India have low productivity increases which is measured as Total Factor Productivity [TFPG]— as a growth rate of the residual after accounting for the contribution of capital and labour in the increase in output. This residual in both countries has been less than one-third of the rate of growth in GDP, when it ought to be more than 65%.

In 1998 China had a significantly higher labour productivity than India only in food processing and wood products, while India had a significant productivity advantage in coke, chemical products, basic metals, office computing and electrical machinery. Grouping industries as consumer non-durables sector and consumer durable and producer goods sector it is evident that China had a productivity advantage over India in the former group of industries while India had an advantage in the latter.

By 2003, however, China gained in terms of labour productivity relative to India in all 2-digit level industries. Differences in labour productivity could be due to differences across industries in utilization of capital for production. Over the 1998-2003 period China gained in terms of TFP relative to India in all industries. Over the 6 year period, not only did China increase its productivity advantage over India in the consumer non-durable sector but also caught up with, and in some cases exceeded, the productivity of industries in the Indian consumer durable and producer goods sector. Productivity in China relative to India increased substantially over the 1998-2003 period for almost all manufacturing industries judged by production function based regression to estimate the difference in average TFP growth for manufacturing industries between the two countries.

Productivity of manufacturing industries in China relative to that in India improved substantially over the 1998-2003 period. In 1998 manufacturing industries were largely owned by the private sector in India while the Chinese government still held a substantial equity in manufacturing industries.

Perhaps an explanation for this superior productivity performance of China relative to India could be the enormous ownership restructuring with the Chinese government selling off its equity to private individuals and delegating authority to the provincial level and shop-level managers. Having more autonomy to hire and fire workers would lead to increased efficiency for firms in the manufacturing sector. This may be another reason for productivity increase in China relative to India, since there were no changes to the outdated labour laws in India. But most of all, it is the FDI-induced technology transfer from the US in foreign-owned and foreign-funded enterprises in China that is the reason for this spurt in productivity growth.

Table 43: Sources of Growth: China, India and East Asia 1978-2004

Annual percentage rate of change

					Contribution of:			
Period		Output	Employment	Output per Worker	Physical Capital	Land	Education	Factor Productivity
Total Economy								
1978-04	China	9.3	2.0	7.3	3.2	0.0	0.2	3.8
	India	5.4	2.0	3.3	1.3	0.0	0.4	1.6
1978-93	China	8.9	2.5	6.4	2.5	−0.1	0.2	3.6
	India	4.5	2.1	2.4	1.0	−0.1	0.3	1.1
1993-04	China	9.7	1.2	8.5	4.2	0.0	0.2	4.0
	India	6.5	1.9	4.6	1.8	0.0	0.4	2.3
East Asia Excluding China								
1960-80		7.0	3.0	4.0	2.2		0.5	1.2
1980-03		6.1	2.4	3.7	2.2		0.5	1.2
1980-93		7.3	2.7	4.6	2.6		0.6	1.4
1993-03		4.5	2.0	2.5	1.8		0.5	0.3

Table 44: Sources of Growth by Major Sector, 1978-2004

Annual percentage rate of change

Period		Output	Employment	Output per Worker	Contribution of: Physical Capital	Land	Education	Factor Productivity
Agriculture								
1978-04	China	4.6	0.3	4.3	2.3	0.0	0.2	1.8
	India	2.5	1.1	1.4	0.4	−0.1	0.3	0.8
1978-93	China	5.2	0.9	4.3	2.5	−0.2	0.2	1.8
	India	2.7	1.4	1.3	0.2	−0.1	0.2	1.8
1993-04	China	3.7	−0.6	4.3	2.1	0.2	0.1	1.8
	India	2.2	0.7	1.5	0.7	−0.1	0.3	0.5
Industry								
1978-04	China	10.0	3.1	7.0	2.2		0.2	4.4
	India	5.9	3.4	2.5	1.5		0.3	0.6
1978-93	China	9.3	4.4	4.9	1.5		0.2	3.1
	India	5.4	3.3	2.1	1.4		0.4	0.3
1993-04	China	11.0	1.2	9.8	3.2		0.2	6.2
	India	6.7	3.6	3.1	1.7		0.3	1.1
Service								
1978-04	China	10.7	5.8	4.9	2.7		0.2	1.9
	India	7.2	3.8	3.5	0.6		0.4	2.4
1978-93	China	11.3	6.5	4.7	1.8		0.2	2.7
	India	5.9	3.8	2.1	0.3		0.4	1.4
1993-04	China	9.0	4.7	5.1	3.9		0.2	0.9
	India	9.1	3.7	5.4	1.1		0.4	3.9

Source: Author's estimates as described in text. For China, the output data are the official series of the national accounts for agriculture and services, and the series for industry is based on the alternative price deflator discussed in the Barry Bosworth and Susan M. Collins. *Accounting for Growth: Comparing China and India,* Working Paper 12943 http://www.nber.org/papers/w12943.

Table 45: GDP and its Determinants, India, 1950-2006

Growth (in %)

	Capital	Labour force	Income per worker	TFPG
1950s	4.3	1.1	1.9	0.8
1960s	5.7	2.2	2.9	1.3
1970s	4.4	2.2	0.2	−0.7
1980s	4.8	1.9	4.0	2.7
1990s	5.7	2.1	3.6	2.1
2000s	7.2	2.0	4.8	2.5
2003-06	8.6	2.0	6.3	3.4

Source: Maddison (2006); Penn World Table version 6.1; World Development Indicators, World Bank (2006); World Economic Outlook, IMF (2006).

Table 46: GDP and its Determinants, China, 1950-2006

Growth (in %)

	Capital	Labour force	Income per worker	TFPG
1950s	5.2	2.1	2.8	1.5
1960s	1.4	1.6	1.9	1.9
1970s	7.2	2.5	2.1	0.0
1980s	9.5	2.2	4.2	1.0
1990s	10.7	1.3	6.9	2.8
2000s	9.9	0.8	9.8	5.7
2003-06	10.8	0.8	9.9	5.5

Source: Maddison (2006); Penn World Table version 6.1; World Development Indicators, World Bank (2006); World Economic Outlook, IMF (2006).

Table 47: Annualized growth (%) and TFPG, India

Growth (in %)

	Population	GDP	GDP, pc	TFPG
1950s	1.6	2.9	1.3	0.8
1960s	2.2	5.0	2.9	1.3
1970s	2.1	2.4	0.3	−0.7
1980s	2.0	5.9	3.9	2.7
1990s	1.8	5.7	3.9	2.1
2000s	1.7	6.8	5.2	2.5
2003-06	1.7	8.3	6.8	3.4

Source: Maddison (2006); Penn World Table version 6.1; World Development Indicators, World Bank (2006); World Economic Outlook, IMF (2006).

Notes:
1. TFPG is calculated as a residual from a panel data for developing countries for the period 1960-2006. See Appendix I for details. Coefficient of capital and labour were 0.40 and 0.60 respectively (e.g. 1960-69).
2. Each decade ends in the ninth year except 2000s which is from 2000-2006.

Table 48: Annualized growth (%) and TFPG, China

Growth (in %)

	Population	GDP	GDP, pc	TFPG
1950s	1.6	4.9	3.3	1.5
1960s	2	3.5	1.5	1.9
1970s	2	4.6	2.6	0
1980s	1.5	6.4	4.9	1
1990s	1.1	8.2	7.2	2.8
2000s	0.6	10.5	9.9	5.7
2003-06	0.6	10.7	10.1	5.5

Source: Maddison (2006); Penn World Table version 6.1; World Development Indicators, World Bank (2006); World Economic Outlook, IMF (2006).

Notes:
1. TFPG is calculated as a residual from a panel data for developing countries for the period 1960-2006. See Appendix I for details. Coefficient of capital and labour were 0.40 and 0.60 respectively (e.g. 1960-69).
2. Each decade ends in the ninth year except 2000s which is from 2000-2006.

Graph 17: TFPG, India

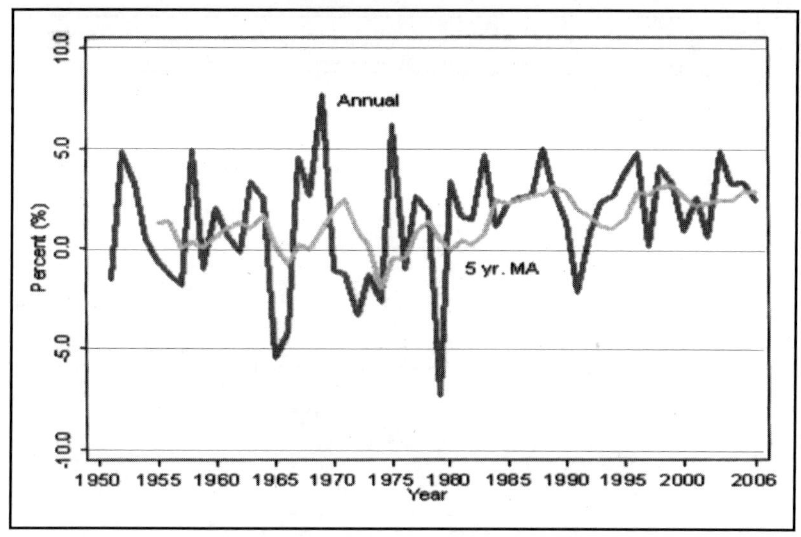

Graph 18: TFPG, China

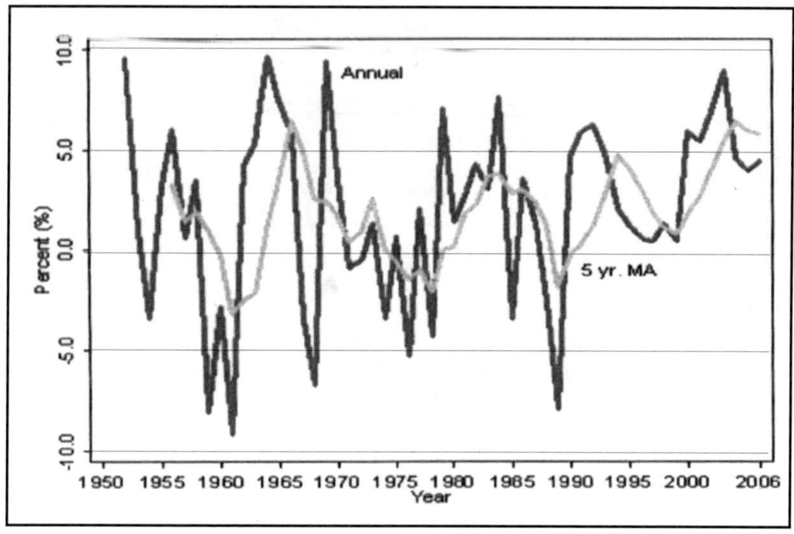

Graph 19: Capital growth, India

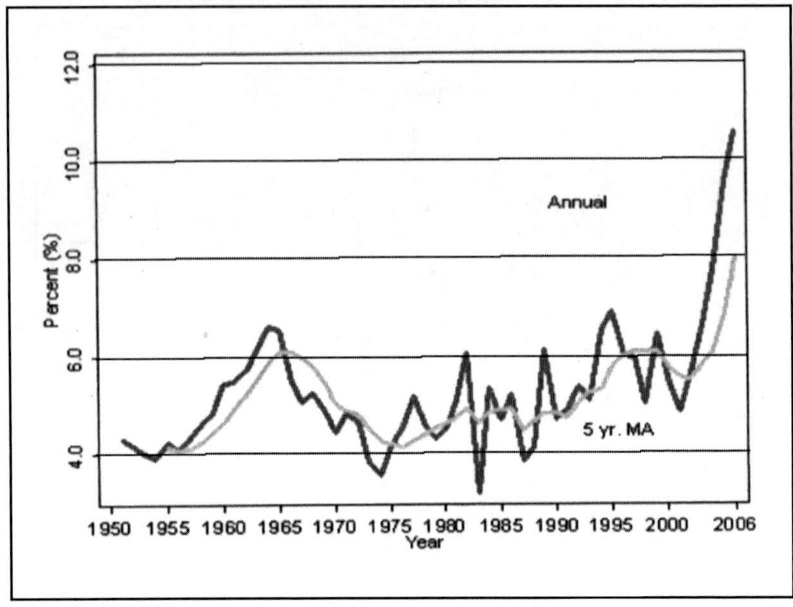

Graph 20: Capital growth, China

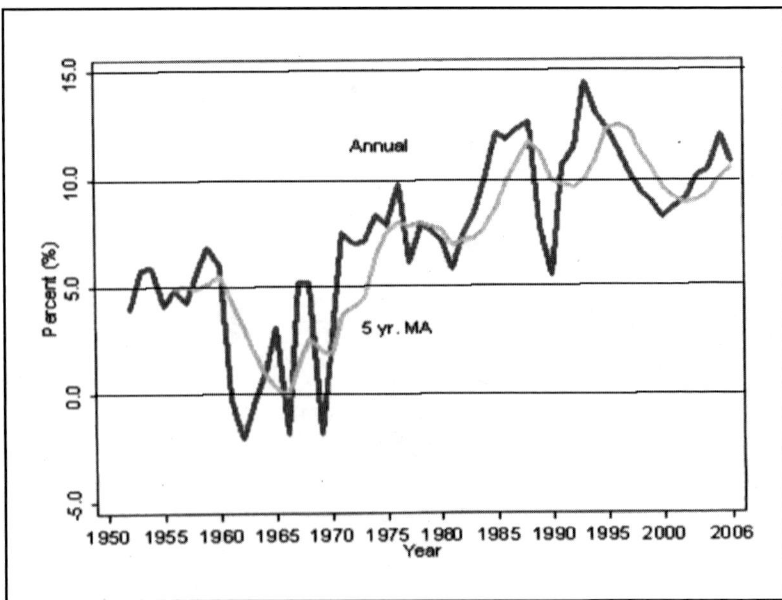

Table 49: Labour Productivity in India and China (Employees), by Industry (2002)

Industry	(US = 109)		China = 100	Share in VAD
	China	India	India	India
Food, beverages and tobacco	25.4	7.1	28.0	12.5
Textiles	25.5	11.0	43.0	8.3
Clothing	12.5	8.6	69.2	2.0
Leather and footwear	30.9	13.8	44.6	0.7
Wood, products of wood and cork	26.5	4.5	17.0	0.2
Pulp, paper and paper products	14.8	9.0	60.8	2.2
Coke, petroleum and nuclear fuel	3.6	13.6	377.6	10.9
Chemicals	5.8	15.0	259.3	20.2
Rubber and plastics	13.0	16.8	129.1	3.7
Non-metallic mineral products	24.5	12.7	51.8	5.0
Basic metals	15.9	25.6	161.0	12.5
Fabricated metal products	16.8	19.9	118.6	2.5
Machinery and equipment	40.2	15.3	38.2	5.3
Office, other elect mach, radio, TV and comm eqpt.	40.9	13.0	31.9	5.1
Scientific and other instruments	10.3	11.4	111.1	0.9
Motor vehicles	40.9	13.0	31.9	5.1
Furniture and other mfg**	26.6	21.1	79.5	1.3
Total manufacturing*	13.7	12.6	91.7	100.0

*Sum of the industries in the table.

**Simple average for furniture (43.7) and other manufacturing (9.5) in the case of China. VAD is nominal value added.

Source: Szirmal et. al. (2005) for China and own calculations for India of Abdul Azeez Erumban in "Productivity and Unit Labour Cost in Indian Manufacutring: A Comparative Persp. (April 11, 2009) Vol. XLIV No. 15, EPW, *Economic and Political Weekly*.

Graph 21: Output per Worker by Sector, China and India, 1978-2004

International dollars of 2004

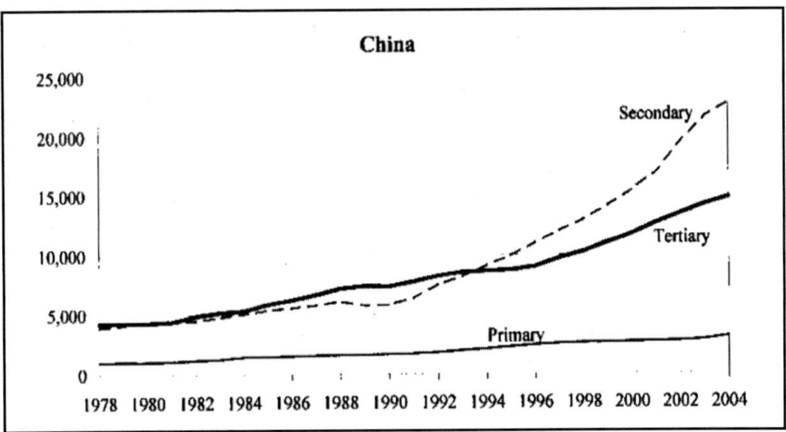

Graph 22

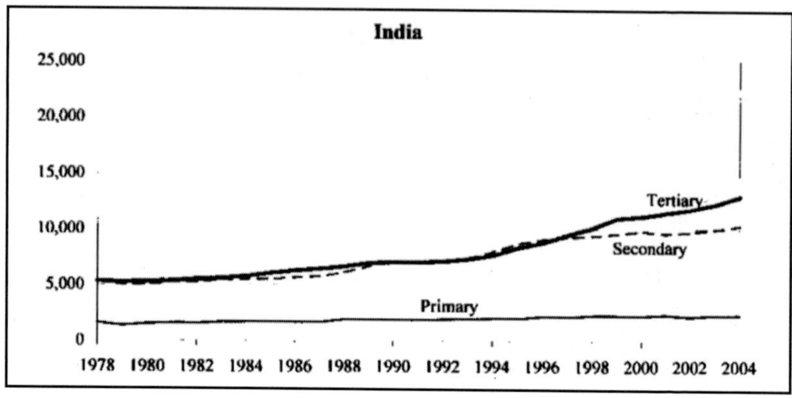

Source: China Data Center and CSY; India National Accounts; India NSSO.

EQUITY

While the initial conditions at the advent of economic reforms in 1978 placed China as a country of similar per capita income and of GDP growth rates same as India's, China had a more equitable distribution of income. The Gini coefficient in the size distribution of income of households for 1979-80 was estimated at 0.33 for China and 0.42 in India. But, with the advent of reforms, China's Gini coefficient rose 1980s and 1990s, and now is at the Latin American levels of over 0.45. This is mainly due to the inter-regional increase in inequality in China, but nevertheless is well above the Indian level, which declined since 1980 to less than 0.35.

Such an unexpected result can be explained theoretically [see Swamy (1965)]. If the urban income per capita relative to rural income per capita is sufficiently large, then the national inequality index will exceed both the urban and rural intra-sectoral inqualities, which is what now obtains in China, where it is estimated that the urban-rural disparities accounted for more than half of the inequality level in China, and as the World Bank estimates, urban-rural disparities also explains 75 per cent of the increase in income inequality.

Using this author's mathematical equation developed in 1964 in his Ph.D thesis at Harvard University under the supervision of Nobel Laureate Simon Kuznets, inequality at the national level was shown to be decomposed into two parts: a contribution of rural and urban inequalities, and of the relative urban-rural income differences. Based in that equation, it can be mathematically demonstrated that if the urban income per capita as a ratio of rural income per capita is sufficiently large, then the national inequality index (coefficient of variation) will exceed both the urban and rural intra-sectoral in qualities.

This now obtains in China, where it is estimated that the urban-rural disparities accounted for more than half of the inequality in China between 1984 and 1995. Using adjusted data, the World Bank estimates that urban-rural disparities explained 75 per cent of the increase in income inequality. With, urban incomes now rising at 6.4 per cent per year, and rural income crawling at 2.1 per cent per year there is a distinct possibility of a further sharp increase in national inequality in China, making it even more iniquitous than India.

With, urban incomes now rising at 6.4 per cent per year, and rural income crawling at 2.1 per cent per year in China, there will be further sharp increase in national inequality making it even more iniquitous compared to India. Economic reforms in China has led to a sharp increase in urban incomes in the east coast areas, in India, urban incomes have not relative to rural incomes risen sharply despite a slow reduction in the number of people below the poverty line. China has out-performed India in the number of people lifted above the poverty line, despite

Thus, China is a case of rapidly reducing poverty levels but of significantly widening income distribution, while by contrast, India is one of slow reduction in poverty but also of narrowing income inequality. The faster growth strategy has, hence, meant that China has lost its 1970s 'USP' in the developing world, of being an egalitarian society by which China sought to mitigate the unfavourable international reactions about Chinese authoritarism and closed society. But today, while China has received kudos for its economic growth following reform, it is still an authoritarian society but now with an in egalitarian income distribution.

China's policymakers are certainly concerned nowadays about the increasing regional polarization in incomes. High inequality can impede growth, de-legitimize market reforms, and contribute to social tension. However at present the matter is at the threshold. The current growing labour unrest and increasing protest in China as a result of this, has the potential of spiraling out of control. The increasingly skewed income distribution in China since reforms, signals an unsettling and deep impact.

In the first half of the last century, Chinese and Indian societies were characterized by extremes in income levels and had large numbers of both urban and rural poor. In the mid-1950s and until the late 1970s, China's main 'unique selling proposition' (USP) was the achievement of a low level of inequality below that which typically exists in developing countries. In the urban sector, the populace was guaranteed employment, housing, low priced subsidised food, education, and health care. In the rural areas where the vast bulk of the population lived, the commune system met the basic needs of most rural families. The closeness of political system and media censorship enabled China to propagate the world over an exaggerated version of this achievement. On the other hand, the relatively more open society of India was seen as the epitome of poverty, malnutrition, and inequality during this period. Indian democracy and freer media made that ever more stark and obvious, and India suffered in sharp contrasting comparison with China.

But during the last two decades of reforms, there is a paradigm shift in this contrasting equity situation. After twenty years of economic reforms, China has changed from being an egalitarian society to a polarized in-egalitarian economy—polarized between urban and rural; interior and coastal areas; and the growth of a small but very rich class in urban areas. Significantly, any income inequality index in China now exceeds today the levels in India, Indonesia and Taiwan.

Unlike East European countries and the former USSR republics where large income gaps between the rural and urban sectors were absent or negligible, income inequality in China is pronounced in terms of urban-rural income differentiation and regional disparity of rich coastal and poor interior provinces.

Thus, despite a dramatic fall claimed by official sources in the number of poor below the poverty line in China, from 239 million (or 31 per cent) to in 1979 to 71 million (or 6.6 per cent) in 1996, it needs however to be pointed out that if one uses the World Bank poverty standard of $1, then the number of poor in China would be 300 million in 1996. The Gini index of inequality also rose consistently during this period as Table-22 summarized the position based on official data: Chinese and Indian level of inequality fall between Denmark (0.25) at one end and Brazil (0.60) near the other end of the inequality spectrum.

Thus, China's income distribution has become increasingly skewed since reforms, and is now, more so than in India. A change of this magnitude is highly unusual and signals an unsettling and deep structural transformation in the distribution of assets and their returns on these assets. According to *Xinhua,* the 1999 Gini ratio is 0.46. While Economist (June 26, 2001) quotes economist Ms. He Qinglian to place it at 0.60! Of course, during the first three decades of Communist rule, and at the height of fervour for egalitarianism, individual remuneration barely reflected productivity and thus inequality was curbed. In 1978, the government introduced individual incentives, and market forces immediately began to increase returns to capital and land, diversify employment, and increase factor mobility. Inequality became a consequence of rapid growth in China that followed the adoption of reforms. Government policies are thus exacerbating inequalities because these favour urban over rural areas, the coast over the interior, and those with access to education, health care, and labour mobility. Unlike in India, in China, rural inequality (0.34) measured by official based Gini ratio is higher than the level in urban areas (0.28).

China's Gini coefficient is now at a level in excess of the "capitalist" United States, and higher than the East Asian average, and substantially higher than in Eastern Europe an on par with Sub-Saharan Africa and Latin America.

The size distribution of incomes had become clearly wider in China by the late 1990s. The Lorenz Curve of China is now more convex and outward than India's. The Gini coefficient in China as a consequence is higher at 0.45 than in India's at 0.34.

China's policymakers are certainly concerned nowadays about the increasing polarization of regional incomes. High inequality can impede growth, de-legitimize market reforms, and contribute to social tension. However the matter is at the threshold. Income inequality in China is still moderate by international standards. Professor Xavier Sala-i-Martin of Columbia University quoted in *Business Week* [May 6, 2002] estimates World's Gini coefficient was at 0.63 in 1998 (down slightly from 0.66 in 1970) which is much above China's level. But still, the 1990s Gini coefficient for China has been above 0.40, i.e., above the warning level internationally. Hence, China though warned, is not yet into the ranks of the notoriously unequal, while benefits of growth, even if unevenly distributed, have indeed reached the poor, as indicated by the fall in percentage of people below the poverty line.

Since the start of reforms in 1978, China has without doubt lifted millions of people out of absolute poverty despite increasing inequality. Without rural income growth, the number of absolute poor in China would have increased by more than 100 million between 1981 and 1995 because of adverse distributional changes. Instead, the ranks of the poor fell by more than 150 million. *But that is thus so far.* If as stated earlier, the challenge of increasing inequality is not met and the problem mitigated in China, then it may imperil future growth and stability. The preset growing labour unrest and increasing protest in China as a result has the potential of spiraling out of control.

As the World Bank studies suggest, the extraordinary growth of TVEs early in the reform period initially offset the impact of these policies on rural incomes. However, the conditions that favoured this growth—particularly excess demand for mass consumption goods—began to erode in the mid-1980s, and TVEs and the rural sector more generally have been in relative decline ever since. Relative rural incomes rose again for a brief period in the mid-1990s in response to higher grain procurement prices, but resumed their decline in 1997 as a result of overproduction, depressed prices and declining rural industrial employment. Real per capita income growth in rural areas has fallen continuously since then, to just over 2 per cent in 2001, its lowest rate of increase during the reform period.

Concerned, and in order to combat this rising inequality, the Chinese government in 1994 launched a programme—known as the "8-7 Plan" —to completely eradicate poverty by the year 2000, but so far has achieved limited success. Using the Chinese-defined poverty line i.e., \$0.6 per person per day, the latest available figures suggests that the number of absolute poor has been reduced to about 71 million in 1996; although using the higher World Bank standard of $l per person per day, the figure stands at about 300 million. By 2000, thus, poverty even if substantially reduced, had not been eliminated as China in 1994 targeted to do.

In India, over the last two decades, the poverty level has declined significantly. Despite this progress, around 230 million people still live in acute poverty, which continues to present a major policy challenge. Between 1974-2000 incidence of poverty (i.e., percentage of population below the poverty line) fell from 55 per cent to 26 per cent. Rural poverty, constitutes roughly three-fourths of the total poor, and declined from 56 per cent in 1974 to 27 per cent in 2000, while during the same period urban poverty dropped from 49 per cent of 24 per cent. Interstate differentials in poverty remain large, although the differences have narrowed over time, even if per capita state incomes diverged over the same period (see **Chart-4**). China's Gini coefficient is now at a level that exceeds the "capitalist" United States and close to the East Asian average, and substantially higher than in Eastern Europe although somewhat lower than in Sub-Saharan Africa and Latin America.

The size distribution of incomes had become clearly wider in China by the late 1990s. The Lorenz Curve of China is now more convex and outward than India's. The Gini coefficient in China as a consequence is higher at 0.403 than in India's at 0.378.

Graph 23: Gini coefficients for income inequality in China

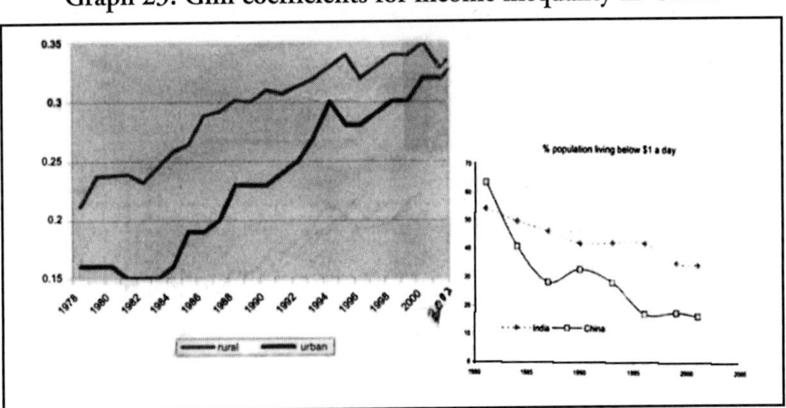

Review of Income Inequality in China, China Economic Quarterly (Chinese).
Source: Chen and Ravallion 2004 (L.H.S graph); Ravallion and Chen 2004 (RHS graph).

Graph 24

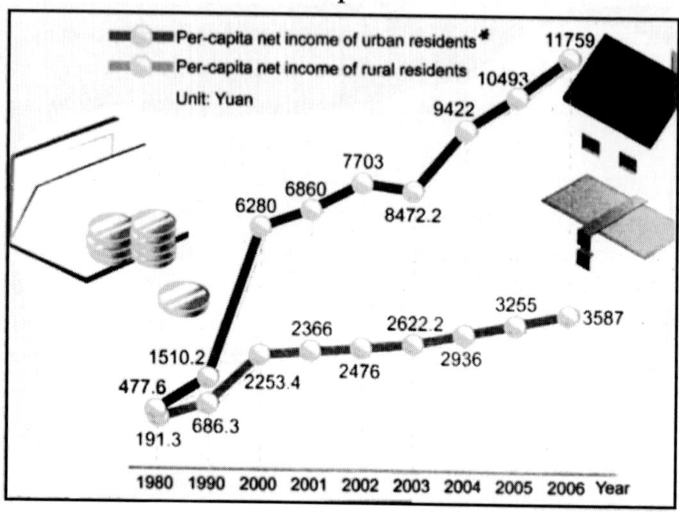

**Perks not quantified.*

Chart 16

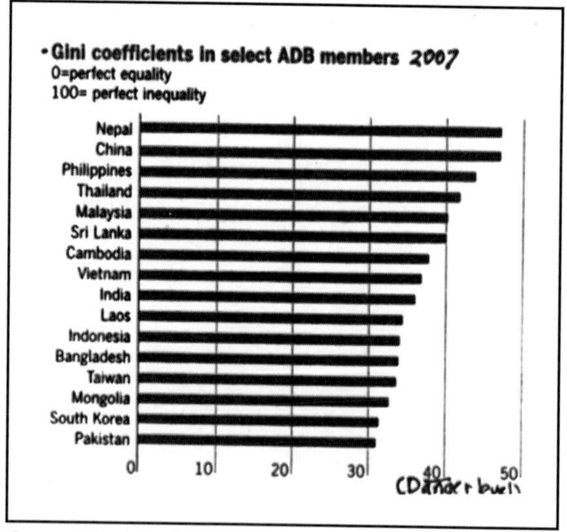

Source: Asian Development Bank.

Chart 17: Urban-rural income ratio: China

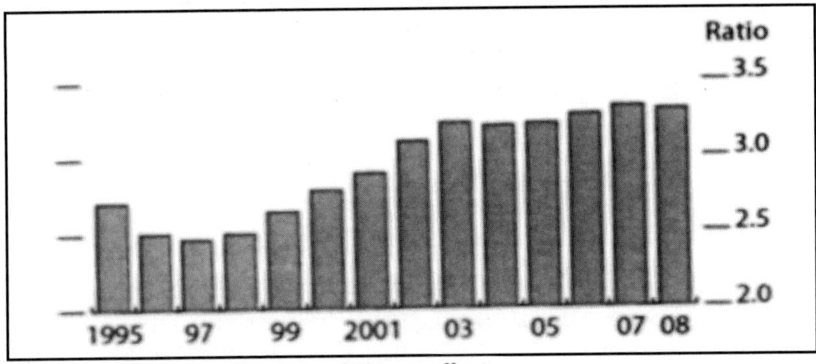

Source: national Bureau of Statistics of China; staff estimates.

Graph 25: Poverty Measure for India, 1951-2006

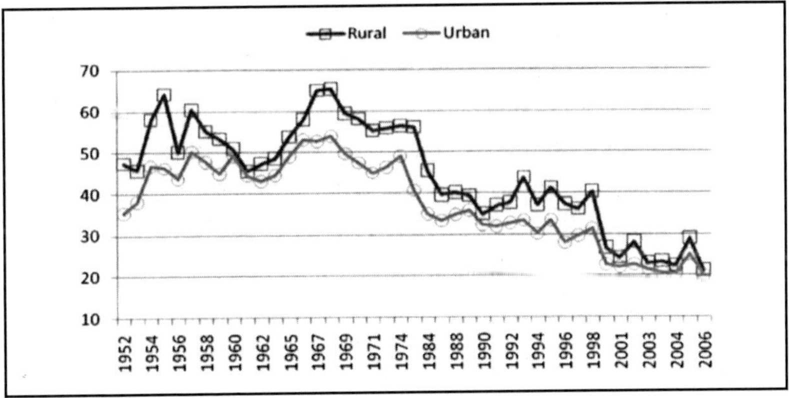

Graph 26: Squared poverty gap index (%): India

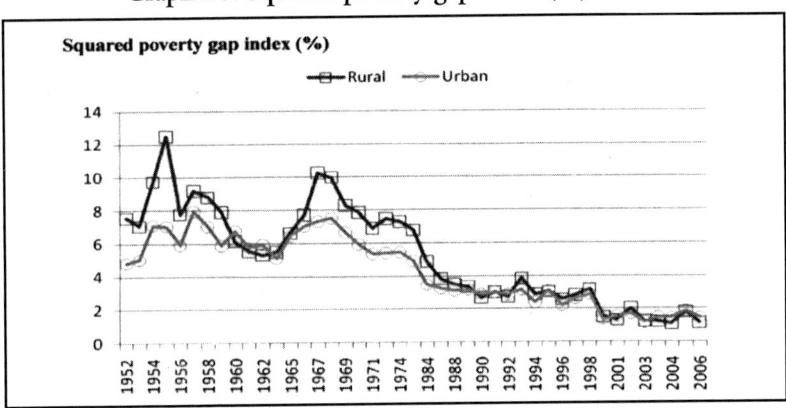

Source and notes: Authors' calculations.

Table 50: Gini Coefficients in China and India

Year	China	India
1979	0.33 (234)	0.42 (329)
1988	0.38 (110)	0.38 (272)
1996	0.42 (71)	0.36 (230)
1999	0.46 (65)	0.34 (210)
2005	0.48 (55)	0.32 (185)

Figures in brackets represent no of poor in millions according to official standard.
Source: Swamy, Subramanian: [2003] p.67; 1999 & 2005 are author's estimate. See also: Azizar Rahman Khan and Carl Riskin "Income and Inequality in China", The China Quarterly No.154, June 1998.

Unlike in India, in China, rural inequality (0.34) measured by official based Gini ratio is higher than the level in urban areas (0.28)!

Table 51: Regional Dispersion of Percapita Incomes

	Gini Coefficient	
Year	China	India
1980	0.198	0.152
1991	0.218	0.168
1997	0.252	0.225

Source: China: Zhang, Z, Liu,A; and S.Yao: "Convergence of China's Regional Incomes 1952-97" China Economic Review, Vol.12, No.2/3, 2001 p. 243. India: Author's estimate

India defines in poverty line at roughly Rs.15 a day. The government says this is enough to maintain a 2,200-calorie diet required to prevent death. The new World Bank poverty line is $1.25 or Rs.53 per day. This nearly doubles the number of poor in India from the government's official figure of 280 million.

Controversies about the poverty numbers are however not new to India, and arc quickly seized upon by opponents and proponents of reform. Regardless of which version will be proven right, however, the fact remains that India has not been a star performer in poverty reduction by the standards of some nations of East Asia where poverty ratios are typically between 8 to 15 per cent.

Graph 27: Gini coefficients for income inequality in China

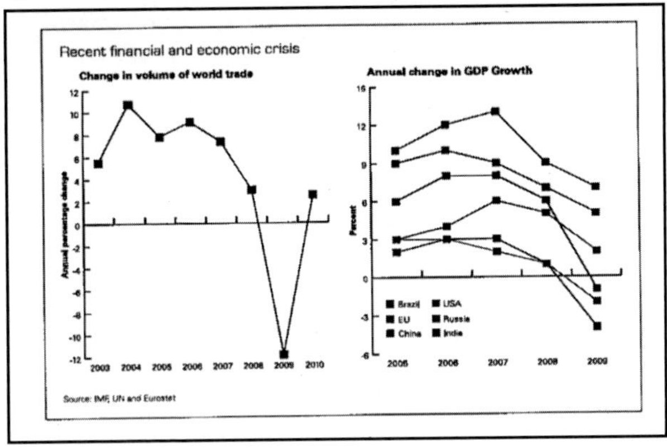

Measures of poverty in India, however, have also not been free of controversy. Although, aiming developing countries the quality of data on poverty in India is among the best (and goes as far back as 1951 when the first National Sample Survey (NSS) was conducted), there is concern that the NSH carries out two types of consumer surveys—an annual survey with limited sample size and coverage, and a more comprehensive survey with a larger sample conducted roughly every 5 years. Although estimates from the smaller samples are made public, they are not officially accepted. Consequently, official poverty estimates are available only in 5-year intervals, making it difficult to study their time series properties.

Table 52: India-Poverty Statistics (World Bank Criteria)

Year	1981	1984	1987	1990	1993	1996	1999	2002	2005*
$1/Day	296.1	282.2	285.3	282.5	280.1	271.3	270.1	276.1	266.5**
$1.25/Day	420.5	416.0	428.0	435.5	444.3	441.8	447.2	460.5	455.8
$2.0/Day	608.9	635.6	669.0	701.6	735.0	757.1	782.8	813.1	827.7
$2.5/Day	650.3	686.1	725.0	766.5	808.8	841.1	875.2	914.4	938.0

Note: *India's population was 1080 million in 2005. ** All figures are population in millions. One dollar is equivalent to about Rs 40 (now about Rs 45)

Despite data shortcomings, poverty statistics in India, unlike in China, has been extensively researched. The broad consensus conclusion from these studies is that in India, poverty and inequality have reduced during the reform period while it had increased in the earlier socialist phase. This contrasts with China where during the phase of socialist planning, poverty and inequality declined more sharply, A major contributor in reducing poverty in India has been growth acceleration iii GDP. Empirical studies show that both higher agricultural yield and increases in per capita nonfarm output were significant determinants of rural poverty reduction. But, the almost halving of the growth rate of real agricultural wages in the 1990s compared to the previous decade suggests that the poverty-reducing impact of agricultural growth was muted.

China's HDI rank has always been better than India's, but the gap has been narrowing since 1980. China is also likely to meet all its Millennium Development Goals, whereas India is not likely to do so [Chapter I].

UNEMPLOYMENT

State Council adviser Chen Quansheng said at a forum in Beijing in December 2008 that about 6.7 million jobs vanished due to the global crisis, many in the export hub of Guangdong, pushing unemployment well above the official figure of 8.3 million. India has faced no such consequence of the global crisis, reflecting the difference in the two economies.

"The major conflict in China now is employment, especially for university graduates and young migrant workers," Chen added.

Urban unemployment it is estimated has risen to about 9.4 percent, double the official figure, the Chinese Academy of Social Sciences said in a report this week. A quarter of China's 6.1 million rising college graduates could have trouble finding a job next year, it said:

In these way, China was able to offer global investors a unique combination of 19th century business practices and 21st century infrastructure, which enabled the country to attract more than $800 billion in foreign direct investment since 1979.

But China's economy is now so open that further reforms will bring only marginal benefits. The country's environmental devastation has forced the government to adopt more sustainable policies, and pressure from the West is pushing Beijing towards enforcing intellectual property rights. Lastly, China's WTO commitment to privatise and reform its banks means they cannot be used to subsidise its gargantuan state-owned companies and public works projects. This leaves China's as yet sullen and dis-empowered labour force as the country's only unchanged competitive advantage.

Despite the hype surrounding the might of China's new multinationals, the fact is no Chinese company can be globally competitive if it had to pay globally competitive wages. The primary reason Chinese firms can keep western, and even Indian, competitors at bay is that in China the absence of collective bargaining means wages are not priced by market forces but by a de facto government mandate. Officials and industrialists however realize that in the long run, wages cannot be controlled beyond a point without serious unrest and that China must move its economy up the value chain if it wants to compete.

Thus, this "policy" advantage allows China to build grant buildings for about 20 percent of what they would cost in the US. Activists who try to challenge these circumstances face harsh reprisals. About 45 known labour activists are currently languishing in Chinese prisons, according to Human Rights Watch. What is interesting is, as Table below shows, it is the private sector which has generated the fastest growth in employment, and not the state enterprises.

Table 53: Changes in Urban Employment 1995-2005 (by main sectors)

Year	(Urban and Rural) Total	Urban Total	SOEs	Collectives	Limited Liability Companies	Share-Holding Companies	Private Companies	Hong-Kong and Foreign Companies	Self-Employed
1995	680.65	190.40	112.61	31.47	—	1.64	6.20	5.13	17.09
2005	558.25	273.61	64.88	8.10	17.50	6.99	34.58	12.45	27.78
Change	+77.6	+82.9	-47.8	-23.4	+17.5	+5.35	+28.38	+7.32	+10.69

Table 54: Changes in Rural Employment 1995-2005 (by sectors)

Year	Total	TVEs	Private	Self-Employment
1995	490.25	128.62	4.71	30.54
2005	484.94	142.72	23.66	21.23
Change	-5.3	+14.1	+19	-9.3

Cynical counter arguments are often advanced by defensive Chinese scholars: The US, which was rich in resources, imported slaves; and the Europeans, who had no resources, colonized other countries with natural resources. Since China cannot do either, is its only option to exploit its own workers? China's construction boom would have been impossible without cheap almost bonded labour. For example, while a bricklayer in the US makes about $40 an hour, his peer in China makes $1 a day. In India, a high class construction labour would fetch $3 a day.

CONCLUSIONS

The main conclusions of the foregoing review of the economic growth in India and China are: [1] The GDP growth rate, calculated on corrected data and averaged and filtered on a three year moving average, over three decades before and since 1980, at about 4% each[1950-80], 10% per year for China and 5.5% for India respectively [1980—93], 8.0 and 6.5 during 1993-2003 and 8.7 and 8.5 in the period 2003-2008, thus placing China ahead of India marginally, but in per capita terms decidedly so, because of a much lower growth rate of Chinese population. [2] The structural changes in output and employment of GDP seen in terms of the changing shares of Agriculture, Industry and Services, are quite different. China's growth depended largely on labour-using manufacturing sector, which India's was founded on the Services sector. Agricultural sector was equally non-performing in both countries, but the shift out of labour to other sectors was substantial and larger in China. [3] In terms of productivity increases measured as Total Factor Productivity [TFP] and its growth [TFPG], China and India for the period prior to, and after 1980 for years for which have adequate data, TFP and TFPG were less for China prior to, and about the same, after 1980. Both thus have perspired and been inspired about the same over the last six decades.[4] China after 1998 had gone far ahead of India in infrastructure, while measured by Gini coefficient, China has slipped behind India in equity, although in terms of BPL population ratio and HDI rankings, China is better and ahead of India, while those gaps are narrowing.

Because of India's open media and freedom of movement, India has relatively to China a consistently poorer performance image and perception in public opinion. But the future economic growth of the two nations in the next four decades should now however be seen in the context of implementing new structural reforms, and both nations thereby catalysing a re-structuring of the global economic order.

Nevertheless, the prediction sometimes made that India will grow in the coming years at a rate of growth to exceed China's, is based on the main reason that India's high savings rate has risen close to 40% of GDP and has a lower capital-output ratio than China's, which incidentally already has a savings level of 43% and is, according to Nobel Laureate Modigliani, at a saturation level. And so is China's export potential near a ceiling of quantum jumps, whereas India's strategy of growth is not export-led.

The two economies will need however to progress in the future by a different route than hitherto, that is by innovation, productivity increases, energy and land use efficiency, and by protecting their environment, but not by piling in more capital and cheap labour. And this is true more so for China. That may mean convergence of the development and growth trajectories of the two nations not only in rates of growth but in policies as well. This could set the stage for a India—China, or 'Chindia' joint strategy for a new global economic order, a precursor of which was the 2010 Copenhagen summit.

The current pattern of development has therefore got to change. China, in effect, needs to repeat what it did after 1978 – move out of the investment-led export-fueled growth to more balanced, more diversified and consumption-led home-grown pattern of growth.

The question remains as to what caused the spurt in growth in China and India during the last three decades since 1980 however remains unanswered. Short answer is of course: *Economic Reforms.* But a detailed answer is required in order to answer the next question: *Will China and India be able to retain these high growth rates of the last three decades or dissipate in the coming decades?*

As for the answer, in case of China, three main factors can be identified as responsible for this spurt:

First, the rise in rate of investment from 25 percent of GDP to almost 50 percent today, that is, nearly double the rate enabled by gigantic domestic savings rate of over 42 percent, which is much higher as the Graph and Table below shows. As a corollary, it can be safely said that it is impossible that this rate of investment can increase much further.

Second, exports as we shall see from next Chapter, rose from 20$ billion in 1980 to $200 billion in 1994, i.e., a jump by a factor of ten. In

2008 it was a peak of $ 800 million i.e., a jump of a factor of four over the same length of time. It is most unlikely that over the next 15 years the US, EU, and other countries can absorb another large multiple—4 or less, leave alone ten fold—of Chinese exports. This fact highlights the need for re-balancing of the Chinese economy.

Third, the Chinese have kept the cost of capital down by state intervention and increase in money supply. These are hidden subsidies. This certainly aided the acceleration of investment and hence of growth. But the weak performance of SOEs has burdened banks with a large amount of nonperforming loans. Chinese banks have thus been saddled with at least $ 400 billion in NPLs, completely wiping out their capital. This cannot be continued without risking a major financial crisis. Already the Capital Adequacy Ratio which should at least 12% [Basel II] is less than 4%.

In the case of India, first, the growth in acceleration came essentially from the fast growing services sector. This attested by the fact that the share of the Services sector in GDP rose to over 50%, which is unprecedented for an emerging economy[see table below]. This however signals that employment generation in India may be being provided only for the highly skilled such as software engineers.

Second, during 1950-2008, the only sub-period during which China had, after carrying out necessary data corrections in the scope, netness and valuation of their national accounts data, a significantly higher growth rate than India was in 1980-93 . This was due to the fact that China was carrying out reforms while India was mostly still shackled by the most unsuited Soviet model of planning.

Third, while India may continue to grow at this rapid growth rate in GDP, it must generate employment for the young freshly skilled and semi-skilled working population to sustain the development. Hence India will need to re-balance its economy towards manufacturing growth so that the excess labour in agriculture and the semi-skilled cannot also get employment.

China presently is presently better placed in this regard compared to India, but since 2005, India's corporate sector after re-tooling itself is poised to enter into the cost effective manufacturing boom compared to China. Building managers, engineers and product managers in India, who will man it, will cost between one-half and one-third of what it is in China today. Gross hourly net wages in Beijing at $2.6 is more than double India's at $ 1.2 in Mumbai. This provides a strategic advantage to India.

Fourth, India chose a more consumption and domestic demand driven path relying on local entrepreneurial energy and high end service industry such as outsourced IT software. China instead chose an US-EU destination export-led foreign direct investment-based, labour-intensive manufacturing sector-driven, joint ventures that value-add to semi processed imports from East Asia. The indigenous capacity was not built commensurately, and now in global crisis poses a major threat to the Chinese economy.

Because of India's more domestic demand driven growth, India is much less affected by the US meltdown than China. In fact, had India not permitted Participatory Notes a derivative that facilitates money laundering, the effect on India would have been negligible. China also minimized the effect 're-exporting' the contagion to East Asia, by cutting down imports from those nations.

Briefly summarizing thus, the macro-features of economic growth in China and India reveal that in the last three decades, following different methodology of growth and reforms, differentially helped by transfer of technology from the West [via FDI, as we shall see in the next Chapter], favoured access to US and EU markets, and by what Princeton's Krugman calls as "perspiration" viz., by raising the rate of savings and using cheap skilled labour in workshop milieu, and not so much by "inspiration" i.e., innovation that leads to rising productivity. This latter is measured by Total Factor Productivity [TFP] and its growth [TFPG].

In China cheap labour, a near disdain for intellectual property rights, disregard for the environment, and cheap capital from state-controlled banks that are not subject to strict prudential norms—have long been essential ingredients in China's economic growth.

The route of the past six decades can be no more efficacious since the current levels of levels of investment and cheap labour deployment are near their limits, more so in China than India. China has been more energy using per $ GDP, polluting and with higher ICOR than India.

Both nations appear however to be headed for a major financial crisis [Chapter IV]. It is my considered opinion that over the next four decades it is India that is better poised to meet the requirements of these four factors and carry out the necessary reforms to prevent the crisis or get out it quickly largely because of the greater accountability inherent in the democratic system that India has adopted. China, I estimate, because of the same reason, or more accurately, the lack of it, will not be able to do so as quickly, just as Japan because of the cronyism of *Keiretsu* has been mired still in the after effects of the 1997 Asian financial crisis, and hence fall behind India after 2020 following the aftermath of a financial crisis that will arrive during this decade.

The future growth trends in China and India will then depend on the differential impact, depending on the policy emphasis and constraints, of the following three factors that will re-route the reform strategy arising from: [1] moving away from *ploughing in more capital and cheap labour* i.e., by "perspiration", *to raising productivity through induction of epochal innovation* such as IT, by "inspiration" [2] the resolve to carry out politically unpopular financial reforms to move back from the precipice of banking and fiscal bankruptcy. [3] reaping the demographic dividend by modernizing the educational system, empower the young population with skills essential for a 21st century knowledge economy and a commensurate productive employment generation.

This re-routing will depend on four factors: [a] *Reforming the Financial Architecture* and moving away from hidden and overt subsidies of soft-budget constraints and moral hazard, as also of illegal round-tripping flows, and a more realistic exchange rate. [b] *Securing the demographic dividend* by skill-empowerment and R&D orientation—requiring a major overhaul of the education system that China has already begun. [c] *Triangular cooperation of* the American innovating eagle, Chinese hardware dragon and India's software elephant, in IT, Biotech, Pharmaceuticals, Nanotechnology, and new energy systems including hydrogen fuel cells and Thorium reactors. [d] *Loosening the Political Constraints*—that is by greater democratization, transparency in decision-making, and accountability. This China will find much harder to do.

How all this will pan out over the next five decades is a subject matter of the next three Chapters.

Chapter 4

Globalisation, Information Technology and Financial Architecture

Globalisation of an economy today may be defined as a process in three dimensions, *first* of restructuring, especially in re-location and outsourcing of economic activity in a transnational framework of decision making, and characterized by increasingly free movement of factors of production, technology, services and knowledge.

Chart 16: Process of Globalisation

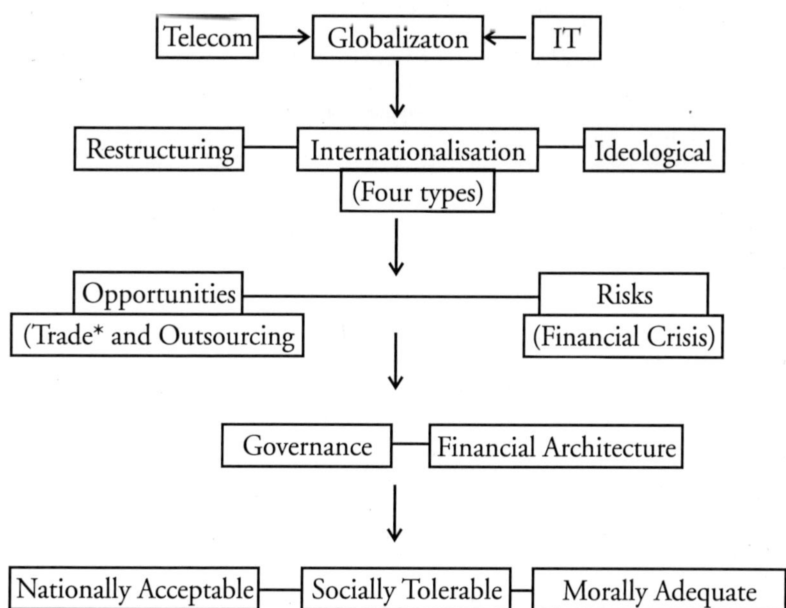

Box 6: India Goes Global – The Boom is Overseas Acquisitions

The Emergence of globally- Competitive private corporates in India has triggered an unusual boom: its corporates have started to acquire foreign firms. Such acquisitions amounted to $7.2 billion in the first three quarters of 2006. then doubled in a single deal in October, when Tata Steel announced it would be spending $8 9billion to take over Corus, a U.K./ Dutch steelmaker. Such large acquisitions mark a coming of age for Indian companies. If sustained, they could also rewrite the development mark a coming of age for Indian companies. If sustained, they could also rewrite the development textbook, For when Japan and Korea began their overseas investment drives, their GDP per capita was ten times higher that of India today. And although China and Russia have begun expanding overseas at a much earlier stage of development, their GDP per capita is still much higher than India's. Equally striking, India's outward FDI is exceptionally large relative to its still –small inward FDI. So, what explains India's outward FDI is exceptionally large relative to its still-small inward FDI, So, what explains India's sudden surge in acquisitions?

To begin with, Indian corporates have been taking over foreign firms, primarily in Europe and the United States, to gain direct access to advanced markets and technology. In other words, while other countries have imported technology through inward FDI, India is obtaining it through acquisitions. One reason why Indian corporates have been able to do this is that their business models are very similar to western ones, both in terms of framework and governance, they have managers who have been trained in western universities and speak English.

A Second factor has to do with finance. After a decade of restructuring, the profitability of Indian corporates is very high, while their leverage-unlike in East Asia-is quite low. Consequently, international financial firms have been willing to help fund these acquisitions, especially given the current benign global financial environment. In many cases, acquisitions have taken the form of leveraged buy-outs, whereby a special purpose vehicle (SPV) is incorporated in the country of acquisition, and then borrows against the cash flow and assets of the acquired company. This mechanism not only allows the Indian company to take over foreign companies of much large scale, but also leaves financial room for the parent company to make further acquisitions abroad and expand domestically.

A third factor has to do with competitiveness. India's shopping list belies the conventional perception that India has a comparative advantage only in information technology and related services. Initially, the overseas boom was indeed triggered by software companies, which wanted to enlarge and diversify their customer base, establish an on-site presence for their clients, and move up the value chain. But over the past few years, as manufacturing companies have also emerged as internationally efficient and low-cost producers, they have also started to acquire foreign firms, including in the textiles, auto parts, chemicals, and now joined the race overseas, too.

Better information is needed to monitor and manage any attendant risks. Banks should be aware of their clients' worldwide financial exposures, including leverage taken on through overseas financial activities. In addition, macroeconomic data on outward FDI can be improved, specifically to include outflows financed through offshore vehicles.

1/ According to Dealogic.

Source: World Bank/IMF.

Table 55 : M & As China and India

Year	Value of Cross-Border M & A's, By Region/economy Of seller (in Millions)		Number of Cross-border M &A's, by region/economy of seller		Value of Cross-border M &A's, by region/economy of purchase (in million)		Number of Cross border M &A's, by region/economy of purchaser	
	China	India	China	India	China	India	China	India
1987	0	49	1	1	0	49	1	1
1988	0	0	0	1	17	91	4	2
1989	0	0	1	1	202	9	6	3
1990	0	5	0	3	1,340	23	5	1
1991	270	0	6	2	185	1	9	4
1992	517	35	9	5	1,152	3	14	8
1993	672	95	34	12	2,187	208	39	2
1994	828	424	59	23	1,155	269	28	7
1995	502	261	58	49	759	36	21	13
1996	1,502	230	64	33	2,139	22	27	7
1997	3,539	1,597	90	40	6,699	88	58	13
1998	5,213	949	101	63	1,198	7	51	9
1999	9,190	1,381	108	95	784	316	9	31
2000	38,798	1,904	132	144	3,787	869	47	56
2001	3,072	1,661	136	125	2,023	2,120	54	40
2002	17,247	1,888	196	102	16,332	213	79	48
2003	4,940	1,407	285	115	5,256	1,362	112	70
2004	9,127	1,927	314	105	2,725	947	110	77
2005	10,131	7,144	334	160	9,546	4,958	102	122
2006	11,452	7,119	304	200	14,906	6,586	88	162
2007	12,185	18,830	357	187	4,452	30,414	122	194
2008	3,672	2,882	157	86	26,492	8,556	51	110
Mean	6,039	2,263	125	71	4,697	2,598	49	45
Median	3,305	1,165	96	56	2,081	211	48	13

Source: UNCTAD (2008)

Besides the restructuring dimension, globalization has *two other dimensions*: of internationalization, and ideological. Chart 16 above summarises the structure of the globalization process.

Internationalisation means openness, increased world trade [8% in 1913 to 20% in 2000 of world output at $ 6 tr], and financial leveraging [$1.5 tr exchanged daily] in a multinational discipline of rules [going on since gold standard 1870, enabled by telegraph, Bretton Woods in 1944 enabled by jet engines and telephones, and 1994 enabled by IT], global standardization of business practices, disclosure standards and corporate governance, spread of technology, and managing of westernization of tastes[through 700 m English speakers]. Trade interacts with Growth in three ways: (a) Encourage resources to move to high returns areas (b) Exports & Imports lead to technology transfer, standards and rise in TFP (c) As demand pull, exports employs excess capacity.

The *ideological* dimension [shared ideas, patterned beliefs, guiding norms, and a coherent view of world as it is and should be] lies in accepting market economy as a norm and global competitiveness within the international rules of the UN, IMF, WB and WTO. Of course it is recognized that there are market failures that need to be corrected by state intervention.

It also implies the acceptance of democracy as the ideal political framework which in turn means any reform process must guarantee sufficient social inclusion and empowerment. We thus need to recognize that "one size fits all" globalization process does not exist. Nor can autocratic kleptocracies prosper in globalisation.

The challenge of globalization is how to make it first *nationally acceptable* especially the security concerns, arising from the issue of size. For example, Nokia's $25 billion budget is larger than Finland's national budget, Sony's is bigger than Pakistan, IBM is larger than Ireland, and of the 50,000 MNCs, 200 account for 50% of world industrial output, 142 of which are headquartered in just three countries: US, Germany and Japan; next *socially tolerable* since survival of fittest theology is no more acceptable, and finally *morally adequate by not* glorifying acquisitive materialistic individualism that could erode the binding sense of community and acceptance of responsibility for the underprivileged.

The downsides of globalization are: non-level playing field arising out of capital-labour differential mobility, digital divide or skill fault lines arising out of skewed skill empowerment that will further accentuate global disparities ratio [it was 3:1 in 1900, 30:1 in 1970, 86:1 in 1998 in top 20% to bottom 20% ratio] and job insecurity, greater volatility with shorter boom-bust cycles, e-crimes, even disease. Thus the task of government becomes even more demanding, complex, and sophisticated calling for a new mindset for governance.

Essentially then, the task in the globalization process is to maximize the opportunities [trade, technology transfer, FDI] and to minimize the risks [of volatility, disease transmission, sophisticated crimes], inherent in globalization. But globalisation is here to stay—thanks to IT which has made the world into a global village

Problems have arisen in re-location and outsourcing especially developed democratic countries which find matching the cheap labour costs of developing countries hard. There is also the ideological issue, of now jettisoning the *Washington Consensus* on dos and don'ts of economic policy authored by Williamson for the World bank and IMF, as also the *Golden Strait Jacket* [to downsize government, commit to free markets, capital account convertibility, free M&A etc.] because those who adhered to these prescriptions have suffered. Thus, Nobel laureate J. Stiglitz argues for a new style of governance of smarter government intervention, i.e., through a Competition Policy and a financial architecture.

Globalization process been on balance beneficial to all countries. It is now *inevitable* because of the efficacy of internet based solutions, *irresistible* due to falling transaction costs of communication and travel, and *irreversible* because of the essentiality of WTO membership FOR Most Favoured Nation trade status. Three factors however may cause globalisation to auto destruct: [1] shorter boom bust cycles, i.e., increased volatility. [2] backlash from those on the wrong side of the digital divide or are former rentier class and now losers. [3] failure for institutions to make it socially tolerable and morally adequate.

Box 7: Special and differential provisions in WTO agreements

WTO trade agreement	Special and differential provisions
GATT	Developing countries entitled to take measures not consistent with provisions of GATT to promote the establishment of a particular industry (subject to prior consultations and within time limits)
Agreement on Agriculture	The requirements to reduce budgetary outlays for export subsidies and the quantities benefiting from such subsidies are lower for developing countries
Anti-Dumping Agreement	Constructive remedies must be explored before applying antidumping duties where these would affect the essential interests of developing countries

(Box 7 contd...)

Technical Barriers to Trade Agreement	Developing countries are not expected to use those international standards, which are not appropriate to their development needs, as a basis for their technical regulations
General Agreement on Trade in Services	In negotiations for specific commitments, there shall be appropriate flexibility for individual developing countries to open up fewer sectors
Agreement on Trade (related Aspects of Intellectual Property Rights (TRIPS)	Developing countries are entitled to a delay in implementing most TRIPS obligations, Incentives should be provided to encourage the transfer of technology to developing countries.

India, China and rest of East Asia ranked in this process of globalization is as follows: India is, by Globalisation Index 2004, in the bottom of the heap of 62 countries, ranking 61. China is also way down. Ireland is on top of the list, followed by Singapore. US is sixth. India is poorly ranked because of tariff levels still high, labour laws, higher transaction costs, poor connectivity including infrastructure, and the laws.

Nobel Laureate Paul Samuelson in 2007 has pointed four paradoxes of modern globalization: First, the market mechanisms necessary and sufficient to propel total factor productivity, will invariably, simultaneously, exacerbate inequalities between winners and losers. Second, the fruits of science, which improve health and quality of living, also worsen our environment and ramp up our vulnerability towards war and terrorists' malevolence. Third, what can preserve economics as the non-dismal science, are the considerations that the potentialities of science itself can: (a) enable us to limit contamination of air and water and (b) rectify (somewhat) the degree of worsening inequalities. Fourth, our current political systems will not achieve these offsets against environmental evils, and income and wealth inequalities. It will happen only if voters, purely out of altruistic impulses, agree to tax the winners' winnings and use these to reduce the losses that the market will mete out to the losers. No democratic government anywhere can successfully second-guess the market mechanism by extreme transfer programmes from rich to poor in the hope of levelling out family differences in wealth and income. At best, the Golden Mean of the feasible best must utilise limited state-enforced income redistributions.

The current era globalisation has features in common with the international trade wave the world had experienced at the end of the 19th century. But there are differences too between then and now.

During the *earlier wave of globalization*, tensions arose mainly between the then established colonial powers (primarily Britain, France and Russia) and new industrialising nations (mainly Germany and Japan).

The imperialist controlled nations, including China and India, were too weak economically and politically to be active during this period on the world scene. A combination of domestic and international tensions, predominantly within and between European powers, is what eventually led to World War One (WWI) and the concomitant disruption of the first wave of globalisation.

Today, there are three major differences. First, The initial wave of globalisation that began in 1870, the now two largest emerging countries, China and India, had then still accounted for about 30 per cent of world GDP in purchasing power parity (albeit declining from their previous historical level of about 50 per cent till 1820). At the close of the first wave brought about by the outbreak of WWI, the combined share of China and India had fallen to barely 16 per cent, and this share continued to decline even thereafter, staying below 10 per cent from about 1940 until 1980.

From the end of the 19th century till late in the 20th century, the "centre", i.e., Western Europe and Japan, specialised in manufactured goods while the "periphery", i.e., colonies was confined to the role of producer and exporter of raw materials. Trade was facilitated by new technologies of mass production, jet engines and telexes. As recently as 1975, developing countries accounted for only 9 per cent of world manufacturing exports, and manufacturing goods accounted for barely 16 per cent of these countries' total merchandise exports.

The *second and the latest wave of globalisation*, which commenced around this time, has fundamentally altered patterns of production and trade, with large parts of the periphery assuming centre stage. The difference, the second, was made by the new epochal innovation of information technology, which made it possible to re-structure the production framework, re-location of stages of production across the world, and communicate instantly. By 2005, developing countries aided by foreign direct investment, already accounted for 45 per cent of world manufacturing exports and manufacturing accounted for two-thirds of their total exports.

The third difference between the current and the earlier wave of globalisation is in the quality and reach of national and international institutions. The domestic and international confrontations that brought the first wave of globalisation to an end happened in an environment where nations lacked adequate institutions to resolve conflicts. It took WWI, the great depression and WWII for countries, mainly in Europe and the United States, to set up domestic welfare states and international institutions of global economic governance, such as the World Bank, the IMF, and recently the WTO and new GATT to moderate and resolve disputes.

The new GATT (1994) has now global acceptability. Not one country in the world has refused to sign it. The few Left Opponents of GATT in India must explain why even. China was so keen to rejoin the GATT a persistent applicant to GATT membership since 1984, and after having walked out in 1950. China has enacted a Patent Law which is even more stringent than required by Trade Related Intellectual Property Rights (TRIPs) in GATT (1994). China was admitted only on December 2, 2001, seventeen years after applying, conforming and reapplying.

The GATT is a vehicle to take us on the path of development in the 21st century. To get on this vehicle is not all that easy, nor is it simple to stay on it without losing balance because of the WTO's unique power of "cross retaliation". The wisdom of the nation's leadership will be tested fully on how to stay on course with the GATT vehicle and reach our destination of full development. Thus implementing the GATT and abiding by the WTO rules will mean an upheaval in our attitudes to work and quality. Transparency and audit will be the order of the day under WTO oversight. When fully implemented, WTO Rules will ensure a jump, a rise in global trade by US $ 600 billion. India should try and carve out 5 per cent 'of this increased trade.

Hence we can conclude that Globalization as a process has come to stay since technological innovation has made it possible to cut transaction coats and take instant decisions of global significance through the communication industry. The question remains for each country as to how to make globalization as economically rewarding, social tolerable and morally adequate.

In the context of Globalization, while China has a in areas made tremendous advances, the spread of globalization is limited by the desire of the ruling Communist Party to retain control over the polity of China. Hence, no counter railing institutions can be allowed to emerge. This limits ultimately the full import of globalization as the recent Google episode reveals. India being a democracy and used to the functioning of an open society is much more attuned to globalization process. The only road blocks is the legacy of soviet socialism whose fetters have yet not been completely dismantled with the advent of reforms.

Today, the choice is: either to go along with the international consensus that has emerged which we in India should intelligently shape to our advantage in the future, or be forced to quit the WTO because if we refuse to accept the international consensus, the—cross—'retaliation measures' with the WTO under the new GATT are such that we would pay an unbearably heavy price. India is a founding member of 23 nations which signed in 1947 the original GATT Agreement. Today, 150 countries are members of WTO and another 40 are in the queue to join it. To quit for any country would invite disaster and terrible tribulation for the its people, because then exporters and importers would be at the mercy of bilateral trade agreements and will also lose the automatic MFN status with other countries.

However no one can however argue that the GATT is all good either. The crucial point is that the GATT has its plusses and minuses. Thus each country has to take steps to realise the plusses and swamp out the minus to achieve overall plus. The plus in GATT is for farmers, textile companies, computer software, and Indian multinationals. Indian farmers can, under the new WTO mandate, if Doha Round is successfully concluded, export to US and EU such commodities as cereals, fruits, dairy products, vegetables and cut flowers in a big way because Indian prices are about one fourth that the developed countries are paying. Indian producers can thus earn on an average four times what they would in India. And if they do that, then farmers would for example not have to beg the government for small increases in purchase prices or subsidies on fertilisers.

The increased revenue from exports could then be used for new investment in agriculture, which sector has one of the lowest productivity in the world. This new investment can double or triple agricultural output for further export as well as to create abundance within the country. Of course this cannot be achieved unless we set up the marketing infrastructure such as internet connections, fax machines, feeder airlines, cold storages, and low cost air freight services. We have to seriously get on with this, because the world is not going to wait for us. Similarly, the textile industry will have to be fundamentally modernised within the next three years to benefit from the new GATT because the quotas under the MFA systems will be phased out then. The competition from China, South Korea and Phillipines will be severe, and therefore we cannot assume that the GATT will automatically benefit us. Along with agricultural and textiles export possibilities, the GATT 1994 also provides opportunities to our companies to take our abroad Indian labour for construction projects. This hitherto unavailable opportunity will enable Indian companies to become competitive bidders in global tenders. All these opportunities together have the potential of satisfying mass aspirations for rural development and employment both directly through globalisation of the agricultural economy and indirectly through linkages in the industrial and service sectors.

Of course, the developed countries have already realised the profound effect of low wage skills of India, and hence have already began planning new concepts to smother the comparative advantage of such countries. The US for example has raised the issue of labour standards in international trade, by which it proposes that goods produced by exploitative labour practices such as using child labour, bonded labour or by labour unfairly below minimum wage be banned for export. India has taken a hard line opposition on linking attainment of internationally acceptable labour standards of a country to the trade privileges it is entitled to under the new GATT. But the linking would really hurt other countries of Asia and Africa more than India. Therefore there is some argument for us taking the lead in formulating acceptable labour standards that meets the US concerns without losing drastically our comparative advantage in trade. After all India is one of the world leaders in labour legislation and guaranteeing constitutionally freedoms of association and collective bargaining. In fact we have ratified 36 labour conventions formulated by the ILO, while the US has ratified a mere 11.

At the same time we must be cautious with what is now being known as the Social Clause which if hastily implemented, would cause great harm. Even if such a clause does not become a part of the WTO, nevertheless, defacto, it could be implemented. For example, US and European companies could start to sign export contracts with Indian companies only after ascertaining if they meet acceptable labour standards. In Tiruppur, Coimbatore district, European companies are refusing to renew export contracts with Indian knitwear companies unless they first satisfy them that they meet labour standards especially on child labour. If this continues, then social clause will be a *fait accompli* even before we enter in a WTO sponsored conference for a verbal duel.

In my view, rather than flatly rejecting or completely surrendering on the issue of social clause, we ought to pursue a middle path of seeking to modify the US and European countries rigid stand, and imposing some of our own labour standards on them such as requiring a more liberal immigration policy, or asking from the developed countries for funding a programme to raise labour standards. In any case we should not be defensive since we have one of the better labour standards in the world.

Thus on this inevitable unpleasant issue, by a moderate stand India could enhance its moral image of a truly democratic country. The issue of banning child labour for example, and in fact upholding the ILO Conventions on labour standards in general, are worthy of full support by India. Mere vocal advocacy however is not going to stop the practice of child labour. To be effective, deterrence of child labour practice has to be linked to trade privileges and subject to "cross-retaliation" measures under the WTO. It is morally enlightened to stand up firmly to declare that children must be in schools and not in factories. To say that poverty and unemployment, or even family tradition in crafts are responsible for child labour is to implicitly justify it and is a recipe for doing nothing. Child labour is really a capital market failure because banks lend on basis of a mortgage instead of on discounted future income stream after an education of the child.

But to eradicate this shameful blot on society requires a huge commitment of funds, for creating accessible primary schools and for empowering families to be able to send their children to such schools. My study on this subject that I did for the Government in 1996 as Chairman of the Commission on Labour Standards, shows that such an arrangement would require US $ 15 billion (i.e. Rs. 65,000 crores), which we can afford in instalments over a 20 year period.

Thus what we should propose to developed countries is that India is prepared to abolish child labour in 20 years, i.e., 2020 AD, but if the developed countries feel so strongly as to require that we achieve this task by 2005 or 2010, then they should finance the project, either wholly or substantially. This approach is more workable and would enhance India's stature in WTO. A flat refusal to consider the social clause, namely the linking of trade privileges under GATT for abolishing child labour is counter-productive and immoral. Besides, the child labour issue apart, India has a good record on upholding ILO's labour standards conventions. Why should we therefore not agree to the punitive measures of social clause under WTO, especially when the offending countries are India's competitors.

The minus point in the GATT is mostly in the lack of "level playing field" in the WTO Rules, in the asymmetry in treatment of capital and labour (the former in free flow and the latter blocked from free movement) and of course trips. But even here, the current propaganda is way out of line with the reality, and is unnecessarily alarmist.

The demand that our intellectual Property laws not be changed, for example, arises from a fear psychosis that we cannot compete internationally without enjoying the handicap of copying and plagiarism.

Underlying this demand is the negative perception of Indians that we should remain permanently a copying country having very little original research to protect. We should, therefore, some argue principally the Left, steal the research and development fruits of the West without paying them compensation. One view suggests that this is justified since the West had taken our concept of zero and decimal system without paying us compensation! But under TRIPs, unpaid-for-borrowing of zero, calculus decimal system etc., would actually be justified because TRIPs requires payment of compensation only for those inventions that were patented not more than 20 years ago. Our invention of zero and decimals is more than a 1000 years old! In the case of medicines, about which there is a scare that it's price's would go up due to TRIPs, the same consideration applies.

Medicines based on patented research that is older than 20 years, will not become more expensive. Medicines in the essential category, as classified by the WHO that would require payment of patent fees and royalty would be a mere 2 percent of the total. Ninety eight percent would not have any price increase due to TRIPs, since their patents would be more than twenty years old and thus beyond protection. In any case, at Doha Ministerial Conference of WTO, it was agreed public health considerations will override the TRIPs requisition.

India can also advance her interests in those areas and issues where the develop countries are not united. In market access in agriculture for example, India, US and Australia have common interests. It is Europe which has a problem in cutting down subsidies and tariff walls for agricultural exports which is now required under the new GATT Agreement. India however in the past in the Uruguay Round deliberations had without merit, supported the Europeans on this issue for no other reason than knee-jerk antipathy to the United States, an attitude that we had developed during the Cold War. Now we should abandon this disastrous basis.

Another vital area where India and the US are on the same side is on the WTO guidelines for e-commerce and for creation of cyber world. Most of Europe and the non-democratic countries of the world are resisting this for differing reasons. But India can cooperate with the US on this issue, and perhaps get a deal through to press for other issues of special interest to India. One such special interest area is the free cross-border movement of skilled and semi-skilled labour. The West is united in resisting putting immigration policies on the WTO agenda. India has only once pressed for this, and that was at the Uruguay Round in Brussels in December 1990, when I was Commerce Minister. But the West while wants to have free access for capital, it is cold about relaxing immigration laws. There is no reason therefore for India not to press for free movement of its surplus labour and make a deal with the US for this purpose. Conferences are meant for such negotiations and deals.

FOREIGN DIRECT INVESTMENT

FDI is a part of the Globalisation process. FDI inflow and outflow have helped the Indian and Chinese economy to grow, and the governments, continues to encourage more of this sort of investment. Tables and Graphs below bring out the magnitude of these flows.

Economists of the IFC headquartered in Washington have pointed out that the figures for China and India are not really comparable. For instance, in 2000, China received $40.7 billion of FDI while India received a measly $3.2 billion. But adjusting these figures to conform with the International Monetary Fund's (IMF's) definition of FDI brings the Chinese figure down to $20.3 billion and raises the Indian to $8.1 billion. A proportionate adjustment to the inflows from 1992 till 2003 would therefore bring China's cumulative FDI down to $233 billion and push up India's to $70 billion. In 2006, against China's $69 billion, the FDI that flowed into India added up to $23 billion *(China Statistical Yearbook* 2007 and Government of India's Economic Survey 2007-08). The gap India as a ratio of China FDI therefore, remains large, but about one third.

Hence the gap between China and India in FDI not that wide as is popularly perceived. Furthermore, if real estate-invested FDI is removed, then the gap is even less. The difference, thus between China and India in FI lies not in the quantum received, but in the content (Portfolio Vs FDI) and the deployment of FDI to secure development goals such as exports. China has done better in that respect.

While we ought to recognize the need to adjust the data on FDI, to make them comparable, it is important not to lose sight of the fundamental truth: After all is said and done about the definitional issues in FDI statistics, there exists a significant gap between the FDI received by China and India.

Graph 28: Outward FDI/GDP: China-India-US

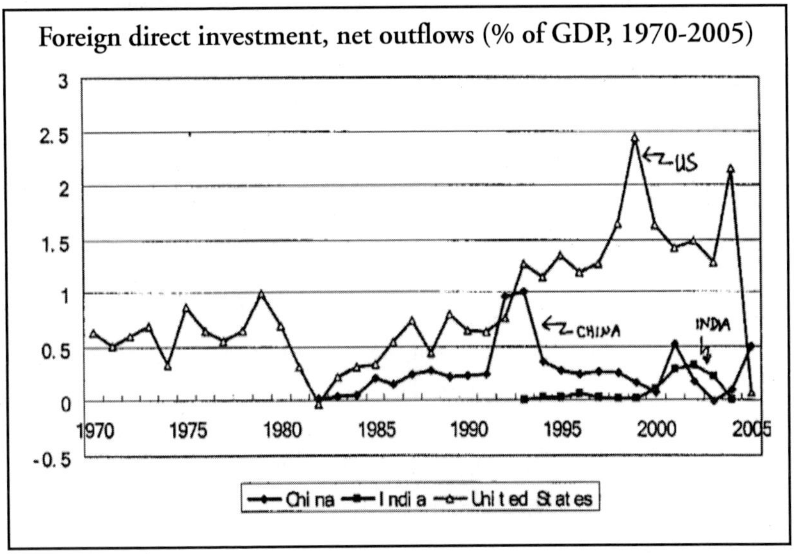

Foreign direct investment, net outflows (% of GDP, 1970-2005)

China — India — United States

US / CHINA / INDIA

Chidus Triangular

By definition, foreign direct investment is a financial flow from one country (originating) to another host/target that involves long term-relationship of lasting interest, and control over assets in the target country. Consequently an investor is able to exercise influence in the management of enterprise. Since minimum equity share holding of 10 per cent is reckoned as the threshold for control of assets, hence Equity participation of less than 10 per cent is treated as portfolio investment.

It is the ability of the investor to exercise management control that distinguishes FDI from portfolio investment. The IFC defines Reinvested earnings as part of FDI. Thus, the scope of FDI has to be delineated, which IFC has now settled. Returns on short-term portfolio investment are through capital gains and dividends. Portfolio investment in the emerging economies e.g., China and India began only in the early 1990s. Foreign equity in an enterprise can go up to 100 per cent, if entry conditions so permit. In that case, it would be a fully foreign owned enterprise. But the usual pattern of investment is in the form of a joint venture rather than wholly owned enterprise, even if 100% is permitted.

Joint ventures are preferred since interdependence is likely to be mutually beneficial. Joint ventures can also reduce production and transaction costs. Generally speaking 100% FDI or wholly owned enterprises are usually favoured in countries with cultural and geographic affinity or proximity. This is exemplified by China where wholly-owned foreign enterprises have eventually emerged as the dominant mode of investment for nations of East Asia, which accounted for 71 per cent of inflows during 2005, and cumulatively 45 per cent as of 2005.

Foreign direct investment includes 'greenfield' investment (new enterprises) as well as M&As i.e., acquisitions and mergers of existing firms, and both comprise non-debt flows. Host or target countries prefer equity participation over foreign debt, since it involves sharing of risks. Inflows through M&As are concentrated mainly in the developed countries. M&As accounted for as high as 85 per cent of inflows to developed countries during 2006. These are dominant in pharmaceuticals and service sectors, particularly in the banking and finance industry. On the other hand, greenfield investment continues to be the primary mode of inflows for developing countries. Their share in worldwide mergers and acquisitions is less than 15 per cent. Pursuit of privatisation policies by many countries has accelerated the flow of investment through M&As. Acquisitions do not enhance the productive capacity of the host economy, but result in transfer of ownership and control from domestic to foreign enterprises. From the perspective of developing countries, greenfield investment is considered more beneficial, as it generates fresh employment. M&As may also exert competitive pressure on domestic enterprises resulting in improvement in their product quality variety and innovation. Inflows through M&As have been rising in India since 2002 and accounted for over 20 per cent of inflows during 1991 to 2006.

Inward FDI global flows have gone up from US$ 154.8 billion in 1991 to US$ 1305.08 billion in 2006. These are, however, concentrated in a handful of high and middle income home and host countries. Top ten developed countries accounted for 71 per cent of outward FDI flows during 2006. Outflows from developed countries have mostly remained in developed countries, in particular in Triad countries (Japan, European Union and the United States). As a result of liberalisation measures initiated during the 1990s, the share of developing countries in inflows has been rising steadily. It was 29 per cent of total inflows during 2006.

However, inflows to developing countries are also confined to a few countries. Top ten developing economies had 71 per cent share in the inflows to developing economies during 2006. It may be a matter of some satisfaction that the degree of concentration has come down, since top five developing countries in 2001 had 62 per cent share in inflows. China accounted for 18.33 per cent of inflows to developing countries during 2006, while India's share was 4.45 per cent. Poorer countries have remained marginalised in the distribution of FDI. This is due to their weak institutions, inefficient governance, and small markets and underdeveloped infrastructure.

Box 8: Revised FDI definition in India

Conceptually, the main difference between FDI and portfolio investment is in the lasting interest expressed by a non-resident direct investor in a resident enterprise of the domestic economy. The lasting interest underlines a firm desire on part of the non-resident investor to be associated with the long-term business activities of the resident enterprise by exerting significant influence on the management of the enterprise. Accordingly, the international best practice systems have focused on recording of FDI data in balance of payments statistics in terms of three main categories as mentioned below:

1. equity flows (equity in branches, shares in subsidiaries and other capital contributions),
2. reinvested earnings (retained earnings of foreign subsidiaries and affiliates), and
3. inter-company debt transactions (inter-corporate debt transactions between associated corporate entities).

(Box 8 contd...)

There are, however, considerable variations among countries as far as their reporting systems of FDI flows are concerned. China and India are good examples in this regard. The Chinese system of reporting FDI is much more broad-based. Apart from equity capital, reinvested earnings, inter-corporate debt transactions, China includes short-term and long-term loans, trade credits, bonds, grants, financial leasing, investment by foreign venture capital funds, earnings of indirectly held enterprises, non-cash equity acquisition, control premium and non-competition fee within FDI. It also includes project imports as FDI flows, which, in India, are recorded as imports. As compared to China, it is clear that till some time back, the reporting of FDI in India's balance of payments statistics, which was confined only to equity capital, represented a much narrower coverage of FDI flows.

It is interesting to note that adoption of a broader coverage system for FDI flows has resulted in upward revision of annual FDI inflows into India for the years 2000-01 and 2001-02 by US$1.7 billion and US$2.2 billion respectively, representing on average, a 70 per cent increase over previously reported data. While this is not to suggest that the difference between volume of FDI inflows into China and India is attributable only to the disparities in coverage of data, comparisons between the two nations in terms of their abilities to attract FDI, should take note of this point.

Graph 29: FDI/GDP: China vs. India 1950-2006

FDI/GDP: China vs. India (1970-2005)

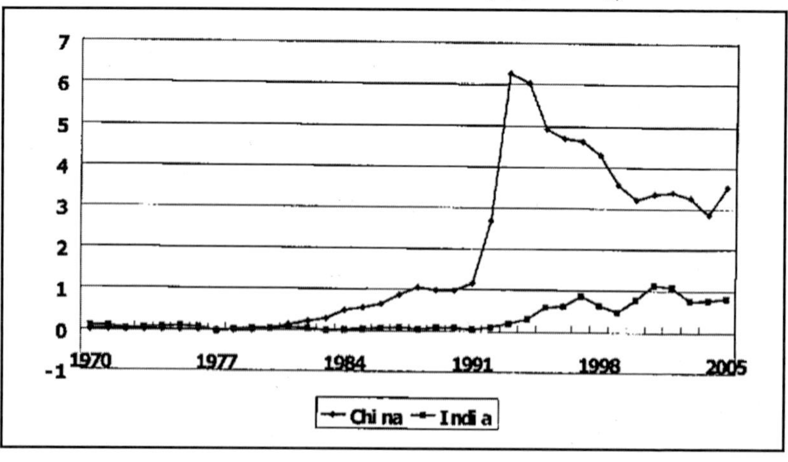

Table 56: FDI Performance Index

Year	Inward FDI Performance Index				Inward FDI Potential Index				Outward FDI Performance Index			
	China		India		China		India		China		India	
	Rank	scores	rank	scores	rank	scores	rank	score	rank	scores	rank	scores
1988-1990	46	1,033	98	0.066	45	0.176	72	0.120	36	0.214	82	0.003
1989-1991	50	1.184	103	0.073	43	0.179	71	0.123	39	0.213	84	0.001
1990-1992	43	2.162	118	0.088	52	0.196	97	0.138	35	0.524	86	0.002
1991-1993	19	4.672	113	0.144	56	0.190	94	0.194	30	0.843	94	0.002
1992-1994	43	2.162	118	0.088	59	0.190	95	0.152	35	0.776	91	0.013
1993-1995-	11	5.780	108	0.378	55	0.212	93	0.163	39	0.453	87	0.019
1994-1996	16	4.667	104	0.467	45	0.225	84	0.165	60	0.243	90	0.035
1995-1997	20	3.678	105	0.534	41	0.238	92	0.158	60	0.200	86	0.030
1996-1998	30	2.761	113	0.417	42	0.251	88	0.167	61	0.158	95	0.019
1997-1999	43	1.806	116	0.265	42	0.256	87	0.165	64	0.099	107	0.008
1998-2000	51	1.198	119	0.155	42	0.255	91	0.156	69	0.055	91	0.015
1999-2001	56	1.134	121	0.166	44	0.255	91	0.153	60	0.092	71	0.045
2000-2002	50	1.331	121	0.215	39	0.273	89	0.159	59	0.111	63	0.080
2001-2003	37	1.969	114	0.357	38	0.269	85	0.157	58	0.150	61	0.114
2002-2004	45	2.134	112	0.410	33	0.289	82	0.166	72	0.052	54	0.131
2003-2005	62	2.020	121	0.451	30	0.307	85	0.159	61	0.217	65	0.171
2004-2006	75	1.320	110	0.615	32	0.304	84	0.163	58	0.244	50	0.327
2005-2007	88	0.986	106	0.629	32	0.304	84	0.163	59	0.240	50	0.368

UNCTAD (2008)
P. Prime, 1 bid

FDI in Service Sector

Historically, FDI has been associated with manufacturing and industry. During the 90s, sectoral distribution of FDI has undergone significant change. The share of services in inflows now exceeds that of manufacturing. The share of primary sector in inward FDI stock went down from 9 per cent in 1990 to 6 per cent in 2002, and that of manufacturing from 42 per cent to 34 per cent. On the other hand, share of services increased from 49 per cent to 60 per cent during the same period. In developing countries, share of primary sector in FDI stock remained unchanged at 7 per cent in 1990 and 2002, while for manufacturing sector it decreased from 46 per cent to 38 per cent and for services it went up from 47 per cent to 55 per cent. The stocks of FDI in services are mostly held in developed countries and that of most of the international production in manufacturing are in the developing countries. The share of service sector in the GDP of developing and developed countries has also gone up. In 2001, it was 72 per cent for the developed countries, against 52 per cent for the developing countries.

Deregulation of service sector by many countries has stimulated investment in activities like financial services, telecommunications and utilities. The industry composition of FDI in service sector is undergoing rapid transformation. Trade and financial intermediation which remained dominant until the mid-1990s have yielded place to business services and communication. A feature of service sector is that many non-equity forms of participation, such as franchising, management contracts, concessions and partnerships are also prevalent in a number of service industries. The share of services in FDI inflows is rising due to growing service intensity in production of goods and as a result of "tradability revolution" of services, offshoring of export-oriented services such as call centres and business processes and research and development.

Developing countries have immense export potential in a variety of services. These include tourism, ports and shipping, audio-visual, construction and health services. Ireland in the developed world and India amongst developing countries have been successful locations for software development. Computer and related services and other highly skilled activities can be of export interest to developing countries. Rapid growth of outsourcing business in India demonstrates that foreign investment and trade can benefit developing countries. India has emerged as a preferred destination for off shoring of whole range of IT services. It enjoys the first mover and agglomeration advantage. Software and business process outsourcing are expected to attract one-third of all foreign investment to India by 2008 and generate US$ 60 billion a year in exports and nearly a million new jobs. The Indian outsourcing firms control over half of the intensely competitive global IT and back office outsourcing market. Service sector exports from India have risen from US$ 4.9 billion in 1991 to US$73.84 billion in 2006. In China, these have increased from US$ 6.86 billion in 1991 to US$ 91.42 billion in 2006 (Annexure A-2.7a).

India's services sector attracted USD 17.45 billion foreign direct investment in the last three years, the highest in the said period, leaving computer and telecom sectors to trail behind.

The services sector accounted for 27 per cent of the USD 64.40 billion total FDI received during April 2006 - March 2008, according to the data provided by the Government in Parliament.

Computer software and hardware industry was a distant second, receiving USD 5.7 billion followed by housing and real estate (USD 5.4 billion) and construction activities (USD 4.75 billion) and telecom (USD 4.29 billion), it said.

FDI inflows in the country have increased from USD 5.5 billion in 2005-06 to USDJ 27.31 billion in 2008-09 and that despite the economic slowdown, inflows in 2008-09 showed a growth rate of 11 per cent over the previous year's USD 24.58 billion.

As a result of foreign direct investment, China has now become the de facto global leader in light manufacturing and has been able to distance India in many dimensions, including per capita income, power availability, telecom subscribers, bandwidth, and exports, but most important of all-in technology upgradation. China is strict in ensuring that firms with foreign participation, export a substantial portion of its output. Today, 40 percent of China's exports are from such firms, while in India this ratio is a mere 8 per cent.

Considering that in China nearly 58 percent of the FDI comes from China's 'Sinic' neighbours, the question is why India is not able to tap its diaspora and neighbours. The fact is that India does not have developed or NICs as neighbouring countries (as Hong Kong, Singapore, Korea or Taiwan are to China) or neighbours which have grown faster than India itself. It could also be due to what Yasheng Huang as stated as the 'institutional bias'. China has created institutions such as SEZs to overplay the FDI as a substitution to moving toward market decisions, while India's vested interests the rentier class from socialism, underplayed FDI to moderate the natural tendency of a democracy towards the market.

It is an established fact that while the Chinese non-resident Community (NRC) is primarily responsible for large and increasing FDI inflows in China (NRC share rising from 1.1 percent in 1985 to 31.5 percent in 1995, (see Table-49) the non-resident Indians (NRIs) have shied away from India despite the advent of economic reforms (NRI share falling from 48.9% to 3.9%) [see also Chart-41 and 42]. Both NRIs and NRCs took advantage of incentives provided by the respective governments. Indeed, NRCs were driven by a need to relocate labour-intensive units from rising wage NICs such as Taiwan, Hong kong and Singapore to China, while NRIs chose the safer and familiar alternative of deposits in Indian banks. By contrast the diaspora of China in her neighbouring areas consists of businessmen with a strong representation of billionaire tycoons with wide practical experience in Asian markets (see Table).

China's success in attracting FDI is partly a historical accident-it has a wealthy diaspora. During the 1990s, more than half of China's FDI came from overseas Chinese sources. The money appears to have had at least one unintended consequence: the billions of dollars that came from Hong Kong, Macao, and Taiwan may have inadvertently helped Beijing postpone politically difficult internal reforms. For instance, because foreign investors were acquiring assets from loss-making organizations, the government was able to drag its feet on privatization.

After decades of keeping the Indian diaspora at arm's length, New Delhi is now embracing it. In some circles, it used to be jokingly said that

NRI, an acronym applied to members of the diaspora, stood for "Not Required Indians." Now, the government policy has changed and hence the term is back to meaning just "Non-Resident Indian." The change in attitude was officially signaled in 2004 when the government held a conference on the diaspora that a number of prominent NRI attended.

Until now, the Indian diaspora has accounted for less than 10 percent of the foreign money flowing to India. With the welcome mat now laid out, direct investment from nonresident Indians is likely to increase. And while the Indian diaspora may not be able to match the Chinese diaspora as "hard" capital goes, Indians abroad have substantially more intellectual capital to contribute, which could prove even more valuable.

The Indian diaspora has famously distinguished itself in knowledge-based industries, nowhere more so than in Silicon Valley. Now, India's brightening prospects, as well as the changing attitude vis-à-vis those who have gone abroad, are luring many nonresident Indian engineers and scientists home and are enticing many expatriate business people to open their wallets. With the help of its diaspora, China has won the race to be the world's factory. With the help of its diaspora, India could become the world's technology lab.

The Indian diaspora consists mainly of semi-skilled workers and salaried professionals. Moreover, even NRI (Non Resident Indian) investment, because of discouragement by local authorities, has been declining in the 1990s from 49% of FDI to about 4% in 1999 [see Table-50]. Standard 85 Poor's Joydeep Mukherjee and Indian Council for Research on International Economic Relations (ICRIER) have tried to figure out the reasons for this difference in mindsets, and came to the following conclusion:

(1) NRIs are risk averse since most of them are salaried professionals and wage-earning labourers. Even those in business don't have much experience. Only 9.3% of NRI investment is in manufacturing of machinery.

(2) NRIs lack experience in dealing with low-wage labour to produce low-cost, export-oriented manufactured goods, and hence, are unable to relocate units.

(3) NRIs have to constantly deal with bureaucracy at both the Centre and the state levels. That is one reason for the delays in investment inflows in projects promoted by NRIs.

(4) Most NRCs, on the other hand, have been in the manufacturing business for more than two-three decades and are, therefore, more experienced than their Indian counterparts.

(5) NRCs manage to side-step the red tape of the central and provincial bureaucracies due to decentralised policy-making in China. Thus, NRCs do not require multiple clearances from different government department, as is the case in India.

(6) NRCs manage to save both time and money as they do not have to give bribes (at the provincial level), which becomes a major inducement for investments inflows.

Besides, dynamic neighbours and well placed diaspora, there are other reasons as well. The high FDI in China is a product of favourable taxation policy, good infrastructure in special economic zones, and the delegation of investment approval authority to the local level. India has as yet no special zones for FDI. Its investment clearance procedures remain cumbersome and centralized. Tax norms are complicated and infrastructure is decidedly poor. According to investors there are other reasons as well as to why China has been preferred to India: its non-state sector pays almost no taxes; its labour market regime is more flexible; and its imports of intermediates are virtually tariff- free as long as they fall under the class of inputs for exports. China has also emphasised infrastructure even ahead of economic growth whereas India's policy on infrastructure is ambiguous and haphazard. This made China a much more attractive destination for FDI.

Nevertheless despite these draw backs, India does receive two-fifths of China's FDI—after data adjustments—and since 2006 the gap is rapidly narrowing.

Thus, with an effective and familiar legal system, a large market potential, and adequate institutional capacities, India can play a key role in information technology and other such cutting-edge sectors where FDI would be attracted. Its educated middle class of 300 million can provide the necessary demand level to sustain rapid industrial growth.

India already has an impressive industrial base and a tradition of private enterprise with 7,000 listed companies. It is accustomed to the rule of law, English is widely used, property rights defined, and financial systems conform to international standards. India's capacity to absorb FDI specially in knowledge-based products will make it an attractive destination for exports, and this may ultimately put India ahead of China in the year ahead. With those kinds of advantages should forge ahead of China in FDI in the future if the foreign investors had welcoming objective conditions obtaining such as infrastructure and flexible labour laws.

East Asian countries were able to build export manufacturing capabilities and enhance their export competitiveness through export-oriented FDI. Their export growth has been driven mainly by non-resource manufacturing. The most dynamic products in the world trade are found mainly in three manufacturing industries viz., electronics, automotive and apparels. The development policies pursued by these countries combined intervention with export promotion and control on the volume and quality of capital inflows. Industries not yet ready to compete internationally were granted protection and export-ready industries were promoted. However, TNC activity has been limited in Japan which has made full use of other routes for acquiring technology.

It has demonstrated that it is possible for a country to move through the initial stages of investment development path without undue reliance on FDI. However, to be able to do so, a country needs to have a strong technological base and entrepreneurial and work ethic dedicated to improvement of product quality. Following the Japanese example, South Korea also encouraged import of technological and management skills and promoted indigenous R&D. Indian experience also testifies that economic progress can be made with modest FDI inflows, albeit at a slower pace. Export-oriented FDI is a special type of FDI which is driven by different factors. It is particularly sensitive to the availability of quality infrastructure. It is of footloose nature and moves from country to country depending upon changing comparative advantage. India has not been able to attract export-oriented FDI due to lack of requisite infrastructure.

The last two decades have seen a significant rise in the internationalization of firms from developing economies. According to the 2008 *World Investment Report*, outward flows of FDI from developing countries rose from about US$6 billion between 1989 and 1991 to US$225 billion in 2007. As a percentage of total global outflows, the share of developing countries grew from 2.7% to nearly 13.0% during this period.

Within this the growing internationalization of firms from two fast-growing developing countries, China and India, is particularly notable. Table 1 illustrated the size of outward FDI flows from China and India in 2007. Firms from China and India have also been involved in significant and growing levels of mergers and acquisitions abroad. The recent high-profile overseas acquisitions by India's Tata group and China's Lenovo and Haier groups stand out as examples. Between 2005 and 2007, cross-border purchases by Chinese firms averaged about US$3.5 billion per annum, while those by Indian firms averaged US$1.5 billion per annum. As some of these acquisitions were financed through raising money in international markets or in the host economies, measures of outward FDI flows probably underestimate the extent of internationalization of firms from these two countries.

However, the quantitative significance of these trends needs to be kept in perspective. Although outward FDI from both countries has increased in recent years, the levels remain paltry relative to the size of these economies and relative to global FDI flows. Both countries also rank quite low in terms of UNCTAD's outward FDI performance index, which measures a country's outward FDI relative to its GDP.

So why have these fledgling flows commanded so much attention? For one, both China and India are large and populous developing countries and their recent growth spurt has captured the popular imagination. Further, the emerging outward orientation of these countries reflects a distinct break from their historical trajectories: both China and India were inward-looking economies for much of the period after the Second World War and these trends may mark their arrival on the international scene.

Within the context of these trends, two features stand out. First, the pattern of internationalization by Chinese and Indian firms does not conform to the conventional form where firms expand overseas to exploit their firm specific advantages; rather, these firms have largely been driven by a search for resources, technology and other strategic assets. This has significant implications for traditional industrial policy in recipient countries, which have tended to encourage such investments to boost local employment and economic growth. Second, the overseas expansion was to some extent fed by the availability of easy credit in international financial markets, and the emerging pattern may well prove fragile in the wake of the global financial crisis.

New Patterns of Internationalization

The patterns of internationalization followed by Chinese and Indian firms share a number of common elements. Both countries have experienced rapid growth in recent decades, which has led to large inflows of FDI and portfolio capital and, for China, a sustained current account surplus too. These inflows, combined with high rates of domestic saving, created large reserves of capital at the macroeconomic level, which in turn led to a relaxation of policy restriction on capital outflows. Many outflows in recent years took place under easy credit conditions in global financial markets, though this situation has changed dramatically since the summer of 2007.

At the same time, there are significant differences in the international behaviour of firms from the two countries. Whereas Chinese overseas acquisitions are more commonly carried out by state-owned enterprises, Indian outward FDI involves mostly private sector firms–typically the large, diversified business houses. Chinese overseas investments are more likely to have been in primary sectors, notably minerals and energy, whereas Indian investments are more distributed across a range of sectors.

These differences are probably closely linked to the underlying policy environment that has guided the industrial evolution of each economy. Despite the economic liberalization that started in China in the 1980s, state-owned enterprises continue to play an important part in the Chinese industrial sector. Given the dependence of the economy on sustained exports, many Chinese overseas investments aim to secure access to critical raw materials, especially energy. By contrast, India's industrial sectors have experienced many policy gyrations over the decades. India was remarkably open to inward FDI throughout the 1950s, allowing a substantial stock of foreign investment to build up. Through much of the 1960s the policy of import-substituting industrialization allowed considerable scope for private enterprise, creating a significant pool of private firms that have taken advantage of a more liberal regime to internationalize abroad.

Motivating Factors

What are the specific factors that have driven Chinese and Indian firms to venture abroad, and have enabled them to do this with a degree of success? Judging from recent survey data (for instance the 2006 *World Investment Report*), most developing country multinational corporations (MNCs) report that they invest abroad to access overseas markets or to gain proximity to potential clients. Although Chinese manufacturing firms can gain access to international markets through exports, overseas investments are used as a means of improving access to markets or pre-emptively securing access against potential protectionist barriers. Indian technology firms realize that proximity to their clients can help them understand and service their overseas markets better.

A second key motivation for firms to invest abroad is to secure access to strategic assets, including natural resources and raw materials, as well as new technologies and brands. Because security of access to essential raw materials is considered important for economic growth, state-owned enterprises have been at the forefront of acquiring ownership stakes in overseas mining and energy sectors. China National Petrol Corporation and China National Offshore Oil Corporation are typical firms in this category, but India's Oil and Natural Gas Commission has also made substantial forays abroad.

Technology disseminating FDI is not peculiar to China and India. In the past, Korean firms such as Samsung and Hyundai combined foreign investment with international technology licensing to build their technological capabilities. However, the stronger international intellectual property regimes that have emerged in recent years could have created a bias towards technology-seeking overseas acquisitions. In part, this is because ownership of technology assets allows more experimentation. Technology and the related desire to acquire brands and distribution networks are important elements in the internationalization of Indian pharmaceutical and software companies. For China, Lenovo's acquisition of IBM assets and Haier's investments in the United States have provided footholds in overseas markets as a stepping stone to develop their own brand identity. Additionally, in some sectors overseas acquisitions may enable firms to exploit economies of scale and scope, for example, Indian firms' investments in steel.

Graph 30: Export-GDP Ratios

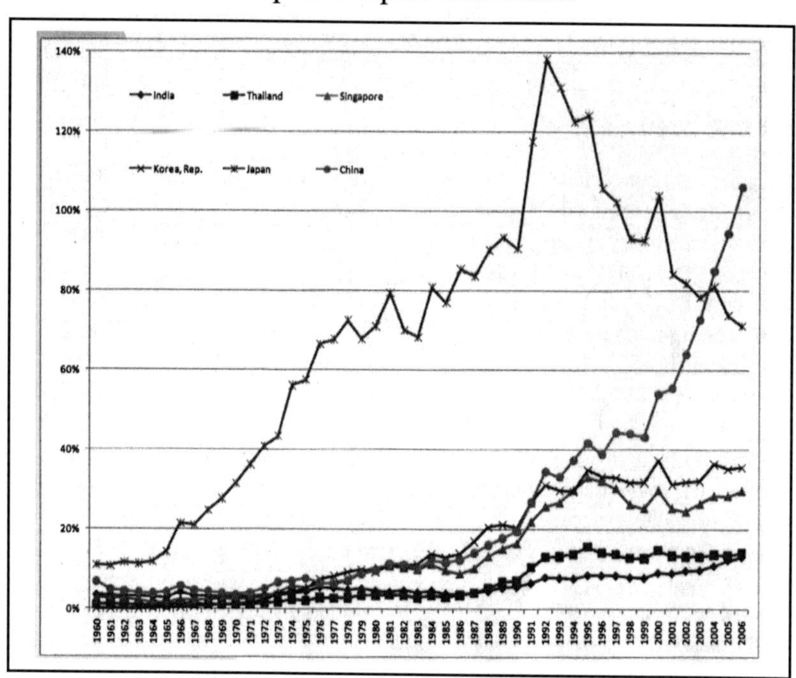

Table 57: Annual Growth in Exports, China India, 1995-2004

Percent

	1995-04	1995-00	2000-04
China			
Total Exports	18.1	13.7	23.8
Goods	18.6	14.2	24.2
Services	14.0	9.7	19.7
India			
Total Exports	12.6	9.5	16.6
Goods	10.1	6.7	14.5
Services	20.6	19.8	21.6
Memo: Share of Goods in Total Exports			
	1995	2000	2004
China 87.0	89.1	90.5	
India 82.2	72.2	67.1	

Source: World Bank. 2006. World Development Indicators.

Table 58: Top 25 Exports for China and India, 2004

China	Percent
Product	Share
Parts of automatic data processing	4.0
Digital auto data processing machinery	4.0
Input or output units	4.2
Transmission apparatus	3.1
Parts suitable for use solely or prese	2.3
Monolithic integrated circuits	1.9
Storage units, whether or not prese	1.5
Video recording or reproducing appa	1.5
Optical devices, appliances	1.4
Video recording or reproducing appa	1.2
Television receivers including video	1.2
Cargo containers	1.1
Static converters, nets	0.9
Parts and accessories of apparatus	0.9
Petroleum oils, etc, (excl. crude)	0.9
Coke and semi-coke of coal, of lign	0.9
Printed circuits	0.9
Footwear with rubber ... soles	0.9
Automatic data processing machines	0.9
Bituninous coal, not agglomerated	0.8

Footwear, nes, not covering the ankle	0.8
Trunks, suit-cases ...., etc.	0.8
Digital process units	0.8
Sound reproducing apparatus, not in	0.7
Jerseys, pullovers, etc, of man-made	0.7
Total	38.4

India	Percent
Product	Share
Diamonds non-industrial nets	12.7
Petroleum oils, etc, (excl. crude)	9.7
Articles of jewelry and parts thereof	4.6
Non-agglomerated iron ores and conc.	4.5
Semi-milled or wholly milled rice	2.6
Other organic compounds, nets	2.1
Flat rolled prod, i/nas, plated or	2.0
Other medicaments of mixed or unmix	1.9
T-shirts, singles and other vests,	1.4
Women's or girls' blouses, shirts	1.4
Frozen shrimps and prawns	1.5
Men's or boys' shirts of cotton	1.3
Imitation jewelry nets of base metal	1.2
Furnishing articles, nes, of cotton	1.2
Oil-cake and other solid residues	1.1
Cashew nuts, fresh or dried	1.1
Made up articles (incl. dress patterns)	1.1
Motor vehicle parts nes	1.0
Polypropylene, in primary forms	0.9
Copper cathodes and sections of cat	0.9
Agglomerated iron ores and concentr.	0.9
Men's or boys' shirts of cotton, knit	0.9
Automobiles with reciprocating piston	0.8
Woven fabrics of high tenacity yarn	0.8
Colleges and similar decorative	0.8
Total	58.4

Graph 31: Trade Surplus/GDP: China vs. India

Net Trade (% of GDP, 1975-2004)
5%
4%
3%
2%
1%
0%
-1%
-2%
-3%
-4%
-5%
1975
1980
1985
1990
1995
2000
CHINA
INDIA
China
India

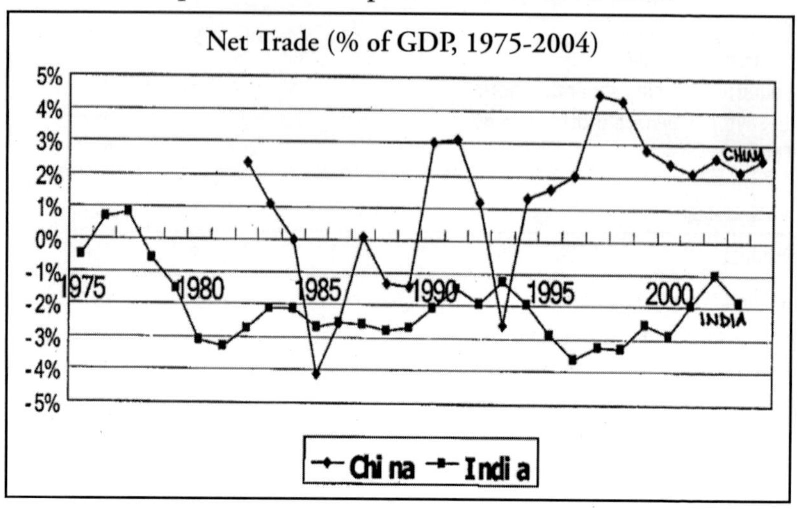

Chart 17

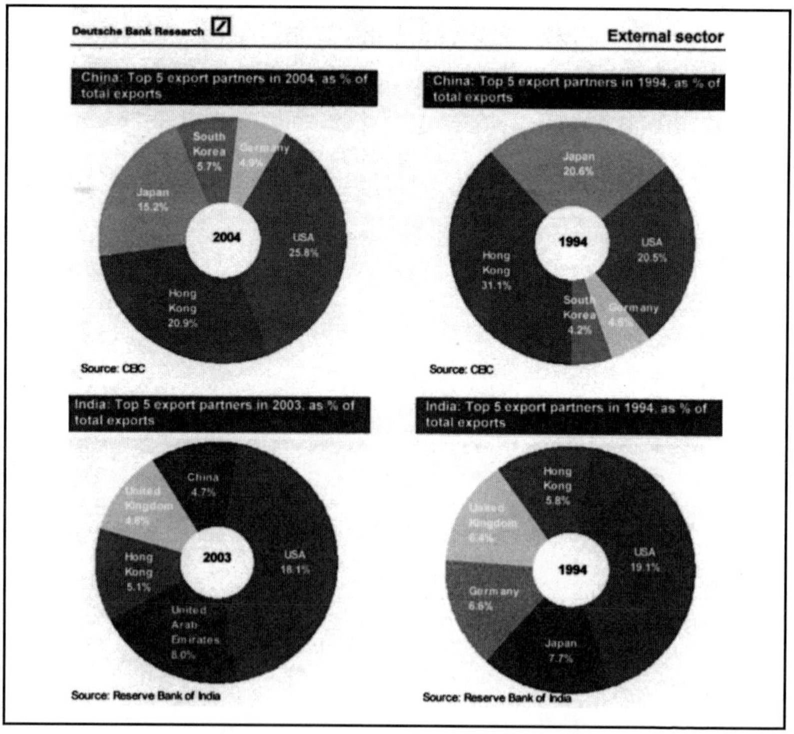

Deutsche Bank Research
External sector
China: Top 5 export partners in 2004, as % of total exports
South Korea 5.7%
Germany 4.9%
Japan 15.2%
2004
USA 25.8%
Hong Kong 20.9%
Source: CBC
China: Top 5 export partners in 1994, as % of total exports
Japan 20.6%
1994
USA 20.5%
Hong Kong 31.1%
South Korea 4.2%
Germany 4.6%
Source: CBC
India: Top 5 export partners in 2003, as % of total exports
China 4.7%
United Kingdom 4.6%
2003
USA 18.1%
Hong Kong 5.1%
United Arab Emirates 8.0%
Source: Reserve Bank of India
India: Top 5 export partners in 1994, as % of total exports
Hong Kong 5.8%
United Kingdom 6.4%
1994
USA 19.1%
Germany 6.6%
Japan 7.7%
Source: Reserve Bank of India

Chart 18

China: Key export products
% of total exports
2000
2004
15
10
5
0
Clothing & garments
Electrical machinery & equipment
Yarn & textiles
Source: EIU
India: Key export products
% of total exports
2000
2004
25
20
15
10
5
0
Non-metallic mineral manuf.
Clothing
Textile, yarn, fabric
Source: EIU

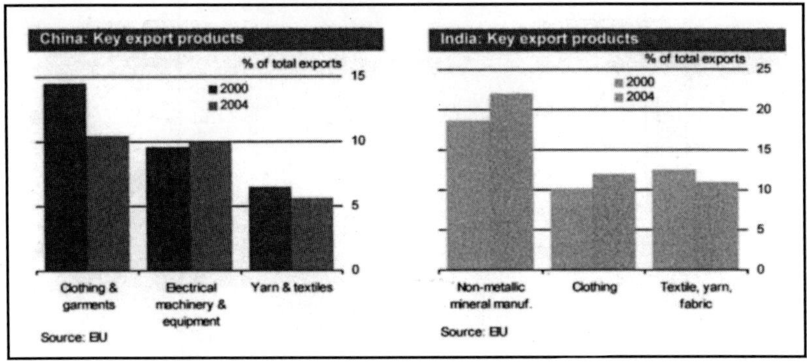

Chart 19

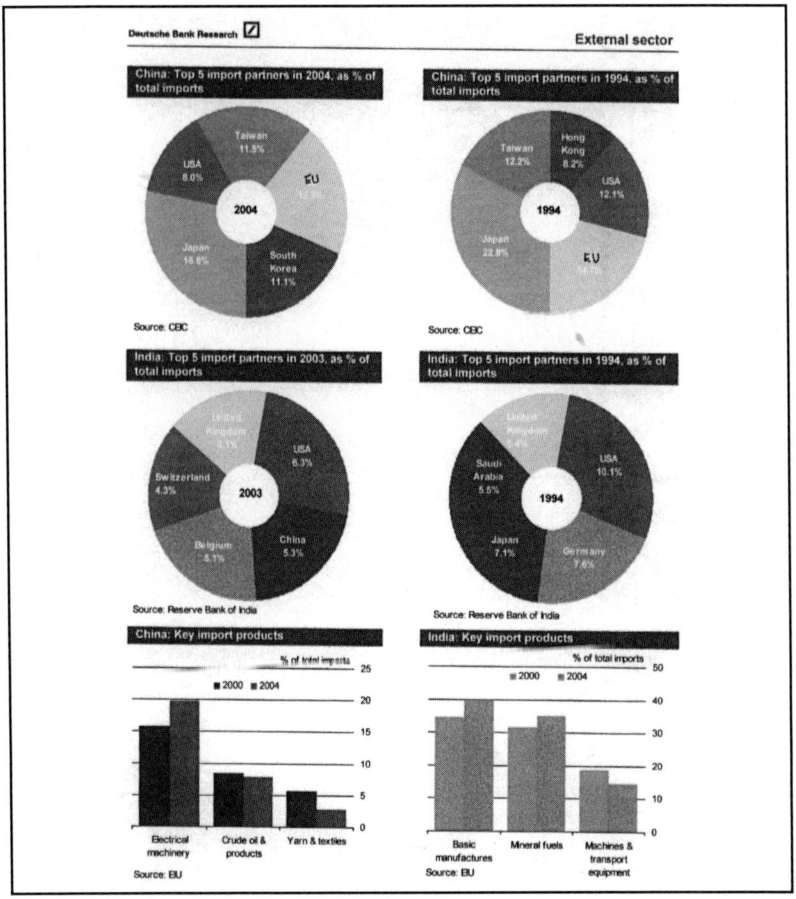

Deutsche Bank Research
External sector
China: Top 5 import partners in 2004, as % of total imports
Taiwan 11.5%
USA 8.0%
EU
2004
Japan 16.8%
South Korea 11.1%
Source: CBC
China: Top 5 import partners in 1994, as % of total imports
Taiwan 12.2%
Hong Kong 8.2%
USA 12.1%
1994
Japan 22.8%
EU
Source: CBC
India: Top 5 import partners in 2003, as % of total imports
USA 6.3%
Switzerland 4.3%
2003
Belgium 5.1%
China 5.3%
Source: Reserve Bank of India
India: Top 5 import partners in 1994, as % of total imports
Saudi Arabia 5.5%
USA 10.1%
1994
Japan 7.1%
Germany 7.6%
Source: Reserve Bank of India
China: Key import products
% of total imports
2000
2004
25
20
15
10
5
0
Electrical machinery
Crude oil & products
Yarn & textiles
Source: EIU
India: Key import products
% of total imports
2000
2004
50
40
30
20
10
0
Basic manufactures
Mineral fuels
Machines & transport equipment
Source: EIU

Table 59: India's Trade with China

Year	Mean	CV	1996-97	1997-98	1998-99	1999-2000	2000=01	2001-02	2002-03	2003-04	2004-05
Trade(USS billion)											
Exports to China			0.6	0.7	0.4	0.5	0.8	0.1	2.0	3.0	5.3
Imports from China			0.8	1.1	1.1	1.3	1.5	2.0	2.8	4.1	6.8
Trade with China			1.4	1.8	1.5	1.8	2.3	3.0	4.8	7.0	12.1
Trade balance	-0.8	-0.5	-0.1	-0.4	-0.7	-0.7	-0.7	-1.1	-0.8	-1.1	-1.4
(percent of trade)	-25%	-0.5	-10%	-22%	-44%	-41%	-29%	-36%	-17%	-16%	-12%
Growth rate											
Export	39%	1.2		17%	-41%	26%	54%	15%	108%	50%	81%
Import	33%	0.6		47%	-1%	17%	17%	36%	37%	45%	76%
Trade	34%	0.8		33%	-17%	20%	28%	28%	60%	47%	73%
Trade share	18%	o.9		27%	-16%	4%	17%	28%	33%	18%	29%
Share in all/total											
Export	2.9%	0.6	1.8%	2.1%	1.3%	1.5%	1.9%	2.2%	3.7%	4.6%	6.6%
Import	3.6%	0.4	1.9%	2.7%	2.6%	2.6%	3.0%	4.0%	4.5%	5.2%	6.2%
Trade	3.3%	o.5	1.9%	2.4%	2.0%	2.1%	2.5%	3.1%	4.2%	4.9%	6.4%

Source: www.dgft.delhi.in,Department of Commerce.

Graph 31: Growth Rate of India's Trade in China

(in percent)

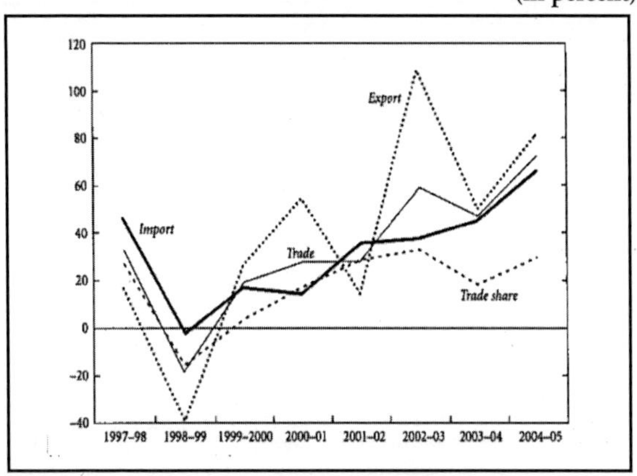

Source: www. dgft.delhi.nic.in. Department of Commerce.

Table 60: Composition of India –China Trade

India's Top 10 Exports to China			India's Top 10 Imports from China		
HS	Commodity	Share	HS	Commodity	Share
26	Ores, Slag, ash	52.1%	85	Electrical machinery and parts	25.6%
72	Iron and steel	11.5%	84	Nuclear reactors boilers, machinery	14.8%
39	Plastic and articles	7.4%	27	Mineral fuels, oils, and waxes	12.0%
29	Organic chemicals	6.5%	29	Organic chemicals	11.7%
28	Inorganic chemicals, compounds	3.9%	50	Silk	4.3%
25	Salt, culphur, lime, cement, etc.	2.6%	71	Pearls, stones, jewelery	2.2%
3	Fish and aquatic invertebrates	1.9%	28	Inorganic chemicals, compounds	2.1%
84	Nuclear reactors, boilers, machinery	1.8%	72	Iron and steel	1.8%
52	Cotton	1.5%	59	Textile fabrics, industrial textiles	1.5%
74	Copper and articles	1.2%	54	Man-made filaments	1.5%

Source: **www.dgft,delhi.nic.in,Department of Commerce.**

Graph 32: China's Share in India's Total Trade

(in percent)

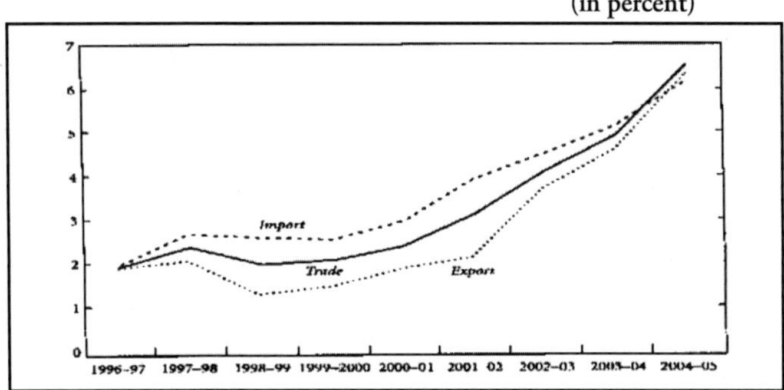

Source: www. dgft.delhi.nic.in. Department of Commerce.

Graph 33: Growth Rate of India's Trade in China

(in percent)

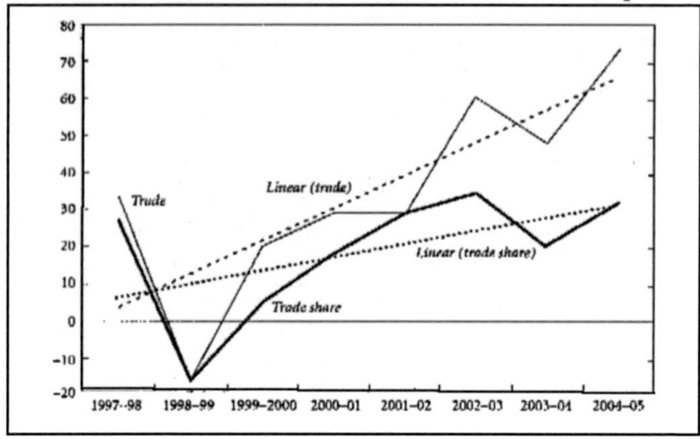

Source: www. dgft.delhi.nic.in. Department of Commerce from Prime, Penelape.

Box 9: Export and Import Statistics

	China	India
Exports	$1.485 trillion f.o.b. (2008)	$187.3 billion f.o.b. (2008)
Exports of Commodities	Electrical and other machinery, including data processing equipment, apparel, textiles, iron and steel, optical and medical equipment.	Petroleum products, textile goods, gems and jewelry, engineering goods, chemicals, leather manufactures.
Export partners 1990	Hong Kong (43.3%); Japan (14.7%); U.S. (8.5%); Germany (3.3%); Singapore (3.2%); Korea (0.7%)	U.S. (15.1%); Japan (9.3%); Germany (7.6%); U.K. (6.2%); Hong Kong (3.1%) Italy (2.8%); UAE (2.6%); PRC (0.1%)
Export partners 2008	U.S. (18.4%); Hong Kong (13.6%); Japan (8.1%); Korea (5.1%); Germany (4.1%)	U.S. (13.1%); PRC (11.1%); UAE (8.9%); Singapore (4.3%); Hong Kong (3.7%); U.K. (3.7)
Imports	$1.191 trillion f.o.b. (2008)	$299.4 billion f.o.b. (2008)
Imports of Commodities	Electrical and other machinery, oil and mineral fuels, optical and medical equipment, metal ores, plastics, organic chemicals	Crude oil, machinery, gems, fertilizer, chemicals
Imports of partners 1990	Japan (14.2%); U.S. (12.2%); Germany (5.5%); Australia (2.5%); Singapore (1.6%); Malaysia (1.6%)	U.S. (11.0%); Germany (7.7%); Japan (7.5%); U.K. (6.9%); UAE (4.0%); Australia (3.2%); Singapore (2.9%)
Import partners 2008	Japan (12.5%); Korea (10.2%); U.S. (6.8%); Germany (4.6%); Australia (3.1%); Malaysia (2.9%)	PRC (11.9%); U.S. (6.9%); Singapore (4.5%); Germany (4.4%); Australia (4.0%); Japan (2.9%); UAE (2.9%); Korea (2.8%)

Source: **CIA World Fact book for major traded commodities and Asia Development Bank, www.adb.org/statistics, for trade partners and trade totals for 2008.**

Graph 34

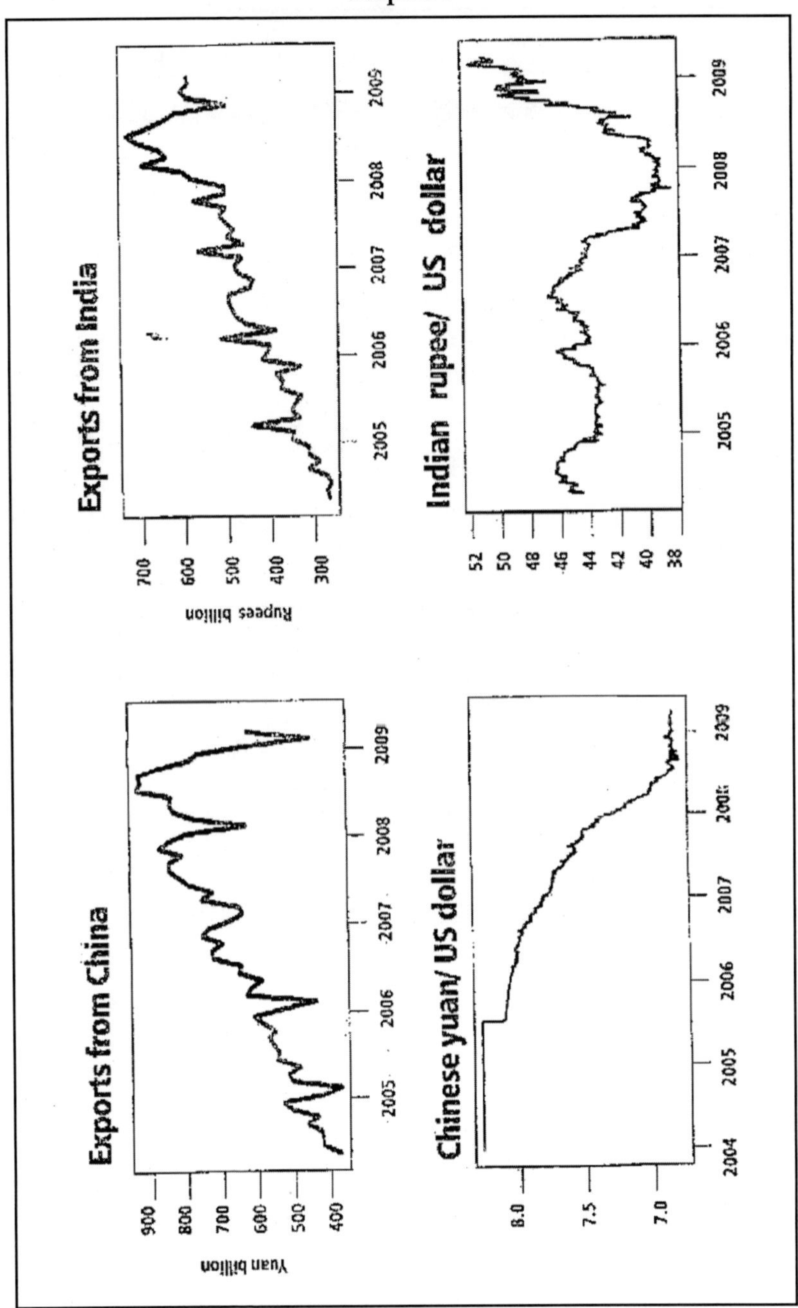
Exports from India
Rupees billion
700
600
500
400
300
2005
2006
2007
2008
2009
Indian rupee/ US dollar
52
50
48
46
44
42
40
38
2005
2006
2007
2008
2009
Exports from China
Yuan billion
900
800
700
600
500
400
2005
2006
2007
2008
2009
Chinese yuan/ US dollar
8.0
7.5
7.0
2004
2005
2006
2007
2009

Chart 19

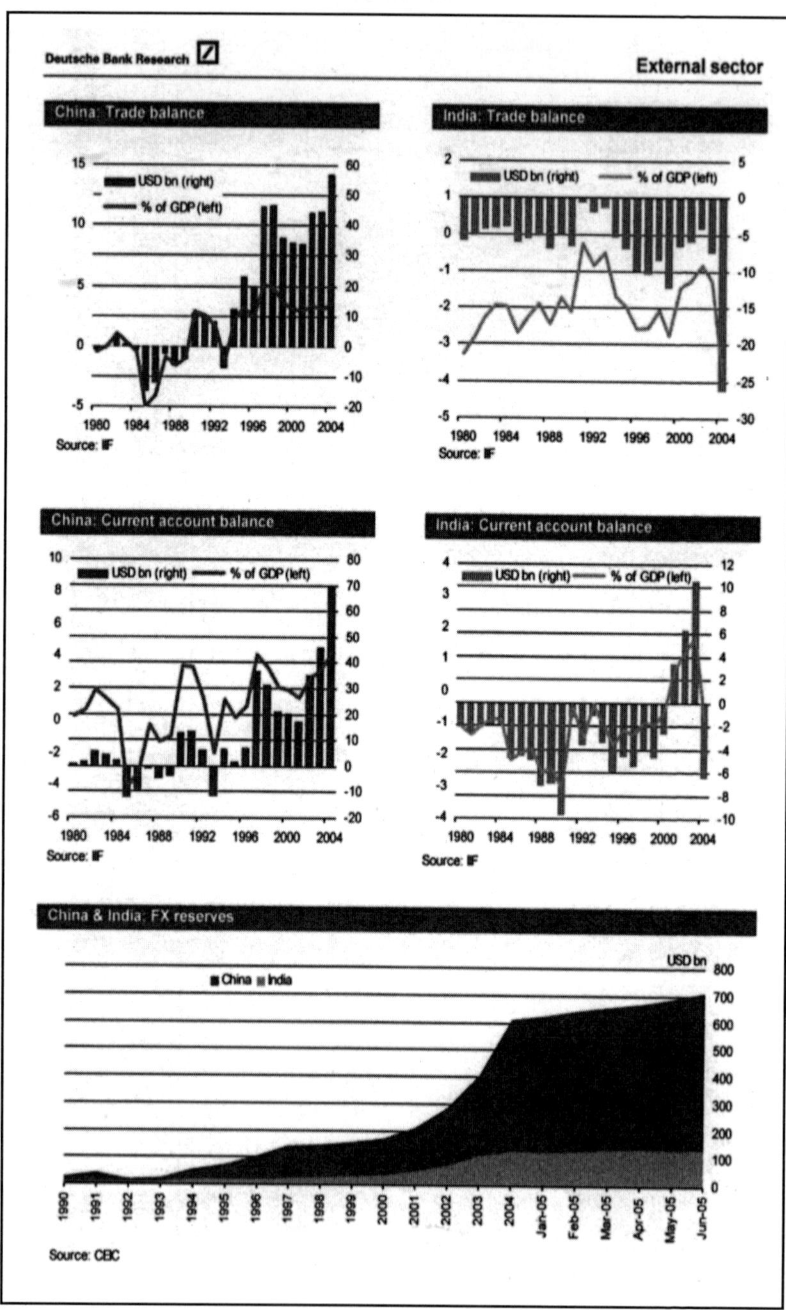
Deutsche Bank Research
External sector
China: Trade balance
USD bn (right)
% of GDP (left)
Source: IIF
India: Trade balance
USD bn (right)
% of GDP (left)
Source: IIF
China: Current account balance
USD bn (right)
% of GDP (left)
Source: IIF
India: Current account balance
USD bn (right)
% of GDP (left)
Source: IIF
China & India: FX reserves
USD bn
China
India
Source: CBC

Table 61: Share of China and India in World Trade

(Per cent)

	1980		1990		2004	
	China	India	China	India	China	India
	World exports					
I. Manufacturing	0.8	0.5	1.9	0.5	8.3	0.9
1. Iron and steel	0.3	0.1	1.2	0.2	5.2	1.6
2. Chemicals	0.8	0.3	1.3	0.4	2.7	0.7
2.1 Pharmaceuticals			1.6[a]	1.2[a]	1.3	1.0[b]
3. Office machines and telecom equip	0.1	n.a	1.0	0.8	15.2	0.6
4. Auto parts	0.0	0.0	0.1	0.1	0.7	0.1
5. Textiles	4.6	2.4	6.9	2.1	17.2	4.0
6. Clothing	4.0	1.7	8.9	2.3	24.0	2.9
II. Commercial services					2.9	1.9
1. Transports					n.a.	n.a.
2. Travel					4.1	n.a.
3. Other					2.4	3.1
	World imports					
I. Manufacturing	1.1	0.5	1.7	0.5	6.3	0.8
1. Iron and steel	2.7	1.0	2.5	1.0	8.2	1.0
2. Chemicals	2.0	n.a	2.2	n.a.	6.5	n.a.
2.1 Pharmaceuticals			0.9[a]	n.a	0.8[a]	n.a.
3. Office machines and telecom equip	0.6	0.2	1.3	0.3	11.2	0.5
4. Auto parts	0.6	0.0	0.6	0.1	1.7	0.3
5. Textiles	1.9	n.a.	4.9	0.2	7.4	0.6[b]
6. Clothing	0.1	0.0	0.0	0.0	0.6	0.0
II. Commercial services			2.5[a]	2.1[a]	3.4	2.0
1. Transports					4.2	2.2
2. Travel					3.3	2.4
3. Other					3.5	2.1

Notes: na = not available, a = pertains to 2000, b = pertains to 2003.
Source: WTO (2005) Tables 1.7, IV 26, IV 27, IV 28, IV 34, IV 39, IV 40, IV 46, IV 47, IV 48, IV 67, IV 68, IV 74, IV 76, IV 83, IV 84, IV 87, IV 90, IV 93.

Table 62: Measures of Integration with the World Economy

		Per Cent of Total		
		1983	1994	2004
Share in GDP of exports of goods and services	China	na	18[1]	34[3]
	India	na	7[1]	19[2]
Share in GDP of imports of goods and services	China	na	16[1]	31[3]
	India	na	9[1]	23[2]

Share in world merchandise exports	China	1.2	2.8	6.7
	India	0.5	0.6	0.8
Share in world merchandise imports	China	1.1	2.6	6.1
	India	0.7	0.6	1.1
Country share in world exports of commercial services	China	na	1.6	2.9
	India	na	0.6	1.9
Country share in world imports of commercial services	China	na	1.5	3.4
	India	na	0.8	2.0

Notes: 1. Shares are for 1990.
2. The figures for India for 2004 do not seem plausible as compared to those in World Bank (2005), Table 4.9 for 2003. National data for fiscal year 2005-06 suggest the shares of exports and imports in GDP at current market prices (factor cost) were respectively 13 per cent (14 per cent) and 18 per cent (19 per cent).
3. The shares of exports and imports were respectively 34 per cent and 31 per cent in 2006 and 38 per cent and 32 per cent in 2006 (Nicholas Lardy, private communication, July 14, 2006).

Sources: 1. For share in GDP, World Bank (2006a), Table 4.8.
2. For shares in world trade, WTO (2005), Tables 1.5 and 1.7.

Table 63: Service Sector Exports and Imports

(USD billion)

	World		China		India	
	Service					
	Exports	Imports	Exports	Imports	Exports	Imports
1991	824.70	850.90	6.86	3.94	4.91	5.80
	(19.00)	(18.98)	(8.71)	(5.81)	(21.67)	(22.09)
1992	924.30	947.10	9.11	9.21	4.89	6.61
	(19.71)	(19.62)	(19.68)	(10.25)	(19.96)	(21.91)
1993	942.00	959.60	10.99	11.56	5.03	6.36
	(19.94)	(19.84)	(10.70)	(10.01)	(18.92)	(21.81)
1994	1033.90	1043.30	16.35	15.78	6.03	8.03
	(19.29)	(19.07)	(11.91)	(12.01)	(19.42)	(23.81)
1995	1183.80	1200.80	18.43	24.63	6.76	10.06
	(18.65)	(18.52)	(11.02)	(15.72)	(18.09)	(22.48)
1996	1270.60	1266.60	20.57	22.37	7.18	11.00
	(19.04)	(18.59)	(11.98)	(13.88)	(17.82)	(22.48)
1997	1319.90	1302.30	24.50	27.72	8.93	12.28
	(19.10)	(18.50)	(11.82)	(16.30)	(20.32)	(22.86)
1998	1351.50	1331.50	23.88	22.47	11.07	14.19
	(19.73)	(18.98)	(11.50)	(15.88)	(24.87)	(24.82)
1999	1406.40	1387.50	26.17	30.97	14.01	17.04
	(19.76)	(18.99)	(11.83)	(15.75)	(28.20)	(26.62)
2000	1493.60	1477.70	30.15	35.86	16.03	18.90
	(18.79)	(18.01)	(10.79)	(13.74)	(27.44)	(26.83)
2001	1498.90	1496.10	32.90	39.03	16.80	19.79
	(19.50)	(18.75)	(11.00)	(13.81)	(27.92)	(28.20)

2002	1608.40	1583.30	39.38	46.08	19.13	20.78
	(19.87)	(19.02)	(10.79)	(13.50)	(27.97)	(26.88)
2003	1842.90	1805.60	46.37	54.85	23.09	25.51
	(19.56)	(18.68)	(9.57)	(11.73)	(28.14)	(26.01)
2004	2212.90	2145.90	62.06	71.60	37.18	36.54
	(19.37)	(18.33)	(9.47)	(11.31)	(32.73)	(26.80)
2005	2458.80	2379.80	73.91	83.17	54.38	49.19
	(19.02)	(18.00)	(8.84)	(11.19)	(35.37)	(26.16)
2006	2755.90	2648.40	91.42	100.33	73.84	63.70
	(18.57)	(17.58)	(8.62)	(11.25)	(38.04)	(26.70)

Note: Figure in parentheses are in percent.
Source: For USED Billion) WTO, Statistic data, Time senses.
(for per cent) WTO, Statistical data, Time series: Derived data.

Table 64:China's and India's Shares of World Exports

	1980		1990		2004	
	China	India	China	India	China	India
	World exports					
I. Manufacturing	0.8	0.5	1.9	0.5	8.3	0.9
1. Iron and steel	0.3	0.1	1.2	0.2	5.2	1.6
2. Chemicals	0.8	0.3	1.3	0.4	2.7	0.7
2.1 Pharmaceuticals			1.6[a]	1.2[a]	1.3	1.0[b]
3. Office machines and telecom equip	0.1	n.a	1.0	0.8	15.2	0.6
4. Auto parts	0.0	0.0	0.1	0.1	0.7	0.1
5. Textiles	4.6	2.4	6.9	2.1	17.2	4.0
6. Clothing	4.0	1.7	8.9	2.3	24.0	2.9
II. Commercial services					2.9	1.9
1. Transports					n.a.	n.a.
2. Travel					4.1	n.a.
3. Other					2.4	3.1

Source: Srinivasan 2006.
Note: n.a. = not available.
a. Pertains to 2000. b. Pertains to 2003.

Table 65: Share of China and India in World Trade

	1980		1990		2004	
	China	India	China	India	China	India
	World imports					
I. Manufacturing	1.1	0.5	1.7	0.5	6.3	0.8
1. Iron and steel	2.7	1.0	2.5	1.0	8.2	1.0
2. Chemicals	2.0	n.a	2.2	n.a.	6.5	n.a.
2.1 Pharmaceuticals			0.9[a]	n.a	0.8[a]	n.a.

3. Office machines and telecom equip	0.6	0.2	1.3	0.3	11.2	0.5
4. Auto parts	0.6	0.0	0.6	0.1	1.7	0.3
5. Textiles	1.9	n.a.	4.9	0.2	7.4	0.6[b]
6. Clothing	0.1	0.0	0.0	0.0	0.6	0.0
II. Commercial services			2.5[a]	2.1[a]	3.4	2.0
1. Transports					4.2	2.2
2. Travel					3.3	2.4
3. Other					3.5	2.1

Source: Srinivasan 2006.
Note: n.a. = not available.
a. Pertains to 2000. b. Pertains to 2003.

Table 66: Industry Exports as a Percentage of Total Exports, China and India

Industry export	1995	2000	2004
China			
Pharmaceutical products	1.1	0.7	0.6
Iron and steel	3.5	1.8	2.3
Electrical equipment	5.9	9.7	10.0
White goods	0.7	1.1	1.3
Road vehicles	1.8	2.6	2.8
Textiles	26.0	21.4	16.2
India			
Pharmaceutical products	2.3	2.8	2.9
Iron and steel	3.0	2.9	6.0
Electrical equipment	1.3	1.8	1.9
White goods	0.0	0.0	0.1
Road vehicles	2.8	2.0	2.8
Textiles	27.0	27.2	17.4

As Athreya and Kapur have noted in their UN University Policy Brief (2009) typically, firms from China and India have only limited technological or ownership advantages to exploit. Rather than exploiting existing assets, their outward FDI may reflect attempts to acquire or augment these assets.

The newfound outward orientation in India and China is noticeable for two of its qualitative aspects. First, the time profile of FDI flows does not conform to the conventional investment development path for developing countries. Traditional theories envisage an initial stage where inward FDI allows developing country firms to acquire technology and other capabilities; they then progress to a stage where they exploit their acquired ability in export markets and only in time to the stage where they invest overseas.

In contrast, both China and India developed their industrial bases through policies of import-substitution without recourse to massive inflows of FDI, China even more so than India. And, for both countries, outward FDI flows have emerged much sooner than expected, whether compared with the trajectory of early industrializing nations or with more recent cases such as South Korea.

Second, traditional patterns suggest that developing country multinationals focus their internationalization activity in economies that are lower down the development ladder. In contrast, and somewhat surprisingly, some of the international investments and acquisitions of Chinese and Indian firms have been in developed economies such as the United Kingdom and the United States. The outward flow of capital from developing countries to acquire assets in developed countries presents a theoretical conundrum. Yet in India the rate of return on capital is surprisingly higher for investments than for overseas ventures in relatively developed economies. To put it simply, the "uphill flow" of capital from labour-rich developing countries to the developed world does not fit textbook economic theory.

The 'fast route' to economic development is via foreign direct investment (FDI), or so it is widely believed. Thus, the ubiquitous "Made in China" label obscures an important point: Few of these products are made by indigenous Chinese companies. In fact, one would be hard-pressed to find a single homegrown Chinese firm that operates on a global scale and markets its own products abroad.

That is because China's export-led manufacturing boom is largely a creation of foreign direct investment (FDI), which effectively serves as a substitute for domestic entrepreneurship. During the last 20 years, the Chinese economy has taken off, but few local firms have followed, leaving the country's private sector with no world-class companies to rival the big multinationals.

But a comparison with India suggests that FDI is not the only path. India's relatively larger homegrown entrepreneurs it is now increasingly held, gives it a long-term advantage over a China, which because of availability of funds from abroad has caused it to be hamstrung by inefficient banks and capital markets. FDI has, as Yasheng Huang pointed out, been a sedative for inefficiency. The MIT Professor also pays high tribute to Indian native enterprise.

India has not attracted anywhere near the amount of FDI that China has. In part, this disparity reflects the confidence international investors have in China's prospects and their skepticism about India's commitment to free-market reforms. But the FDI gap is also a tale of two diasporas. China has a large and wealthy diaspora that has long been eager to help the motherland, and its money has been warmly received. By contrast, the Indian diaspora was, at least until recently, resented for its success and much less willing to invest back home. New Delhi took a dim view of Indians who had gone abroad, and of foreign investment generally and instead provided a more nurturing environment for domestic entrepreneurs.

In the process, India has managed to spawn a number of companies that now compete internationally with the best that Europe and the United States have to offer. Moreover, many of these firms are in the most cutting-edge, knowledge-based industries-software giants Infosys and Wipro and pharmaceutical and biotechnology powerhouses Ranbaxy and Dr. Reddy's Labs, to name just a few. Last year, the Forbes 200, an annual ranking of the world's best small companies, included 13 Indian firms but just four from mainland China.

India has also developed much stronger infrastructure to support private enterprise. Its capital markets operate with greater efficiency and transparency than do China's. Its legal system, while not without substantial flaws, is considerably more advanced.

China and India are the world's next major powers. They also offer competing models of development, one export-led (China) and the other consumption-led (India). It has long been an article of faith that China is on the faster track, and the economic data largely bear this out. The "Hindu rate of growth"-a pejorative phrase to camouflage the Soviet Planning future referring to India's inability to match its economic growth with its population growth-may be a thing of the past, but when it comes to gross domestic product (GDP) figures and other headline numbers, India is still no match for China.

In the macroeconomic statistics, at the micro level, things look quite different. There, India displays every bit as much dynamism as China. Indeed, by relying primarily on home-grown development organic growth, India is making fuller use of its resources and has chosen a path that may well deliver more sustainable progress than China's FDI-driven approach. "Can India surpass China?" is no longer a wild question.

The fact that India is increasingly building from the ground up while China is still pursuing a top-down approach reflects their contrasting political systems: India is a democracy, and China is not. But the different strategies are also a function of history. China's Communist Party came to power in 1949 intent on eradicating private ownership, which it quickly did. Although the country is now in its third decade of free-market reforms, it continues to struggle with the legacy of that period-witness the controversy surrounding the recent decision to officially 'allow' private capitalists to join the Communist Party and thus bring them within party discipline.

Developments at the microeconomic level in China reflect these historical and ideological differences. China has been far bolder with external reforms but has imposed substantial legal and regulatory constraints on indigenous, private firms. In fact, only four years ago, domestic companies were finally granted the same constitutional protections that foreign businesses have enjoyed since the early 1980s. As of the late 1990s, according to the International Finance Corporation, more than two dozen industries, including some of the most important and lucrative sectors of the economy-banking, telecommunications, highways, and railroads-were still off-limits to private local companies.

These restrictions were designed not to keep Chinese entrepreneurs from competing with foreigners but to prevent private domestic businesses from challenging China's state-owned enterprises (SOEs). Some progress has been made in reforming the bloated, inefficient SOEs during the last 20 years, but Beijing is still not willing to relinquish its control over the largest ones, such as China Telecom.

Instead, the government has ferociously protected them from competition. In the 1990s, numerous Chinese entrepreneurs tried, and failed, to circumvent the restrictions placed on their activities. Some registered their firms as nominal SOEs (all the capital came from private sources, and the companies were privately managed), only to find themselves ensnared in title disputes when financially strapped government agencies sought to seize their assets. More than a few promising businesses have been destroyed this way.

This bias against homegrown firms is widely acknowledged. A report issued in 2000 by the Chinese Academy of Social Sciences concluded that, "Because of long-standing prejudices and mistaken beliefs, private and individual enterprises have a lower political status and are discriminated against in numerous policies and regulations. The legal, policy, and market environment is unfair and inconsistent."

Foreign investors have been among the biggest beneficiaries of the constraints placed on local private businesses. One indication of the large payoff they have reaped on the back of China's phenomenal growth: In 1992, the income accruing to foreign investors with equity stakes in Chinese firms was only $5.3 billion; today it totals more than $22 billion. (This money does not necessarily leave the country; it is often reinvested in China.)

For democratic, postcolonial India, allowing foreign investors huge profits at the expense of indigenous firms is simply unfeasible. Recall, for instance, the controversy that erupted a decade ago when the Enron Corporation made a deal with the state of Maharashtra to build a $2.9 billion power plant there. The project proceeded, but only after several years of acrimonious debate over foreign investment and its role in India's development.

While China has created obstacles for its entrepreneurs, India has been making life easier for local businesses. During the last decade, New Delhi has backed away from micromanaging the economy. True, privatization is proceeding at a glacial pace, but the government has ceded its monopoly over long-distance phone service; some tariffs have been cut; bureaucracy has been trimmed a bit; and a number of industries have been opened to private investment, including investment from abroad.

As a consequence, entrepreneurship and free enterprise are flourishing. A measure of the progress: In a recent survey of leading Asian companies by the Far Eastern Economic Review (FEER), India registered a higher average score than any other country in the region, including China (the survey polled over 2,500 executives and professionals in a dozen countries; respondents were asked to rate companies on a scale of one to seven for overall leadership performance). Indeed, only two Chinese firms had scores high enough to qualify for India's top 10 list. Tellingly, all of the Indian firms were wholly private initiatives, while most of the Chinese companies had significant state involvement.

Some of the leading Indian firms are true start-ups, notably Infosys, which topped FEER's survey. Others are offshoots of old-line companies. Sundaram Motors, for instance, a leading manufacturer of automotive components and a principal supplier to General Motors, is part of the T.V.Sundaram group, a century-old south Indian business group that has been winning over several years the Deming Prize instituted in Japan for high quality.

Not only is entrepreneurship thriving in India; some hi-tech entrepreneurs there have become folk heroes. Pro-Soviet intellectuals in India are appalled at the adulation the Indian public now showers on captains of industry. For instance, Narayana Murthy, the 56-year-old founder of Infosys, is often compared to Microsoft's Bill Gates and has become a revered figure. Profit is no more a bad word, although philanthropy has yet to keep apace.

These success stories never would have happened if India lacked the infrastructure needed to support Murthy and other would-be moguls. But democracy, a tradition of entrepreneurship, and a decent legal system have given India the underpinnings necessary for free enterprise to flourish. Although India's courts are notoriously inefficient, they at least comprise a functioning independent judiciary. Property rights are not fully secure, but the protection of private ownership is certainly far stronger than in China. The rule of law, a legacy of British rule, generally prevails.

These traditions and institutions have proved an excellent springboard for the emergence and evolution of India's capital markets. Distortions are still commonplace, but the stock and bond markets generally allow firms with solid prospects and reputations to obtain the capital they need to grow. In a World Bank study published last year, only

52 percent of the Indian firms surveyed reported problems obtaining capital, versus 80 percent of the Chinese companies polled. As a result, the Indian firms relied much less on internally generated finances: Only 27 percent of their funding came through operating profits, versus 57 percent for the Chinese firms.

Corporate governance has improved dramatically, thanks in no small part to Murthy, who has made Infosys a paragon of honest accounting and an example for other firms. In a survey of 25 emerging market economies conducted in 2000 by Credit Lyonnais Securities Asia, India ranked sixth in corporate governance, China 19th. The advent of an investor class, coupled with the fact that capital providers, such as development banks, are themselves increasingly subject to market forces, has only bolstered the efficiency and credibility of India's markets. Apart from providing the regulatory framework, the Indian government has taken a back seat to the private sector.

In China, by contrast, bureaucrats remain the gatekeepers, tightly controlling capital allocation and severely restricting the ability of private companies to obtain stock market listings and access the money they need to grow. Indeed, Beijing has used the financial markets mainly as a way of keeping the organizations afloat. These policies have produced enormous distortions while preventing China's markets from gaining depth and maturity. (It is widely claimed that China's stock markets have a total capitalization in excess of $400 billion, but factoring out non-tradeable shares owned by the government or by government-owned companies reduces the valuation to just around $150 billion.) Compounding the problem are poor corporate governance and the absence of an independent judiciary.

If India has so clearly surpassed China at the grass-roots level, why isn't India's superiority reflected in the numbers? Why is the gap in GDP and other benchmarks still so wide? It is worth recalling that India's economic reforms only began in earnest in 1991, more than a decade after China began liberalizing. In addition to the late start, India has had to make do with a national savings rate half that of China's and 90 percent less FDI. Moreover, India is a sprawling, messy democracy riven by ethnic and religious tensions, and it has also had a longstanding, volatile dispute with Pakistan over Kashmir. China, on the other hand, has enjoyed two decades of relative tranquility; apart from Tiananmen Square, it has been able to focus almost exclusively on economic development.

That India's annual growth rate is only around 20 percent lower than China's is, then, a remarkable achievement. And, of course, whether the data for China are accurate is an open question.

The speed with which India is catching up is due to its own efficient deployment of capital and China's inefficiency, symbolized by all the money that has been frittered away on SOEs. And China's misallocation of resources is likely to become a big drag on the economy in the years ahead.

Graph 35

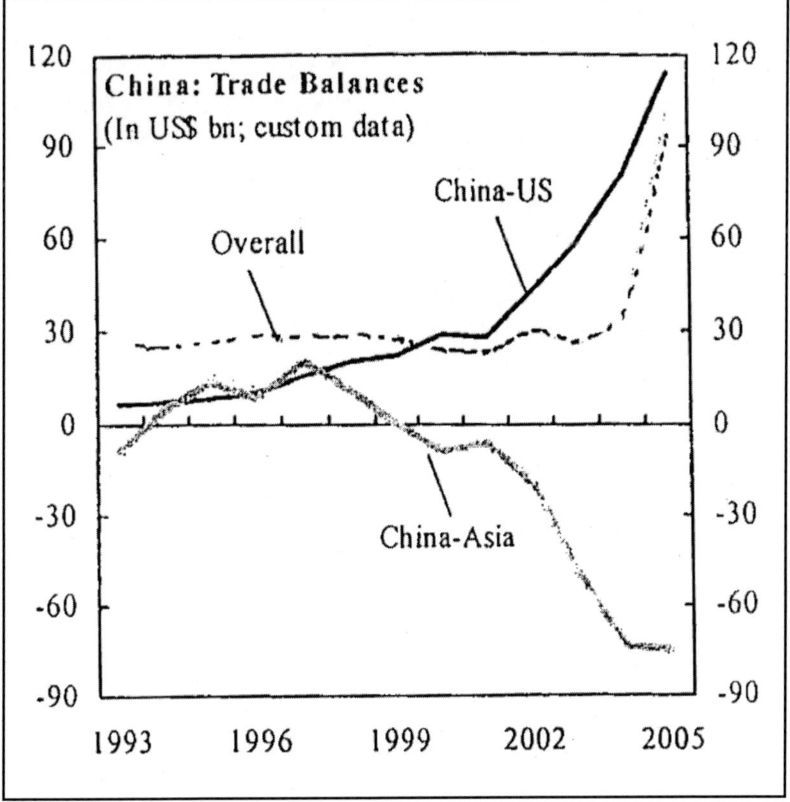

Table 67: Geographic Origin of China's imports, various years

Percent

Origin	1995	2000	2003	2004
Asia	47.1	50.6	66.1	65.8
ASEAN	7.4	9.8	11.5	11.2
Japan	21.9	18.4	18.0	16.8
Korea, Rep. of	7.8	10.3	10.4	11.1
Taiwan, China	11.2	11.3	12.0	11.5
European Union	17.0	13.7	13.2	12.5
United States	12.1	9.9	8.2	8.0

Source: **For 1995 and 2000, Rumbaugh and Blancher 2003; for 2003 and 2004, National Bureau of Statistic of China, *China Statistical, 2005.***

In the early 1990s, when China was registering double-digit growth rates, Beijing invested massively in the state sector. Most of the investments were not commercially viable, leaving the banking sector with a huge number of nonperforming loans-possibly totaling as much as 50 percent of bank assets. At some point, the capitalization costs of these loans will have to be absorbed, either through write-downs (which means depositors bear the cost) or recapitalization of the banks by the government, which diverts money from other, more productive uses. This could well limit China's future growth trajectory.

India's banks may not be models of financial probity, but they have not made mistakes on nearly the same scale. According to a recent study by the management consulting firm Ernst & Young, about 15 percent of banking assets in India were nonperforming as of 2001. India's economy is thus anchored on more solid footing.

China's development strategy has been to pull the economy by exports, and use the imports and Joint ventures for transfer and/or augmentation of technology. It has worked so far very well for China.

However the sustainability of China's export-oriented growth over the medium to longer term is of concern. It would require for example, significant gains in market share through lower prices in a range of industries to keep it going. Thus, in turn, could be achieved through a combination of increases in productivity, lower profits, and higher implicit or explicit subsidies to industry.

The evidence of Guo and N'Diaye (2009) suggest that it will prove difficult to accommodate such price reductions within existing profit margins or through productivity gains. Instead moving up the value-added chain, shifting the composition of exports, diversifying the export base, and increasing domestic value added of exports is required for further export expansion. This is a tall order. Experiences from other East Asian economies that had similar export-oriented growth suggest there are limits to the global market share a country can occupy. Thus, rebalancing growth toward private consumption is the only option China has over the next decade (2010-2020).

As [Guo an N'Diaye, (2009)] in their study infer, there is a growing sense that China's export-oriented growth will be difficult to sustain over the medium to longer term and that shifting toward a more consumption-based economy, where the nontradable sector plays a larger role than it does now, would be a more viable alternative.

A successful rebalancing of China's growth will require action on several fronts, including structural reforms (to level the playing field between the tradable and the nontradable sector, opening up further the economy to foreign competition, etc.), developing the domestic financial market, and increasing government spending on health and education.

It has been argued [Swamy (2003]] that China's rising influence and clout in world markets may be overstated because a significant portion reflect processing trade.

More importantly China's trade comprises two rather different components: (1) imports that is processed and re-exported and (2) "domestic" or "own" trade, i.e., exports of goods primarily originating in the domestic economy, and imports for domestic consumption and production use, The former reflects China's rising role as a labour-intensive processing and assembly centre, fueled by outsourcing and external final demand, while the latter is more strongly influenced by domestic economic trends.

If we divide China trade into its component parts, we find two very revealing trends, as Figure .... reveals. The current trade surplus is due completely to the positive balance on processing trade, i.e., value added in China before re-exporting to final—destination markets, which reached,

US$40 bn last year—At the same time, China's own domestic trade is increasingly in deficit, with the balance declining from a positive level of nearly US$20 bn in 1998 to a deficit of the same magnitude in 2001 [**See Graph below**}.

The primary driver of this deficit has been rapidly growing domestic imports, which more than doubled over the last three years compared with domestic export growth of only 50%—a testament to the strength of ongoing import liberalization and domestic demand growth in China.

Graph 36: Expanding horizons

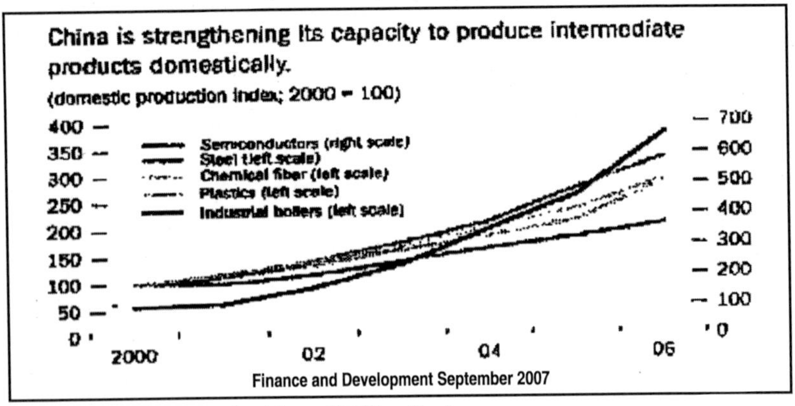

China is strengthening its capacity to produce intermediate products domestically.
(domestic production index; 2000 = 100)
Semiconductors (right scale)
Steel (left scale)
Chemical fiber (left scale)
Plastics (left scale)
Industrial boilers (left scale)
400
350
300
250
200
150
100
50
0
700
600
500
400
300
200
100
0
2000
02
04
06
Finance and Development September 2007

Source: CEC, Chinese authorities and IMF staff estimates.

Chart 20: Greater domestic content

China is increasingly using domestic materials in its processing operations.
(Percent of total processing trade)
(per cent)
Margin of processing with imported materials (right scale)
Share of processing with imported materials (left scale)
100
90
80
70
60
50
50
40
30
20
10
0
1993
94
95
96
97
98
99
2000
01
02
03
04
05
06

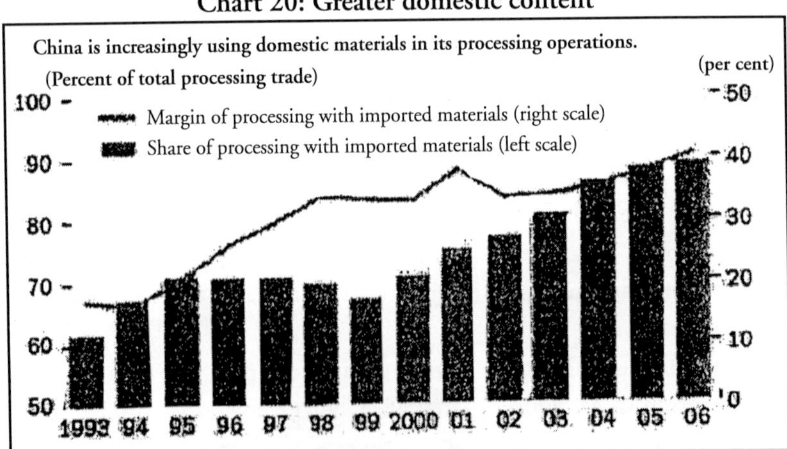

Source: CEIC, Chinese authorities and IMF staff calculations. The domestic value added for each dollar exported or the trade balance divided by exports.

Chart 21: Shifting export structure

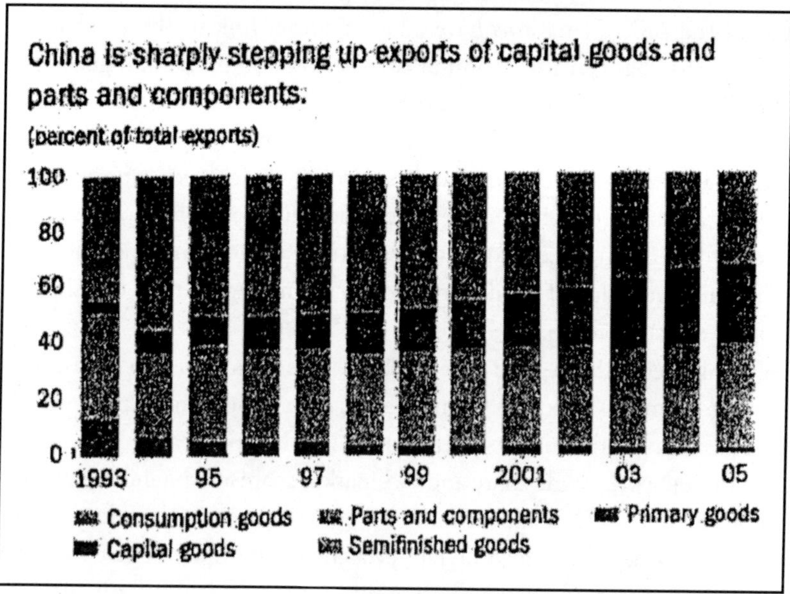

Source: CEIC: Chinese authorities; and IMF staff calculations.

Chart 22: Technological upgrade

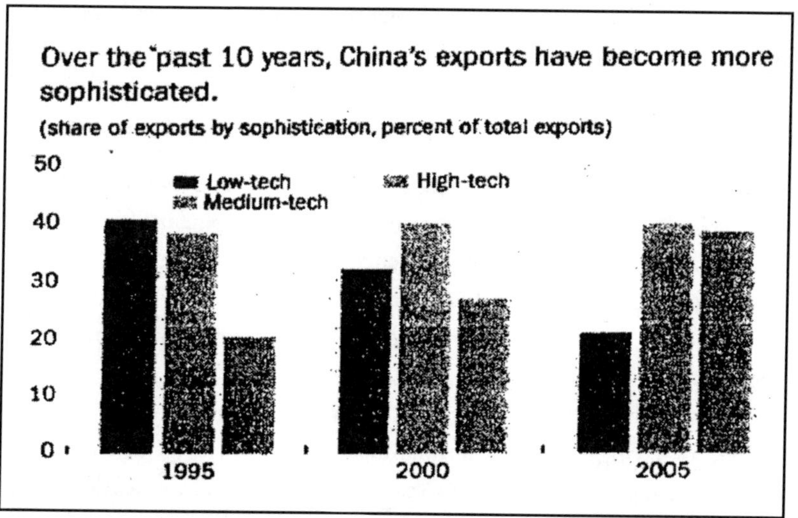

Source: CEIC: Chinese authorities; and IMF staff calculations.

Over the past 15 years, the opening of the Chinese economy and the rise of the ASEAN nations have added another link to the production 'chain' that changed the region al division of labour. Capital goods are now shipped from Japan to economies like Taiwan and Korea, which in turn send semi-finished or processed capital-intensive inputs to China for labour-intensive processing and assembly before re-exporting to developed markets. Thus, each time a new link is added to the Asian production chain, recorded infra-Asian trade value jumps significantly, while the final value of goods exported to end markets outside of Asia may not have risen at all.

This means that a good part of China's rapid trade growth is, in effect, 'double-counting'. Because China records high import and export growth and has become the main exporter to the G3, it appears as though China is grabbing world trade share and US market share at a phenomenal pace while the Asian NICs appear to be losing out. Over the last decade, the Chinese mainland has recorded an ever-increasing trade deficit with the Asian NICs, and an ever-increasing and a bigger surplus with the US, giving China an over all surplus in the balance of payments.

This, then, makes China vulnerable to challenge from India, which could, *ceteris paribus,* substitute for China in this chain. Hence amity and collaboration between China and India is to both's mutual advantage. But then there is an urgent need for China to rely less on export-led growth and engage in re-balancing its economy.

Re-balancing Indian and Chinese economies for sustained global growth

To assess the need for re-balancing of the economic strategy of India and China, C.P. Chandrasekhar and Jayanti Ghosh *Business Line* (news daily) have examined the long-term evidence on manufacturing in the two economies. The need is to help correct global imbalances while sustaining global growth, and reduce external account deficits in countries burdened with them such as the U.S.

From their study, it appears that this rebalancing is required more in China, as having sustained its manufacturing growth by acting as the manufacturing export hub and sweat shop for Asia and the world. India, on the other hand, has been a services exporter, while its manufacturing sector grows largely on domestic demand, and at a lower, though significant rate.

Statistics analysed over the three time periods 1980-89, 1990-96 and 1997-2003, reveal that total manufacturing value added in China grew at compound rates of 8.1, 11.8 and 14.1 per cent respectively in the case of China, whereas the corresponding figures for India were 5.6, 8.7 and 4.7 per cent. While India's manufacturing growth was much lower than that of China's, it was significant and relatively stable even after the Asian crisis of 1997.

According to Chandrasekhar and Ghosh, an index of *home market dependence* is the proportion of internal flows (defined as production minus exports) in total production, which is presented here for three digit level industries for the three periods defined above [**see table below**].

Chart 23: China: Rate of growth of Value Added (1997-2003)*

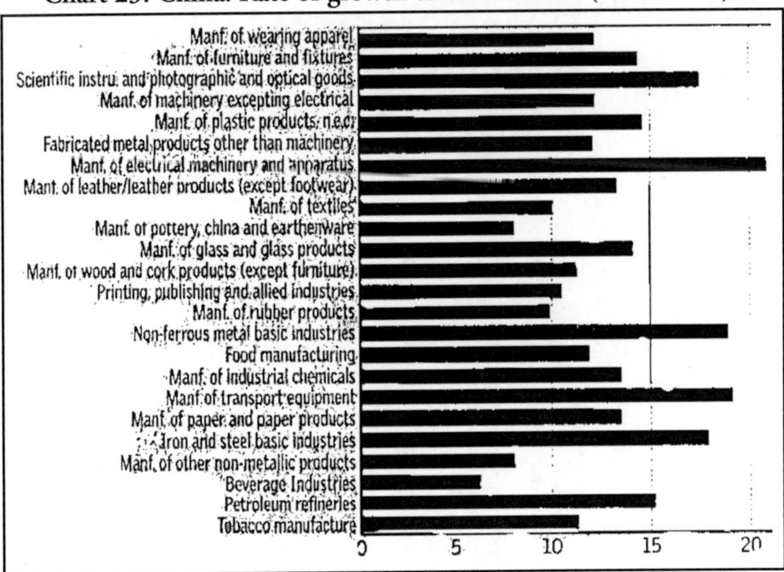

*by industries ranked according to export market dependence (%).

From the this Table we see that China's manufacturing sector during the 1980s was based almost wholly on the domestic market (except for the wearing apparel sector).

Table 68

China: Average internal flow by industry (%)	19080 to 1989	1990 to 1996	1997 to 2003
322: Manufacture of wearing apparel	44.4	– 48.0	– 48.3
332: Manufacture of furniture and fixtures	914	516	126
385: Scientific instruments and photographic and optical goods	95.9	65.3	39.3
382: Manf. of machinery excepting electrical	99.0	88.4	47.4
356: Manufacture of plastic products, n.e.c.	94.8	66.5	58.2
381: Fabricated metal products other than machinery	95.0	79.3	60.3
383: Manf. of electrical machinery and apparatus	99.5	71.5	64.3
323: Manufacture of leather and leather products (except footwear)	83.6	57.0	66.5
321: Manufacture of textiles	89.3	75.8	67.0
361: Manufacture of pottery, China and earthenware	93.8	82.6	75.9
362: Manufacture of glass and glass products	98.3	91.7	79.2
331: Manufacture of wood and cork products (except furniture)	97.3	85.7	79.3
342: Printing, publishing and allied industries	99.4	94.5	83.8
355: Manufacture of rubber products	99.2	96.2	87.9
372: Non-ferrous metal basic industries	95.9	91.1	88.0
311: Food manufacturing	92.8	88.5	88.8
351: Manufacture of industrial chemicals	95.1	91.9	91.9
384: Manufacture of transport equipment	98.8	96.0	92.8
341: Manufacture of paper and paper products	97.8	96.0	93.8
371: Iron and steel basic industries	98.5	94.6	94.3
369: manufacture of other non-metallic products	99.3	97.3	95.1
313: Beverage industries	98.2	97.6	97.8
353: petroleum refineries	88.2	95.5	98.0
314: Tobacco manufacture	99.8	97.5	99.2
352: Manufacture of other chemical products	96.1		
354: Misc. products of petroleum and coal	99.6	99.7	

India: Average Internal Flow (%)	1980 - 1989	1990 - 1996	1997 - 2003
322: Manufacture of wearing apparel	–53.9	–86.2	–76.0
323: Manufacture of leather and leather products (except footwear)	74	–29.4	–30.4
321: Manufacture of textiles	90.4	78.2	676
381: Fabricated metal products other than machinery	90.2	81.0	71.5
390: Other manufacturing industries	89.0	82.6	72.7
362: Manufacture of glass and glass products	95.6	88.5	79.0
351: Manufacture of industrial chemicals	96.7	88.6	81.3
385: Scientific instruments and photographic and optical goods	93.8	88.4	82.9
382: Manf. of machinery excepting electrical	95.1	90.8	83.7
331: Manufacture of wood and cork products (except furniture)	92.9	85.2	84.5
355: Manufacture of rubber products	97.7	91.9	86.0
352: Manufacture of other chemical products	97.9	94.5	87.8
383: Manufacture of electrical machinery and apparatus	98.3	95.6	89.9
311: Food manufacturing	94.9	91.4	91.2
369: Manufacture of other non-metallic products	99.0	95.3	91.7
384: Manufacture of transport equipment	95.8	93.3	92.4
342: Printing, publishing and allied industries	98.7	97.6	94.8
356: Manufacture of plastic products, n.e.c.	98.3	95.2	95.6
341: Manufacture of paper and paper products	99.6	98.1	95.7
354: Misc. products of petroleum and coal	100.0	99.9	97.3
314: Tobacco manufacture	97.8	98.3	98.2
353: Petroleum refineries	96.8	96.3	98.6
313: Beverage industries	87.8	98.9	99.1
332: Manufacture of furniture of fixtures	86.4	–8.3	
361: Manufacture of pottery, China and earthenware	97.8	91.1	
371: Iron and steel basic industries	98.8	93.7	
372: Non-ferrous metal basic industries	98.1	94.8	

But there were a number of sectors in which there was a sharp decrease in the share of domestic sales in production both during the first half of the 1990s and in the period after the 1997 East Asian financial crisis. This increase in the share of exports could not have been directed at crisis-affected Asia, and hence it points to the importance of developed countries' markets for Chinese exports. In the case of wearing apparel, the internal flow figure in fact turns negative, possibly because of the importance of re-exports in this sector.

Third, the industries of China that were the most export dependent consisted of a combination of traditional export sectors and new sectors such as scientific instruments and photographic equipment, manufacture of electrical and non-electrical machinery, and the manufacture of plastic products. This diverse structure tallies with the notion that China had become an exporter of high-tech manufactures as well, even if this was mainly because of the role of foreign firms.

Finally, it emerges that of the 24 three-digit industries for which data was available for the last period (1997-2003), there were only seven for which less than a third of the output was being diverted away from the home market on account of exports.

That is, it can be said that China's manufacturing growth was largely and significantly export-led. If we examine the rank of the leading exporting industries in terms of the rate of growth of value added in the three periods, it can be argued that the more export-dependent sectors were driving manufacturing growth (Chart 1), though not necessarily in rank.

The home market appears more important when we examine 'apparent' consumption, *defined* as production minus exports plus imports, since imports both feed into domestic production within individual industries as well as cater directly to consumption in an increasingly liberalized environment. This is the phenomenon of semi-processed imports from East Asia.

The ratio of apparent consumption, which is a proxy for domestic demand, to production, which is significantly high in a large number of industries, strengthens the impression that the home market has been an important element in China's export growth. The implication of this should be clear. China's presence in global markets and the volume of and rate of growth of its manufactured exports do imply that China's growth is overwhelmingly driven by exports.

This has consequences for internal "rebalancing" in China, because a reduction in the investment rate and an increase in the share of consumption in GDP, would expand the domestic market and accelerate growth, even as the foreign reserves would reduce. But the rebalancing will sustain China's growth while redistributing its benefits in favour of workers and peasants.

Nevertheless, since the demand for manufacturers is from both investment and consumption, redistributing from one to the other may not make too much of a difference to aggregate manufacturing demand. Since investment is substantially in infrastructure, it generates direct and indirect demand for manufactured goods. Hence redistributing national output in favour of consumption is unlikely in itself to raise the level of manufacturers demand. This may make China's growth less dependent on exports at the margin, but it need not imply any net increase in the rest of the world's exports to China.

In the case of India, there were fewer industries characterized by substantial export dependence during 1997-2003 (**Table**). In fact there were only three industries in whose case the level of exports exceeded or was near a third of production. And all of these were traditional industries like wearing apparel, leather and the production of textiles. In most three-digit industries, exports were less than a fifth or a tenth of production. But the fact that domestic production caters largely to domestic consumption does not mean that there is no space for imports.

Unlike in the case of China, in a very large number of industries, apparent consumption which takes into account imports was significantly higher than domestic production, pointing to the role of imports in servicing domestic productive or final consumption.

This is a consequence of liberalization, of the demand for imported luxuries resulting from income inequality and of the inability of Indian producers to compete with their foreign counterparts in certain markets. The result is that manufactured imports do and will continue to service domestic consumption in India.

Thus, if growth remains high in India, more so if it accelerates, it would have a positive effect on the global economy by drawing on its production. India, then rather than China, has the characteristics needed to serve as an engine of growth for other countries.

Moreover, India unlike China, runs trade and current accounts deficits in its balance of payments with the West, whereas China runs large surpluses that underlie the global imbalances. This is an additional reason for India being a bigger factor in powering world growth.

The real issue, of course, isn't where China and India are today but where they will be tomorrow. The answer will be determined in large measure by how well both countries innovate and utilize their resources accordingly, and on this score, India is presently doing a relatively superior job. Is it pursuing a better road to development than China? We won't know the answer for many years. However, some evidence indicates that India's ground-up approach may indeed be wiser-and the evidence for that view, ironically, comes from within China itself.

Consider the contrasting strategies of Jiangsu and Zhejiang, two coastal provinces that were at similar levels of economic development when China's reforms began. Jiangsu has relied largely on FDI to fuel its growth. Zhejiang, by contrast, has placed heavier emphasis on indigenous entrepreneurs and organic development. During the last two decades, Zhejiang's economy has grown at an annual rate of about 1 percent faster than Jiangsu's. Twenty years ago, Zhejiang was the poorer of the two provinces; now it is unquestionably more prosperous. India may soon have the best of both worlds: It looks poised to reap significantly more FDI in the coming years than it has attracted to date due to its world class human capital in cutting edge technological sectors, and yet it has laid emphasis in home consumption led growth..

But for that to continue to happen in India, it has to do better in R&D despite its demonstrated capacity to produce islands of excellence in innovation and individual endeavours. In the Patents area, for example, India has fallen behind China.

The Indian Patent Office ranks 9th in the number of patents filed and 12th in the number of patents granted, according to the World Intellectual Property Organisation's (WIPO) latest data.

The total number of patents filed in India amounted to 28,940, according to the Geneva based organisation's recently released World Intellectual Property Indicators-2009 report.

This was behind the US (4,56,154), Japan (3,96,291), China (2,45,161), the Republic of Korea (1,72,469), European, Patent Office (1,40,763), Germany (60,992), Canada (40,131) and the Russian Federation (39,439).

In terms of the number of patents granted, India (at 7,539) stood behind Japan (1,64,954), the US (1,57,283), the Republic of Korea (1,23,705), China (67,948), European Patent Office (54,699), the Russian Federation (23,028), Canada (18,550), Germany (17,739), France (12,112), Australia (11,236) and Mexico (9,957). The WIPO-compiled data pertains to 2007.

What is significant about India, however, is not just its overall ranking, but also the fact that a majority of patents filed and granted by it was to non-residents (whether companies or individuals). Thus, of the 28,940 patents filed in the country, as many as 23,626 (82 per cent) were by non-residents. This was unlike China, where 1,53,060 out of the total 2,45,161 (62 per cent) patents filed originated from resident applicants.

Table 69: Inventions Patented

	[2006]	
	Patents	
	Filed	Granted
The US	4,56,154	1,57,283
Japan	3,96,291	1,64,954
China	2,45,161	67,948
The Republic of Korea	1,72,469	1,23,705
European Patent Office	1,40,763	54,699
Germany	60,992	17,739
Canada	40,131	18,550
The Russian Federation	39,439	23,028
India	28,940	7,539

Indeed, if one looks at purely resident patent filings, India's ranking falls to 11th (5,314), behind Japan (3,33,498), the US (2,41,347), China

(1,53,060), the Republic of Korea (1,28,701), Germany (47,853), the Russian Federation (27,505), the United Kingdom (17,375), France (14,722), Italy (9,255) and North Korea (6,922).

In terms of resident patent grants, India (at 1,907) stands at the 13th place, behind Japan (1,40,040), the Republic of Korea (91,645), the US (79,527), China (31,945), the Russian Federation (18,431), Germany (12,977), France (9,748), Italy (5,257), North Korea (4,235), Ukraine (2,505), Spain (2,325) and the UK (2,058).

The substantial increase in patent filings by China and the Republic of Korea is a major development of the last 10 years or so.

In fact, for the first time, a Chinese company - Huawei Technologies - topped the list of applicants to have filed patent applications through the Patent Cooperation Treaty (PCT) in 2008.

The Chinese telecom equipment major made 1,737 filings under the PCT, which is a WIPO-administered agreement (to which India is also a signatory) that enables patent protection for any invention simultaneously in a number of countries by filing a single 'international application' with a single patent office.

Huawei filed more PCT applications last year than Japan's Panasonic Corporation (1,729), the Netherlands' Philips (1,551), Japan's Toyo-ta (1,364), Germany's Robert Bosch (1,273) and Siemens (1,089), Finland's Nokia (1,005), Korea's LG (992), Sweden's Ericsson (984), Japan's Fujitsu (983), Qualcomm of the US (907), Japan's NEC (825) and Sharp (814), Microsoft (805) and Motorola (778) of the US, Sweden's BASF (721), 1MB (664) and 3M (663) of the US, Korea's Samsung (639) and Dupont of the US (517). *Not a single Indian company features in this list.*

Bilateral Trade between India and China

In terms of total bilateral trade, the flows between the two economies have increased since 1991, accelerating rapidly after 2001(**see figure below.**). When Chinese Premier Wen Jiabao visited India in April 2005, he set a goal of $30 billion in bilateral trade between the two countries by 2010. Clearly it is already well beyond that. Total trade between the two countries was $264 million in 1991 and increased gradually to $7.6 billion in 2003. By 2008, bilateral trade had reached $55 billion.

Although both countries have been shown to have a revealed comparative advantage in similar manufactured goods at the global level, the majority of India's exports to China are intermediate industrial goods and primary products (especially iron ore), whereas China sells an increasing amount of manufactured equipment to India. But it is not all smooth just yet.

In fact, India leads all members of the World Trade Organization (WTO) in the number of antidumping cases it has filed against China in its domestic market. It has banned imports of Chinese toys, milk, and chocolate, citing safety concerns, and has launched investigations into China's exports of truck tires, chemicals, and power equipment. In recent years, India's trade deficit has grown with China. In the background, there also are strategic concerns, ranging from the border issue to China's foray into Indians backyard with its development assistance to Pakistan, Thailand, Bangladesh, and Myanmar. In general, however, the geostrategic relations between the two countries have improved sufficiently to allow for a blossoming bilateral economic relationship.

In recent years, the speed at which the commercial relationship between the two of the world's fastest growing economies has grown has been impressive. A decade ago, bilateral trade between India and China stood at a paltry few million dollars. Today, China is India's largest trading partner. In 2001, bilateral trade between India and China stood at US$ 2billion. In 2008 the figure crossed $52 billion, and has in the last decade grown at a stunning 50 per cent a year. Trade has so far has been largely driven by the huge demand for Chinese machinery from India's fast-developing manufacturing sector, and China's growing demand for 'raw materials, chiefly metal ores. Now, business in India and China need to the relationship to the next level. More and more Indian companies in sectors like banking, IT and manufacturing are setting up shop in China and ready to take on the Chinese market. And, in equal measure, Chinese investments in India are surging, from infrastructure projects to telecommunications.

The biggest names in Indian software and education, from NIIT and Infosys to Tata Consultancy Services and Wipro, have all begun making inroads into the Chinese market in the last two years. In a major watershed for Indian IT in China, TCS was recently awarded a $100million contract to provide IT services for the Bank of China. The floodgates, many say, have now been opened. Perhaps the biggest success story has been that of NIIT, the IT educator. The success of NIIT is lesson for any company on how to tackle the Chinese market. Through a brilliant strategy of local tie-ups and localisation, the company has built an impressive network in China. By 2011, NIIT will produce more Chinese IT graduates than all of China's universities combined.

Other sectors are not far behind. In manufacturing, many Indian companies have been sourcing parts for China, particularly in the Auto sector. In 2005, Sundram Fasteners of the TVS opened a new page by launching its impressive state-of-the-art facility in Zhejiang province. Now, No.1 Sundram Road in Wuyuan town in Zhejiang has in recent years been shipping out high-tensile fasteners, bearing housings and other supplies to a range of overseas customers as well as multi-national companies such as John Deer that operate out of China.

China's reform policies, launched three decades ago. has also gradually paved the way for Indian companies to lend their expertise in other sectors, such as banking. India's largest bank, the State Bank of India, which has 130 overseas branches, has opened a branch in Shanghai that has provided invaluable services by fostering the expanding trade; between the growing number of Indian businesses in China's prosperous south-east. In addition to its Shanghai branch, SBI has also opened a representative office in the northern industrial city of Tianjin; and has also opened two branches in Hong Kong. Mutual investment between the two countries is also Son the fast track. India has become an increasingly important destination for Chinese companies, which have in recent years secured contracts from infrastructure projects to manufacturing to the tune of $26 billion.

Telecom major ZTE, which has been in India since 1999, has established a major presence here, providing state of the art telecom equipment to Indian customers. ZTE's unprecedented success in India has created waves in China, encouraging more Chinese companies to turn their sights to India. ZTE's sales revenue in India has rapidly grown, to $650 million in 2008 up from $ 100 million in 2004. The company aims to cross $ 1 billion this year. Telecom giant Huawei is poised to expand its already significant presence in the Indian market. The global giant recorded an impressivel00% revenue growth last year, and is targeting doubling its India revenues. Huawei has an impressive Research and Development Centre in Bangalore, where it employs more than 2,000 young professionals.

A shining example of the success of Indian enterprise in China is the success story of NIIT. The well-known IT training and software solutions provider has enjoyed unprecedented success in the Chinese market, and has become a well-recognised brand among Chinese professionals. By 2011, NIIT, remarkably, will be producing more IT graduates than all of China's universities combined. Starting with only two centres in the commercial hub of Shanghai in 1997, Today, NIIT has 183 cooperative education and training sites across 25 provinces and cities in China, an unmatched national presence. NIIT currently trains more than 50,000 Chinese students in software skills every year, and has become the unrivalled choice among Chinese students looking • for an IT education. The company, which has fostered close relationships with every software company in China, has a 100 per cent placement record. By next year, NIIT will be training 100 students a day.

NIIT, leading Global Talent Development Corporation and Asia's largest IT trainer, was recently honoured for its contribution to the IT Training industry in China, by the Chinese Society of Educational Development Strategy (CSEDS), under Ministry of Education of PRC, at a recently held function in Beijing, to mark the 60th Anniversary of the People's Republic of China. Besides being honoured as the as the most Influential IT Training Brand in China, NIIT received a total of five Education Awards as below:

- The most influential IT Training Brand in China
- Top 10 Brand in overall Training industry of China
- Top 10 Brand in student placement within Training industry in China
- Most influential Brand in Franchising within Training industry of China

- Celebrity award to Prakash Menon, President, NIIT China, for influencing the development of Training industry in a China.

NIIT's success story holds lessons for any company that seeks to penetrate the Chinese market. Prakash Menon, the head of NIIT China, says the key to the company's success has been a strategy that has combined localisation to suit the needs of the domestic market and a network of local tie-ups. NIIT works with dozens of China's premier universities, training students in its state-of-the-art laboratory class rooms and making tens of thousands of China's graduates industry ready. China's IT and outsourcing industry is steadily growing at more than20 per cent every year, even in tough financial times. And India's NIIT is leading the country's IT revolution.

The potential for future growth in the Indian and Chinese domestic markets has not gone unnoticed, and a new consumer orientation is emerging in both economies. The middle class may be as large 250 million in China, and at least as large in India. The McKinsey Global Institute (2007) estimates that by 2025, China's middle class will reach 612 million people and India's as much as 583 million.

INFORMATION TECHNOLOGY

It is now widely accepted that the computor enabled new techniques called information technology has the potential to become the Kuznetsian 'ephocal innovation for accelerating growth and raising productivity. Information Technology has three main contributions to make in China and India: (1) It can cut transaction and inventory costs; (2) through backward and forward linkages, it can increase employment; (3) through rise in factor productivity it can accelerate very substantially the growth rate of the economy, for the same level of investment.

Although India has received world attention for achievements in IT software area, China is ahead in quantum of information technology utilized and especially in hardware. India however scores in quality rating. India's advantage over China in software emerged when 185 of the Fortune 500 outsourced to India. Of the 23 software companies in the world with SEI-CMMS Certification, 16 are Indian, and of the startups in Silicon Valley, USA, 40 percent had Indian partners. This quality consideration is making GE and Google to set up their R & D centers in Bangalore, India to benefit from low cost world class engineers and scientists in India. China has no far none. While average wage for a Chinese software developer today is more than for an Indian one, the lower Chinese cost of physical and telecom infrastructure wipes out this out in competitive terms.

Fluency in English language and world class institutes of technology that train them, make Indian software engineers more innovative and of world class excellence. Hence, in IT-enabled services and outsourcing, India may retain its advantage for years to come. India has access then upto $10 trillion in outsourcing from developed countries on comparative advantage logic.

Table 70: Information Communication Technologies: India Versus China

	March 2002		March 2006	
	India	China	India	China
PC Population (million)	6.5	16.3	16.6	39.9
Internet users (million)	9.8	30	50	200
Fixed line phones (million)	32	189	60	320
Cellular phones (million)	6	165	44	400
C&S households (million)	37	75	70	210
International bandwidth (Gbps)	1.5	50	N.A	N.A

Source: Nasscom, Morgan Stanley, CLSA, China Telecom, Business, Week, Oct 21, 2002.

The turnover of the Chinese computer industry as a whole is expected to cross $46.1 billion in 2001, an increase of 36.8 per cent over the previous year, while sales of software are expected to be over $3.6 billion, an increase of 31.7 per cent over 2000. India riding on the IT wave, recently hiked its targets from $50 billion to $87 billion by 2008. If this has to be achieved, India's IT contribution will require to grow from 1.3 per cent of GDP to 7.8 per cent of GDP, as high as the US today.

China is already occupying No.3 position in the IT hardware supply to the world, far ahead of India in the area. India can close the gap by the same technique as the Chinese had succeeded by, namely by re-processing and value-addition activity. This would require a well developed telecom industry to provide domestic demand for the hardware.

In five years since 1996, the number of main telephone lines in India and China rose from about 12 million and 57 million respectively to around 34 million and 164 million lines respectively in 2001. In this five year period, China registered an annual average growth rate of 32.5% while India has registered a growth rate of 22.5%. In mobile phones, China has around 165 million units while India has around six million. China had plans to reach 400 million mobile phone users by 2006 and has an ambitious target of 800 million mobile phone users by year 2010. India's target for 2010 is 50 million, and is currently set at 44 million for 2006. But recent de-regulation of the Telecom Sector in India has raised hopes of a sharp acceleration, and possible closing of the gap with China. But it still requires enormous effort on part of India to close the quantity gap in this sector.

Table 71: Telephone and Transportation

	Telephone		Transportation					
	Main lines in use	Cellular	Airports	Airports with paved runways	Heliports	Railways	Roadways	Ports and terminals
China	365.4 Million (2007)	547.386 Million (2007)	477	64	35	75438 km	1,930,544 km	8
India	37.75 Million (2009)	362.3 million (2009)	345	251	30	63221 km	3,316,452 km (2006)	9

UNCTAD, 2008

Table 72: Internet Usage: India versus China

	Internet Users (Year 2000)	Internet Users (Latest Data)	Penetration (% Population)	User Growth (2000-2008)	Users (%) in Asia
China	22,500,000	298000000	22.40%	1224.40%	45.30%
India	5000000	81000000	7.10%	1520.00%	12.30%

Internet World Stats, 2008.

India's growth of information technology (IT) has attracted international attention for a number of reasons. First, the pace of growth has been rapid, albeit from a low base. Total IT output today is 3 percent of India's GDP. Over the 12-year period 1990-91 to 2001-02, the annual compound rate of growth of output was 37.4 per cent. That is, output was doubling every 2.2 years and accelerating since 1996 because f the Y2K research. Second, this rapid growth unlike in the rest of the economy has essentially been the result of a rapid expansion of exports. During the period 1990-91 to 2001-02, exports have been growing at 54 per cent per annum or doubling every 18-24 months, and now constitutes 61 percent of software output.

The IT sector's growth has been driven largely by the Indian private sector on both the supply and demand sides, though government support in terms of IT infrastructure investments, duty-free access to hardware for software exporters and hitherto zero taxation of export profits has been a factor.

Almost all the IT firms producing for the domestic and international markets are private firms and, the private sector has accounted for a dominant and rising share of domestic IT spending since 1995-96 and contributed as much as 73 per cent of the total in 2001-02, as compared with 15 and 12 per cent by the government and public sectors respectively. In China the share of government owned corporations in IT spending is over 80 percent.

The ability of the IT sector to "unleash growth" in the future in India depends on diversification of its end-use. The problem is that though software services dominate the export of IT services (ITeS is registering a rise in share), India's software exports are still concentrated in terms of sources and destinations. Of the 1,250 companies exporting software services in 1999-00, the source of those exporting more than Rs.100 crore (about $22.5 million) stood at just 37. The top 25 exporters accounted for 61 per cent of export revenues. And the US market dominated in terms of destination accounting for 62 per cent of exports as compared with Europe's 23.5 per cent. Finally, Indian firms are finding it increasingly difficult to migrate up the value chain, so as to ensure a growing share of the market as well as enter into segments that offer higher value per employee. Generation of customised software or generating code for systems specified by clients dominate the export software services market. As has been repeatedly emphasised, this often involves just body-shopping in the form of temporary export of software professionals to undertake specific jobs in large projects designed and executed in the West.

Thus, conceptually, India's software thrust of the 1990s is not as spectacular as it appears. It is substantially export of lower end software facilitated by the availability of cheap skilled labour. And it is in large part a technology-aided extension of the earlier waves of migration by service-providers of different descriptions: doctors, nurses, and blue-collared workers of various kinds. An expansion of that kind cannot be self-sustaining. Even in quantitative terms the latter development is not spectacular. The 'net foreign exchange revenue' to the country from migration of the old kind, captured by the volume of remittances into India, is in the range of $10-12 billion. The gross foreign exchange revenue from software exports is just around $8 billion.

The big constraint for India is that Indian software companies have not been able to persuade Indian industries to become their customers, hence exports is the basis for growth. This puts a cap on the software growth unless India turns its attention in IT to the internal industrial market.

Table 73: Software Levels in China and India

(@ 2005)

	China	India
Software exports	$0.85 billion (+112.5%)	$6.2 billion (+37.78%)
Software exports as a % of total exports	0.37%	14.17%
2005 software exports growth target	$ 15 billion	$20.42 billion
IT professionals graduating each year	50,000	73,218
Current IT professionals	150,000	522,000
Demand for IT professionals	350,000	400,000
No. of software companies	6,000+	3,000+
Domestic software sales	$4.3 billion (+55%)	$2.06 billion (+31%)

Note: **Percentage increase/decrease figures in brackets are for a one-year period.**

Although there is no doubt that at present China, by outsourcing for Taiwan, Korea and Singapore, has outstripped India in IT hardware, but China lags behind India on most counts of software development, as the Table-17 above shows.

But the crucial question is how India holds up to serious price competition—whether from China or any other low-cost region such as Ireland China's basic infrastructure remains superior to India's—because the former government systematically ensured that deployment of telecom infrastructure and power grids are carried out. Chinese telecom facilities are at least 10 years ahead of what India has developed. On the macro level, Chinese engineers are arguably more or less at par with Indian engineers, or perhaps even greater capabilities—judging by advances in Chinese nuclear and defense industries. Moreover if the Chinese government decides to teach Chinese engineers in numbers English in the next five years is probable that the program will be rigorously carried out, unlike in India.

Having made its mark in the low-end assembly business, China is now all set to focus on the high end of the IT manufacturing including semiconductor manufacturing and design. For instance, the Beijing University recently patented China's first 32-bit and 16-bit microprocessors, and the General Research Institute of Non-Ferrous metals has developed an 8-inch mono-crystalline silicone chip. China is deploying abundant funds in R&D in its universities to create high-end technical manpower.

At the coding and body shopping level of the value chain, India is likely to face intense competition from China over the next few years. However, IT is one area where there is considerable scope for India and China to work together to exploit complementarity and comparative advantage and carve a large world market share China is front runner in hardware, and India is in software. Even in hardware and IT - enabled service area such as banking and telecom the Chinese market is to vastly expand beyond its reservoir of talent, project management skills and domain expertise.

In particular, it is becoming less and less true that China is at the low-tech end software developer, of not so highly qualified personnel, and largely non-English speaking. Judging by Chinese per hour billing rate it already higher than that of India's at $15.90 an hour. Of late, India has made strides in moving up the value chain and managed a 75 per cent growth in its hourly billing rate.

A new study sponsored by the Ewing Marion Kauffman Foundation on the globalization of the pharmaceutical industry shows that big pharmaceutical companies such as Merck, Eli Lilly and Johnson & Johnson are now counting on these countries for advanced research and development as well.

According to the study, "The globalization of innovation: Pharmaceuticals: Can India and China Cure the Global Pharmaceutical Market?", Indian and Chinese scientists are rapidly developing the ability to innovate and create their own intellectual property as a result of the movement of research and development (R&D) to their countries. Several firms in these countries are performing advanced R&D and are moving into the highest-value segments of the pharmaceutical global value chain.

According to Vivek Wadhwa, executive in residence at Duke University and a fellow at the Labor and Worklife Program of Harvard Law School, who led the team of researchers conducting the study, this report is the first in a series which shows how India and China are becoming major players, in global R&D. "Even though China is investing hundreds of billions of dollars into next-generation plants to turn the country into an export power in semiconductors, passenger cars, and specially chemicals, India is ahead in innovation and R&D", he says.

"We observed that in the aero-space industry, Indian companies are designing the interiors of luxury jets, in-flight entertainment systems, collision-control/navigation-control systems, fuel-inverting controls, and other key components of jetliners for Americans and European corporations," Wadhwa adds. "In the automotive industry, Indian engineers are helping to design bodies, dashboards, and power trains for Detroit vehicle manufacturers. In telecom and computer networking, Indians are developing futuristic technologies for the intelligent cities which are being constructed in the Middle East.

Since, 1995 in India, the factor for spurt in growth has been the rise of high-end technology of IT software and the financial services sector. IT software however is but of the blue-collar variety. This too cannot go on because of the rising competition from Phillipines, Russia and Ireland. India has to move up the value chain of IT software to keep the revenues coming home. Indians have also earlier benefitted by the slack in manufacturing industry built during the 1980s in the manufacturing industry. That has been exhausted now; India now needs more reforms, and especially world class information friendly infrastructure in telecom.

Hence, to borrow a phrase from Professor Krugman, India and China have to stop relying on "perspiration" for growth and move onto "inspiration" i.e., innovation to keep the growth momentum going. Both countries need to go for innovations to raise productivity.

IT in India is spread across four key sectors- IT services; IT enabled services (ITES), software, and e-business. These sectors combine for a 2008 annual revenue forecast of $87B (source: NASSCOM) with numerous analysts suggesting higher revenue.

Highlighting the rapid growth of IT in India, software was a small $150 million industry in 1991, but grew to $5.7B in 2000, which is an annual growth rate of 50% (NASSCOM). The public and private sector factors that have contributed to this hyper growth of IT provide lessons for possible replication in China and other developing countries. One important policy lesson can be that high tech areas, driven by the market, can pull in global capital even if domestic opportunities are limited. India's IT sector growth also provides a fine example of how foreign-bom or out of country immigrants provide linkages to capital, technology and culture to emerging entrepreneurs in the native country.

Information technology, unlike technologies of the industrial age requires freedom and openness. The greater the political and economic freedom of a society, all else being equal, the greater its capacity to be an information age power.

India, because of its democratic political system the willingness of its government to stay out of over-regulating the IT sector, and because of the relative younger population is suited to become an IT *Power to reckon with in the 21st century "knowledge economy."*

The involvement of the Chinese in the US IT industry needs to be studied in detail by India. About half of the 1900 technology transfer cases investigated annually on the West Coast of US involve the Chinese.

India, on its part, needs to network with the Indian Diaspora in the US to ensure that there is a free flow of information technology, especially since India, Israel and US share-similar global strategic concerns, and are inherently non-antagonistic.

India also needs to take many lessons from the Chinese in the management of the telecom sector. In Asia, India like China, a large nation with a significant rural population, had a small and inefficient telecommunication system at its independence in 1947. The British left India with 82,000 working lines for a population of 350 million. In 1986, new policies were introduced and the monopoly Posts and Telegraph Board was partially split. A new Department of Telecommunications (DoT) continued to play the roles of regulator, service operator and equipment manufacturer. The year 1991 saw the opening up of the Indian economy and 1999 saw the declaration of a New Telecom Policy (NTP'99).

India's recent success in the IT industry, the development of indigenous satellite and other electronic technologies, *the* ability to creatively use the Internet and the increasing success of Indian entertainment exports—film, TV, and music—draw attention to India's competitive advantage in these fields. The Indian media's self-confidence has been built in the face of decades of free competition in the cultural marketplace since India has remained a relatively open society. Indigenous talent in the information and media has always been willing to benchmark itself against international competition and has not just survived but in fact thrived.

A Democratic and liberal nation can make more effective use of various IT media than an autocratic and insular country. The early 21st century has already seen a debate on whether the flow of information via IT should be blocked or censored or whether its diffusion should be encouraged. While dedicating the supercomputer "Param 1000" (the fastest computer developed in Asia barring Japan), Indian scientists voiced, their fears of being subject to technological colonialism and blackmail, even information apartheid.

India changed its strategy which was earlier followed of high tariffs on IT products and is increasingly reducing tariffs on the import on IT. The growing competitiveness of the software industry in India and the new market dynamics in the IT industry have enabled more open trade for IT products. India must now concentrate on the development of infrastructure in the IT and telecom sectors because of the burgeoning market in the IT services industry. If India can build a good information infrastructure, capable of supporting sophisticated, fast and cheap communication technologies, it has the potential to become the Asian hub for all services-related activities in the region. There is a potential Rs.55,000 crore market that will provide employment to 4.1 million office workers by 2020. India runs the risk of giving away this ITes market to China and South-East Asia due to the lack of an advanced information infrastructure. Though, India must continue to reduce tariffs on IT products, developing infrastructure and Import of necessary is technology.

In the area of software exports, India, like China is targeting the low-end, low technology software for exports (i.e. the $2 per hour variety like Y2K solutions, etc.), while India's comparative advantages ties in its core competence is in the high-end software exports. If India, with increased FDI and M & A switches over to the high end and brand software exports, the revenue received will tremendously rise by several multiples.

Software is one of China's fast growing service industries too. The Chinese software industry however is inherently different than India's. The majority of Chinese software services producers are companies with domestic consumers. Another major difference between the Chinese and Indian software sector is the fact that the latter is more export oriented whereas the former serves primarily domestic demand. A mere 5.6% of China's software industry was exported versus approximately about 70% in India.

The Chinese IT market is structured differently from India's. It is 70 percent hardware, 12 percent software and 17 percent ITes, while the Indian market is almost the reverse—20 percent hardware, 60 percent software, and 17 percent ITes. While China's IT is mostly used domestically, India's is largely exported. China's software is almost entirely used internally and is of relatively lower quality. Indian software companies graded by SEI-CMM ratings from a lowest 1 to a highest 5, number 36 companies of ratings 5 even higher than for US, while China has only 1 company of rating 5. China however is working hard and to a plan to rectify this, ironically in collaboration Indian companies such as Tata Consultancy and NIIT.

But all said and done, it is today the United States which is the global leader in new innovations such as information technology. And innovations are key to rising growth rates achieved by rising capital and labour productivity.

The factor determining the future trend of economic growth in China and India would depend on how the American innovating Eagle, the Chinese hardware manufacturing Dragon and the Indian IT software Elephant are going to engage in expanding their commonalities and address their differences to harness new innovations which will have epochal impact of future economic growth by raising productivity in all sectors and the factors of production.

China, India, and the United States have been the main destinations of global foreign direct investment (FDI) in Information and Communication Technologies (ICT), accounting for more than 50 percent of the overall investment. However, the profile of these investments varies across these countries. While India is preferred for research and development (R&D) and IT-enabled services, IT services projects are concentrated in the United States and China is considered the hub for ICT manufacturing.

For example, India is a country with the largest variety of gene pool, large number of English speaking physicians, and support staff which make India an irresistible destination for conducting clinical trials. India is today ranked third—after the US and China—in terms of attractiveness as a clinical trial destination. After the call center book, it is now the clinical trial outsourcing business that is all set to redefine the market rules.

But India does not have the regulatory framework to ensure that poor and illiterate patients are not exploited. No studies are being conducted in India so that unsafe drugs can be ruled out.

Some efforts to regulate the market have been made – new laws have come into force, amendments have been made to the existing ones. The regulatory landscape has undergone a dramatic change in the past 18 months with the passing of several amendments and Bills in the Drugs and Cosmetics Act. Recent reforms include mandatory Registry of

Clinical Trials, Review of Ethical Committees, Registration of CROs, transparency in the regulatory system and pharmacovigilance activity across medical colleges in India.

The two most important factors making India a worthy destination for clinical research organizations are English speaking physicians and the presence of six out of seven genetic variations. The Government of India has however been cautious and conservative as far as the clinical trial industry is concerned, to ensure that the people are not exploited.

The clinical trial industry is valued to go up to $1 to 1.5 billion in the next five years. The offshoring of clinical trials brings with it allied services, and hence more opportunity in clinical data management (CDM), biostatistics, pharma-covigilance and medical welfare.

Currently, seven of the top 10 global CROs have an established presence in India. Trials for a standard drug in the US can cost about $150 million. A similar drug could be tested in India for 60 percent less.

Since India stands to benefit from these trials by much-needed investment into healthcare and access to beneficial drugs, there is an urgent need to create an agreeable environment by raising awareness and ensuring ethical clinical practice.

As per Ernst and Young Survey Report, 2008, India can attract up to 10 per cent of the global contract research out-sourced market in the next five years. The industry is valued to go up to $1 – 1.5 billion (Rs.4,800 – Rs.7,200 crore) from the current $300 million (Rs.1,440 crore). In 2005, only 100 clinical trials were being conducted in India.

At present, the figure stands at 350. It is now being said that the new Health Care plan brought in by President Obama is going to benefit India the most. Already for the UK Health system India's IT is playing a significant role. The Obama Plan calls for spending $20 billion on healthcare technology services, bulk of which it is cost-effective route through India.

Whereas India and the United States are yet to succeed in attracting ICT manufacturing investments, China has been successfully garnering investments in the IT services projects as well as for R&D. This is mainly due to the well-educated and cheap labor force in China. The high influx of foreign investors into China has ensured the high demand for ICT products and services in the country.

Global IT outsourcing was estimated to be around $39.6 billion in 2004 India's share amounting to nearly $17.2 billion while China garnered nearly $1.9 billion of the outsourcing revenues.

Chart 1 indicates the share of IT outsourcing revenues by region in the year 2004.

Chart 24: IT Outsourcing: Share of revenues by region, (World), 2004

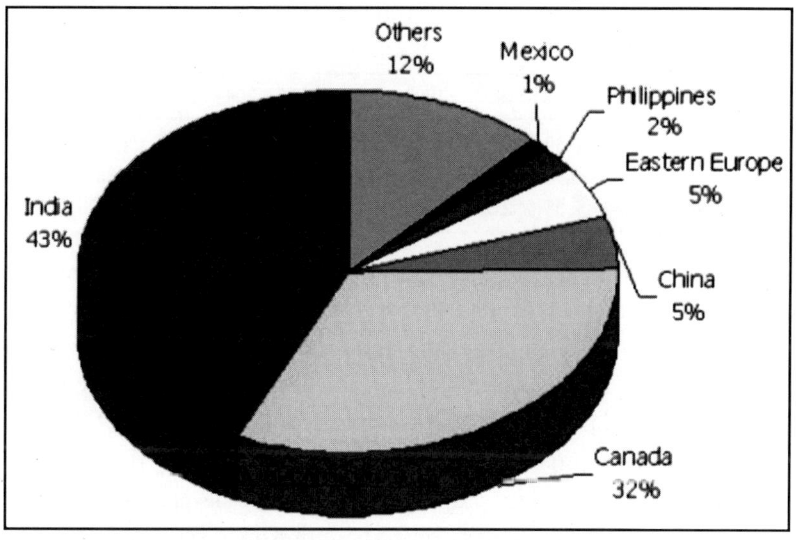

Source: National Association Software and Service Companies (NASSCOM), India.

The Chinese Government and the IT service providers are working at various levels to compete with the dominant Indian participants in the global IT outsourcing market. India with its 44.0 percent share of IT outsourcing projects is considerably ahead of China in the global outsourcing market but this gap in revenues is estimated to reduce soon as China leverages on its advantages.

Towards this end, the Chinese Premier, Wen Jiabao, visited several Indian IT outsourcing hubs such as Bangalore and also visited the premier Indian Institutes of Technology (IITs) in 2004. The Chinese Vice Foreign Minister, Wu Dawei, was quoted as saying "The Premier Wen would like to know more about the experience of India in developing science and technology."

India has had tremendous advantage with around 813,000 knowledge professionals being employed in the IT software and ITES BPO sectors during the years 2003 and 2004. More than 65 IT companies achieved SEI CMM Level 5 assessment at the end of 2003 and many more companies are expected to follow. China till 2008 did not have any. Now there is just one.

Table 74: Research and development expenditure: China and India

(% of GDP)

Country Name	1996	1997	1998	1999	2000	2001	2002	2003	2004
China	0.60	0.68	0.70	0.83	1.00	1.07	1.22	1.31	1.44
India	0.55	0.70	0.74	0.78	0.85	0.88	0.89	0.86	0.88
United States	2.55	2.58	2.61	2.65	2.72	2.73	2.66	2.67	2.68

China shares many of India's advantages in the outsourcing market such as cheap labor costs and favorable government policies. However, the Chinese lack English language skills and the expertise in western business practices. The Indian Government has gained from years of investment in IT education and from lenient policies toward the IT industry.

While the Chinese IT companies are increasingly bidding for international outsourcing projects, they are also leveraging on their proximity to markets such as Japan and South Korea, where they have an advantage both due to the geography and language. Nevertheless, China has to still gain expertise in project management as well as achieve economies of scale before it can compete with countries such as India in the global outsourcing market.

Indian firms are increasingly setting up operations in China in order to capitalize on the future prospects that the country might offer in IT outsourcing. As of June 2005, nearly 18 Indian companies had operations in China and had a workforce of nearly 2000, with investments estimated to be nearly $50 million. By the end of 2005, Indian companies are expected to expand their Chinese operations as well as double their employee base in China.

Frost and Sullivan's recent report on the 'Chinese Information Technology Industry' analyzes the trends affecting the industry in view of the political policy and cultural environment as prevalent in China.

Some of the trends in favor of Chinese expansion in the outsourcing market are the liberalization of government regulations, the growing middle class, large-scale investments in technical education, a vibrant economy, and the availability of cheap labor force. However, China needs to build its workforce capabilities in terms of English language proficiency and project management skills in order to emerge as a viable alternative to India in the global outsourcing market. Moreover, both China and India will also have to deal with the mounting competition from other low cost countries such as Russia, Philippines, Ireland, and Israel.

Within a very short time, India has made its major presence in the global biotech industry. India is ranked among the top 12 biotech destinations in the world and is the third biggest in Asia-Pacific in terms of the number of biotech companies (CII-KPMG report). More than 350 companies of India's USD 2.5 billion industry developed the sector at an average 30% annually for five consecutive years -and even 18% last year against the background of the global financial crisis.

That's an impressive performance by any standards. The Indian biotech sector's overall turnover in 2008-09 was USD 2.51 billion, as compared to USD 2.13 billion in 2007-08 and is expected to reach 5 million marks in2010(Report by CII and KPMG). Bio-pharma contributed USD 1.6 billion; bio-agri nearly USD 311.28 million, bio-industrial segment USD 99.19 million and bio-informatics grew 15% to touch USD 45.65 million.

The reasons for this bio boom are not unique. With a huge base of talented, skilled and cost competitive manpower, and a well-developed scientific infrastructure, India has become a leading global player in biotechnology. In the health sector, Indian firms are developing novel biotech treatments for cancer, diabetes, and other conditions. In agri-bio, India is also innovating in bio-energy, with experiments using advanced biofuels to power trains and buses and with plans to meet more of India's energy needs with bio-diesel derived from the jatropha bush.

The global clinical research outsourcing market is projected to touch USD 23 billion by 2011, with consultancy firm KPMG estimating that India will comer 15% of this in two years. The Stem Cell Global

Foundation, a New Delhi-based organisation promoting stem cell research, estimates the business to be growing at a compounded annual growth of 15% and cross USD 450 million next year.

Moreover, India has joined an elite group of six countries which have successfully decoded the human genome indigenously. Biocon, Serum Institute of India, Panacea Biotec, Nicholas Piramal, Wockhadrt Limited are the names of the top ten biotech companies of India that have broken new ground and given new products and technologies to the world.

The government of India is planning to create separate National Biotechnology Regulatory Authority. The Indian government and the UNESCO, fully realising the need of training and education for generating interdisciplinary human resource relevant to biotechnology, took a joint decision to establish the Regional Centre for research, training and education in biotechnology under the auspices of UNESCO.

Financial Architecture

Globalisation can be managed if the economy's financial system has a secure foundation on a well designed financial architecture. In Tokyo in 2000, the G-7 had made a declaration on "Strengthening of Financial Architecture", and described this foundation.

The volatility in the international system arises from combination of freer financial flows, IT, and WTO enabled market access.

The essential fragility of finance arises out because: [1] A commitment to lend is a leap into the uncertain future. [2] Risk hedging is imperfect because of asymmetry in information available with lender and borrower. [3] Lending and borrowing is based on expectation which is fickle. [4] Investors suffer from cut-your-losses mentality and hence contagion, and therefore volality is inevitable.

The global economy therefore needs a Financial Architecture: consisting of prudential norms, institutions to enforce the norms, transparency, governance rules, and better predictor models based on continuous research. It may require a new world institution, long over due, viz., World Financial Agency (WFA) to monitor the new norms.

Norms encompasses:[1] International Financial Standards on stabilization, disclosure, containing moral hazard, soft budget constraints [China's policy loans, India's loan melas], and auditing. [2] Basel Standards of capital adequacy and core principles—CAR=bank capital/ risk weighted assets > 8%, China less than 3%.[3] Crisis management set up for internal risk leveraging, debt, pension reform, NPAs, and securities insurance. [4] Reform of IMF. Besides this, three important question in a China India comparison: (1) Exchange Rate-appreciate or not. (2) capital account convertibility. (3) How much in reserves to hold. (4) How high a fiscal deficit to maintain since it affects capital accounts balance.

As far as holding reserves is concerned, these have to cover the precautionary [6 months], transaction [amortization of foreign debt, CAD], speculative [portfolio, short-term loans, NRI/NRC, currency fluctuation] concerns.

As indicated in Table below, China's foreign exchange reserves have increased sharply in recent years, both in absolute terms and as a percent of gross domestic product (GDP). Those reserves rose from $216 billion in 2001 to nearly $1,069 billion in 2006[2] China's reserves as a percent of GDP grew from 18.1% in 2001 to 38.6% in 2006. According to Global Insight, China's FER may have hit $1,540 billion in December 2007, which would equal about 47.3% of China's estimated GDP in 2007. By year-end 2010, China's FER are projected to reach $1,865 billion.

Table 75: China's Foreign Exchange Reserves: 2001-2010

Year	Billions of U.S.Dollars	As a % of Chinese GDP
2001	215.6	18.1
2002	291.1	22.1
2003	403.3	28.1
2004	609.9	31.5
2005	818.9	35.5
2006	1,068.5	38.6
September 2007	1,433.6	N/A
Projection for 2007	1,539.9	47.3
Projection for 2010	1,865.0	32.1

Source for actual data: International Monetary Fund (IMF) and People's Bank of China.

Source for 2007 and 2010 projections: Global Insight, Country Intelligence, China, October 2007. Note: Year-end or month-end values.

We define the main function of the financial system as mobilization of resources through financial assets or debt instruments and to facilitate the allocation and deployment of these mobilized resources spatially and over time efficiently and optimally in an uncertain environment to maximize the growth rate of the economy and achieve the highest rate of return on the resources deployed. This function encompasses a 'financial architecture', i.e., payment system with a medium of exchange, a transfer mechanism for resources mobilized from savers to borrowers/ investors/other users of resources, and eventual repayment to savers, with a reduction of risk through insurance and diversification.

Financial architecture is constituted by the following: (i) Institutional regulators such as the Security Exchange Commission (2) International standards of accounting to ensure transparency in transactions (3) Corporate governance norms for management, shareholders and stakeholders, and (4) Sound banking and prudential norms such as those posted by Based IT norms which limit moral hazard and soft-budget constraints.

The Financial system's ability to perform the main function stated above, and be stable, depends on the following three factors:

(a) Macroeconomic fundamentals
(b) Structural Parameters
(c) Institutional Quality

By current international standards, both China and India have impressive macroeconomic fundamentals such as a high growth rate in the range of 6 to 8 percent per year, a relatively low annual inflation rate below 5 per cent, foreign exchange reserves of $1 trillion and $380 billion respectively.

The two economies differ on structural parameters and institutional quality, besides a declining headcount ratio of poor people. The perception today is thus that both economies are going strong and will fuel global growth in the future.

Box 10: Reserve adequacy

India's total foreign exchange reserves (including gold, Special Drawing Rights (SDR) and reserve with the IMF) have increased from US$ 5.8 billio9n at the end of March 1991 to US$118.5 billion at the end of April 2004. The rate of accretion to total reserves has been particularly remarkable during the last three financial years. In the three years since 2001-02, annual addition to total reserves has been US$ 11.8 billion, US$21.3 billion and US$36.9 billion. The spectacular rise in reserves has drawn attention to the issue of what is an 'adequate' level of reserves for the country.

There are certain common indicators for determining the adequate level of reserves for an economy. These indicators aim to determine the extent of external vulnerability of a country and the capability of reserves in minimizing these vulnerabilities. These indicators are:

1. Import adequacy: The number of months of imports that can be financed by the reserves held by the country.
2. Debt adequacy: The ability of reserves to cover external payment obligations, particularly short-term debt liabilities. This is measured by the ratios of reserves to total external debt and short-term debt.
3. Monetary adequacy: The extent of capital flight that can occur in the event of financial crisis. This is measured by the ratio of reserves to broad money and reserve money.

Since 1991-92, India has made significant progress in all the reserve adequacy indicators. The import cover of reserves has increased from just over five months in 1991-92 to almost 14 months in 2002-03. The reserves to external debt ratio has shot up from 10.8 per cent in 1991-92 to 72 per cent in 2002-03. Over the same period, the reserves to short term debt ratio has gone up from 130.4 per cent to 1650.9 per cent. The ratios of reserves to reserve money and broad money have improved from 24 per cent and 7.5 per cent respectively in 1991-92, to 97.1 per cent and 20.8 per cent respectively in 2002-03.

While the level of foreign exchange reserves held by India at present can be termed comfortable in terms of all the commonly applied adequacy indicators, it is also important to reflect upon the costs of holding reserves. Two issues are significant in this regard. These are the returns earned from deploying the reserves in various securities (according to the guidelines laid down by the RBI Act, 1934) vis-à-vis the interest paid on external debt and the costs of building up reserves through sustained open market operations. While the first issue entails the direct economic cost of holding reserves, the second apart from involving costs of intermediation for the banking system, includes the consequences of prolonged sterilization on domestic money supply and price levels. Given the trends of sustained accretion, the issue of reserve adequacy requires to be addressed in the light of the costs and benefits likely to manifest from holding on to the current high level of reserves.

While today's popular perception of China and India in this regard may be pleasing, it is important to remember that economic history is lull of such favourable perceptions evaporating before the reality that dawns with a bang. At one stage in the nineteenth century, many countries of Latin America were considered more wealthy than North America, Now, the exact opposite is true. In the 1980s, it was widely perceived that Japan would overtake the US. In fact Japanese business bad begun to buy up prized US real estate, and became owners of major corporations in North American mainland. That trend has now been completely reversed. In the case of the 'Asian Tigers', the World Bank had published with a volume titled The East Asia Miracle which was an unabashed prescriptive advocacy of the export-led free trade; strategy of East Asian economies. The celebrated World Bank remark that these economies had got their "basics right" "by implication other developing countries had not-come back to haunt the World Bank after the 1997 financial crisis. East Asia, especially Japan, has yet to fully recover from that crisis.

Although the Bank did attempt damage limitation by subsequently publishing another volume tilled Rethinking East Asia's Miracle, the institution's credibility was hit hard because on the contrary the very area where the East Asian countries had got their basics quite wrong was in the financial system, to monitor which under the 1944 Bretton Woods Charter, the World Bank and IMF were set up in the first place.

Are China and India two more examples of the same phenomenon? Or have China and/or India now embarked, as Europe and the US did in the late nineteen century, on a stable sustainable economic growth path, and can the two countries, in the medium term accelerate growth, and ultimately in the foreseeable future attain developed country status? The answer from the researches of Professor Richard Sylla of NYU as reported in 2001 in his Presidential Address to the American Economic History Association is that it would depend on the appropriateness of the financial architecture in the two economies.

Thus to ensure that post-reform impressive growth performance of the two countries achieved during the last two decades of the twentieth century, does not in the coming two decades of the twenty first century, evaporate in a financial crisis, 'bubble burst' as in 1997 East Asian melt down, it is essential for China and India to make the transition to a new modern financial architecture.

Earlier to Sylla, in 1980, Richard Easterlin, had posed a question in his Presidential address to the Economic History Association (EHA) titled: "Why Isn't the Whole World Developed?" Easterlin's answer was that historical differences in development around the world could be explained by historical differences in the spread of formal mass schooling. Mass schooling, he argued, facilitates the acquisition and application of knowledge of new production techniques associated with the modern economic growth. East Asia of 1997 showed that his answer was incomplete and insufficient.

Richard Sylla proposed a more complete answer, namely that past and current differences in development around the world can be explained by historical differences in the spread of modern financial systems, which serve to facilitate the acquisition and application of both nonhuman and human capital—new production techniques and mass schooling, if you like—and a lot of other improvements as well. Sylla's theory thus is not only more comprehensive, but persuasive as well.

Sylla suggests the key institutional components of a modern financial system are: sound public finances and public debt management; stable monetary and payments arrangements; sound banking systems (more generally, institutional lenders); an effective central bank; good securities markets for debt, equity, and money-market instruments; and sound insurance companies, more generally, institutional investors.

It is easy to identify six functions of a financial system: clearing and settling payments; pooling resources and subdividing shares; transferring resources across time and space; managing risk; providing information; and dealing with incentive problems. While there is substantial overlap, explicit and implicit, between the two perspectives, these components and functions together constitute the financial architecture. Most successful nation-state economies of modern economic history had in common these components and functions.

Easterlin's question however has become crucial ever since the eruption of the Asian financial crisis in mid-summer 1997. China and India are economies that display many of the symptoms the East Asian economies had prior to the crisis. The two nations have list of acute economic problems, including excessive government interference in the economy, inefficient state owned industry, a sick banking sector, a near bankrupt Central Budget, real estate bubbles and rampant corruption. But China and India have so far managed to avoid a catastrophic financial crash from which its other Asian neighbours failed to escape in the large part due to structural and macroeconomic fundamentals:

(i) Like other Asian countries, China and India have been beneficiaries of increased capital inflows in recent years, but unlike others what China and India have attracted is predominantly foreign direct investment rather than short-term portfolio capital. This is however changing since 2006. There has been a spurt in portfolio inflows.

(ii) China and India have from time to time resorted to foreign borrowing, but the present value (PV) of foreign debt as a share of GDP stood at less than 20% of GDP at the end of 1997. Even after the crisis, at the end of 1998 PV to GDP stood at 15 percent and 20 percent respectively, well below the 48 percent level above which debt level becomes moderately high. Also more than 80% of China's and India's foreign debt outstanding is long-term, in sharp contrast to countries such as Thailand, Indonesia and Korea which had relied on short-term foreign currency debt.

(iii) One can also cite the two nations' relatively closed capital account which offer a firewall protecting the currency from speculative attacks in times of crisis.

(iv) The biggest different, however, lies in the current account positions of China, India and the Asian "crisis countries" during the years prior to the crisis. China turned a current account deficit to a surplus while India reduced her's, whereas other Asian countries had incurred high levels of current account imbalances. China and India steadily built up their foreign exchange reserves, crossing $1 trillion, and $1.45 billion for India. China's and India's favourable external performance was brought about by strong and timely macroeconomic adjustments, initiated in 1992.

In China's case, beginning in 1992, the Chinese economy became overheated, with very rapid credit expansion, dwindling fiscal revenues and frenetic investment in development zones, commercial real estate and the stock market. Inflation soared to a record high of 28%. And China's external balance deteriorated sharply. Even though real GDP grew at a breakneck pace the deteriorating macroeconomic imbalances indicated such growth was simply not sustainable.

The government set up an emergency economic team, led by Zhu Rongji, and introduced an austerity program. Under the austerity program, China vigorously pursued tight monetary and fiscal policies. The government enforced credit quotas, hiked interest rates, raised taxes and cut government spending. China also relied on old administrative methods to force the unruly provinces, cities and enterprises to scale back many investment projects. Investment in real estate, mostly financed by unauthorized bank credit, and leading to property price bubbles, was the primary target of the crackdown.

These strong measures, a mixture of old-fashioned administrative directives and market-based policy instruments, sharply curbed investment demand and restored macroeconomic balances in China. Inflation has since fallen rapidly, and China's current account has turned into surplus. By 1997, when Asia was hit by the worst financial crisis since World War II, China's economy had already achieved a successful soft landing.

Without the austerity program and decisive macroeconomic policy adjustments made since 1993, the problems China would have been facing today would have made south-east Asia's financial troubles look small. But the question remains! whether the financial architecture in China and India will prevent a future blow up triggered by international factors?

Table 76: East Asia Current account balances. Uphold the Asian Crisis (1997) (% of GDP)

	1993	1994	1995	1996	1997
China	-2.0	1.4	0.2	0.9	2.5
India	-2.5	-2.3	-2.0	-1.7	-1.2
Indonesia	-1.1	-1.5	-3.4	-3.6	-2.4
Korea	0.1	-1.2	-2.0	-4.9	-2.0
Malaysia	-4.4	-5.7	-8.5	-4.9	-4.3
Philippines	-5.5	-4.6	-4.4	-4.7	-5.8
Thailand	-5.1	-5.6	-8.0	-8.0	-2.1

Sources: **IMF and Goldman Sachs**

There are analysts such as Joe Studwell, Gordon Chang and recently Edward Chancellor who indeed think that China is the next "bubble" waiting to burst. In 1994, well before the 1997 East Asian melt down and early in China's trend of declining growth rates, Richard Hornik wrote that China has "its fundamentals wrong" because the Deng's reforms 'have played themselves out". A bipartisan US Congressional Staff team after a research trip to China in December 1997 found that "many of the economy's fundamental structural weaknesses make predictions of China's unrelenting economic rise problematic."

But as of now, the fundamentals of both China and India for averting a 1997 type melt down are strong. They could weaken if reforms are not continued. Indeed they have weakened since 2008, after both countries chose "stimulus" package instead of more reforms. A range of macroeconomic and structural factors explained why China and India were relatively unscathed by the 1997 East Asian crisis. But for the future, estimates of crisis probabilities based on macroeconomic venerability indicators of the IMF which was relatively small in late 1996 when compared to other Asian economics, would have to be monitored. The crisis probabilities are estimates of the probability of balance of payments crisis 24 months hence, and are based on a model maintained by the Developing Country Studies Division of the IMF'S Research Department. These studies have tended to identify a range of variables that can signal crisis including: real exchange rate appreciation, banking crisis, growth of M2/reserve growth, stock price inflation, export growth weakness, output growth slowdown, excess M1 balances, falling external reserves, excess domestic credit growth high real interest rates, and a decline in the terms of trade.

Sample countries are: Argentina, Bolivia, Brazil, Chile, Colombia, India, Indonesia, Israel, Jordan, Korea, Malaysia, Mexico, Pakistan, Peru, Philippines, South Africa, Sri Lanka, Taiwan, Thailand, Turkey, Uruguay, Venezuela, and Zimbabwe. A crisis is defined to have occurred when a weighted average of monthly percentage depreciations in the exchange rate and monthly percentage declines in reserves exceeds its mean by more than three standard deviations. The independent variables in the model include: real exchange rate overvaluation relative to trend; current account deficit as a percentage of GDP; reserve and export growth; and the ratio of short-term debt to reserves. The probability of a crisis is found to increase when the bilateral real exchange rate is overvalued relative to trend, reserve growth and export growth are low, and the ratio of the current account deficit to GDP and short-term debt to reserves are high.

The estimated coefficients from the model can then be used to generate predictions in the form of the probability of a crisis occurring in any one country during the next 24 months, given the current values of the explanatory variables. Predicted probabilities above a certain threshold (typically taken as either 25 or 50 percent) indicate that the model is signaling the likelihood of a crisis (assuming unchanged policies) within the next 24 months.

In effect the signaling of an imminent crisis is tantamount to the model indicating that under unchanged policies, the path of external sector imbalances is unsustainable. Of course, a crisis may not eventuate if appropriate policy actions are taken to address the underlying problems.

The estimated crisis probability for India was high and rising during the second half of the 1980s and well above the 25 percent threshold. If the threshold level was instead taken as 50 percent, this was crossed on two occasions, in mid-1988 and late 1990. Crisis as defined in the model occurred in April and July 1991, and also in March 1993. These results are in line with evidence that India was in breach of its solvency constraint prior to 1991. The crisis probability reached a peak in May 1991 at over 60 percent, just five months before the formal commencement of new reforms. The crisis probabilities declined quickly following the wide-ranging reform program introduced in the wake of the 1991 crisis, and have generally remained low since that time. It is notable that during 1997 and 1998, when the economy was buffeted by the Asian crisis, the crisis probability was quite low.

The aggregate crisis probability can be decomposed into the contributions made by each of the five variables. The steadily rising probabilities during the second half of the 1980s were largely due to the widening current account deficit and the increase in short-term debt.

On this criteria i.e., estimates of crisis probabilities based on macroeconomic fundamentals—including the real exchange rate, the current account, reserves, export growth, and short term debt exposure—were relatively benign in the case of India and China in late 1996, especially when compared to other Asian economies.

Besides these relatively good macroeconomic fundamentals, China and India were ironically also insulated from financial market contagion and trade spillovers by the relatively closed nature of their economies a long history of capital controls, and its modest financial links with the region.

Although the near-term risks to Chinese and Indian economies appear limited since the standard external vulnerability indicators are favourable i.e., the current account ratio is low, external debt is early manageable and official reserves and high (6-8 months imports), nevertheless since 1997 China's venerability has slightly increase while India's has diminished. This is mainly because export growth is a much larger part of China's economic growth than India's Global slowdown has sharply reduced China's current account ratio from +4.1 to +1.9, and the official reserves cover for imports has reduced from 10.4 months to 8.1. Hence, there is a definite urgency for financial reforms. Indeed, compared with neighbouring countries, China's export growth has held up somewhat better and its growth momentum is fairly robust. However, a more prolonged global slowdown than presently envisaged would pose a greater risk, especially as slower GDP growth in China could make progress with reforms more difficult due to social constraints.

Table 77 A: External Vulnerability Indicators: 1997-00

	1997		2000	
	INDIA	CHINA	CHINA	INDIA
Current account balance/GDP (in percent)	-1.6	4.1	1.9	1.1
External debt/GDP (in percent)	23.4	19.4	15.2	22.2
External debt/exports (in percent)	278.6	95.6	66.1	166.3
Official reserves (US$billions)	36.0	143.4	168.9	42.3
Official reserves (in months of imports and gnfs)	6.0	10.4	8.1	6.0
Official reserves/short-term debt (residual maturity) (in percent)	190.0	227.3	843.7	160.1
Official reserves/total external liabilities (in percent)	30.1	82.1	102.6	31.4

Much has been made by Chinese and Indian planners about the high level of foreign exchange reserves in the two countries. Although at present these reserves cover more than eight months import bill that by itself is not a reason for complacency. Given the uncertainty of the future, how much is enough cover, if not eight months?

On the question of how much cash to hold, John Maynard Keynes had suggested three motives for holding cash: transaction, precautionary and speculative. Thus, enough reserves to cover the import bill of a few months is the transaction motive. There are reserves necessary for other motives as well. Reserves are essential to cover the payment obligations on maturing debt. This is the precautionary motive. Finally, short-term commercial credit and portfolio investment, i.e., not money could move inspite of the restrictive capital mobility regimes in the two countries. If indeed capital account convertibility is accepted by both countries, then faced with a global slow down China and India could rise above the levels of risk and currency crisis, and plunge into a financial crisis.

The fact that macroeconomic and other fundamentals were not uniformly strong, may suggest that it were the capital controls that could have contributed to India and China's relatively favourable experience during the 1997 East Asian crisis. The closed capital account meant that external debt—especially short-term external debt—was modest, and restrictions on capital movements also helped mute the impact of the sharp turnaround in investor sentiment on the capital flows.

India and China maintains relatively strict control over capital flows—the IMF's index of capital control places these two countries, with Chile among the most restrictive economies. In general, outflows by residents are prohibited, and inflows by nonresidents are subject to constraints. Although a timetable for the phased withdrawal of most capital account controls over the 1997/98- 1999/2000 period was established in June 1997, progress toward capital account liberalization has slowed considerably after the East Asia crisis. This reflected concern that the Asian crisis had exposed the vulnerability of emerging markets to shifts in investor sentiment and its volatility. It also reflected a recognition that many of the pre-conditions that have been identified for successful liberalization—including significant fiscal consolidation and a strengthened financial system—were not yet in place. This is of even greater concern for the future.

Consistent with the discussion above, most of the variables that provided a significant indicator of crisis vulnerability in other countries did not signal vulnerability for China or India during the 1997/98 period. Notably, reserves, current account deficit, real interest rate, and exchange rate movements were not typical of the behaviour shown by crisis economies of East Asia. In addition, crisis economies typically were significantly more exposed to a common creditor—i.e., had a larger proportion of international bank loans from a single creditor country—but this was not the case for India or China. Real interest rates were high enough not to signal a crisis risk. A 4 percent real interest is considered internationally competitive.

The global economic meltdown not a valid excuse for the subsequent impact on the Indian economy. That crisis need not have affected the Indian economy at all. China had got affected because its economic boom was export—led, enabling that country its huge trade surplus with US and EU, and consequently rising foreign exchange reserves. A slump therefore in the demand for Chinese goods hurt China. But India's exports to US and EU as a ratio of GDP is still small. Then why did Indian economy, which was not export-led like China, get affected?

Nor the sub-prime loan default-crisis in US caused it. The general financial crisis in the US was possible because of weak oversight of banks. But the Indian banks are strictly regulated by the Reserve Bank of India, and banks are forced to hold reserves in the name of SLR and CRR, and to purchase of government treasury bonds. In fact except for HFDC, due to their own foolishness, no bank in India collapsed or even made losses during this period.

Then why did India suffer? That is the key question to answer.

Indian economy had a set-back *not because of* financial contagion spreading from US, or because of the interdependent global trade system, *but because of our own perfidious financial derivative called Participatory Notes [PNs]* compounded by an anti-national agreement with Mauritius to permit even $ 1 paid-up companies incorporated in that country to invest in Indian stock markets and not be subject to capital gains tax.

In fact so large PNs have become in value, that the movement of the stock market, bulls and bears, can be manipulated by the free entry and exit of this derivative. *Today thus, our stock market has become rigged.* It can be made to rise and fall at will of PN holders' cartel of corrupt politicians and business persons. The sufferers are middle class who hang on to shares to improve on the yield of their pensions and provident funds but then who cares for them in India? Even the media has been muffled or compromised to remain silent on PNs by this cartel.

Hence the PN continues without any accountability. Thus, billions of dollars of "hot"money enter every year into the Mumbai stock exchange, and are used for buying and selling shares with PNs almost as with cash transactions. In fact it is better because cash purchases of over Rs.10,000 have to be reported with details to the Income Tax Department. Moreover if PNs came via Mauritius, one did not have to pay capital gains tax. By September 2008, PNs accounted for 60 percent of the FII funds in the stock market from near zero in 2003.

The financial crisis in the US was officially acknowledged following the collapse of Fannie Mae and Freddie Mac, the two US government owned loan providers, followed by Lehman Brothers in September 2008. A liquidity crunch developed in US and later in Europe. Interest rates rose as liquidity froze and funds were in demand.

The PNs, which were "hot money", the just shipped out of India without any hindrance to the tune $60 billion in October 2008-January 2009 causing a stock market crash in India symbolized by the steep fall in the Sensex index. *It is this that caused the financial crisis in India and not the US sub-prime loan defaults or exports drying up.*

However, the unexpected 1997 East Asian crisis, and it's contagion effect on other countries has led to considerable research in the IMF under the umbrella topic of "financial architecture" that has vastly improved our understanding of the financial system. Measures of crisis vulnerability and crisis prevention have been developed [e,g,, Compilation Guide to Financial System Indicators. IMF 2004] that now enables the IMF to estimate the probability of a financial crisis.

The Financial System in China and India

The current macroeconomic fundamentals have been secured in China and India by milking the financial system, without nurturing it by more reforms, and by sweeping the malaise in the system under the carpet. That is, macroeconomic fundamentals have been ensured in both countries increasingly at the cost of deteriorating structural parameters and institutional quality.

As a consequence, now in 2010, the structural parameters in the banking and fiscal sectors indicate a looming crisis. More crucially, *as* presently structured, the banking sector in the two economies is internally ill-equipped to meet the challenge inherent in the developing financial crisis. The institutional quality of the financial system of the two countries is out of sync with the needs of increasing globalization, because even today Soviet vintage prudential norms and opacity in transactions are present in the system.

The financial systems of the two countries are bank and budget centric because their capital markets are under developed, and prone to insider trading, rigging and scandal. Their respective bond markets are in its infancy (see Swamy [13]).

Table 78: External Vulnerability Indicators: 1997-00

	2001/02	2002/03	2003/04	2004/05	2005/06
Measures of financial strength and performance					
1/Risk-weighted capital adequacy ratio (CAR)	12.0	12.7	12.9	12.8	12.4
Public sector banks	11.8	12.6	13.2	12.9	12.2
Domestic private banks	12.5	12.8	13.7	12.5	12.2
Foreign banks	12.9	15.2	12.0	14.0	13.0
Number of institutions not meeting 9 percent CAR 2/	3	2	2	2	2
Public sector banks	2	0	0	0	0
Domestic private banks	1	2	2	2	3
Foreign banks	0	0	0	0	0
Net nonperforming loans (percent of outstanding net loans) 3/ 4/	5.5	4.4	2.9	2.0	1.3
Public sector banks	5.8	4.5	3.0	2.1	1.4
Domestic private banks	5.7	5.0	2.8	2.2	1.3
Foreign banks	1.9	1.8	1.5	0.9	0.7

Gross nonperforming loans (percent of outstanding loans) 4/	10.4	8.8	7.2	5.2	3.5
Public sector banks	11.1	9.4	7.8	5.5	3.9
Domestic private banks	9.6	8.1	5.8	4.4	3.2
Foreign banks	5.4	5.3	4.6	2.9	2.1
Number of institutions with net NPLs above 10 per cent of advances	22	13	9	4	3
Public sector banks	3	2	0	0	0
Domestic private banks	4	2	2	1	0
Foreign banks	10	6	5	4	3
Net profit (+)/loss (–) of commercial banks 5/	0.8	1.0	1.1	0.9	0.9
Domestic private banks	0.7	1.0	1.1	0.9	0.8
Foreign banks	0.7	1.0	1.0	0.8	1.5
Balance sheet structure of commercial banks					
Investment/deposit ratio	39.7	42.7	45.0	43.5	34.0
Credit/deposit ratio	53.4	56.9	55.9	64.7	71.5
Lending to sensitive sectors (in percent of total loans and advances)					
Real Estate Market	1.4	1.7	1.8	12.7	17.2 6/
Capital market	0.5	0.3	0.4	1.4	1.5 7/
Commodities	1.4	1.2	1.1	0.2	0.3

Sources: Indian authorities; and staff estimates of IMF.

1/ Classification differs from that in other countries; for example, sub-standard assets are loans that have remained nonperforming between 90 days and 15 months (verses less than90 days In the Unlted States and South Africa).

2/ The three banks with capital shortfalls in 2005/06 are small, collectively accounting for less than 1 percent of total resident deposits.

3/ Gross nonperforming loans less provisions.

4/ Starting in 2001/02, figure includes ICICI, formerly a large development finance institution, which merged with ICICI Bank Ltd. in 2002.

5/ In percent of total assets.

6/ For 2004/05 and 2005/06, the exposure to real estate sector is inclusive of both direct and indirect lending.

7/ For 2004/05 and 2005/06, the exposure to capital market is inclusive of both investments and advances.

Moreover, (1) the sector is dominated by government ownership. More than BO percent of the deposits in, and in excess of 60 percent of the assets are of banks that arc wholly government owned and not self-regulating on market principles (see Table-A 1-4) (2) a lack of modem prudential and governance norms (3) weak opaque non-independent regulatory bodies, and (4) directed credit and captive finances. Besides, the fiscal budgeting has limited scope because of large contingent liabilities and irreducible heads for fund allocation, e.g., subsidies, interest payments re-capitalization of lending institutions, pensions and defence.

Hence because of these Two factors, the financial system in China and India are subject lo a double jeopardy that causes the systemic under perform and sub-optimise the allocation of resources in conversion to productive investment and by creating excess capacity.

It needs to be stated here however that relatively India's financial system is institutionally better structured than China's, although Indian Regulators have yet to fully emerge out the shackles of the Soviet-style command mindset of yesteryears, Fur example, even today, government-owned banks which as stated above, receive 80 percent of all deposits, are compelled to deploy about half of the funds in low interest, albeit low risk, government securities [to finance the government budget's fiscal deficit]. Another 20 percent is directed credit, and 25 percent is kept in mandatory reserve. Such straitjacketing of fund dispersal on government direction applies to other financial institutions such as insurance, provident funds etc.

While capital controls undoubtedly played an important tole in helping to insulate China and India from the financial contagion that afflicted other countries in the Asia region, the pervasive government control over the banking sector and the relatively modest pace of liberalization in the domestic financial sector, i.e, high reserve and liquidity requirements, priority lending regulations, and an underdeveloped domestic debt market, discouraged the asset price inflation seen elsewhere in Asia. However, as reforms continue, the systemic vulnerabilities to contagion will necessarily increase. The danger is balance of payments becoming increasingly dependent on gross private inflows of portfolio investment, as well as investments by nonresidents Indians. This only increases the importance of ensuring that the prudential and supervisory systems covering the domestic financial sector are strong, and that macroeconomic imbalances are addressed to avoid a future threat of a meltdown.

Thus, though China and India have emerged from the tightly controlled Soviet type command economy, and despite the de-regulation since 1980, government control still dominates the financial sector and non-market factors influence the sector dominates through guanshi (influence with officialdom) in China or cronyism (capitalist-politician nexus) in India. Thus, "soft budget constraints" operate in China and India quite extensively, which severely distorts the marginal conditions essential for the efficient allocation of scarce resources.

The Possibility of Financial Crisis In China and India

Empirically, it has been observed that a financial crisis envelops an economy via three different routes of causation:

(1) A run in the foreign currency market that *induces* a banking collapse which in turn triggers a fiscal crisis.

(2) A banking collapse that causes a fiscal crisis which then *induces* a foreign currency run.

(3) A fiscal crisis that triggers a banking crisis which subsequently *induces* a foreign currency run.

The first route was observed in the 1997-99 East Asia crisis. Gerard Caprio and Daniela Klingebiel of the IMF have documented 117 systemic banking crises in 93 countries since the 1970s. A subset of these 117 cases document the second and third route listed above to a financial crisis, A financial crisis thus is not of a one-way causation. The alternative routes of causation mutually reinforce, that could richochet or cascade to a bubble and which bubble can theoretically implode by any of the nine possible alternatives, which each represent permutations of causation of foreign exchange, banking and fiscal crisis [3x3].

By which routes are China and India respectively likelyy to head into an expected financial crisis? Both countries presently do face severe financial systemic problems but of different kinds that require different corrective measures to rectify them and slave off a crisis.

It is the thesis of this study that the imminence of a financial system crisis in China will be triggered by a banking, failure, and in India by the unsustainable fiscal deficit in the union and state government budgets.

Based on a predictor model of two IMF economists, Andrew Berg and Catherine Pattatilo, it can be ruled as improbable that a financial crisis in China or India will come via the 1997 East Asian route, that is, triggered by a currency crisis. The structural parameters in the balance of payments accounts are today such in both countries that the estimated probability of a currency crisis is low. Thus a crisis is indicated if:

Table 79: International Comparison of Top Twenty Debtor Developing countries, 2007

Sl. No.	Countries	Total Debt Stocks (US$ million)	Short term Debt (US$ million)	Ratio of Total debt tto Gross National Income (%)	Debt Service Ratio (%)	Ratio of Short term debt/Total debt(%)	Ratio of Foreign Exchange Reserves/ Tota Debts(%)	Foriegn Exchange Reserve/ (US$ million)	Principal (US$ million)	Interest (US$ million)	Total Debt Service Payments (US$ million)	GNI (US$ million)	PV of debt (US$ million)	Ratio of PV of Total debt to Gross National Income(%)
1	2	3	4	5	6	7	8	9	10	11	12	13	14	15
1	China	373,635	203,698	14.0	2.2	54.5	413.9	1,546,365	20,734	5,444	26,178	3,229,841	363,630	13
2	Russian Federation	370,172	79,103	37.0	9.1	21.4	129.1	477,950	24,249	13,719	37,968	1,258,578	381,401	39
3	Turkey	251,477	41,803	46.0	32.1	16.6	30.4	76,496	31,629	10,226	41,855	648,739	257,109	47
4	Brazil	237,472	39,248	23.0	27.8	16.5	75.9	180,334	40,341	13,016	53,357	1,272,274	261,702	25
5	**India**	**220,956**	**43,662**	**23.0**	-	**19.8**	**125.2**	**276,578**	**32,544**	**5,898**	**38,442**	**1,171,444**	**194,337**	**20**
6	Poland	195,374	60,365	56.0	25.6	30.9	33.6	65,725	41,439	4,291	45,730	409,270	184,939	51
7	Mexico	178,108	9,006	19.0	12.5	5.1	49.0	87,208	28,316	11,302	39,618	1,008,694	181,722	20
8	Indonesia	140,783	34,943	41.0	10.5	24.8	40.4	56,936	9,617	3,676	13,293	415,694	147,835	43
9	Argentina	127,758	38,067	60.0	13.0	29.8	36.1	46149	5,074	2,899	7,973	257158	135,691	63
10	Kazakhastan	96,133	11,745	133.0	49.6	12.2	18.4	17,641	23,596	3,537	27,133	92,709	94,263	131
11	Romania	85,380	30,505	67.0	19.1	35.7	46.8	39,974	8,199	1,956	10,155	165,781	85,293	53
12	Ukraine	73,600	22,914	67.0	16.9	31.1	44.1	32,484	8,407	2,305	10,712	139,060	73,134	66
13	Phillippines	65,845	7,084	50.0	13.7	10.8	51.2	33,740	6,343	3,790	10,133	157,087	66,459	42
14	Thailand	63,067	21,640	31.0	8.1	34.3	138.7	87,472	13,473	905	14,378	237,576	58,506	29
15	Chile	58,649	13,302	46.0	14.2	22.7	28.7	16,843	9,276	1,721	10,997	145,638	57,202	45
16	Malaysia	53,717	15,250	35.0	4.6	28.4	189.9	101,995	7,818	1,615	9,433	182,716	52,738	34
17	Croatia	48,584	5,099	113.0	33.0	10.5	28.1	13,675	7,482	1,437	8,919	49,721	46,784	109
18	Colombia	44,976	5,349	27.0	22.0	11.9	46.6	20,951	5,832	2,835	8,667	199,900	45,908	28
19	South Africa	43,380	16,558	17.0	5.9	38.2	75.9	32,919	3,806	1,332	5,138	274,141	48,323	19
20	Venezuela, R. B.	43,148	11,700	23.0	7.4	27.1	78.2	33,759	3,005	2,545	5,550	230,636	48,087	26

Note: As per World Bank's Global Development Finance, 2009, all the above 20 countries are classified as Middle Income Countries.

Source: World Bank's Global Development Finance, 2009.

-: Data not available.

(i) Short-term foreign debt, including portfolio investment, the diaspora's repatriable deposits, loans which become due for payment within the fiscal year, and short-term foreign exchange loans of banks and companies reach a level such that the foreign exchange reserves falls below 80 percent of that level, At present, this ratio is estimated in China and India lo be well above that level [in fact, exceeding 100%], But since 2002, the foreign exchange reserves as a ratio of short-term debt has been falling became of a sharp acceleration in the latter. In 2003, short-term debt in China rose 38.1 percent to $ 78 billion while total current value external debt rose by just 13 percent to $ 194 billion. In India, since 2002, short-term external debt has doubled.

It could be argued that the 80 percent level is too low as an indicator of potential crisis, since in terms of the three Keynesian motives to hold reserves, the present level of foreign exchange reserves in China and India

(ii) Net present value of foreign debt is more than 37 percent of GDP. At present, this ratio is 16 percent in India and 13 percent [of uncorrected official GDP] in China.

Table 80: Adequacy of Foreign Exchange Reserve: 2000

($US billions; year-end)

Motive	CHINA		INDIA	
	2000	2003	2000	2003
Transaction[1]	65.07	149.00	25.60	38.62
Precautionary[2]	21.42	22.34	6.24	15.09
Speculative[3]	57.25	95.40	7.90	19.11
Total Required	122.04	266.74	39.74	72.82
Available	157.80	412.00	42.30	107.45

1. Four months import cover 2. Deht Service 3. Portfolio and other short-term debt including errors and omissions.

Source: Statistical Abstract of China, National Bureau of Statistics, Beijing, 2001. Statistical Abstract of India, Central Statistical Organization, New Delhi 2001 updated from IMF Article TV records.

(iii) Current account delimit in the balance of payments accounts is larger than minus 2.5 percent of GDP. At present this ratio is + 1.1 percent in India and +1.9 percent in China. Although both ratios are positive i.e., in surplus, it has declined in China from 4.1 % in 1997. In case of India it has risen from a negative 2.0 % but it is not yet a sustainable trend.

(iv) Foreign Direct Investment is less than 60 percent of the total capital inflow. At present FDI corrected for scope is 62 percent in India and 67 percent in China, But this ratio due to rising portfolio investment has been declining during the last four years in both countries and on present trend could fall below the 60 percent mark by 2007.

Fitting these parameters into the Berg-Pottatilo model, it con be inferred the probability of an imminent currency crisis—of liquidity—is low in China and India, less than 10 per cent unless the crisis is exogenously induced by a banking or fiscal crisis or both, but as of now or in the foreseeable future currency crisis cannot be die trigger for the general financial crisis.

It is now on accepted view in the literature that even with healthy macroeconomic fundamentals, an economic system can experience a financial crisis induced by a policy mismatch such as the "unholy policy trinity". Thus, If in an economy, capital account convertibility [CAC], a fixed or pegged exchange rate regime, and an expansionist monetary policy [M3 rising at a rate exceeding 15 percent annually] are seen together, a currency crisis is likely.

At present, China has the first two of the trinity and India just the third. Recent credit squeeze policy in China has brought M3 below the 15 percent cut-off level [In 2004, it was 14.5%, below the 2003 level of 20%].

Mismatches in loan disbursement norms of financial institutions had also helped trigger The East Asian crisis (see Desai [ ]). These 'policy' mismatches were: (i) currency mismatch—issuing local currency loans against foreign currency deposits (ii) maturity mismatch— issuing long-term loans against short-term deposits, and (iii) management mismatch—following prudential norms in receiving deposits and practicing cronyism ["guanshi" in Chinese] in loan disbursement. At present, the third mismatch is present in the Chinese and Indian financial systems.

Banking System in China

Chinese banks have been nearly bankrupted by an apparently unshakeable State commitment to a soft-budget constraint, and "policy loans" that are allocated on non-market principles and on government directives.

By the end of 2002, the total assets of the Chinese banking sector were 26.4 trillion yuan [$ 320 billion approx], representing 85 percent of the total assets of the entire financial sector. Although the role of capital markets is growing, the size of these markets remains quite small, with a capitalization of 1350 billion yuan by end June 2003. Hence the Chinese financial system is bank-centric. Since the banks have a total NPL exceeding the assets, China has today a banking crisis that is hidden by the monopolistic system and the State's commitment to bail it out.

China's banking sector comprises of many institutions. These include state-owned banks, joint-stock banks, city commercial banks, and credit cooperatives etc. However, banking is dominated by the four state-owned commercial banks, which account for 61 percent of the loans. Some academics argue that this is typical of an oligarchic market, which tends to lower the efficiency for allocating financial resources and result in distortions in the system. Further, dominant state ownership in the banking sector tends to erode the credibility of the threat of market failure and the effectiveness of the banking supervisory authorities to enforce prudential rules and requirements.

The second tier of the banking market comprises eleven joint-stock commercial banks with a diversified ownership structure. However, the key shareholders of these banks are local governments and the state-owned or state-controlled enterprises- in September 2003, their assets represent 13.7 percent of the total banking sector assets of 26.4 trillion yuan. These banks have expanded rapidly in recent years. For example, in 2001 alone, their assets increased by 24 percent. At present, five joint-stock banks are already listed in local stock exchanges.

In September 2003 there were 112 city commercial banks, most of which were created by way of restructuring and consolidating urban cooperatives. These banks represent 5 percent of the total banking assets. In addition, there were 35,588 urban and rural cooperatives, accounting for 10 percent of the total banking assets.

Foreign banks for now play a rather limited role in the system. In September 2003, there were 191 licensed foreign banking institutions in China, among which 157 were foreign bank branches, 11 sub-branches, and 15 subsidiaries incorporated locally with 8 branches. Foreign banks represent 0.3 percent in the local currency lending market and around 13 percent in the foreign currency lending market.

Despite the improvement of the asset quality in recent years, the size of non-performing loans (NPLs) is a major threat for the banking system in China. In September 2004, the NPL of the banking sector, including state owned banks, policy banks and joint stock banks, amounted to 2,532 billion yuan ($309 billion) measured according to the five-category supervisory loan classification system, and the NPL ratio thus was 18.7 percent. The non-performing loans of state-owned commercial banks reached 1,999 billion yuan and the NPL ratio was 21.4 percent, an equivalent of 20 percent of GDP of 2002.

The asset quality of the joint-stock banks varies. Some have healthier balance sheets than the state owned banks. The NPLs for joint-stock commercial banks is 8.5 percent on average. The asset quality of other banking institutions is just as worrisome.

Most of them are still using the four-category loan classification system based on the status of past-dues. This old classification system is less stringent. Although the figure for NPLs for these banks is not comparable with that for the state-owned banks and shareholding banks, it is generally believed to be higher.

However, data weaknesses and judgment bias adopting the supervisory loan classification also suggest that the scale of problem—loans may be higher. These weaknesses include the relatively large share of loans classified as special mention and doubtful, the lack of proper treatment of restructured loans and foreclosed assets, and not to mention, losses from non-credit activities.

At present, the capital adequacy ratio for most Chinese banks is below regulatory requirements. At the end of September 2003, the composite capital adequacy ratio of the state-owned commercial banks was merely 4.61 percent, significantly below the minimum regulatory requirement of 8 percent (Basel I) and 12 percent(Basel II). The same ratio for joint-stock commercial banks and city commercial banks are 6.83 percent and 6.01 percent respectively. Capital adequacy should however be calculated on the assumption of sufficient provisioning for loan losses. Therefore, allowing for deficiency of provisions for loan losses, the capital adequacy ratio for Chinese banks becomes much smaller than stated above. As Luo Ping of China Banking Regulation Commission in a speech in New Delhi at a seminar [November 14, 2003] stated, pre-provisioning CAR for SOBs would be just 2%.

The resolution of the problems in the banking sector depends critically on the reform of the state-owned enterprises (SOEs). These enterprises represent the vast majority of the state-owned commercial banks' loan book and recurring non-performing loans. In this contest, the structural problems of these banks cannot he successfully addressed unless the SOEs are at least partially rehabilitated and have become credit-worthy borrowers.

In the interest of social stability, banks largely bear up the reform cost of the SOEs. For example, by the end of 2000, 51.2 percent of the 62,000 firms that had completed their change of ownership failed to repay bank loans. In fact, there has been so much stress on the appropriate terms of settlement for employees of the bankrupt enterprises that some restructuring of SOEs proceeds at the expense of banks when enterprises are closed down or declared bankrupt.

A banking crisis as a consequence is already at hand because: Firstly, of a huge amount of NPLs [$309 billion; according to S&P $864 billion] lo maintain status quo would require 40% of GDP or $600b as work out requirement in SOBs and at regional cooperative banks' level [with higher NPLs because exposure arises out of a lack sound risk analysis and more on "policy considerations" the local level].

Secondly, Chinese banks do not have any prudential norms for bank exposure to real estate investments that are prone to asset bubbles building up quickly. There is also considerable pump priming for automobile credit purchase.

At present, 17% of new loans arc going to real estate activity [India's is 1.5%] which activity is highly leveraged, and since 2000 these prices have been rising sharply. Property bubbles do burst—Japan in the 1980s is a case in point, not to mention other East Asian nations in the 1990s. Overall urban land and property prices in China rose by end 2004 to 70% above the 2001 level (Business Week USA April 4, 2005). In Shanghai properly values doubled in 2004, while rentals fell.

Besides, it is estimated by Automotive Resources Asia [Economist March 20, 2004], that at the present rate investment in the sector, the gap between capacity and sales will widen from half a million on sales of 2.2 million to a gap of 3 million excess in automobiles alone by 2007. Profit margins at 8% are comfortable but has been moving downwards since 1999.

Provisioning for these bad loans has of course meant a less tight monetary policy. China had already been pump priming for the last five years. Broad money to GDP ratio rose from 62.3% in 1990 to 171.4% in 2002 to 183.2% in 2003 [for India it was 43.5% to 69.3%. In the US, it is 65%]. China's government debt including quasi-fiscal liabilities [e.g., bonds to recapitalize banks, pension] is now at 95% of GDP [uncorrected], much higher than India's 81%. In ten years 1990-00, China's pension fund contributors doubled, while retirees tripled. The contribution at 227.8 billion yuan is slightly higher than the distribution of 211.5 b Y. By 2007, the former will fall short of the latter.

This has meant creating inflation potential since the rate of growth of fixed assets in China has declined from 24.3% in 1998 to 10.9% in 1999 to 9.9% in 2000, and to even lower [9.8%] in 2003. In that, more than half is accounted for increases in capital construction and property related projects. China estimates [News From China, April 2004, p.20] that of the 8% growth rate in 2002, real estate contributed 1.85% points].

Consumer price official index in China has also accelerated to 5% an y-o-y basis, up from 3.6%.

Consequent Fiscal and Currency Crisis in China

As a result of the soft budget constraint facing the SOEs and above mentioned factors, China's corrected fiscal deficit at the central level is now 6% of GDP [uncorrected has risen to 3.6%]. Government total fiscal deficit including provincial deficits may be as high as 13% today. This is one of the highest in the world [In 2000, out of 74 countries tabulated, only 7 had fiscal deficits exceeding 7%, and only four including China and India had deficits exceeding 10%]. The ensuing banking crisis thus has thus already affected fiscal budgetary health of China.

The consequent inflation and the continued fast export-led growth will mean commensurate wage increases to sustain consumer demand and to meet demand for skilled labour in exporting firms. This can induce a currency crisis because of the peculiar and precariously balanced structure of China's foreign trade, in which imports from East Asia are reprocessed and exported to US and EU. And thus a surplus on the current account earned with the developed West is covering the deficit with East Asia.

More importantly China's foreign trade comprises of two rather different components: (1) imports that is processed and re-exported and (2) "domestic" or "own" trade, i.e., exports of goods primarily originating in the domestic economy, and imports for domestic consumption and production use. The former reflects China's rising role as a labour intensive processing and assembly centre, fueled by outsourcing and external final demand, while the latter is more strongly influenced by domestic economic trends.

It can be expected therefore that China's current account will turn negative in the second first decade of the 21st century because of a rapidly increasing deficit in domestic trade and rising wages rates of skilled labour in export oriented industries. That is, even without a crisis, continued high growth rates will cause skilled workers' wages to rise which could put Chinese exports at comparative disadvantage against South Asian countries or even East Asian countries, thereby slowing exports, upsetting the regional trade balances, and thus cause a currency crisis especially following a banking collapse.

Furthermore, it is China's high domestic saving which is keeping the State owned banks [SOBs] flushed with funds. Two problems will however arise soon. First, China's the rate domestic saving has peaked (see Modigliani. Franco, and K.Cao). Moreover, China's incremental capital-output ratio is estimated after conforming data to international practice at 6.0, which is very high. Further, if China is unable to keep it's commitments to the WTO on the financial sector, FDI which is already very high at $ 50 billion could consequently taper off.

Second, savers will have alternatives if and when China implements it's WTO assurance to open to foreign banks on "national treatment" basis by 2007. That will hit the SOBs and undermine the Communist Party's main controlling weapon of financial authority.

So far economic reforms have been successful in legitimizing the CCP which it had lost during the GPCR. But the implementation of this particular assurance to the WTO on opening the banking sector to foreigners will undermine the authoritarian political control that financial patronage affords to the CCP. Therefore will this assurance be implemented? I am doubtful.

But if China does keep it's commitments to the WTO, the State owned banks [SOBs] would suffer a sharp drop in depositors because the thus WTO enabled foreign banks would be able to attract them better by a higher deposit interest rate. At present, SOBs give merely 2 percent as interest on deposits. Such a desertion by depositors will make the SOBs wholly untenable financially and would lead to their crash. Already in 2004, bank deposits growth has slowed with the advent of limited foreign bank freedom to operate.

In turn, the State owned enterprises [SOEs], of which two-thirds are in the red and surviving because of loans from SOBs that are not paid back [soft-budget constraint], would have to wind up and render millions unemployed.

Furthermore, foreign banks in China would find it profitable to lend to the private sector which at present gets less than five per cent of all bank loans. According to *Beijing Review* 8, 2004, 77 per cent of the private enterprises are facing financial difficulties. This sector is relying on informal sources for finances. Enterprise will have to, as the Review suggests to commercial banks for their existence in the near future. This would enable the private sector to emerge as serious competitor to the

SOEs, but with less padded employment potential. Will the prevailing political constraints permit that? According to George Gilboy, that is unlikely since it will mean permitting the private sector to emerge as an independent economic power and the consequent Party's control over the financial system decisively weakened.

A Financial Cleft Stick or Catch -22 for China

It is thus a Catch-22 situation for China. It means either being resigned to an inevitable financial crisis arising from:

(i) 50% NPL
(ii) 2% CAR
(iii) Fiscal deficit of 13% of GDP implying inflation
(iv) Contingent liabilities to provide for enhanced pension, increased social security to meet the rising layoffs & migrants, and rural subsidies to contain food prices.
(v) M2/GDP rising towards 200%.
(vi) A depleting current account surplus.
(vii) The deteriorating balance of trade in Chinese-origin products and switch processing trade..

or to face and political upheaval arising from the consequences of essential financial sector reforms.

The Chinese financial system thus is now prone to a crisis if adequate correctives are not applied immediately. Interestingly, this is recognized by leading officials of China. Speaking at the plenary session of the National Peoples Congress in March 2004, China's Prime Minister Wen Jiabao stated that on banking system reforms "China is engaged in a last ditch fight that we cannot afford to lose".

However, ground level corrective action today does not reflect this official acknowledgment. Whatever action has been taken is quite inadequate to stave off the crisis.

The Communist Party of China had in the past courageously undertaken reforms but more because it was necessary *and which also legitimized the Party* especially after a prolonged disorder which had damaged the party's credibility nationally and internationally. After the

Great Leap Forward, the Great Proletarian Cultural Revolution and the Gang of Four, the Communist Party's standing with the people was eroded. Chairman Deng had understood that and skillfully launched reforms.

Dramatic as the financial crisis scenario appears, it is the reality in China. There is today clearly a Catch-22 type political bind on the financial system. Either China will have to carry our financial reforms and face a possible political upheaval arising from a large number of urban workers being laid off, or retain the political levers on the financial system and face an economic crisis caused by a banking bankruptcy that cannot be bailed out by fiscal measures.

With a peaked domestic saving rate, a high incremental capital ratio, and an uncertain FD1, there is no scope for raising or even sustaining the present growth rate in GDP without reforms that are able to increase total factor productivity. The last few years of sustaining demand by "pump priming" has already been reversed since June 2004 by new credit restrictions, leading to open discussion of whether a "soft-landing" of the economy is possible.

Hence, consider a banking crisis deepened by this credit squeeze, which is accentuated by the ticking pension bomb that will require funding of $600-800 billion [by 2025, China's 65+ years population will have risen from 10% to 25%]. At present, the IMF estimates that there are 105 million contributors and 32 million beneficiaries. But the implicit pension liability is 90% of GDP with a financing gap of 70% of GDP. At present, the pension system however covers only 20% of the workforce. Beijing cannot print more money to meet these gaps.

Add to it the threat of private savings shifting to foreign banks as per WTO mandate for 2007, plus a rise in wages of skilled workers caused by continued high growth and through increased labour demand of more and more multinationals coming to China, that will erode China's comparative advantage.

On lop of it all, the off loading of the yuan equivalent of the $300 billion exports net of deductions parked in US Treasury bonds plus FDl of $50 billion, and the inflow of S by the continued speculation especially by the diaspora, that the *yuan* will appreciate, thereby flooding China with more speculative dollars for windfall profits in a future exchange for yuan, the bubble burst scenario is clearly visible. It is well known that defending a fixed rate has been everywhere a cause fur crisis. Even if the WTO assurance on foreign banks is not implemented, these ingredients (and add the need to finance food and oil imports) are sufficiently fissile to cause a bubble burst.

Last March at the NPC, the Chinese authorities had hoped for a soft landing [lower inflation and growth rates], but hard landing appears certain to most analysts [unemployment, inflation, recession, slump in growth rates]. A foreign banker was quoted by Wall Street Journal as saying: "If Chinese banks can't be fixed, then the government will not open up the banking industry, because they know local banks can't compete".

To me therefore a crash not soft or hard landing of the Chinese economy seems probable by 2010,

The Fiscal Crisis in India

In India, unlike in China, it will not be the bankruptcy of the banking sector that will be trigger the crisis. That will come from the failure of fiscal budgeting system.

It is also widely recognized that major new generation of reforms are required to stave off this failure but which political constraints will not permit to be implemented. In my view, as on the last occasion of a balance of payments crisis in 1990-91, it will be only at the brink of the precipice when Indian political constraints will melt and allow the new generation reforms to be initiated. As before, it may require a regime change, of course brought about democratically.

The malaise in the Indian financial system as we saw is not in its macro economic fundamentals per se. It is that these fundamentals have been attained by running the fiscal system to the ground, e.g., inflation has so far been contained by financing the large government deficit by a surplus of private saving over private investment. Growth rate in GDP has been sustained by disproportionate rise in the service sector which is now 52% of GDP.

However, Indian financial institutions are in place even if straitjacketed by the government. India has a long functioning central bank [The Reserve Bank of India], a well-defined capital market regulator [The Securities and Exchange Board of India], and a modern IT —savvy paperless stock market.

The banking system is also not in shambles as in China. NPL is not more than 15% and the bad debt is about $15 billion. Capital adequacy ratio requirement of 12% is also met by most banks.

India's problem is as stated above, that the government budget is a can of worms. At the Central government level, the budget finances are in a debt trap, made inflexible by politically irreducible commitments-for amortization, defence subsidies, counter guarantees and pensions-which account for 95% of all revenue mobilized in the Budget.

This is compounded by the political inability to prune what can be pruned with greater political determination: defence, subsidies, and government administration expenditure, or to raise new taxes substantively.

Moreover, the provincial governments are increasingly dependent on transfers and grams from the Centre, and are getting close to defaulting on their employees' salaries. Early in 2004, the Supreme Court ordered the state government of Bihar to pay employees their six months overdue salaries. The order was complied with thanks to an extraordinary grant from the central government which is run by a new coalition in which the state party is also a constituent.

Moreover, most public sector enterprises units are in the red, and the State Electricity Boards are bankrupt. The Central government is making the provisions for these government enterprises out of loans squeezed from the SOBs. This has had a negative effect on the private industry investment [as a ratio of GDP] which ratio has been declining since 1995.

Total investment in agriculture has also declined, while a small rise in the service sector investment has neutralized the decline in public sector savings to keep the total domestic savings ratio roughly constant. In fact, in the Central Budget, the Capital Account Budget has to be increasingly, year after year, be in surplus to finance the Revenue Account Budget deficit.

The trigger thus will be this Budgetary cleft stick:—the impossibility of finding new resources, coupled with the rising demand for funds from a newly invigorated private corporate sector. At present, 90 percent of the financial household saving is being deployed to finance the gap between public saving and public investment. The former is negative at -21/4% of GDP. The economy will not be able to find the resources for both. Therefore:

(i) real interest rate will rise to exceed the growth rate in GDP, causing investment decline, followed by the growth rate falling further below the real interest rate. This can then spiral the economy onto a tail spin to depression, and a return to the "Hindu" growth rate [derisively termed to be below 4 percent growth rate that is below unemployment clearing poverty reducing rate of a minimum of 6 percent].

(ii) The rise in interest rate will put the debt dynamics on an explosive path as well. According to a study of Dr. Kalpana Kochhar of IMF, the real effective interest rate on government debt [defined as the ratio of interest payments in a year to outstanding liabilities at the end of the previous year] has risen already from 3¼% in 1997-98 to 6¼% in 2000-01. As Martin Feldstein showed mathematically, when the rate of interest exceeds the growth rate, debt will swell on the explosive path.

(iii) This will send the government budget headlong into an internal debt trap. At present the Budget is already on the verge of a debt trap. Hence, this will mean a down grading by international rating agencies as it happened in 1990-91.

(iv) The NRIs, as studies show behave just as any other nervous investor, will hence begin pulling out their deposits because of what is called 'a herd mentality'. Along with "hot money", this withdrawal will be sizeable and enough to cause a currency crisis.

(v) The rising fiscal deficit will impact on the external current account balances either by the private sector reaching out abroad for funds or for the government seeking financing of debt through floating bonds or asking SOBs to seek short-term loans from abroad, both of which will carry heavy servicing obligations.

(vi) To rescue the Indian economy from this inevitable spiral, it will need a paradigm shift in current political outlook and require a non risk—averse leadership as in 1990-96 India had, to complete the reform process to totally dismantle the remaining Soviet style controls on the economy.

(vii) The task of reforms was interrupted in 1996 once well past the crisis, by an electoral defeat of pro-reform Prime Minister Narasimha Rao, a defeat organized by the rentier class and Ac crony capitalists. Since then, successive governments have made ad hoc and sporadic efforts to reform but no new generation reforms have been initiated to succeed the first generation de-regulating liberalization 1991-96.

(viii) The provinces in India are also equally in the red, getting close in some states to defaulting on payment of salaries to its own employees. Table below shows that, according to a tabulation obtained from the Planning Commission that majority of the provinces of India are "debt-stressed", i.e., close to insolvency. Most of the state public sector enterprises are making losses while the State Electricity Boards with monopoly on transmission are deeply in red with accumulated losses that are staggering, India is clearly headed towards a budgetary dead-end.

Given the decade long constancy in the domestic savings ratio, the long term decline in the agricultural investment rate, a stagnant private investment because of a record 11 per cent of GDP being the fiscal deficit, there is no way the growth rate of the Indian economy can be raised or prevented from falling due to the law of diminishing returns, unless productivity is increased by modernization of domestic industry for' example by using IT software. FDI which on the most inclusive definition does not exceed $ 6 billion per year, is unlikely lo increase to raise the level ff investment unless infrastructure and labour laws are brought to international standards. Both these at the very least require new legislation which under the present political dispensation appears a remote possibility.

CONCLUSION

In India and China, political factors had led to economic reforms being implemented during the two decades since 1980. Growth rates thus accelerated and exports boomed. Increased foreign investment was seen and many poor people were lifted above the poverty line.

However, since the late 1990s, both countries have experienced severe problems in the financial system. In China, the government owned banking system is in crisis and almost bankrupt. It is being kept afloat by liberal recapitalization by the State. In India it is the fiscal budgetary system that is locked in a debt-trap and inflexible commitments for current expenditure, that require large pre-emption of bank funds for meeting the revenue deficit, funds that otherwise would have been available for private investment.

To rectify these imminent bankruptcies, a banking one in China and fiscal one in India, would require a new generation of financial reforms that may hurt political interests that are very difficult to ignore. Hence politics in the coming decade would be the constraining factor in the implementation of these reforms.

A crisis, ceteris paribus, appears probable in both countries. India is institutionally better equipped to fire fight the crisis once it envelopes the economy because of the flexibility of democracy in being able to replace failed leadership. The Chinese institutional system is still underdeveloped, and it political order is more brittle, and the leadership is not only not directly accountable but less capable of political change as demonstrated during the 1989 Tiananmen incidents.

As **Gordon Chang** has aptly observed the collapse of the Soviet Union came about because it reformed politically "too fast", China would collapse, according to Chang because it erred by moving too slow. India will fumble but its democratic institutions will throw up a new leadership as in the past when a crisis descended, which would be empowered to take bold decisions and come out of the crisis.

Chapter 5

GOVERNANCE, DEMOGRAPHIC DIVIDEND AND EDUCATION

For a modern State, the management of a globalised economy requires sagacity in understanding the casual links and assumptions underlying policy tradeoffs and choices; about the institutional capacity needed to implement reforms, Social consensus and alliances that will have to be built with different parts of society to successfully carry out the reforms. For this is required room to maneuver against narrower political interests; identify and develop needed compensatory mechanisms for the poorest and most adversely affected citizens. This is Governance.

Governance is structured to provide access to information as a fundamental right, accountability, empowerment i.e. inclusiveness and participatory democracy, and devolution of power.

Definition of Governance

There are several definitions of governance, as given below:

The World Bank

Governance is defined as the manner in which power is exercised in the management of a country's economic and social resources. The World Bank has identifies three distinct aspects of governance (1) the form of political regime; (2) the process by which authority is exercised in the management of a country's economic and social resources for development; and (3) the capacity of governments in design, formulate and implement policies and discharge functions.

United Nations Development Programme

Governance is viewed as the exercise of political, economic and administrative authority in the management of a country's affairs at all levels. It comprises mechanisms, processes and institutions through which citizens and groups articulate their interests, exercise their legal rights, meet their obligations, and mediate their differences.

Organization for Economic Cooperation and Development

The concept of governance denotes the use of political authority and exercise of control in a society in relation to the management of its resources for social and economic development. This broad definition encompasses the role of public authorities in establishing the environment in which economic operators function and in determining the distribution of benefits, as well as the nature of the relationship between the ruler and the ruled.

Commission on Global Governance

Governance is the sum of the many ways individuals and institutions, public and private, manage their common affairs. It is a continuing process through which conflicting or diverse interests may be accommodated and cooperative action may be taken. It includes formal institutions and regimes empowered to enforce compliance, as well as informal arrangements that people and institutions either have agreed to or perceive to be in their interest.

Mahbub ul Haq Human Development Centre

Humane Governance is governance dedicated to securing human development. It must enable the State, civil society and the private sector to help build capacities, which will meet the basic needs of all people, particularly women, children and the poor. It requires effective participation of people in state, civil society and private sector activities that are conducive to human development.

Citizens' access to information is for setting priorities for national expenditure, for enabling access to quality schools, ensuring for example that roads once financed actually get built, or seeing to it that medicines are actually delivered and available in clinics.

Access to laws and impartial justice is also critical to protect the rights of poor people and pro-poor coalitions and to enable them to demand accountability, whether from their government or from private sector institutions. Thus it requires a law, the Right to Information act, which India has, but not China. It also requires easy access to courts.

Accountability is a concept that enables the combating of corruption, Corruption is sub-optimization of the allocation of public resources by providing "rent" payments or simply 'greasing palms' to public officials, private employers or service providers. To account, requires that they be answerable and held responsible for their policies, actions and use of funds.

Corruption, also defined as the abuse of public office for private gain, hurts poor people the most because they are the least likely to have direct access to officials and the least able to use connections to get services; they also have the fewest options to use private services as an alternative.

There are three main types of accountability mechanisms: political, administrative, and public or social. *Political accountability* is of public representatives, and generally achieved through elections. *Administrative accountability* of government agencies is through internal mechanisms, both horizontal and vertical within and between official agencies. *Public or social accountability* mechanisms hold government agencies accountable to citizens. Citizen action or social accountability can reinforce political and administrative accountability mechanisms, but generally nowadays the Courts have become the main arena for rectification.

India's Minister of Programme Implementation informed the Lok Sabha (Parliament) sometime ago that out of the 425 Central Sector Projects costing Rs. 20 crores and above on the monitor of his Ministry, 205 projects were running behind their original schedules. Consequently, the cost of these projects had increased to Rs. 84,167 crores from the original estimate of Rs.52,987 crores, that is, by 58.8 per cent!

The actual loss would be much more since a large number of projects costing up to Rs.20 crores are not on the monitor of the Ministry. Besides, similar losses are being incurred by various State level Governments on the projects coming under their jurisdiction.

If one includes the losses incurred on smaller projects under the Central sector and also those coming under the State sector, it is estimated that public funds worth around Rs.50,000 crores go down the drain every year because of the huge time and cost overruns. Much of this wastage can be avoided if only there is a better planning and tighter monitoring of projects.

There is also another dimension in the problem of time and cost overruns. According to Construction Industry Development Council, the disputed amount locked up in all projects, is to the tune of Rs. 52,000 crores over a period of 8-10 years.

The problem of huge time and cost overruns in infrastructure projects has been nagging policy makers and experts for many years now with no solution in sight. Even the creation of a separate Department of Programme Implementation (formerly Ministry of Programme Implementation) in 1985 with the exclusive purpose of independently monitoring Central Sector Projects has not improved matters.

If at all, the losses suffered by the nation have only tended to escalate over the years. It is ironical that while the debate over the ways and means of raising resources for infrastructure projects continues, little attention seems to have gone into the question of efficient use of available funds.

The reasons dished out by the Ministry for the long delays in the implementation of projects remain unchanged year after year. These include funds constrains, land problems, delays in civil works, delay in award of contract, slow progress and the delay in supply of equipment. It need not come as a surprise that of the 205 Central Sector projects running behind schedule, as many as 125 are Railway projects.

Recent survey shows that of the 1,035 infrastructure projects completed between 1992 and 2009, 41 per cent faced cost overruns and 82 per cent time overruns. Currently, time delays on infrastructure projects is estimated to be over 40 per cent while the average cost overrun is estimated to be 13 per cent in any infrastructure project.

In the context of the nearly 46 per cent of the country's total Plan outlay for FY11 allocated to critical infrastructure sectors, and with time and cost playing a critical role in the completion of any construction or infrastructure project, it is important, that technology is adopted to enable governance, save cost and provide faster access to information than ever before.

In India, a lot of construction companies (general contractors, project management consultancy firms, real estate firms and capital project owners) do not give importance to technology and are investing a miniscule 0.15 per cent of their total turnover on IT, while the developed countries are investing 2-3 per cent of their turnover, which is a 20-fold increase in IT investments made by similar sized companies in India.

Infrastructure projects, being the most affected due to project delays and cost overruns which in turn lead to reduced margins for the contractor as infrastructure projects, are generally fixed-price contracts.

It is imperative that Indian infrastructure and construction companies pay heed to technology as an essential investment rather than just treating it as a checkmark purchase.

In 2006, India ranked 134 out of 175 countries in terms of ease of doing business. China ranked 93, and the relatively tiny Vietnam ranked 104 – 30 places higher than India. In terms of dealing with licences and sundry government permissions, India ranked 155, China was only marginally better at 153, but Vietnam was way ahead at 25. As far as registering property was concerned, India was placed at 110, versus China at 21 and Vietnam at 34. Regarding flexibility in hiring, utilising and retrenchment of workers, India was 112, compared to 78 in China and 104 in Vietnam.

In exports and imports, India ranked at 139, China was 38, and Vietnam 75 in the cumbersome procedures. India also fared abysmally in the case of enforcing commercial contracts; ranked 173 (that is, only two countries are worse than us), versus 63 for China and 94 for Vietnam. And our monstrous difficulties in winding-up ranked India at 133 in the case of closing business, compared to 75 for China and 116 for Vietnam.

All these hassles have to do with the government and the judiciary; center, state, districts, municipal entities and courts. All procedures involve multiple permissions—often sequential and occasionally conflicting in their remit—which take for too long to be resolved. Let me now give you a real life example.

The multinational Cairn discovered India's largest on-shore oil reserves in the district of Barmer in Rajasthan. The original agreement was that Cairn would be paid for evacuating the crude at site (the point of delivery), which would then be carried by a public sector company to southern Rajasthan and Gujarat by a pipeline constructed by that enterprise.

By end-2006, it was clear that the public sector company was not going to be able to construct the pipeline. Since no pipeline meant no oil for the nation (you need to ship the crude out of Barmer), Cairn offered to build the pipeline with cost recovery. That required two permissions from the Ministry of Petroleum. The first was to permit shifting the 'point of delivery' of the crude from Barmer to the end-point of the pipeline and hence, right of access. And the second required recognizing Cairn as the pipeline contractor for getting cost recovery.

The file made interminable rounds in the ministry for more than six months. Eventually, Murli Deora, the minister concerned, was given the full picture of the delays and what it was costing the nation. Deora, to his credit, immediately sanctioned the project. Guess what? Even after the minister's approval, a civil servant in the ministry succeeded in putting such onerous caveats in the last paragraph of the sanction letter that it has become impossible to proceed without these being removed.

Bureaucracy thus delayed a project that happens to be India's largest on-shore find and for reasons bordering on a lack of concern about the cost to the nation. The situation in China is similar.

On August 1, 2007 Mattel recalled approximately 1.5 million toys made by a manufacturer in China because of dangerous levels of lead in their paint. The recall makes a continuation of the quality control problems that importers of Chinese-made exports have been experiencing over the past two months in products ranging from pet food to fish to tires. Four days earlier, the Chinese government ordered the country's banks to increase their reserves and thereby reduce the amount of money they can lend to business—part of an effort to cool down an economy that is growing at its fastest rate in 12 years.

But quality concerns and rapid growth are not China's only worries. There are many governments in China, and the ability of the central government to control commerce in China is very limited. There's no Chinese counterpart to the U.S. commerce clause in their Constitution. And so, whatever regulations or laws the central government makes, they are sometimes changed and often ignored by local governments.

Again, it is highly decentralized in China. The provinces and the provincial governors have strong incentives to maximize their GDP. They're rewarded or punished career-wise for the level of their provincial GDP. Advancement within the political system depends upon provincial GDP level achieved. So the provinces tend to fulfill—as in old Soviet Union—they tend to fulfill and over-fulfill their quotas. Often the NBS is in the position of tapping down to the statistics they get from the provinces. The provincial totals and the aggregated NBS numbers are in disparity. The central government has been taking some measures, both administrative as well as fiscal, to try to slow down GDP growth. But can they? Chinese government really cannot control the banks. The banks are themselves fairly decentralized. Every province has a branch of Big Four commercial banks is run (fairly) autonomously. But the banks have become joint stock companies and Western investors have taken positions in them. An just like the central government has trouble controlling local governments, bank headquarters have trouble controlling the branches of the banks!

Now, there's an additional issue called the "perpetual motion machine" in China. China produces goods for export and FDI (Foreign Direct Investment) comes into China as well. When the dollars or Western currencies come into China, they are absorbed by the central bank, viz., the People's Bank of China. The People's Bank of China in turn puts the dollars into China's foreign reserves. The PBC issues RMB in return for the dollars—but because of lack of convertibility these RMB cannot leave China. The RMB is not convertible.

Thus all of this RMB in China has no place to go except China. It ends up in further fixed asset investment—roads, factories and the like. Fixed asset investment leads to more production and more exportable surplus, and hence "the perpetual motion machine". But where is the demand for this rising production? Unless and until there is convertibility of the RMB currency, China's GDP, China's exports and China's fixed asset investment are going to all go up together in a few years in smoke.

Dr. Bibek Debroy has researched on the World Bank produced Doing Business (DB) India is 122nd out of 171 countries, slipping two ranks from 2008. Within South Asia, India performs better than only Bhutan and Afghanistan. **Table below.**

The DB exercise quantifies and measures procedures in 10 stages of a business's life—starting a business, dealing with construction permits, employing workers, registering property, getting credit, protecting investors, paying taxes, trading across borders, enforcing contracts and closing a business. It takes 13 procedures and 30 days. (1 day in New Zealand) to start a business in, India and costs of starting a business are 70.1 per cent of per capita income. Twenty procedures and 224 days 34 in Korea) are required for construction permits and costs are 414.7 per cent of per capita income. The rigidity of the employment index (low is good) is 30 in India (0 in Hong Kong) and firing costs are 56 weeks of wages, Six procedures and 45 days (2 in New Zealand, 5 in Nepal) are required to register property in India and costs are 7.5 per cent of property value.

Table 81: Snapshot of Business Climates in India and China, 2008

Indicator	India	China	OECD Average
Starting a Business			
Number of procedures	10	11	7
Duration (days)	88	46	30
Cost (% of GNI per capita)	49.8	14.3	10.2
Min. Capital (% of GNI per capita)	430.4	3855.9	61.2
Hiring and Firing Workers			
Flexibility of Hiring Index	33	17	49
Conditions of Employment Index	75	67	58
Flexibility of Firing Index	45	57	28
Employment Laws Index	51	47	45
Enforcing Contracts			
Number of procedures	22	20	17
Duration (days)	365	180	233
Cost (% of GNI per capita)	95	32	7.1
Procedural Complexity Index	50	52	49
Getting Credit			
Public Credit Registry operates?	NO	YES	
Year Public Credit Registry established	-	1999	

Public Credit Registry coverage (borrowers per 1000 capita)	0	3	43.2
Public Credit Registry Index	0	56	58
Private Credit Bureau operates?	No	No	
Private Credit Bureau coverage (borrowers per 1000 capita)	0	0	443.5
Creditor Rights Index	3	2	1
Closing a Business			
Actual time (in years)	11.3	2.6	1.8
Actual cost (% of estate)	8	18	77
Goals of Insolvency Index	21	51	77
Court Powers Index	33	67	36

Table 82: Best Practices in China and globally

Indicators	Best practice in China	International ranking of best practice in China	Best practice in the world
Cost to open a business (% of provincial GDP per capita)	3.1 Shanghal	22	0 Denmark
Days to open a business	28 Guangzhou	79	2 Australia
procedures to open a business	12 Hangzhou/Nanjing/Fuzhou	140	2 Australia/Canada
Procedures to register property	4 Shanghai	23	1 Norway/Sweden
Days to register property	3.1 Chongqing	52	0 Sweden/Thailand
Cost to register property (% of property value)	3.1 Beijing	52	0 Saudi Arabia
Days to create and register collateral	7 Fuzhou	n.a.	n.a.
Cost to create and register collateral (% of loan value)	2.1 Nanjing	n.a.	n.a.
Days to enforce contracts	112 Nanjing	2	109 New Zealand
Cost to enforce contracts (% of claim value)	9.0 Shanghai	8	5.5 South Korea

* International comparative data are from *Doing Business in 2008.* "Enforcing contracts" data are from *Doing Business in 2007. How to Reform.*

** n.a. = not applicable. The time and cost of registering collateral were not reported in the global *Doing Business Study.*

Source: Doing Business database.

Table 83: Doing Business - Global Comparisons (2007-08)

Item	India	China	Thailand	Korea	Philippines	Australia	US	Best
1	2	3	4	5	6	7	8	9
Starting a business (no. of days)	30	40	33	17	52	2	6	1 (New Zealand)
Dealing with licenses (no. of days)	224	336	156	34	203	221	40	34 (Korea)
Employing workers (difficulty of firing index)	70	50	0	30	30	10	0	0 (US)*
Registering property (no. of days)	45	29	2	11	33	5	12	2 (Sweden, Saudi Arabia, New Zealand, Thailand)
Getting Credit (strength of legal rights index)	8	6	4	7	3	9	8	10 (Hong Kong China, Kenya, Malaysia, Singapore)
Protecting investors (strength of investor protection index)	6	5	7.7	5.3	4	5.7	8.3	10 (New-Zealand Kenya)
Enforcing contracts (days)	1420	406	479	230	842	395	300	150 (Singapore)
Closing a business (years)	10	1.7	2.7	1.5	5.7	1	1.5	0.4 (Ireland)

*Hong Kong, China, Singapore, Maldives, Marshall Islands also have the same status. Difficulty of firing index 0 (zero difficulty) to 100 (highest difficulty) . Strength of legal rights index 0 (no strength) to 10 maximum strength).

Source: World Bank *Doing Business Database (2009).*

For getting credit, India scores 4 (high is good) on a credit information index (New Zealand is 5) and 8 on a legal rights index (Malaysia is 10). India scores 6 on an investor protection index (high is good), New Zealand is 9.70. India requires 60 tax payments a year (2 in Sweden) and 271 hours per year (59 in Luxembourg) are spent in paying taxes. Tax rate is 71.5 per cent of profits in India and 8.4 per cent in Vanuatu, Eight export documents are needed in India (2 in France) and 17 days are required to export (5 in Denmark). Cost of exporting is $945 per container ($450 in Malaysia). Nine import documents are needed in India (2 in France) and 20 days are required to import (3 in Singapore). Cost of importing is $960 per container ($439 in Singapore). Forty-six procedures (20 in Ireland) and 1420 days (150 in Singapore) are required to enforce a contract in India and costs are 39.6 per cent of claim (6.2 per cent in Ireland). Ten years are required for insolvency proceedings in India (0.40 in Ireland), cost of insolvency is 9 per cent of estate value (1 per cent in Singapore) and recovery rate is 10.4 per cent (92.5 per cent in Japan).

Chart 25: Governance Indicators: India's Ranking within 75 Countries and China's

India Ranks better than China in 15 Indicators, equal to in 3 and worse in 21, out of a total of 39. In two parameters, India ranks within the first 20 countries out of the 75. China is better of, with seven parameters in teh first twenty countries. In the top 10 countries, India scores only in one indicator. Details below:

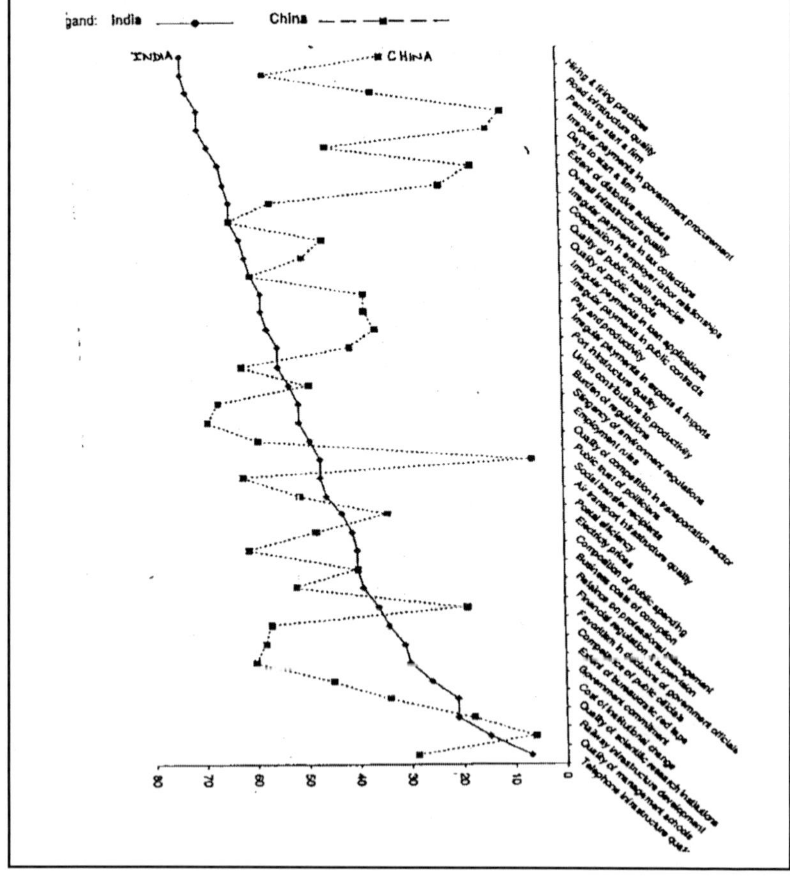

Ranking of India and China within 75 World Countries
(No. 1 is the best)

First, not everything relevant for doing business is captured directly in DB indicators—I physical infrastructure, law and order, macro-economy, institutions are instances. Second, information is based on subjective responses to questionnaires and this raises issues of sampling biases.

An Indian Chamber of Commerce (ICC) found that it takes 105 days to register property in West Bengal, compared to 2 days in Karnataka and 1 in Gujarat and there are similar results for other business transactions.

China's mandarins embattle a dubious and incriminating dairy scandal. The dairy scandal—of infant formula laced with industrial addictive, melamine—claimed three infant lives and rendered an estimated 53,000 infants sick. The scandal has raised critical questions regarding the credibility of one-party control and China's systemic weakness to provide appropriate, adequate regulatory safeguards.

It also brings to the fore the act of a free press and opposition. It also puts a spotlight on the underside—the costs of doing business with China.

China has been riddled with scams and scares—ranging from pork scare, to contaminated toothpaste and even life-saving and essential drugs. Last year, almost 200 Chinese cancer patients were found to have been treated with spurious leukemia drugs. Recently, pet-food for the US market, made by two Chinese animal feed companies was found contaminated with melamine (an ingredient which fakes protein content) and which in turn triggered off pet deaths in US. The adulteration was done to meet prescribed protein requirement to increase profit margins. Other recent cases have been an estimated 100 deaths in Panama after patients took an adulterated cold medicine, manufactured in China. There have also been two recent high profile cases involving a 3 million toy recall as toys made for the Fisher-Price and Thomas and Tank Engine Products label were found tainted with excess level of toxic lead paint.

Ironically, just a year ago, when China was reeling under the spectre or scams and ensuing cover-ups, Prime Minister Wen Jiabao pledged to get at the root of the serial scandals. The government authorised $1.1 billion and sent 300,000 inspectors to examine quality control. Besides, it also took the unprecedented step of issuing a White Paper on "Quality and Safety of Food in China" in August 2007 and another on the "Status Quo of Drug Supervision in China" in July 2008, ostensibly to smoothen and assuage ruffled business feathers, as Anurag Vishwanath found.

China has a stringent licence system, compulsory inspection system, the China National Accreditation Service for Conformity Assessment (CNAS) with various other safeguards thrown in. However, China's specific laws, administrative regulations and specific departmental rules create a virtual maze. While the government claims that integrated food supervision and safety is through departmental cooperation such as between the State Food and Drug Administration (SFDA), Health Ministry, Agriculture Ministry, Commerce Ministry and the General Administration of Quality, Supervision, Inspection and Quarantine, in reality jurisdiction is overlapping and blurred.

China's competitive economic milieu where the buck stops at the cheapest manufacturer has led not only to dismal working conditions but also ingenious cost cutting methods. Also in a social culture where *guanxi* or networking plays an important role, laws, licenses and loopholes are for a price.

The public outrage is palpable given that the dairy scandal comes months after China's top good quality watchdog SFDA, rated dairy companies as the safest—and gave them a clean chit saying that 99 per cent of them passed safety inspections for infant formula As the matter stands, almost 22 dairy companies, including export companies such as Yili Industrial Group (a sponsor of the Beijing Olympics) and Mengniu Dairy Co. stand incriminated, tangled in a web of questionable manufacturing practices. Reports suggest that a slew of dairy companies were exempted from mandatory inspections.

Countries such as Japan, Singapore, Hong Kong and Taiwan have recalled dairy products—ranging from cheese, baby formula, non-dairy creamer amidst increasing food scare. The scandal has left a trail all the way across Asian markets to the US which has recalled a few instant coffee and tea drinks containing Chinese made non-dairy creamer. Health experts are speculating whether the contaminated dairy products have seeped into other food products, fanning food fear.

The scandal initially centered on the Sanlu Group, a joint venture with New Zealand dairy giant Fonterra, which owns a 43 per cent share. Sanlu headquartered in Hebei province (surrounding the Beijing municipality) was chaired by a Communist Party official, appointed by the provincial party authorities. What also appears to be the case is that the complaints regarding the baby formula began filtering in by December 2007. Sanlu, the worst offender, did not take adequate steps to investigate and form the public. In fact, the company made a high profile $1.25 million donation of baby food, presumably toxic, to the Sichuan earthquake infants.

President Hu Jintao's conceded that "some leaders lacked a sense of responsibility and had a loose governance" and called for cadre "self-improvement". But according to the *Financial Times,* the Prime Minister of New Zealand Helen Clark has said that local officials knew about the contamination but did not act until her government took it up with. Beijing.

China's recurring scandals are clearly not stray incidents anymore, but systemic. China professors that it has adequate regulatory safeguards but the lack of transparency and suppression of information is increasingly becoming an embarrassment. China's reputation as a reliable factory of the world at stake.

Population in India and China

Since 1980, both countries have progressively reduced the population growth rate to levels at which projection of convergence to a stationary or zero population growth by 2020 appears credible and an attainable target. At present China's population growth is at less than 1 per cent per year, while India's is at 1.7 per cent, and the trend is downward. The comparative international perspective may be seen in Table below, which reveals that China's growth rate is below developing countries average, while India's is about the same level.

Table 84: Some Demographic Indicators

Country/Region	Annual Population Growth Rates (Per Cent)		
	1960-92	1992-2000	2000-2010
China	1.9	1.0	0.8
India	2.2	1.8	1.7
Indonesia	2.1	1.5	1.5
Arab States	2.6	2.9	3.0
Sub-Saharan Africa	2.8	2.9	2.9
Latin America and the Caribbean	2.4	1.8	1.6
Developing Countries	2.3	1.8	1.7
World	1.9	1.5	1.4

Table 85: Demographic profile: China: India

	1995		2020	
	China	India	China	India
Indicator				
Population (million)	1,200.24	916.09	1,425.29	1,470.14
Labour force (million)	811.40	346.72	987.78	798.07
Fertility rate (percent)	1.95	2.50	2.00	2.10
Life expectancy (years)	69	62	73	70
Children/population	26.0	32.3	19.9	28.1
Elderly/population	6.4	4.8	10.8	6.9
Dependency ratio[a] (percent)	47.9	58.1	40.9	48.4
Decadel Population Growth rate (%/year)	1.2	1.8	0.9	1.2

a. Ratio of nonworking-age population to working-age population

Source: World Bank data & Statistical Yearbooks.

The factors causing steeper decline in population growth rate in China compared to India are the follows:

(a) The implementation of family planning programmes, particularly in the rural areas, has reduced the infant mortality rates tremendously in China to 3 per 1000, in contrast to India at 80 per 1000. In China, 94 per cent of child births are attended by trained health personnel as compared to 33 per cent in India. Cross Section data confirm statistically that infant mortality rates are positively correlated with birth rates. This is the hedge against risk of infant mortality.

(b) Family planning education to women: By extending education to women, China could increase the age of women seeking marriage and convince them to adopt methods to avoid early child birth. For instance, the percentage of married women of child-bearing age using contraception is as high as 83 compared to 43 in India.

(c) Health and nutrition standards: By improving the health and nutrition levels of the people, especially women, China increased female life expectancy well beyond India's. This with reduction in infant mortality removed the need for a mortality hedge against risk which hitherto meant a larger than desired family size.

China is projected to remain the fastest growing BRIC economy over the next few years, but is expected to be overtaken in growth rates (though not levels of GDP) by India in around 2015 and Brazil in around 2025. The decelerating growth profile in China reflects the factors discussed above, in particular China's rapidly ageing population (the same factor accounts for the marked deceleration in projected growth in Russia over the next 20 years). In contrast, the much younger and faster growing Indian and Brazilian populations are able to sustain a more stable rate of growth up to around 2030, although after that they too experience a gradual deceleration as their populations also begin to age.

Of course, what happens if, in the near future, China changes its "one-child" policy to, say, a "two-children" policy? The implications are not as yet clear.

Figure 38: India overtakes China in 2030

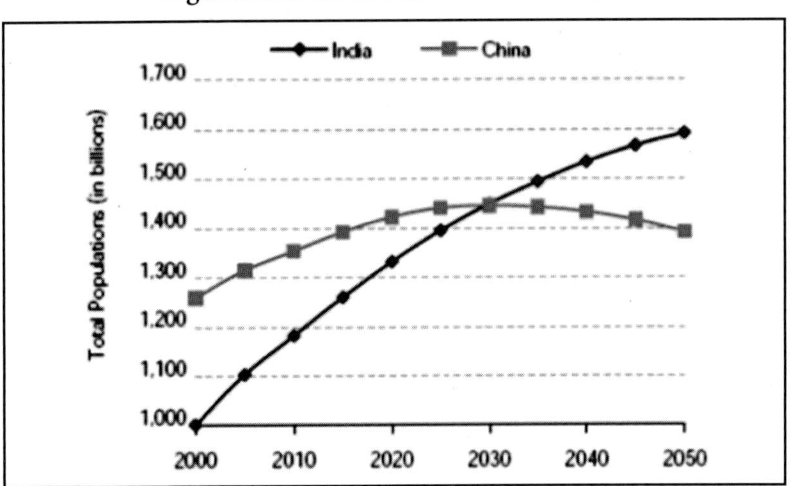

Source: UN Population Division: Medium variant.

Figure 39: Dependency Ratio

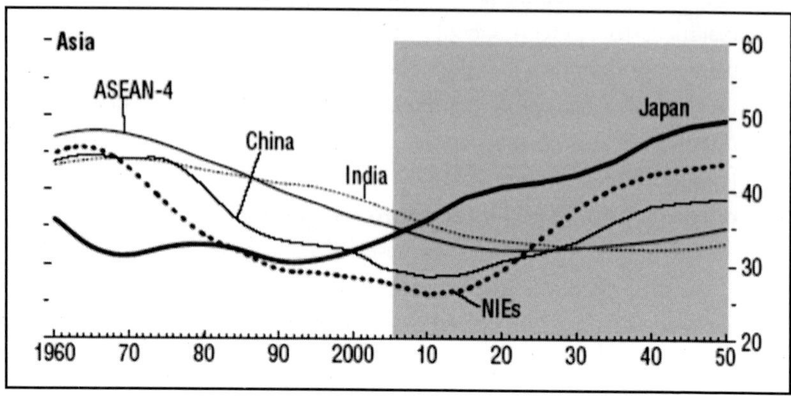

Dependency Ratio= 100 - (%ratio of working-age (15-64) population to total population).

Note it can be inferred from the above given graph that the ultimate growth rate of India and China have downward sloping with china having more volatility in slope compared to India and projected to have a positive growth till 2050 with China growing at a faster rate than India. However the variation factor in growth rate is more in case of China compared to India .The projected growth rate assumes to be subjected to change until the assumptions taken for the growth projection has been satisfied.

DEMOGRAPHIC DIVIDEND

The present population in India is approximately 1.1 billion and 1.315 billion in China, and by 2050 it expected to rise to around 1.392 billion in China but overtaken [Figure 2 in Annexure 1] by India's 1.592 billion at the present projected rates of growth of population. India is expected to overtake China in population size by year 2050 as Figure 2 above depicts. The two most populous countries of the world also have a large share of the young. By 2020, 50 per cent of India's population and 30 per cent of China's population will be under 30 years of age. With those enormous numbers of young people bursting with newfound cultural confidence, the chemistry of the world will change immeasurably.

For India and China the population explosion and its control, about which we were patronizingly advised by intellectuals and governments of the West, and sometimes lauded or often berated for, became thus a matter of serious concern for planning in both the countries. But now the young population resulting from high population growth rates caused by rapidly declining death rates, is being perceived as one of their strengths.

The share of working age population in India is expected to grow until 2050 and decline thereafter, but in China, it is expected to start declining from 2015 due to the excesses of a one-child per family norm for which earlier China was much lauded.

The share of working age population in India is expected to grow until 2050 and decline thereafter, but in China, it is expected to start declining from 2015 due to the excesses of a one-child per family norm for which earlier China was much lauded internationally. India's and China's earlier had much emphasized liability from population growth, but now is being viewed to be their asset—thus termed as *Demographic Dividend.*

India's earlier much criticized failure to control population growth compared to China is turning out to be its future asset, a demographic dividend to be reaped, which China's earlier much lauded success has become its 'time bomb' and failure since its working age population ratio is expected to decline from as early as 2015. As it is now being said, China may grow old before it gets rich. India has a potential advantage over China in the reaping of its Demographic Dividend.

Thus the factor in the future trend in economic growth of China and India -will be on how soon and how effectively the two nations reap their demographic dividend by an economic strategy that raises the GDP growth rate while generating jobs for the young labour force.

Once considered the biggest stumbling block in the country march towards development, India's population is today being hailed as its most promising resource. By 2020, the average Indian will be only 29 years old (by 2015), 54 per cent of India's population will be in the 15-49 years bracket, compared with 37 in China and the US, 45 in West Europe and 48 in Japan, which would mean that while US will be short of 17 million people of working age, China 10 million, Japan nine million and Russia six million, India will have a surplus of 47 million, working age people. This 'bulge' in the working age group is India's potential demographic dividend. But inadequate educational opportunities coupled with unemployment may turn this dividend into deficit.

Table 86: College Enrollment/Population: "Chindus"

Series Name	Country Name	1991	1999	2000	2001	2002	2003	2004	2005
School enrollment, primary (% gross)	China	125.15	-	-	117.73	116.01	115.02	117.62	112.78
	India	98.11	97.35	98.80	98.30	98.95	107.43	116.20	119.25
	United States	103.39	101.24	100.52	101.33	99.46	99.68	98.98	99.03
School enrollment, secondary (% gross)	China	48.69	61.75	62.86	65.10	67.20	70.26	72.53	74.34
	India	44.18	46.17	47.94	48.02	49.80	52.29	53.51	56.56
	United States	91.91	95.16	93.97	94.33	93.26	94.53	94.68	94.75
School enrollment, tertiary (% gross)	China	2.97	6.39	7.60	9.82	12.61	15.42	19.10	20.31
	India	6.03	-	10.23	10.49	11.04	11.50	11.76	11.41
	United States	73.62	73.15	69.16	70.09	80.68	82.59	82.44	82.72

Chindus Triangular

According to a recent report by Bangalore-based Team Lease, the country's second largest private employer, around 53 per cent of India's employed youth suffer from some degree of skill deprivation.

A recent study by Nasscom says while 3 million students graduate from Indian universities each year, only about 25 percent of engineering graduates and 10-15 percent of general college graduates are considered suitable for employment in the offshore IT industry, which faces a shortage of 500,000 professionals by 2010.

Thus, of an estimated population of 205 million in the 6-14 age group, some 82 per cent were enrolled in schools in 2006. But this enrolment rate, impressive as it is, is totally nullified by the horrendous dropout rate. Between primary school and 10+2 class, over 90 per cent drop out of schools. Only 6 per cent of all students actually go to college, and of that, nearly three-fourths do arts. The rest are split up among engineering, medicine, science, management, law, and other special subjects.

If for years Corporate India has been wondering why an overpopulated India, with 70 percent of its population under 35, is facing a talent crunch, the answer is evident in the above statistics, India may reach a 10 percent growth rate, there is no way India can sustain this growth rate for the next 10 years or so-which is what is needed if we are to join the ranks of developed nations by 2025.

There is little doubt that Corporate India and other organizations of civil society like trusts, etc. will have to steps in, if not for the nation's sake then for its own.

India is one of the few countries in the world where the dependency ratio will improve in the coming years. There are 570 million people in India under the age of 25. When most of the developed world is be-set with the problem of ageing, India has a uniquely young population.

But if we have a large group of young uneducated people without the ability to participate in the workforce, it will be a demographic disaster.

India's workforce today has 484 million people. Of these 273 million are working in rural areas primarily in agriculture (many of them dearly underemployed), there are another 61 million working in manufacturing and about 150 million in services. Shockingly, 40% of the current workforce is illiterate and another 40% is below 12 class pass. That means 200 million workers cannot even sign their name! Given that 60% of our workforce is in rural areas, which provides only about 18% of our GDP and the growth engine for our economy is the services sector, these simple statistics condemn our rural workforce to penury or destitution.

What is worse, given their skill levels it is very difficult for them to escape their fate by migrating to the services sector. However the openings in modem India, even in modem retail and more mechanised construction, will seek a basic education. It is hard to use uneducated people in the productive parts of India's economy. At the higher end in IT, financial services and healthcare the problem is different—it needs high quality graduates.

Currently about 23 million children are eligible for entry into the school system yet only six million finish the 12 standard and only about

2.3 million graduate. Thus 17 million do not even finish school. The quality of education on offer is abysmal. On any day 25% of the teachers are absent and 50% of children in class V cannot read a story and 21% of them cannot recognise numbers. Little wonder that parents dependent on government schools do not see the relevance of sending their children to school. Child labour results. One estimates show that there are 89 million people expected to join the work force in the next five years. However, 47 million of these will be school drop-outs. Only 13 million of these will be graduates and above. While the demand over the next five years is met by the supply on offer in overall numeric terms, if we disaggregate this by sector, we find that there will be a shortage of 600,000 graduates by 2012. However, if we adjust for employability, which is about 60% for graduates, we find the overall shortage will be in excess of five million for graduates.

The reasons have been known to all in the government for a very long time. Report after report has highlighted the issues. The root cause in education that plague over regulation, under-funding, and no accountability for performance delivery.

In primary education, we spend about $280 per pupil to $1,000 in Thailand, and $8,000 in the US.

There is an urgent need both to increase funding with more accountability for government school (as well as to allow private provision of education for profit.

Its role from being a provider of education to becoming a financier of the student in obtaining education. Families empowered with vouchers which they could spend in private schools providing quality education. If the education quality falls, the parents could vote with the feet and move their children to other schools offering better education. Government provision itself must have more performance oversight.

Presently our university education system is contributing 3 million graduates and post graduates every year find students seeking employment after completion of 10th class and 10+2 class are around 7 million per year. Thus nearly 10 million youth are injected into the employment market, every year. In the 21st century, India needs a large number of talented youth with higher education for the task of knowledge acquisition, knowledge imparting, knowledge creation and knowledge sharing. At present India has five hundred and forty million youth-under the age of 25. This will continuously be growing till the year 2050. Keeping this resource in mind, the universities and educational systems should create two cadres of personnel; (i) a global cadre of skilled youth with specific knowledge of special skills. (ii) another global cadre of youth with higher education. These two cadres will be required not only for powering the manufacturing and services sector of India but also will be needed for fulfilling the human resource requirements of various countries. Thus, the universities and secondary school education system will have to work towards increasing the through put of the higher education system from the existing 11 per cent to 20 per cent by the year 2015, 30 per cent by the year 2020 and 50 per cent by the year 2040. Other Indians who are not covered by the higher education system should all have world class skill acts in areas such as construction, carpentry, electrical systems, repair of mechanical systems, fashion design, para-legal, para-medical, accountancy, sales and marketing, software and hardware maintenance and service, software quality assurance to name a few.

The University Grants Commission (UGC) has come up with a startling admission: Over half of the students who pass Class XII don't even enter the higher-education sector; 90 per cent of colleges and 60 per cent of universities across the country are of middling or poor quality. On almost all indicators, from faculty standards to library facilities, from computer availability to student-teacher ratio, higher education is in crying need for an up-grade.

The "quality gap" in both universities and colleges is alarming: 25 per cent faculty positions in universities remain vacant; 57 per cent teachers in colleges do not have either an M Phil or Ph D; there is only one computer for 229 students, on an average, in colleges.

These results of the first-even official assessment of the higher education system, conducted by UGCs Bangalore-based National Assessment and Accreditation Council (NAAC), have been presented to Prime Minister Manmohan Singh. The assessment was conducted on 123 universities and 2,956 colleges across India—an estimated 60% of these institutions were private, the rest government run.

Institutions participated on a voluntary basis. It was based on seven broad parameters: curriculum, teaching, research and consultancy, infrastructure, student support, management and innovative practices.

The data acquire extra significance given the boom in the higher education sector and the exponential rate of growth expected. The number of universities has risen from 20 in 1947 to 378 in 2006; colleges, from 500 to 18,064 during the same period. And yet, little more than half, 52.61 per cent, of those who passed the 12th standard get into colleges and universities, the other half drops out.

The dropout rate among Scheduled Tribes is maximum (61.5 per cent), followed by Scheduled Castes (51.21) and Other Backward Classes (50.09). Thus, poverty is the reason.

Of 123 universities, only a third is of "good quality", over a half are B-grade and a sixth C-grade. Among 2,956 colleges, only 10 per cent made Grade A cut; 66 per cent were B-grade and 24 per cent C-grade.

We have to focus on bridging the quality gap between A-grade and the rest. There are mainly two reasons for this quality gap: availability and quality of facilities quality of faculty."

One key factor behind *the* quality gap the under-investment in higher education since 1980s. Between 1951 and 1980 the government spending on higher education sector grew at the rate of 17 per cent, but the dipped to 10 pc between 1981 to 2003-04.

The world over today, there is talk of the "demographic dividend" that India will receive over the next forty years. For decades since Independence in 1947, we were told that India's demography was her main liability, that India's population was growing too fast, and what India needed most was to control its population, even if by coercive methods. In 1975-77 the government even experimented with forced sterilization. Now how did India billion—plus population become a dividend?

Such was the atmosphere created since Independence that when noted demographer. Dr. Ashish Bose of the University of Delhi published in 1972 my research as a chapter in his book titled: India's Population, the results of which research had contradicted the view that population growth is innately a negative factor in economic development of a nation, and on the contrary, a growing population could be an asset if the youth of the nation is we well educated and properly motivated. That is, the youth of India would be an asset to the country's development and not a liability, because modern science—imbibed youth, and through their scientific innovations, can overcome the limitations of land, natural resources and production. I had then also called coercive family planning as "an obsession of developed nations".

But the negative view of population prevailed till the 'nasbandi' [vasectomy] fiasco of the Emergency in 1975-77 forced Indian politicians to become less vocal about the need for coercive family planning. But the prejudice about population growth in India continued into the beginning of the 21st century.

During this same period, China had earned international praise for coercively controlling population by it's short-sighted one child per family scheme. Indian Left academics how ever kept exhorting us to follow the China example. Thank our good fortune, that our democracy protected us from the China disaster. Even China accepts today that their one-child programme was wrong and is now hurting their development.

The world view has since completely changed with the shift in focus in the theory of economic development. Now development is no more thought of as capital-driven, but as knowledge-driven. For application of knowledge, we need innovations, which means more original research, and hence we need more fresh young minds out of universities—the cream of the youth. But most of all, the nation needs a modem world class system across the spectrum of primary, secondary, and higher education.

India today leads in the supply of youth, i.e., persons in the age group of 15 to 35 years, and this lead will last for another forty years. We should not squander this "natural resource". We must therefore by proper policy for the young, realize and harvest the demographic potential. China is the second largest world leader in young population today. But the youth population in that country will start shrinking from 2015, i.e., less than a decade from now because of lagged effect of the one-child policy.

Japanese and European total populations are fast aging, and will start declining in absolute numbers from next year. The US will however hold a steady trend thanks to a liberal policy of immigration, especially from

Mexico and Phillipines. But even then the US will have a demographic shortage in skilled personnel. All developed countries will experience a demographic deficit. India will not. Our past liability, by a fortuitous turn of fate, has now become our potential asset.

Thus, India has now become, by unintended consequences, gifted with a young population. If we educate this youth to develop cognitive intelligence to become original thinkers, imbibe emotional intelligence to have team spirit and rational risk-taking attitude, inculcate moral intelligence to blend personal ambition with national goals, and cultivate social intelligence to defend civic rights of the weak, gender equality, the courage to fight injustice and spiritual intelligence to connect the mind to the cosmos and think out of box then we can develop a superior species of human being, and Indian youth who can be relied on to contribute to make India a global power within two decades.

India must therefore structure a national policy for the youth of India so that in every young Indian, the four dimensional concept of intelligence, viz., cognitive, emotional, moral and social, manifests in his character. Only then, our demographic dividend will not be wasted. These four dimensions of intelligence constitute the ability of a person to live a productive life and for national good. Hence, a policy for India's youth has to be structured within the implied parameters of these four dimensions. This inculcation must begin at the primary schooling level, and develop over the secondary schooling period.

Western education was introduced into India through foreign rulers. After Independence, thanks to Nehru and early demise to Gandhi and Patel, public schools in India continued the modern Western model, while Islamic institutions (madrasahs) were allowed to keep teaching the way they had been doing, sometimes going back to the seventeenth century.

The Western educational model is not appropriate for India and cannot serve the spiritual and cultural heritage that is India's real gift to the world. India does not need to follow the Western educational model any more than it should follow Western dress. In fact as long as it does, the country is likely to drift like a person who has forgotten who he really is.

Even the West is moving away from institutional models of education towards a more intimate instruction that resembles the gurukula system. Real education depends upon personal instruction, not state run schools that mass-produce students like industrial products with nationally uniform curriculums that ignore native student ability and that depend on government dispensed funding.

The challenge for the coming century—for India to revive itself as a nation and a culture—is to recreate the Indic model of education in the modern context, in which the dichotomy between science and religion is resolved. We must move beyond not only dogmatic and exclusive religions on one hand, but also materialistic science on the other. We must recreate religion as a form of science and science as a form of spirituality.

Although the pattern of education varies from State to State, its basic elements are:

(a) Eight years of elementary education, covering Classes I-VIII in the age-groups of 6-14 years.

(b) Three years of Secondary education, covering Classes IX-XI in the age groups of 14-17 years.

(c) Three years of University education, leading to the first degree.

There are five dimensions of the current crisis:

1. Student, faculty and supporting staff unrest.
2. Over-crowding in higher education.
3. Declining quality and standards.
4. Diminishing social rate of return on educational investments.
5. Suffocating politicization.

The curriculum should have a blend of three aspects of education: mind-building for further abstract and advanced study, practical training towards some vocation, and an inculcation of the spirit of service and innovation.

However, the curriculum in Indian education system has undergone very little change since the days of British. During the freedom struggle, Mahatma Gandhi had observed what still applies as follows:

"Almost from the commencement (of school) the textbooks deal, not with things the boys and girls have always to deal within their homes, but with things to which they are perfect strangers .... He (a boy) is never taught to have any pride in his surroundings. The higher he goes, the further he is removed from his home, so that at the end of his education he become estranged from his surroundings. He feels no poetry about the home life. The village scenes are all a sealed book to him. His own civilization is presented to him as imbecile, barbarous, superstitious, and useless for all practical purposes. His education is calculated to wean him from his traditional culture. And if the mass of educated youths are not entirely denationalized, it is because the ancient culture is too deeply embedded in them to be altogether uprooted even by an education adverse to its growth".

This does not mean that India should wipe out English from study. On the contrary, as the most prized international language, English should be taught as a third compulsory language but not for use as the medium of instruction. This process has, however, to be slow and steady, but determined by the aim to replace English by an Indian language.

Chapter 6

Conclusion: Need for a Future Strategy for Economic Growth and Reforms

India and China are today amongst the world's fastest growing economies with their GDPs increasing at the trend rate of over 9 percent each over the last five years on the basis or corrected data. Together these two most populous countries, having more than a billion plus people each, which together constitute 38 percent of the world population. They are referred as the non-identical twins of the east, and equally, erstwhile economically developed and ancient civilizations.

Both countries with ancient unbroken civilizations have common histories of checkered foreign invasions and plunder, imperialism, Soviet socialism, and the recent phase of three decades of rapid and accelerating, economic growth which has uplifted their world status.

Measured by GDP, in purchasing power parity (PPP) terms, China is the second largest economy in the world—the first being the United States followed at the third place by India. At current growth rates, China is expected to be the world's largest economy in three decades hence overtaking the US, while India will remain the world's third largest economy but close to the US.

Economic reforms since the 1980s have helped in unleashing the massive potential of both the countries, China and India. Both have witnessed spectacular growth rates with India and China at 9% p.a., or thereabouts, in recent years. But the future will be determined by innovation, in which the US has to date unchallenged supremacy.

Hence these two nations are invariably compared and contrasted in any debate on the future of global economic development and growth.

India with a relatively more open and free press suffers in the media induced perception about the relative economic performance, but that is a hazard we have to live with.

But the question now is about the future of India's and China's economic development based on their recent past performance. Latin American and East Asian had been forecasted to become world leaders in development, but unforeseen financial crisis crashed them en route—the former in the 1980s, while the latter in the late nineties. Japan was expected in the 1980s to overtake the US by AD 2000, but it fizzled out in the 1997 Financial Crisis. Today Japan is crawling at 2% per year far behind USA much less overtaking it. Does the same future uncertainty cloud the economic future of India and China? I shall summarise the findings of the last four Chapters here before attempting an answer.

India and China up to eighteenth century they were legendary seats of immense wealth and wisdom for Europeans travelers and traders. Somewhere between the middle eighteenth century and early nineteenth centuries both these countries came under Imperialist European control.

After gaining independence in the late 1940's, both countries adopted different political frameworks, with India becoming the world's largest democracy and China becoming a communist purist. But despite having different political ideologies, both embraced similar economic ideas.

Both had in the past suffered exploitation, economic stagnation, impoverishment and innumerable injustices of so-called capitalist and free trade policies of the imperialist forces. This had instilled a deep rooted fear of capitalism. Both saw capitalism as an inefficient mechanism which perpetuated inequalities. The level of poverty and deprivation in both countries had grown steadily during that Imperialist phase, more than half the population being poverty-stricken. During those days, the Soviet model of socialism, due to press censorship in the USSR apparently was working wonders in rapid industrial development and in providing safety nets for the poor.

This portrayal of socialism along with inherent distrust for capitalism led to both countries adopting centralized planned economic planning. On one hand China became a state controlled autarky since its private sector was almost non-existent. Indian policies, on the other hand, were influenced by a more moderate form of pro-poor socialism, sometimes known or caricatured as Fabian Socialism.

Hence, India chose the path of a mixed economy where both the public and private sector were allowed to co-exist. However, the public sector was accorded the more dominant role, 'the commanding heights' in reviving the economy with the bureaucracy being put in charge of regulating the private sector.

The pursuit of self-sufficiency or autarky however failed. By the 1970's, neither had even begun to regain its historic position. Good intentions but bad policies, proper allocation but improper implementation, massive inefficiency of the corruption plagued bureaucracy was all to blame for this. Both economies were performing dismally at a 3.5 per cent annual growth rate in GDP.

In mid-twentieth century thus they though became independent republics, the two nations launched on the path of planned development on a borrowed ill-suited Soviet growth model that called for squeezing an already emaciated agriculture to finance capital-intensive producer goods industry that had few buyers.

During the forty years of "planned" economic .development (1950-90) the Soviet economic strategy adopted by India envisaged a large benign Government setting the pace of development through public sector investments in five year plans, and by directing the volume of private sector investments through the rigid State regulations on financial institutions, licensing, foreign exchange control, and tax policy. India, in name, had been a mixed economy.

In reality it had been a state-directed economy-a hybrid "command" economy. Even today, after the introduction of some deregulation measures initiated by the Narasimha Rao Government, the underlying "command" economic structure is largely intact, especially at the state level. The current government is struggling to get even marginal changes approved because of the opposition from allied parties and the Left.

The results of the Soviet economic strategy were not anywhere been commensurate with either the resources mobilized from the public, or in terms of India's potential for growth. During the period since 1947, till

1980, the Indian economy had grown at the average rate of four per cent per year or less, while countries adopting a different and a more market oriented strategy had achieved rapid development in the same period, growing 10-12 per cent per year. The so called "Four Tigers", namely South Korea, Taiwan, Hongkong and Singapore, with less trained manpower and a lot fewer natural resources, had moved from the Third World category to First World status *in just one generation!* The per capita income of South Korea, for example, in 1962 was $82, comparable to India's $70 at that time. Today South Korea's per capita income is about 13 times that of India's current level! Even after allowing for certain advantages enjoyed by South Korea, such as assured markets in the US, there is no convincing explanation for the difference in performance of the two countries except that the economic strategy was different. In a nutshell, ours was inferior, and South Korea's superior!

The 1997 East Asia crisis has not dimmed this performance. It was a lack of an adequate financial architecture to contain cronyism that had set the East Asia Tigers back. Cronyism in capitalism is something all market economies need to guard against.

China took up reforms in 1978, to effect the transition from state-controlled to market economy and from an autarky to international economic integration. India, reluctantly took up partial reforms in the late 1970s and 80's such as import liberalisation. Growth rate accelerated, but it was not sustainable since it was powered by short-term loans from abroad. Huge Government short-term borrowings were led to high fiscal deficits, and due to lagging exports a worsening current account.

Major economic transitions have occurred in both China and India over the last three decades. Both countries moved from autarkic, planned economic systems to more liberalized, open economies. The phases and significance of these reforms have been documented in many accomplished studies. [**See Prime**].

Potentially the toughest competition for the manufacturing powerhouse that is China today, is from the re-tooled born again Indian manufacturing sector. Slowly and steadily two different core competencies seem to be emerging in the competitive environment between China and India. While China has become a world class manufacturing hub, characterised by economies of scale, India is climbing the value chain in quality at a rapid pace. India today harbours world's second largest forging company, world's second largest optical storage media company and the world's largest two-wheeler manufacturers. All three defined by cutting-edge quality. China produces toys, apparels, footwear in millions and billions.

In terms of convergence factors today, India relative to China faces ten major competitive disadvantages in this major area of growth difference: manufacturing, which could block India closing the gap in the first two decades of the 21st century:

(1) In labour and financial environment, privately-owned Chinese companies are allowed to hire and fire workers at will as also foreign invested or owned companies especially in SEZs.

(2) Competitive disadvantage of Indian manufacturing sector is because power is prohibitively expensive in India about two and a half times China's rate. Generally, cost of inputs in manufacturing is about 30 peer cent less in China than India because of this factor.

(3) China was able to generate a much higher industrial growth than India by higher rate of structural transformation, by shifting a considerable proportion of labour force from agriculture to industry, consistently building up the rural industrial base through town and village industries (TVEs), through much higher labour-intensive exports as Table 80 shows.

(4) China was able to inspire much greater international confidence in its policies and commitment to reforms than India thereby attracting much higher FDI, which was deployed for exports.

(5) The Chinese government followed a selective interventionist policy which was limited in policy changes. It encouraged economic decentralization in decision-making and a provincial level industrial and investment policy-making environment in the country, which was quite unlike India.

(6) Deregulation of the non-state industrial sector, reform of labour and land laws, and entry and exist policy for firms have gone further in China than in India.

(7) Although both countries have promoted small-scale enterprises, the performance of Chinese TVEs has been far more impressive, thanks to greater market incentives.

(8) China's special economic zones (SEZs) were far more successful in promoting trade and attracting foreign direct investment (FDI) than India's export-processing zones (EPZs) due, inter alia, to the positive role played by the overseas Chinese in Hong Kong, Macao, and Taiwan. The reasons for India's failure seem to be a lack of adequate infrastructure.

(9) Indian ports are serious bottlenecks for external trade especially in industries which are facing acute international competition such as garments. China's overall handling of freight is four times more than India's.

(10) China has not only managed a high rate of investment, but has kept the prime lending rate (PLR) at a relatively low 8 per cent; the interest rate spread between lending and deposit rates confined to 12.6 per cent. In India, the PLR has been not less than 12 per cent for most of the two decades while the interest rate spread is at 3.4.

But Chinese products have taken a massive hit in quality over the last few years while Indian products still stand out as a seeker of six-sigma black belt standard let alone merely meeting every ISO specification. Recall the fiasco over quality of Chinese batteries in Indian market selling at just 4 cents, when its inputs cost alone would have been twice that price. Even bigger fiascos on the quality of Chinese goods were toxic toys and contaminated baby milk.

In contrast, Indian entrepreneurs have focused more and more on innovation and quality on their own. Tata's Nano, Moser Baer's cine storage and film media, and Ranbaxy's generic drugs are only part of this unfolding story. As many as 14 Indian auto makers have received the prestigious Deming Award, the highest number outside of Japan for any country in the world.

However, the Chinese in their rush to create massive manufacturing units, without too much regard for a price which would give a clear margin of profit, have fallen into a trap of horrendous non-performing assets (NPAs) on bank loans—the average NPA in China could be as high as 25%—in other words, a big capital subsidy. In contrast, NPAs in India are between 1.5% and 3%. They have, undoubtedly, made major strides in high technology absorption, particularly in export items. But what is not known is that 88% of China's high technology exports take place from MNCs located in China. Furthermore, 56% of China's total exports originate from MNCs.

China market economy status is marred by non-transparent pricing mechanism, very high non-performing assets in Chinese banks resulting in massive capital subsidies and opaque public sector institutions. Contrast this with India, where pricing mechanisms are market driven and subsidies if any are absolutely transparent.

It is rarely articulated that Chinese economy ticks because of massive foreign direct investments over a sustained period crafted by multinational corporations (MNCs) of the world while Indian economy to a very large extent is driven by entrepreneurs, at times joint ventures with MNCs.

Thus, both countries have accomplished a great deal as a result of the reforms that they have undertaken. In terms of statistical comparisons, China is further ahead than India, but when seen in the context of institutions of social and political importance these statistical differences lessen considerably in importance. In this connection, the researches of Nobel Laureate Douglas North become relevant for us. Despite the similarities in reforms to create markets in both countries, India's path although has been more market-oriented but is still shackled by the remnants of the Soviet legacy, whereas China's has been more government directed and much more and in some ways dangerously de-centralised.

To a large extent China's better performance in terms of growth, exports, and FDI can be attributed to timing and location. China began its reforms earlier than India and at a time when private capital flows were beginning to surge globally. China's leaders decided to implement a major economic reform program at the Third Plenary Session of the 11th Chinese Communist Party Central Committee meeting in 1978.

The initial reform measures involved increasing prices for agricultural output and shifting production into consumer goods. In the early 1980s, the reform gathered momentum with the establishment of special economic zones in southern China (e.g., see Yeung et al., 2009). In India, some domestic economic reforms were begun in the early 1980s, but the measures to open India's trade and investment sectors were not launched until after the foreign exchange crisis in 1991.

China was also able to take advantage of the East Asian production process that was poised to move manufacturing to lower-cost locations. The effect of a 10-year difference in start times for reforms in India and China will most likely fade as the decades advance, and production locations tend to move as global business conditions change. Hence, even while these advantages have been substantial for China, they are temporary.

In terms of these attributes and historical facts, therefore, these two nations are unique in the world. Whether they cooperate or confront in the decades to come it will have cataclysmic restructuring convulsions for the world. Hence these two nations are invariably compared and contrasted in any debate on the future of global economic development and growth.

Is China's property market a bubble? Nothing, not even massive government infrastructure spending, has driven China's growth more than real estate investment. In 2009, total fixed-asset investment accounted for more than 90% of China's overall growth; residential and commercial real estate investment comprised nearly a quarter of that. "China's property market", says economist Andy Xie, "is a *massive* bubble." As Xie points out, residential prices in China relative to per capita income are far and away the highest in the world. The housing price-to-income ratio in urban China is over 20, which means it takes the average citizen's total wages for 20 years to buy an average dwelling. By comparison, the highest housing affordability ratio for a U.S. city—Honolulu—is 8.2.

It has become clear that such concerns are shared by the central government in Beijing, which is seeking to tighten credit growth generally, and property loans in particular. The latest budget report from the Ministry of Finance, draws attention to debt levels being incurred by local governments forging headlong into massive infrastructural and development projects.

The key challenge facing India thus remains: to raise and sustain the rapid growth rates needed to eliminate poverty over the longer term. Roughly 60 percent of the population is still employed in the agricultural sector where productivity and educational attainment are weak and poverty is endemic. Although the service sector has successfully contributed to India's relatively strong growth performance during the past decade—it already accounts for nearly half of India's GDP—the scope for this sector to provide sustained income increases for the rural poor is limited at present level of infrastructure.

Thus, achieving faster growth and poverty elimination will require new policies of major "second generation" reforms that generate employment, sustain income growth in the agricultural sector, and modernize rural infrastructure. This could bring IT enabled services to farm areas, and invoke the WTO mandated opportunities for agro-export. Indian farm products are the cheapest in the world, but lack the necessary infrastructure to effectively market abroad.

In India, the 1980s spurt in the rate of growth from 3.5 per cent per year to 5.8 per cent per year, had been primarily due to external commercial loan-financed imports, bank credit-pushed public investment that built industrial capacity, and the rise in exports in textiles, gems and chemicals due to special factors. This growth rate was however at a heavy cost, e.g., of accumulating short term debt burden that caused the balance of payments crisis of 1990-91. In the 1990s, following the deregulating reforms, by utilizing the excess capacities built earlier in the 1980s the spurt in industrial production in public and private sectors was enabled and through the substantial rise in the service sector (now nearly 50% of GDP) took the Indian economy to the end of the 20th century at an impressive 6.4 per cent average annual growth.

But the industrial sector boom of 1993-97 could not be sustained beyond 1997 since the fundamental and hard reforms to enable industry to become globally competitive or at least survive international competition in the face of WTO commitments, were not implemented. In India, during the late 1990s, economic growth rate weakened substantially. Growth in 2000/01 was only 4 per cent, and in the five years to 2001/02 averaged 5¼ per cent. As a result, industrial growth recently has slumped to 2.5 per cent (in 2000-01) while the scandal ridden financial system milked by crony capitalism and poorly supervised capital market, is on the verge of a major crisis.

In India, as of now, economic reforms introduced in 1991 have been exhausted. Thus, ironically, China and India may be on converging paths to a crisis because of the stalled financial reforms in both countries. In the early 1990s in India, wide-ranging structural reforms yielded notable gains, and by several measures, India's economic performance during the decade compared favourably with China. The reforms started the process of unshackling and opening up the Indian economy and resulted in a significant boost to growth, investment, and exports, and in a market reduction in poverty. Growth in the 1990s was second only to China in the region.

The new institutional architecture will also imply strengthening of independent regulatory agencies and start treating their independence at par with an independent judiciary. Such a new institutional architecture may also have an independent monetary authority by giving greater independence to Reserve Bank of India on the lines of autonomy enjoyed by the Federal Reserve in USA or the Bank of England in U.K. This will promote competition since it would end the crony capitalism that plagues India and inundates the economy with mega scandals involving insider trading and plain fraud.

In the reforms initiated in 1991 the emphasis was on reforms of product markets by abolishing industrial licensing and import barriers. These reforms however left out multiplicity of regulations, land market distortions, government control of banks, the factor markets such as labour markets, capital markets, natural resources market such as water, and institutions mostly untouched. Lack of reforms in these areas are well below the rate required to solve the major problems of unemployment, poverty and in equal opportunity to excel.

However, of the necessary factor market reforms, two are crucial at this stage: First, the reforms of labour markets, and second, financial sector reforms. India's present laws of bankruptcy (exit policy) and corporate control require reforms so that the market for corporate control become competitive. The financial sector reforms would involve reforms of banking sector, equity markets, debt markets and foreign exchange markets.

In this, privatization of state-owned banks is perhaps the most essential, but preceded by strengthening of the regulation and supervision of financial institutions and of capital markets, which are really non-existent at present. The recent developments in the Indian stock market vividly show how actions of one private bank, one cooperative bank, major stock exchange management, and giant mutual fund of 20 million subscribers can have deleterious impact on national equity markets and particularly on small shareholders, because of a lack of strong prudential supervision.

But the most deleterious effects are from rogue corporate empires like the Reliance which no government wants to regulate, and whose suffocating tin-tacks are everywhere choking off competition. Thus the downside risks of globalization get amplified if the financial sector is weak and more so as the economy liberalizes and integrates with the world economy. This is the main lesson of the 1997 Asian crisis or the subsequent crisis of Turkey, and the 2001 meltdown in Argentina.

Rapid balanced growth can continue much less accelerate, only if China and India implement two remaining fundamental reforms: (1) complete the remaining transition from planned economy to a market system, and (2) shift from extensive growth (based on increases in inputs) to intensive growth (driven by improvements in efficiency).

To maintain real GDP growth of 7 per cent a year or more over the next few years requires an ambitious agenda to be implemented which should include maintaining the momentum of reforms in the SOEs and finance sector, and developing human resources in the special skills of modern technology.

India's GDP is growing at 8 per cent a year, compared to 10 per cent that is now required. India's working-age population, is expanding faster. Unless, therefore GDP grows at closer to 10 per cent a year, India could face unemployment as high as 16 per cent by 2010.

The McKinsey Global Institute (MGI) has studied India's economy to assess what is holding back growth and what policy changes might accelerate it. This study has shown that, with the new reform policies,

GDP growth of 10 per cent a year is within India's reach today. A 10 percent growth rate for a decade will transform India, and pull it abreast of China.

This study has affirmed that there are three main barriers in India to faster growth: the remaining multiplicity of regulations governing product markets (i.e., regulations that affect either the price or output in a sector); distortions in the land markets; and extensive government ownership of business. It is to be remembered that even today government controlled entities still account for 43 per cent of the capital stock in the economy, and about 15 per cent of the non-agricultural employment.

Together, these inhibit GDP growth by around 4 per cent a year. In contrast, MGI found that the factors more generally believed to retard growth—inflexible labour laws and poor transport infrastructure—while important, constrain India's economic performance by less than 0.5 per cent of GDP a year. Hence, to raise India's growth trajectory, a broader reform agenda is required .

Removing the main barriers to growth would enable India's economy to grow faster than China (at 10 per cent a year). Annual growth in labour productivity would double to 8 per cent. Some 75 million new jobs would be created, sufficient not only to ward off the looming crisis in employment, but also to reabsorb any workers that might be displaced by productivity improvements.

In order to do this, however, India will have to adopt a deeper, faster process of reforms urgently.

Hence, in a nutshell:

- If the current slow pace of reforms continues, India will only be able to maintain GDP growth at around its current 8-8.5 per cent. The Indian economy will not be able to absorb the expected surge in the workforce, which will lead to an increase in idle hours in agriculture from 36 per cent to 45 per cent of economy-wide employment. In such a scenario there will be no convergence in growth paths of China and India. China will remain ahead.
- If all barriers to productivity improvement are removed, India can achieve around 8 per cent growth in labour productivity, which will

translate into a 10 per cent growth in GDP. To translate the productivity gains into a higher aggregate output, India will have to invest in new capacity that will create high productivity jobs.

¶ Contrary to the commonly held belief that a total investment rate of 35 per cent of GDP is needed for 10 per cent growth in GDP, we believe that an increase to 30 per cent from the current 24.5 is necessary for India to achieve the 10 per cent GDP growth target. Capital productivity in the sectors can be increased by around 50 per cent through a 20 per cent improvement in capacity utilization and a 30 per cent improvement in the cost per unit of capacity. This increase will, however, be offset by a reduction of around 15 per cent in overall capital productivity due to a shift in output towards the capital intensive modern sectors. Average capital productivity will thus show a net increase of around 30 per cent.

The question that remains is: where the funds to finance these reforms can come from? Three sources seem feasible in the Indian context: (1) a rise in domestic savings prodded by attractive tax policies (2) a sharp increase in FDI by appealing reforms in regulations and labour laws (3) by tapping the liquidity in the banking sector.

These scenarios paint a complex picture of the future trends in Chinese and Indian growth. Rapid growth over the next quarter-century for both countries is of course possible. But achieving needed savings rates and productivity growth will require maintaining the momentum of reforms and skilled macroeconomic and sectoral management. These supportive reforms and successful management of change are what will make the difference.

Future growth of China can come only through new set of reforms that raise productivity through greater efficiency in use of resources and a re-balance between domestic driven and export led strategies. That requires wide ranging new financial reforms. Two consequences would probably result if China does not undertake further financial reforms. First, growth would further add to the cumulative costs of maintaining increasingly inefficient state enterprises, thus undermine the budget and the banks, overheat the rest of the economy, and thereby reduce international competitiveness. Second, the pattern of growth would reflect rising disparities between regions, rural and urban areas, and state and nonstate employment, which would acerbate social tensions and reduce productivity.

This would lead to what the World Bank terms as "Sinosclerosis", and much of China's promise would then fade by 2020. Because India, despite assigning "commanding heights" to the state owned enterprises, had a captive but structurally positioned market sector and thus developed institutions for individual enterprise, India is poised for its second generation of reforms, given the political will. If indeed India adopts new reforms and removes the remaining main barriers to growth, it is then within India's reach to close the gap with China and come on par within a decade.

In growth rate terms then, the China-India gap can be closed if India reforms its fiscal architecture in such a way that the rate of investment rises to above 40 per cent of GDP from the present 33 per cent while simultaneously reducing the ICOR from 4.0 to 3.5. This requires increasing productivity of capital while maintaining the structural balances for at least two more decades, i.e., stability manifested in five parameters: (a) an appropriate real interest rate; (b) a competitive and predictable real exchange rate; (c) a low and stable inflation rate; (d) a sustainable fiscal policy; and (e) a viable current account level in the balance of payments. The new financial architecture to achieve the same should yield a much faster growth in exports for India, which has already lost a lot of ground to China since 1980s because of a lack of export performance.

The accretion of strength of the Chinese and Indian economies over the past three decades does not however guarantee that two nations would continue to grow as rapidly in the future. After all, for many countries, past growth has been a poor predictor of future performance. The East Asian "tigers," whose growth had been spectacular for many years, show signs now, especially after 1997 meltdown of faltering and stagnating. The same pattern had been visible in Latin America in the 1970s.

It is important therefore to ascertain the probable causes of the Chinese economic growth acceleration from 1980 and the subsequent peaking and slowdown from 1993 onwards. India's growth also accelerated from 1980 to 1997, but 1997 onwards growth rate had been on an erratic trend 2003. Then a re-tooled manufacturing sector accelerated the GDP growth rate to 9% per year. To understand these trends and predict the probability of it continuing in the future, we need to first recognize what caused the spurt in growth during the last two decades. In the case of China three main factors appear to be responsible for the spurt in economic growth since 1980: (a) A sharp rise in the rate of investment, fuelled first in the 1980s by spurt in incomes in the rural sector due to the HRS reforms in agriculture, and later by the five fold rise in foreign direct investment in 1990s which contributed a quarter of the marginal rate of investment; However, China's inflows of foreign direct investment accounting for a significant share of total investment, has made the economy and its rapid growth dependent on continued foreign capital infusions. While Hong Kong and Taiwan accounted for over two-thirds of the cumulative foreign direct investment, U.S companies are the third largest investors, accounting for about 8-10 per cent of the total foreign direct investment, which companies came to China however in the hope of accessing China's domestic market, but so far have been largely kept out by regulations and guanshi networks. The WTO rules may however enable their entry in the coming years but Chinese government appears determined to slow the pace of that entry. These companies may have to review their China-involvement if they are kept out much longer from the domestic market. But allowing foreign companies freer access to the China market could also disrupt the inter-sectoral balances created in the state-directed economic apparatus. Thus, how China resolves this conflict will determine future growth trends since any drop in FDI caused by disenchantment could reduce Chinese growth rate substantially. (b) Galloping exports from $20 billion in 1980 to $200 billion in 1999, which introduced new technology and modernization of the industrial system especially in the collective and private sectors and sustained the necessary demand to clear the supply of manufactured goods; (c) A supporting diaspora that not only made possible the flow of two thirds of the FDI into China but also by re-location in the mainland of overseas Chinese-owned industries in Hongkong, Taiwan and Singapore (to benefit from low-wage Chinese labour), and provided the crucial access to the international financial network and marketing know-how. This network and know-how was severely lacking in the Chinese economy, which had been straited-jacketed by earlier policies of autarky and by political upheavals such as the Great Leap and the Cultural Revolution.

Besides these three healthy factors, a fourth ad hoc off and on factor of pump priming has also been contributory to sustaining the growth spurt in China: i.e., that of deficit financing and State-owned bank-financed credit expansion in a soft budget constraint framework to bolster demand in the face of a glut of goods produced.

In fact, the decline in Chinese growth rate from 1993 till 1998 was arrested by Premier's Zhu Rongji directive to resuscitate demand by the almost reckless expansion of credit. The same method had been used in post-Tiananmen (1989-91) slump as well. In fact, the "roller coaster" growth path of China—Dwight Perkins' characterization— since 1985 is due to this ad hoc factor. This heavy deficit financing has translated itself into a fiscal deficit of between 6 to 7 per cent in the Chinese central budget, just above India's, and equally unsustainable.

Hence, as a first step, a new generation of reforms have to be carried out in China to improve productivity and efficiency in the allocation of resources rather than an increase its size, to sustain in the future the Chinese economic performance of the past two decades. This will pose a dilemma since such reforms could weaken State control of financial institutions and thereby the Chinese Communist Party's control of the economic system. The reforms so far have been successful in having legitimized the Communist Party in China. But future reforms including especially financial sector reforms, would erode the power of the party. As Yasheng Huang has observed in his study [13], even FDI is a proxy for privatization of the SOEs. The party faces thus a "Catch-22" type choice on future reforms. The WTO entry complicates that choice further. Hence some observers see a danger of major upheaval coming in China (see Chang [6]), even a blow up as in East Asia.

Nevertheless, the last two decades of market-oriented reforms in China, have brought visible success and economic transformation. Since the start of reforms in 1978, GDP growth, on corrected data, has averaged

8.4 per cent, raising real per capita income nearly five-fold, and more than 200 million people have been lifted out of absolute poverty. The nonstate sector comprising the private sector, urban collectives and township and village enterprises (TVEs) is now estimated to account for about 60 per cent of GDP; and China has become more integrated into the global economy, with its share of world trade at 4 per cent.

Notwithstanding these achievements, a substantial reform agenda remains. Most importantly, difficult reforms—involving the SOEs and the financial sector—have yet to be accomplished. The weak performance of SOEs has burdened the state commercial banks (SCBs) with a large amount of nonperforming loans (NPLs). This not only hinders the development of sound and competitive corporate and financial sector, but also creates contingent liabilities that could threaten medium-term fiscal sustainability. At the same time, rising unemployment from the reforms is causing social strains which are exacerbated by widening income disparities—between rural and urban areas, and inland and coastal provinces.

Balancing reforms and social stability thus remains the key challenge facing policy makers. The Chinese authorities recognize that China's accession to the WTO has increased the urgency of reforms and they appear determined to push the reform agenda forward. The 10th Five-Year Plan approved by the National Party Congress in March 2001 stressed the efficiency of growth through further reforms and greater reliance on market forces. The Plan officially aims at annual average growth of 7 per cent over the next decade, which is important for absorbing surplus labour released from ongoing SOE reform and from rural areas; to deepen and broaden structural reforms buttressed by an improved social safety net; and to continue China's opening to the outside world.

Thus, the key risks that China's economy faces are complex, and fundamental, and which require urgent attention. Briefly:

First, the link between banks and state enterprises. As the performance of state enterprises has weakened, so has the financial condition of the state banks. Although the full weight of the government behind the state banks precludes the possibility of a banking collapse as of now, nevertheless, the cost of bailing out the banks is high and rising. The government may have to borrow for this purpose, so its debt service payments could increase. That would mean higher fiscal deficit, and thus crowding out resources required for investing in health, education, infrastructure, and the environment, and for financing the reform of pensions.

Second, the nexus between state enterprise reforms, labour markets, and inequality. Rising unemployment in some cities may discourage the government from pursuing state enterprise reforms. China cannot continue to invest in high returns coastal areas while credible reports of unemployed people roaming the countryside looking for work, confront the authorities. To have such mass open unemployment (estimated 14 percent) after 20 years of economic reform at 8 percent or more growth in GDP, spells danger to the system. It obviously signals the need for corrective action. But again, in growing and increasingly market-oriented economy, such action has to be through the fiscal system. Now, with China's entry into WTO, this problem will be more acute and delicate to handle.

Third, as capital accumulates due to the high rate of investment, the economic law of diminishing returns will operate; each additional unit of capital can be expected to contribute less to employment and output. As the economy matures, structural changes will provide a smaller boost to growth than hitherto. In particular, China will reap fewer benefits from transferring surplus labour out of agriculture and from one-shot efficiency gains. At present, India is further away than China from being subject to these limiting or constraining factors. Because of this alone, the classic convergence scenario will thus obtain.

Fourth, China's growth strategy of export promotion, FDI dependent investment, and a surplus on the current account for 12 of the past 17 years (with an average surplus about 0.5 per cent of GDP) is unsustainable. Once the Chinese consumers get a choice in picking banks for deposits, and foreign banks can extend credit to private sector and individuals, the state-guided strategy of export promotion and pump priming will be severely constrained.

Fifth, China has had capital account controls, a current account surplus and rising foreign reserves. Yet without devaluation of the renminbi, China will find it hard to keep exports growing. But, it will be difficult to reconcile devaluation of renminbi with capital account controls, current account surplus and growing reserves.

Sixth, China's labour intensive exports may not remain so competitive, while the capital-intensive exports produced by the state enterprises as of now do not have much of a market abroad without heavy subsidies that would strain an already overstretched financial position. Furthermore, capital-intensive goods are produced by SOEs that are suffering losses. If anti-dumping rules of WTO are vigorously applied, then it would affect exports, and bank loans to SOEs will become deadweight losses or further add to NPLs.

Thus, impressive as the strengths are of the Chinese economy the risks and challenges are strong and varied enough to threaten progress in China. How the balance will be worked out would depend on the ability and resolve of the leadership to maintain the momentum of reforms, and embarking on newer reforms with bold strokes in financial architecture and SOEs.

Visions of China and India as economic superpowers in 2020 thus constantly collides with the reality in the two countries of remaining poverty, considerable regional, north-south, or east-west, or rural-urban inequalities within the two countries, with substantial sections of the people still poor and unemployed, fundamental and ominous structural fault lines especially in the financial sector and a vast extent of reforms yet to be carried out.

The two economies are still shackled by a number of glaring structural weaknesses that could limit this potential from being realised in the future weaknesses such as an overloaded banking system, saddled with high ratios of non-performing loans (NPLs), high fiscal deficit, pervasive corruption, a glut of unsold goods and a bloated and difficult-to-reform 'public' or state-owned industrial enterprises.

Nevertheless, undeniable and innumerable signs were evident for making this prognosis of extraordinary significance: high growth rate achievement of 8 per cent or more—the highest today internationally, success in providing adequate food to obviate starvation or famine of the billion or more people each in the two countries, foreign reserves to sufficiently hedge against uncertainties of the near future, and in raising the Human Development Index (HDI) for their peoples.

During the period of reform, China and India also became front-runners in the cutting edge frontier technology areas of IT, communications, biotechnology, nuclear and space sciences. The two nations also have a vast pool of scientific personnel and technologists with proven capacity for original research and inventions. During the 1990s, there was a clear trend of convergence in growth rates in GDP, although not sectorally. Whether this trend will continue, will depend now on the adoption of the more difficult second generation reforms in the two countries.

Today, a little more than forty years later after the demise of the Soviet economic strategy, interestingly we are discussing China and India not as failures, nor for their 'quaint' ancient wisdoms of globe-trotting monks and holy men, but as dynamic modem economies that are becoming the hope of powering future growth of the globe—besides to recover their pre-modem eminence.

Thus, as we look back on the economic development experience of China and India it becomes clear that decades of economic progress after liberation, and especially 1980, have falsified the prophets of doom who had predicted that the two countries would not be able to feed their huge and growing populations nor be able to earn enough from exports to buy adequate food from abroad, i.e., both economics would converge to a disaster scenario. The Massachusetts Institute of Technology 1972 study: Limits of Growth had in general terms opined in this vein for at least developing countries such as India. China and India have now proved such prognosis wrong; on the contrary both nations constituting nearly 40 per cent of the world's population have already impressive achievements to their credit, as listed below:

More significantly both economies have shown considerable "de-coupling" with Global crisis as the recent data on GDP growth rates show in Table below:

Table 87: Impact of Global Meltdown on Growth

GDP growth rate	2007 (act)	2008 (est)	2009 (frcst)
China [uncorrected]	13.0 %	9.0%	+/- 1%
[corrected data]	10.1%	7.6%	+ -0.75 %
India	9.3%	7.3%	+/- 0.75%

By IMF projections for 2014, India and China together are predicted to account for 22.8% of world GDP, although China's share will be bigger than India's. Economic historian Angus Maddison's estimates of the gross domestic product (GDP) of the world from as far back as the year 1000 shows GDP (in 1990 purchasing power parity terms) of India and China as a percentage of world GDP was above 50%. In the year 1600, together they accounted for 51.4% of world GDP. For India, its share of world GDP according to IMF's projections, are still far below Maddison's estimate of India's share of world GDP in 1900.

This was inspite of, definitely not because of, the stage set by either the contact with foreigners (1870-1950) or planned Soviet style economic development (1950-80). China's relatively superior performance is because of China's head start in implementing market reforms.

It is clear that the integration of the Chinese economy with the world trade system has been much faster than that of India though the latter's economy was more open than the former's in the pre-reform period. However, China initiated economic reforms at least a decade before India's economic liberalization since 1991, while India hesitated despite some early success with de-regulation in 1977-79.

China gained market share in trade in those commodities in which the East Asian economies no longer had any comparative advantage (e.g., toys) due to rising East Asian labour costs. This advantage could also have been seized by India, had it embarked on wide spread reforms in 1980 instead of 1991. Thus, while China's share in world trade rose (1980-1999) from 1% to 3.0%, for India, the rise was from 0.4% to 0.6%.

A very rough assessment of India's foregone opportunities in exports has been made by the World Bank. Since India and China started out in 1980 at roughly the same level of exports, with competition existing between them in many exports, therefore; China's exports can be used as a rough proxy for India's potential export level. In just one labour-intensive product, garments (comprising about 14% of India's exports), India's total exports were $4.6 billion in 1996, compared with $25 billion for China. If the two countries had maintained the same share of exports (that is, India and China had split their current sales evenly), then India's garment exports would be about $15 billion instead of $5 billion in 1996. Thus, India's trade policies, or lack of it, contributed to a potential loss of $10 billion of exports in one product alone (equal to over 25% of current exports).

This translates into millions of lost jobs and opportunities to make a real impact on poverty. The same would be true for many other Indian exports, which are largely labour intensive. Besides this opportunity cost there is also the loss in terms of new technology and consequent total factor productivity gains that India has foregone due to the late introduction of market reforms especially since 1980 when the World began on the view globalization thanks to computers and internet.

Thus, impressive as the strengths are of the Chinese economy, the risks and challenges are strong and varied enough to threaten progress in China. How the balance will be worked out would depend on the ability and resolve of the leadership to maintain the momentum of reforms, and embarking on newer reforms with bold strokes in financial architecture and SOEs.

Presently, we are in the new era of 'Knowledge Economy" due to the advent of information technology (IT). The Indian industry has been the source of much discussion on the successful growth of a knowledge industry in a largely poor and developing country. IT in India is spread across four key sectors- IT services; IT enabled services (ITES), software, and e-business. These sectors combine for a 2008 annual revenue forecast of $87B (*source:* NASSCOM) with numerous analysts suggesting higher revenue.

Highlighting the rapid growth of IT in India, software was a small $150 million industry in 1991, but grew to $5.7 billion in 2000, which is an annual growth rate of 50% (NASSCOM). The public and private sector factors that have contributed to this hyper growth of IT provide lessons for possible replication in China and other developing countries. One important policy lesson can be that high tech areas, driven by the market, can pull in global capital even if domestic opportunities are limited. India's IT sector growth also provides a fine example of how foreign-born or out of country immigrants provide linkages to capital, technology and culture to emerging entrepreneurs in the native country.

Software is one of China's fastest growing service industries too. The Chinese software industry however is inherently different than India's. The majority of Chinese software services producers are companies with domestic consumers. Another major difference between the Chinese and Indian software sector is the fact that the latter is more export oriented whereas the former serves primarily domestic demand. A mere 5.6% of China's software industry was exported versus approximately about 70% in India. But all said and done, it is today the United States which is the global leader in innovations in information technology.

The factor for the future of economic growth in China and India would depend on how the American innovating Eagle, the Chinese hardware manufacturing Dragon and the Indian IT software Elephant are going to engage in expanding their commonalities and address their differences to harness new innovations which will have epochal impact of future economic growth.

Will it be a harmonious triumvirate of Silicon Valley, Bangalore and Beijing—to rephrase President Obama—to power a global economic renaissance or an eternal triangle that will dominate and ensure disequilibrium the new Global Economic Order?

Although both the emerging market giants, China and India, are currently experiencing slower growth as a result of the global financial crisis and subsequent deep world recession, it is expected that together they can help lead the world recovery in the coming decade: China's economic growth has outpaced that of India since the 1970s and many expect this differential gained during 1980-92 to persist over the medium term. But with the world economy probably facing a period of slower growth and lower trade flows than in recent years, the Indian 'elephant' can begin to catch up with the Chinese 'dragon' more appropriately than have and tortoise analogy in the race to challenge the US as the world's leading economic power in the 2050s.

Although it is only since 2000 that the growing economic power of the Chinese 'dragon' has come fully into the media spotlight, its GDP has in fact been growing at an average rate of close to 8% per year for the last 30 years (corrected data). This is not much about the 6.8 % of India. China's GDP on a purchasing power parity (PPP) basis, is the second largest economy in the world, and could overtake the US by 2020 if it continues to grow at rates of around 10% per year. India has emerged third today, and could overtake China due to the favourable factor of demographics.

In comparison, the Indian 'elephant' has progressed at a more sedate pace, but still fairly strongly at just over 6.8% pa in the last 30 years. After 'a modest performance in the 1970s and the 1980s—when growth averaged close to 5%, the pace of expansion picked up following the burst of economic reforms in the early 1990s. And the acceleration has been more pronounced in the last six years, with growth averaging 8.4% per year, although as yet it has failed to pierce the double-digit pace on a sustained basis.

But despite the rapid pace of GDP growth in these two emerging market giants, both still face major problems that their economies are generating. Much of the new incomes generated has not been much evenly distributed causing social tensions, especially in the urban areas, and the vast majority in both countries still live very close to the poverty line. Of the 1.3bn population in China, about 60% or 750m live in the rural areas and some of these areas have taken little part in the economic success of the nation as a whole. Yet although India's GDP per capita has grown impressively at around 4% per year since 1980, poverty level has not reduced as fast. Labour force today is over 60% in agriculture even as the sector's share has fallen below 25% of GDP. Other measures of economic wellbeing—such as levels of malnutrition unemployment and literacy rates—illustrate the lead that China currently holds over India. Although much has been made of India's IT and service outsourcing sector, this employs just 0.2% of the population.

Yet despite the relatively weak role of government in India in terms of steering the economic policy over the last 50 years, one clear advantage over China is the fact that it is a democracy. Yet while democracy has brought more political freedom, it has constrained economic reforms because of the need for consensus, meaning that policy reforms that have taken place in India have been very slow and there is still deep suspicion about privatisation.

In China, the impact of rapid growth has tended to outweigh the potential resistance to policy changes, although there have been notable periods of tension. These have not only been about political and social issues, but most recently these tensions appear to have been driven by economic factors as unemployment starts to mount and some regions have started to feel excluded from the economic success story.

Whatever its frailties and shortcomings, India has a full-fledged and secular democracy, with robust political institutions, as illustrated by successive election results that appear to show that the electorate votes on the basis of economic and political competence. In contrast, China still has a very authoritarian regime. This has stifled political debate and denied the population a means of influencing the direction of policy.

But a centrally controlled system has enabled Beijing to implement reforms more quickly and successfully without having to worry about popular approval or democratic rights. However, in the long term this means that there is greater scope for social unrest, although the government's potential response to this may mean that pressures remain bottled up for longer than might be expected. As a result, the capacity of the Chinese political system to handle such pressures may prove to be less conducive to long-term stability, and hence economic progress, than in India.

The other key role for government in both countries is in setting the business climate. Neither India nor China have particularly good records of governance in terms of establishing a climate conducive to private sector involvement. Decision-making has often been arbitrary and contractual and property rights have been neglected. In addition, both countries have been extremely cautious about opening up sectors considered to be strategic, such as infrastructure and power, in order to complement government supplied services. As with its other liberalising reforms, India has begun to move slowly down this route, which in due course will attract greater foreign investor interest and hence funding. It remains unclear which way China will progress – but it may be even more wary than India about opening up key sectors to foreign investment.

But most of all what is in India's favour are its demographics. With the recent boom in the services sector helping to create a relatively affluent middle class, said to be 300m-strong, the links between rural incomes and industrial activity have weakened. Rising incomes and increased access to credit have led to much higher spending on consumer durables such as cars, phones and other electronic items even in rural areas. For India, the working population ratio will not decline before 2051, providing enough time to empower the young population to innovate and accelerate India's growth rate.

The principal finding in this study of the economic progress of China and India, in comparative perspective, is that the two economies at the end of the twentieth century have disproved all the prophets doom and gloom, and were growing rapidly, and possessed of substantial potential to become world class economic powers in two decades hence.

In national accounting terms, Chinese and Indian agricultural sectors grew at about the same rate, while in manufacturing value added, Chinese growth rate was substantially higher. In services sector, India's growth rate was considerably bigger than China's. Since 1998, the moving averaged rates of growth in GDP was about the same for the two countries–but at an ever than before higher level of 8.5% per year.

When all is said and done, about future projection, the essential and new reforms in the financial system, the inclusiveness of education, and reaping of the demographic dividend if implemented which will determine if India and China will stay the high growth rate course, and regain their global primacy of the pre-Industrial revolution era, or not. Much will depend on how the two countries will cope with and come out of the looming financial crisis on the economic horizon of the two nations. As of now, given the fact of sustained democracy in India, the odds are that India will emerge sooner and thus overtake China in economic development post 2020.

REFERENCES

1. Ackerlof, Garge and Robert Shiller: Animal Spirits, Princeton (2009).
2. Bagchi, Amiya: "The Other side of Foreign Investment by Imperial Powers", Economic and Political Weekly, June 8, 2002.
3. Barro, R.J: "Economic Growth in a Cross-Section of Countries, QJE, Vol. 106, 1991.
4. Bekie, M. M., Huang, R. and G.P. Wilson: "How to Fix China's Banking System", Mckinsey Quarterly, Oct 19, 2005.
5. Berg. Andrew and Cathenne Pattatilo, "Predicting Currency Crisis" Journal of International Money and Finance, Vol. 18, Nos. 1999.
6. Blyn, George, Agricultural Trends in India 1871-1947, University of Pennsylvania Press, 1966, Philadelphia.
7. Chang, G.C.: Coming Collapse of Chna, Random House, New York, 2001.
8. Chao, Kang: The Rate and Pattern of Industrial Growth in Communist China, Univ. of Michigan Press, 1965, Also China Quarterly, June 1980.
9. Chua, Any: World on Fire, Arrow Books, Random House, New York (2003).
10. Desai, Padma: Financial Crisis, Contagion and Containment, Princeton University Press, 2003.
11. Dowrick, Steve and J. Quiggin: "True Measures of GDP and Convergence", American Economic Review, Vol. 77 (1997).
12. Feldstein Martin: "Budget Deficits and National Debt," RBI Bulletin, Mumbai, India, 2004.
13. Feuerweker, A: "China's Nineteenth Century Industrialisation" in Economic Development of China and Japan (Cowan, ed,): London; Allen and Unwin 1964.
14. Gilboy, George: "The Myth Behind China's Miracle", Foreign Affairs, Vol.3 No.4 July/August 2004.
15. Gordon, M.J.: "Is China's Financial System Threatened by its Policy Loans", Journal of Asian Economics, Vol. 14, No. 2.
16. Hatermi, J. and M. Irandoust: "Productivity Performance and Exports", Eastern Economic Journal, Vol. 27, No. 2, 2001.
17. Hu, Zu lin and M.S. Khan: Why is China Growing so Fast, IMF, Washington D.C. 2000.

18. Huang, Yasheng: Foreign Direct Investment in China, Cambridge University, 2002.
19. Jefferson Gary, Rawski, Thomas and Yuxin Zheng: "Chinese Industrial Productivity", Journal of Comparative Economics, Vol. 23, No. 2, 1996.
20. Karacadag, C: "Financial System Soundness and Reform" in Tseng and Rodlauer.
21. Keynes, J.M: "Recent Economic Events in India", Economic Journal (1909).
22. Keidel, A: "China's Economy; A Mixed Performance", The China Business Review, Vol. 28, No.1, 2001.
23. Khan A.R. and Carl Riskin: "Inequality and Poverty in China in the Age of Globalization", Oxford University Press, 2001.
24. Kochhar, Kalpana: "Macroeconomic Implications of Fiscal Imbalances", NIFP/IMF Conference on Fiscal Policy of India, Jan. 16-17, 2004, New Delhi, India.
25. Kuhn, Phillip: Select Papers from the Centre for Far Eastern Studies (Susan Jones, ed.), Chicago 1978.
26. Lardy, Nicholas: China in the World Economy, Institute of International Economics, Washington D.C. 1994.
27. Lardy Nicholas: Integrating China into the Global Economy, Brookings, 2002.
28. Macfarquhar, Roderick: The Politics of China, Cambridge, (1997).
29. Maddison, Angus: Chinese Economic Performance in the Long Rurt, OECD Development Centre, Paris, 1998.
30. Modigliant, F. and Shi, Cao: "The Chinese Saving Puzzle and Life Cycle Hypothesis", Journal of Economic Literature Vol. XLII, No.1, March 2004.
31. North, Douglas: Understanding the Process of Economic Change, Princeton (2010)
32. Paddock and Paddock: World Famine 1975.
33. Pandit, Y.S., India's Balance and Indebtedness, 1896-1913, Allen and Unwin, London (1937).
34. Perkins, Dwight: Agricultural Development in China 1368-1968, Aldine (1969), Chicago.
35. Perkins, D.H.: "Transcribed Remarks in China's Economic Future", Journal of Asian Economics, No. 4, Vol. 8 (1997).
36. Perkins, D.H.: China: The Next Economic Giant? University of Seattle, 1988.
37. Prasad, E and Shang in Wei: "The Chinese Approach to Capital Inflows", IMF Working Paper, April 2005.
38. Prime, Penelope: "China and India Enter (a) deal Markets" Economic Geography and Economics (2010).
39. Rawski, Thomas: "What's Happening to China's GDP Statistics", China Economic Review, (2001).
40. Reynolds, Patricia: "Fiscal Adjustments in India" in {7}.
41. Sacks, J. and W.T. Woo: "The Real Reasons for China's Growth", The China Journal, Vol. 41, 2000.

42. Saez, Lawrence: Banking Reforms in India and China, Palgrave Macmillan, New York 2004.
43. Sala-i-Martin: "I Just Ran Two Million Regressions", AER, Vol. 87, No. 2, 1997.
44. Samuelson P.A. and S. Swamy: "Invariant Economic Index Numbers", American Economic Review, Vol. 64, No. 4 (1974).
45. Sarma, Atul: "Prospects of Trade and Investment in China and India", International Studies, Vol. 39, No. 2 (2002).
46. Saul, S.B.: Studies in British Overseas Trade 1870-1914, Liverpool University Press, Liverpool, UK (1960).
47. Studwell, Joe: The China Dream, Barnee and Noble, New York, 2002.
48. Subramanian S: Statistical Summary of Social and Economic Trends in India (Inter-War Period), Office of Economic Adviser, Government of India 1945, pp. 6-9.
49. Summers R. and A Hetson: "Penn Tables", Quarterly Journal of Economics Vol. 106, No. 2 (1991).
50. Swamy Subramanian: Economic Reforms and Performance: China and India in Comparative Perspective, Konark, 2003.
51. Swamy, Subramanian: Economic Growth in China and India, Vikas (ISBN 0-7069-4687-1), New Delhi, 1989.
52. Swamy, Subramanian: "The Response to Economic Challenge: A Comparative Economic History of China and India (1870-1952)", Quarterly Journal of Economics, February 1979.
53. Swamy, Subramanian: Economic Growth in China and India – A Comparative Appraisal (195270), University of Chicago Press, 1973.
54. Swamy, Subramanian: "Structural Changes and Size Distribution of Income", Review of Income and Wealth, 1967.
55. Swamy, Subramanian: "India China: India International Centre, New Delhi (2010).
56. Swamy, Subramanian: Financial Architecture and Economic Development in China and India: Konark, (2006).
57. Sylla Richard: "Financial Systems and Economic Modernization", The Journal of Economic History, Vol. 62, No. 2, (2002).
58. Wanda Tseng and David Cowen: India's and China's Recent Experience with Reform and Growth, IMP/Palgrave Macmillan, 2005.
59. World Bank: The East Asian Miracle, Oxford, (1994).
60. World Bank: Re: Thinking East-Asian Miracle, Oxford (2001).
61. Young, A: NBER Working Papers (2000).
62. Woo, W.T.: "Chinese Economic Growth: Sources and Prospects", Australian National University RSPAS, 1996.
63. Wu, H.X.: "China's GDP Level and Growth Performance", Review of Income and Wealth, Series 46, No.4, 2000.
64. Wu, H.X.: "Real Chinese Gross Domestic Product {1952-77}", Review of Income and Wealth, Ser 39, No. 1, 1993.

65. Wu, H.X.: "How Fast Has Chinese Industry Grown?", Review of Income and Wealth, Series 48, No. 2, 2002.
66. Zhou Li, Fang Cai and Justin Yi fu Lin: "The China Miracle: Development Strategy and Economic Reform, Chinese University Press, Hong Kong, 1996.
67. Zweig, David: "China's Stalled Fifth Wave", Asian Survey, Vol. XLI, No. 2, 2001.

INDEX